THE RECORD OF SINGING

Music advisor to Northeastern University Press
GUNTHER SCHULLER

The Record of Singing
Volume 2: 1914–1925

Michael Scott

Northeastern University Press
Boston

Library of Congress Cataloging-in-Publication Data

Scott, Michael.
The record of singing / Michael Scott.
p.   cm.
Originally published: London : Duckworth, 1977
Includes bibliographical references and index.
Contents: v. 1. To 1914   —   v. 2. 1914–1925.
ISBN 1–55553–163–6 (pbk.)
1. Singing—History   2. Singers.   3. Sound recordings.
I. Title.
ML1460.S34   1993
783'.009—dc20   92–46984

Contents

PART IV Singers from the English-Speaking World

PART V The German Style in Evolution

Illustrations

Preface

The Record of Singing is an illustrated survey of the art of singing as it survives on gramophone recordings; when completed it will cover the entire period of the 78 rpm record, i.e. until 1951. Volume One dealt with the early years; Volume Two continues the story from the outbreak of the First World War until the invention of electrical recording in 1925. After an introductory essay setting the period in historical perspective, the recipe is as before: I have let the singers' records tell the tale and contented myself with acting as guide to features of technique, style and interpretation. My approach is analytical and except to demonstrate a particular point I have avoided drawing comparisons between singers past and present. No history can be wholly objective—it would not be valuable if it were—but there are undoubtedly degrees of subjectivity. In the interpretative arts generally it is possible to establish certain aspects of technique as matters of fact rather than opinion. I have been especially concerned with these, taking my cue from the standards of contemporary critics, many of whom were students of singing and regarded it as the raison d'être of opera rather than, as their counterparts do today, as just one facet in a total art-form. If scholarship has taught us the value of correct style in performance, it applies equally to criticism: we shall appreciate little of the art of singers of previous generations, or enjoy much of what they sang, if we persist in using modern terminology with its picturesque allusions which, though occasionally suggestive, explains nothing.

The book is organised into five parts, each of which treats a different national style. The titles are, I hope, self-explanatory. Each school embraces not only native-born singers (and here I have bracketed the Austrians with the Germans, the Belgians with the French and so on), but those foreigners who identified themselves with its repertory and whose style and technique were conditioned by it. Thus Marie-Louise Edvina appears among the French; Elena Ruszkowska among the Italians, as do Barrientos, Bori, Zanelli, Làzaro, Fleta and Pareto at a time when Spain, Portugal and South America were in effect outposts of the Italian operatic empire. No scheme, however, is perfect and I make no apologies for including Borghild Bryn-Langaard and Tamaki Miura among the English-speaking singers, for it was in England and the United States that they made their reputations.

Each of the five parts is sub-divided into chapters grouping accounts of the careers, as well as some comment on the singing, of the most important operatic, concert and recording artists of the day. I have endeavoured to consider each of them at the height of his or her career, but this has not always been possible. Maria Farneti, Pavel Ludikar and Mme Charles-Cahier, for example, who should have been included here made no recordings during the period. Thus, faute de mieux, they will appear in Volume Three, by which time their singing, if not their art, was passé. On the other hand, the discovery of some outstanding unpublished acoustic records of Alexander Kipnis accounts for what may seem a premature appearance. Several artists—Elena Gerhardt, Tito Schipa and Lauritz Melchior among them, will be included again.

Biographical information—vital statistics, lists of appearances, roles and so forth—and contemporary reviews, criticism and opinions, which I have quoted wherever it seemed appropriate, have been selected in order to give perspective to the singer's art. I should like to think that I have done this fairly but quite deliberately I have made no attempt at completeness. The sources of most direct quotations and some indirect ones will be found at the end of the book, the principal exception to this rule being the occasional story or anecdote, which I have included when they seemed plausible—se non è vero è ben trovato.

No subject—unless it be economics—is more burdened than singing with technical terms—'gobbledegook' one critic has engagingly termed it. Originally conceived as a language of communication, it too often degenerates into the language of concealment. Any writer has open to him two alternatives. He may avoid it altogether, but this will quickly force him into suggestive prose and its excessive recourse to metaphors, with their oblique analogies about which I have already complained. Alternatively he may do as I have tried to do, use it as sparingly as possible, explaining each of the terms as they arise in the text, or listing them in a glossary (see page 251).

The spelling of proper names in a book of this sort presents certain problems. With the singers I have followed the English custom of common practice (it is, after all, the basis of our spelling), wherever possible preserving the character of opera-house cast lists, programmes and gramophone record catalogues. Difficulties have arisen over the Poles and Czechs, when sometimes their names appear in the original spellings and sometimes in French and German versions, and with the Russians when rendering the Cyrillic into Roman. In such cases logical systems too often lead to absurdities, the kind which abound in Grove's Dictionary— Shaliapin, Rakmaninov, indeed. Wherever possible I have copied the singers themselves—it is surely every man and woman's inalienable right to spell their own name as they please. With the operas, for the sake of brevity I have adopted the usual practice and often dropped the articles in German and Italian, but never in French. In the matter of capital letters, I have here taken the style from the score or libretto, preferring e.g. *Il Barbiere di Siviglia* to the modern way—*Il barbiere di Siviglia*—where Seville appears to be more important than the Barber. When operas have been given in translation, so as to avoid having to repeat constantly that, for example, a particular Italian singer sang a German opera in Italian, I have translated the titles, thus: *Maestri Cantori, Franco Cacciatore, Crepuscolo degli Dei* and so on. Of course, this does not work for *Lohengrin* or *Tannhauser*. In the same way *Pagliacci* in German is *Bajazzo; Trovatore, Troubadour;* and *Guillaume Tell, Wilhelm Tell,* but *Traviata* remains *Traviata* in any language. I have not gone on from there to translate the names of the characters as well, as this would surely have lead to absurdities—'Mi chiamano Mimì, ma il mio nome è Mime!' I have been only as consistent as good sense will allow, in the end

reserving the right of every author occasionally to indulge his own fancy.

This book is for Vivian Liff and George Stuart; but for them, their unceasing enthusiasm, encouragement and generosity, it could not have been written. They placed at my disposal the entire resources of the Stuart-Liff collection, one of the finest and most comprehensive in the world. They permitted me to copy countless of their unique historical recordings, consult their extensive library of books to assist in the research and they provided the vast majority of the pictures, many hitherto unpublished, with which I have relieved the narrative. It is not possible for me to thank them sufficiently for all the time they have spent and for the many days I have enjoyed their gracious hospitality at Tunbridge Wells. If there be any merit in this book then the honour is theirs.

It is a pleasure too, to thank many friends throughout the world for their assistance for providing gramophone records, pictures, books, valuable information and assistance of all kinds. In Great Britain: Richard Bebb, Edward Bridgewater, Bryan Crimp, Christopher Dyment, Syd Gray, Jack Henderson, Edward Johnson, Dr Gareth Lewis, Harold Rosenthal, Patric Schmid, Dr Boris Semeonoff, Robert Walker and Don White. In the Netherlands: Leo Riemens. In Norway: The Chief Librarian, Royal Oslo University. In Italy: Helen Conlon, Marco Contini, Luciano di Cave, Arne Dörumsgaard, Gillian Hodgson, Karen Christenfeld, Andy Miller, Maurizio Tiberi and Prof. Emilia Zanetti, Chief Librarian, Accademia di Santa Cecilia, Rome. In the United States: James Camner, Larry Holdridge, Randolph Mickelson, Mrs John Barry Ryan, Edward J. Smith and Professor L. J. Wathen. Lack of space forbids me mentioning everyone here, but I thank them all the same.

I am particularly grateful to John Freestone for the extended loan of many books and to Michael Aspinall for his support at every stage in the production of this book.

I must, however, absolve all these generous friends from any responsibility for the interpretation I have put on the information they have so kindly given.

Rome 1979   Michael Scott

Introduction

IN the later part of the acoustic recording era, the years between 1914 and 1925, the various national styles of singing were at their most characteristic and sharply differentiated. This period coincided with the ultimate triumph of Nationalism, when its legitimacy was finally acknowledged. During the First World War those mighty dynasties that for so long had sat astride—latterly with increasing discomfort—different nationalities, were gathered to the dust of history. At the Treaty of Versailles in 1919, the great powers formally recognised the right of every people to political self-determination, so writing *finis* to a long chapter of history that had begun more than a century and a quarter previously on the barricades in the French Revolution. Nationalism had been the dominating pre-occupation of nineteenth-century Europe, not only in politics; nationalist sentiments had pervaded the arts: poetry, drama and music, and perhaps nowhere were these expressed so potently, launched on stirring melodies, as at the opera house. On one occasion at least, at the Théâtre de la Monnaie in Brussels in 1830, during a performance of Auber's *La Muette de Portici*, the audience was roused to such a frenzy, that there and then began the revolution that was to separate Belgium from the Netherlands. It may be doubted whether Auber premeditated a *coup de théâtre*, or that Rossini, in setting 'Pensa alla patria' conceived Isabella as a spokeswoman for the Risorgimento; both composers were working a vein of feeling in their audiences, easily accessible and too obviously affecting to ignore. In the next generation, however, Verdi consciously exploited Nationalist aspirations to the full in his early operas with their thinly disguised propaganda, so that the very initials of his name, an acronym for Vittoria Emanuele Re D'Italia, became a call for revolution. In this sense, the works of Wagner were not revolutionary. The unification of Germany was not a matter of casting off the foreign yoke but of finding a national identity. The operas of Weber, Marschner and Wagner set out to glorify German culture, its language and mythology; similarly in Russia, Glinka, Moussorgsky and Borodin turned for inspiration to Russian literature and history.

Out of each national music there evolved a different vocal style, each reflecting at the same time the peculiar characteristics of the language. These gradually came to supersede the time-honoured Italian school, the art of which we can still hear exemplified in the recordings of Adelina Patti and Mattia Battistini, and, albeit somewhat modified, in those made by many of the leading pupils of Garcia, Sbriglia, the elder Lamperti and Mathilde Marchesi. By 1914 these mighty pedagogues were dead and the best years of their pupils passed by; their successors, like Antonio Cotogni, who had himself been an outstanding baritone of the old school, abandoned the attempt to impose the classical virtues on a generation which despised its traditions and had no use for its graces. Instead, embracing the new realism, they busied themselves with giving their pupils sufficient technique, chiefly a matter of power and stamina, to cope with its demands: in Italian opera with the strenuous accents required by 'verismo'; in Wagner with the forceful declamation of 'Sprechgesang'; in French vocal music with a style that preferred literary values. In all of them, the essentially vocal imagination of bel canto was sacrificed. Next to Melba, Battistini, de Lucia and Plançon, the singing of even the finest artists of the succeeding generation—Muzio, Martinelli, Schipa and Vanni Marcoux, for example—was less purely musical. Compare the recordings of 'Ah! non credea' by Patti and Muzio, made when both ladies were in decline; Patti, in spite of the various accommodations she is obliged to make to age, is still able to contrive an ineffably moving effect solely by vocal means: purity of tone, perfection of legato, phrasing informed by eloquent portamento, and exquisitely turned ornaments. Muzio's singing lacks refinement; she relies on a generally lachrymose delivery and mannered enunciation of the text. It may be affecting but it is not stylish; this is Bellini out of Boito and Puccini.

The shift in interpretative emphasis is everywhere apparent. In French opera in the days of Lully and Rameau, French singers had put clarity of pronunciation before everything, with results that were often musically compromising; at the time, France boasted one of the most vigorous and brilliant theatrical traditions and the influence of the declamatory style of the great actors in the tragedies of Corneille and Racine had impressed itself on the lyric drama. Throughout the eighteenth century, as we read in Dr Burney, and as Baron Grimm and other commentators confirm, France was not the home of bel canto. French singing was provincial and lacked the virtuosity that made the Italians supreme. Before science mistook voice production for singing and singers still learned their art by imitation, the French suffered for want of the best examples: the castrati. French audiences in the age of enlightenment found the sight of them distasteful; this did credit to their susceptibility but it did not do their singers any good. It was not until after the revolution and the establishment of the Théâtre des Italiens in 1801, that there was a change for the better. Paradoxically, just at the time when the castrati had become unfashionable in Italy, one of the last, Girolamo Crescentini, came to Paris and enjoyed a great vogue; even Napoleon was much affected by his singing. By 1824 and Rossini's engagement as Director at the Italiens, a whole generation of remarkable French singers had grown up, among them Cinti-Damoreau, Fodor-Mainvieille, Meric-Lalande and Levasseur. In the wake of Rossini came Bellini, Donizetti, and Meyerbeer; during the next half century their works were sung by artists like Nourrit, Falcon, Duprez, Dorus-Gras, Stoltz, Roger and Faure, all of them quite as distinguished as their Italian contemporaries. Throughout this period France was still the dominating country in Europe (Napoleon's defeat at Waterloo had taken the entire allied force), and its cosmopolitan capital, Paris, a Mecca to which even those like Verdi and Wagner who professed to disdain its gods, felt obliged to journey. After the humiliating defeat of 1870 in the Franco-Prussian War and the bloody events of the Commune the following year, Paris lost much of its international prestige and its importance as a cultural, and hence operatic, centre. With Germany in the ascendant and the unification of Italy completed, Wagner and Verdi were content to succeed first in their own countries and wait for Paris to capitulate.

These events did not at once precipitate a sharp decline in French singing and it continued to retain much of its excellence during the last quarter of the century. The most popular composers of the period, Gounod, Bizet, Thomas, Delibes and later Massenet, still followed the Italian example, and wrote effectively for the voice. Unlike Berlioz—who was both untypical as well as unpopular—they did not bother with polemics, nor do we find them, like Wagner, striving to extend the frontiers of their art, or seeking some new balance in the relationship between words and music; they were melodists pure and simple. Unlike Verdi's early works, their operas did not ventilate the popular aspirations of the day. They were unashamedly entertainers, and to succeed with a notoriously demanding public, they needed to marshal all the available artillery, including the best singers; not surprisingly their vocal writing is grateful as well as effective. At the time there were plenty of fine French singers to choose from. In the seventies a number of the world's leading singing teachers settled in Paris, notably Pauline Viardot-Garcia, Giovanni Sbriglia and Mathilde Marchesi, from whose studios emerged a galaxy of stars; the best of them, after triumphing at the Opéra or Opéra-Comique, went on to St Petersburg, London and New York, by then the most important operatic centres, and where the biggest cachets were earned. The decade after 1885 saw the last great flowering of the French school of singing with Fidès-Devriès, Lucienne Bréval, Emma Calvé, Felia Litvinne, Jean and Edouard de Reszke, Jean Lassalle, Victor Maurel and Pol Plançon, all of whom had been trained in the classical Italian style and married to it the sophisticated manners of the French tradition at its finest.

By the turn of the century, however, the breakdown of this tradition was obvious. A variety of reasons may be put forward to account for it. On the wider stage, Paris was no longer the unchallenged cultural capital of the civilised world; French glory was a thing of the past and France a defeated and dismembered country. It was inevitable that there should be a reawakening of national consciousness and a reaction against the taste and style of the previous generation. The younger French composers looked back to what they fancied a golden age, to the days of Gluck and even earlier, before French music and the setting of the language had become corrupted by foreign influences. Chief among these was the Italian style, which had infatuated a whole generation after Rossini's arrival in Paris, and which seemed to prefer melody, to put the music before the words. It was pronounced decadent and the 'French' compositions of Rossini, Donizetti, Verdi and especially Meyerbeer were greatly deplored. It was ironic that the real reaction to the Grand Opera of Meyerbeer began not in Germany or even Italy but in France, the country which he had adopted and which had enjoyed with him his greatest triumphs. In his memoirs, Saint-Saëns writes scathingly of Meyerbeer's 'contempt for prosody and his indifference to the verse (in which) he abused all indulgence in such matters'.[1]

A reaction against the foreign influence was inevitable too, at a time when the French lyric stage was under siege from the music dramas of Wagner on the one hand, and on the other from the operas of the Italian verismo. French composers could not afford to ignore either; they were faced with a dilemma, whether to try and beat them or join them. Victory was hardly possible in the melodic style of Gounod and Massenet, whose indebtedness to the Italian example was too obvious; in any case, it was an exhausted idiom, as Massenet's later works and those of his successors Erlanger, Pierné, Leroux, and the rest amply demonstrate. Something stronger than sugar was needed. But joining them seemed just as unsatisfactory. There was something ridiculous, not to say unpatriotic, about the French Wagnerites: Reyer with his Sigurd, Brunehild and the rest. Nor did Bruneau make a better, or more lasting, impression trying to fashion out of the sensational novels of Zola a French verismo. The younger generation wisely neither rejected Wagner nor did they embrace him; like good eclectics, they took from his works what was useful for their purposes, then turned to the classics for inspiration and set about reviving the long dormant French symphonic idiom. The prime mover in this was Saint-Saëns, who was succeeded by Chabrier, Chausson, Fauré, Duparc and Debussy, all of whom were principally concerned with orchestral and instrumental music; unlike their predecessors, for whom a success in the theatre was everything, opera was but a small part of their activities, sometimes not even that. In their writing for the voice they took their cue from the eighteenth century and looked to the language itself, its poetic and histrionic tradition, to provide inspiration for the musical settings. *Faust* and *Werther* have done well in translation but *Pelléas et Mélisande* is unthinkable in any language but French.

Under the Italian influence, the singer in French opera, throughout the nineteenth century, was expected to hold words and music in balance. The musical line was sustained throughout in a pure tone, to be coloured by the pronunciation of the different vowels and articulated by the consonants. As Gounod put it:

> There are two principal things to observe in pronunciation. It must be clear, neat, distinct, exact, that is to say not permitting any uncertainty of the pronounced word to the ear. It must be expressive, that is to say, it must picture to the mind the sentiment expressed by the word itself. As to all that concerns clarity, neatness, exaction, pronunciation takes rather the title of articulation. Articulation has for its object to reproduce faithfully the exterior form of the word. All the rest is the business of pronunciation. It is this which imparts to the word the thought, the sentiment, the passion, in which it is enveloped. In a word, articulation has for its domain form or the intellectual element. Articulation gives neatness, pronunciation creates eloquence.[2]

In the art of one of the greatest singers at the turn of the century, the bass Pol Plançon, we can note precisely that perfect balance between (as Gounod uses the words) pronunciation and articulation, between vowel and consonant, music and text. In the course of the succeeding generation this delicate balance was to become unhinged. Although Vanni Marcoux's intelligence and histrionic skill made him a picturesque Boris, Scarpia and Don Quichotte, his singing was without the brilliance of his great predecessor—not for him the dashing roulades of Thomas's Tambour-Major. His much-admired recording of Philip's Monologue from Verdi's *Don Carlos* may suit our modern notions of understatement in characterisation, with its dramatic restraint and carefully measured articulation of the text, but the vocal dimensions have diminished; there is not the sonority of tone and imaginatively nuanced legato that we can hear in Plançon's recording of the same music, nor the purely musical intensity that still moves us in the records of the elderly Maurel. It is an outstanding but hardly a stylish interpretation; the dry manner would have been more appropriate to Debussy or Ravel than Verdi. Not surprisingly, Vanni Marcoux is at his best in the music of his contemporaries—in Février's *Monna Vanna*, for example, where he gives a subtly controlled and authentic reading of Guido's soliloquy. As so much of the classical poise disappeared out of French singing and the words were no longer sustained in a firm and rounded tone, so the singers' enunciation became increasingly obtrusive, unmusical and affected. The modified vowels of the

French language which such great singers as Plançon, Calvé, Litvinne and Renaud had not allowed to compromise purity of tone, now contrived to produce the characteristically hard and acidulous quality we associate with Gallic sopranos and, among the male singers, a dry and nasal tone. From this time French singers were chiefly remarkable for their interpretative gifts—personality, histrionic skill, charm and so forth—rarely for the intrinsically musical quality of their singing.

Among the Italians too, in the post-1914 period, personality was frequently required to do duty for technique. If Tito Schipa's voice production was less tremulous than de Lucia's, his singing was also less accomplished; in Almaviva's music he sounds elegant by comparison with much that has been heard since, but his coloratura is without de Lucia's easy limpidity, nor is it as accurate. Where de Lucia's charm resides in exquisite vocalisation, Schipa's rests in a graceful, if sometimes precious, delivery of the words. Traditionally the Italians were as much concerned with a clear pronunciation as the French; the idea—we still see it sometimes repeated—that bel canto and intelligibility are mutually exclusive, has no foundation in fact. Caccini, in his preface to *Nuove Musiche* (1601), tells us that the 'new' vocal music (i.e. Italian opera), arose out of a dissatisfaction with contrapuntal music, precisely because it made the text incomprehensible.[3] A century later, at a time when the vocal art had, by general consensus, reached a pitch which it has never since attained, Tosi wrote:

> Without a good pronunciation the singer robs the auditors of a great part of the charm which vocal music conveys by means of the words. If the words are not uttered distinctly one can find no great difference between the human voice and a cornet or oboe. Singers should not forget that it is the words which elevate them above instrumentalists.[4]

The words, however, were to be placed in the tone and were not permitted to disrupt the underlying portamento of the breath. It was only after the beginning of this century that we find in Italian singing a general slackening of tension in the vocal line. This followed inevitably from the rhetorical style of the verismo school of composers: Mascagni, Giordano and Leoncavallo, in particular, and to a lesser extent Puccini, Cilea and Catalani. From this time dates the popularity of many extra-musical devices: the sob and catch in the breath, the glottal attack, the aspirate and those sudden shifts from a mezza voce that is not always well supported and often crooned, to a forte in which the words are uttered with explosive force. So far from making them clearer, it had the opposite effect; by placing undue emphasis on them at the expense of the line, the musical tone which informed the line was sacrificed, and the purity of the vowels compromised. Since, paradoxically, it is the vowels rather than the consonants that make for intelligibility, the more emphatic the enunciation became, the less intelligible it was.

Even in lyrical music, next to the elegant and perfectly clear yet unaffected diction of de Lucia, Bonci and Anselmi, whose words were blended into the musical tone and delivered spontaneously on the breath, the enunciation of Gigli, Schipa and Muzio, with their curiously distorted vowels, sounds stilted and unnatural. It was in the music of their contemporaries that they were most at home. At any time the interpretative arts echo the creative arts; how stylish and affecting all three sound in a popular 'art' song of the day, an amiable piece of kitsch, Stefano Donaudy's 'O del mio amato ben', which although it has some outward semblance of bel canto with its flowing melody, makes its biggest effect when accompanied by the sentimental harmonies of a tea-shop ensemble. Whatever the technical and stylistic shortcomings of Muzio's Norma and Violetta, as Mimi or Wally her identification with the musical idiom is complete. Tito Schipa's many outstanding recordings prove that it was possible to discriminate between verismo and vulgarity. As Turiddu and Cavaradossi, where so many tenors have been provoked into 'that violent attack, forcing of tone and clarion delivery of high notes',[5] which W. J. Henderson complains of, his graceful yet still ardent singing is balm to sore ears.

In the German repertory the picture is more confused. As the pre-war recordings of Abendroth, Siems, Edyth Walker and Matzenauer abundantly testify, German-trained singers may have been able to encompass a wide variety of roles, execute awkward tessitura and unvocal intervals with seeming ease, but this was only managed by sleight-of-voice. It worked well enough in the smaller theatres in the traditional repertory but it was too artificial and inhibiting to be truly expressive and lacked the strength and endurance necessary to surmount the sonorous current of the Wagnerian orchestra. The great lyrical outbursts in Wagner's operas, to make their proper effect, require before all things two virtues of the old Italian school: spontaneity of delivery and intensity of utterance. A fact that Wagner realised; his directive to singers to use a bel canto style in his music was no mere whimsy. Although he was responsible—perhaps more than any other composer—for reducing the singer from a dominating role to instrumental status (at best to *primus inter pares*), his vocal writing shows a finer appreciation of the natural limitations and range of the human voice, also of its peculiar eloquence, than perhaps any other German composer of the nineteenth century. Surviving recordings made by those singers who came under his own direction, for example Hermann Winkelmann and Marianne Brandt (who created Parsifal and Kundry respectively) or Lilli Lehmann, show their singing to have been more affecting in itself, more musical with a firmer legato than those who were trained in the so-called Bayreuth style after the composer's death, and they were skilled in the use of the traditional graces, mordents, trills and portamento, all of which have their place in Wagner's works. The Italian influence failed to survive after *Tristan*, *The Ring* and *Parsifal* had become a part of the repertory of the world's most important—and largest—theatres. This was partly because conductors found the temptation to unleash the full power of the orchestra increasingly irresistible; save for the most lavishly endowed, the singers were obliged to shout and partly because they were positively encouraged to do so by the so-called 'Sprechgesang', the performing style that originated in Bayreuth after the death of Wagner. It arose from a misconception of the nature of the Wagnerian music drama. It was undoubtedly Wagner's intention that the singer should . . .

deliver the text clearly, using the music just as he would the inflexions of the voice in speaking to bring out the meaning of the sentences . . . With which there should be no quarrel, did it not also include such a use of the vowel sounds that the delivery of those pure, sustained tones which constitute song becomes impossible. I do not believe that Wagner wrote the beautiful voice parts in his music dramas with the intention of hearing them cackled in the Bayreuth staccato . . . He could not write his endless melodies if he permitted the text to prescribe the rhythm and the sectional divisions of the music. He says himself that in order to escape the mastery of word over musical setting, he adopted the iterative verse, the staff rhyme (Stabreim), which he used exclusively in *The Ring* . . . He did it not that the singer might fall upon the iterated consonants with all his enunciative force, but that the iterations should make their own rhythmic effect when the singer was strictly attending to his business of singing.[6]

Recordings indicate that whereas the Bayreuth style singers discarded the virtues of the old Italian style—this far, at least, they resembled their Italian and French contemporaries—they still contrived to retain many of the most unattractive features of the traditional German style: an imperfect attack, uneven scale and, especially when singing softly, white tone, to which they added the characteristically consonantal delivery. It is hardly a cause for surprise that many voices failed to stand up to the strain—those, for example, of Ernst van Dyck, Alois Burgstaller and Erik Schmedes—and Bayreuth became notorious as a graveyard for voices. By the late nineties a reaction had begun to set in; a number of distinguished foreign artists, chief among them Jean de Reszke and Nordica, demonstrated that it was possible to enunciate the text clearly, still sing every note in tune without sacrificing tonal beauty. Outside Germany especially, where Wagner's poetry meant much less than his music, in performances of his works given in London, Paris, New York and Milan (often in the vernacular) during the first decade of this century, Olive Fremstad, Félia Litvinne, Agnes Nicholls, Giuseppe Borgatti, Giuseppe Kaschmann and Clarence Whitehill, among many, preferred a style that took more account of musical values.

From the outbreak of the First World War, the Bayreuth style was in retreat. The war itself was partially responsible; so long as hostilities lasted, in the allied countries Wagner's music was performed, if at all, by local singers and mostly in translation. In its aftermath, the German singers themselves, at any rate those who came to enjoy prominent international careers, abandoned most of its rhetorical exaggerations (perhaps this arose from an instinctive realisation that a lasting peace was more likely through music than words). During the period 1918–1925 emerged some of the greatest Wagnerian artists of the century, in particular: Frieda Leider, Friedrich Schorr, Lotte Lehmann and Lauritz Melchior. Although the first two of these retained in their singing certain mannerisms derived from the traditional German technique, chiefly in respect to attack and tone formation, there was virtually nothing of Sprechgesang. Lotte Lehmann owed little to either school; she escaped being taught to bottle her voice up in the Orgeni fashion, or to bark à la Bayreuth. Her vocal training must have been more rough and ready than the others', and yet she is the most eloquent of them all. Her voice is scarcely free, and cannot cope with all the expressive demands she makes of it, but such was her genius that she transforms her failings—in particular, a rough glottal attack in the upper range and a prevailing shortness of breath—into recognisable components of her style, and in the end we almost come to accept them as virtues. Both the vehemence and the breathlessness seem entirely appropriate to Sieglinde's passionate declarations. Though there is no real legato in the long phrases, for the voice is not properly supported, she declaims with an extraordinary intensity, wholly musical in its effect. Had she been possessed of the technical resources of a Lilli Lehmann, she might have been able to add to her wonderful Fidelio, Marschallin and Sieglinde a whole gallery of other portraits, Norma even, and certainly Isolde—which she so much wanted to sing but knew better than to try.

The last of this quartet, the great Dane Melchior, was one of the increasing number of non-German singers, chiefly Scandinavian and Anglo-Saxon who, in the course of the next half century, were to make such an imposing effect in the big Wagnerian roles. Vocally splendid and technically assured though their singing was—indeed, in some cases still is—it had not the unique fascination of artists like Leider and Lehmann, for all their limitations. In Melchior's case this had less to do with a lack of artistic commitment, as is sometimes suggested, than a lack of character in his technique. He belonged to no school and though he was without the German vices he was also without their virtues; his singing, if not his accent, always sounded foreign. The remarkable technique which sustained him so well over so many years in one of the most taxing and strenuous repertories was a rationalisation of his own prodigious natural talent; it owed nothing to example and has proved impossible to emulate. When a young colleague asked him how he sang, Melchior's reply was short and to the point: 'I open my mouth and I push'.[7] It was true, so far as it went. What he did not tell, perhaps was not consciously aware of, was that he knew exactly how far to open his mouth and how much, or little, pressure to push with. Melchior was the first of the great modern singers; his technique was neither stylish nor unstylish, it had no style at all.

The older German technique persisted outside the works of Wagner, but since it was no longer required to contain everything from the Queen of the Night and Rosina to Sieglinde and Venus, its most contrived and artful mannerisms became modified. Next to Irene Abendroth and Margarethe Siems, the coloratura of Maria Ivogün or Lotte

Schoene is hardly as facile, but their voice production sounds altogether more spontaneous, the harmonics rounding out the tone. Where Siems's intonation so often strays, Ivogün's, though not perfect, is generally more reliable and her vocalism altogether more attractive. It was to the operas of Richard Strauss and Mozart, to Lieder and operetta that this technique was now chiefly confined. It was most suited to the works of Strauss, for he self-avowedly wrote for it. It is his vocal writing rather than Wagner's that is supremely instrumental in inspiration. The wide upward and downward portamento which is so characteristic of his vocal writing imitates a style of violin playing that has now disappeared, where the player swept through the intervals on the same string, without switching from one to the other as he would today. We can still hear it in old recordings, especially well in those made by the Concertgebouw under its conductor Willem Mengelberg, whom Strauss greatly admired. On catgut it produced precisely that silvery tone and shimmering line which Strauss sought to copy in his vocal writing. In the Final Trio from *Rosenkavalier*, for example, in the recording with Siems, von der Osten and Nast the three voices soar aloft like instruments. The effect is undeniable, even if it is hardly a vocal one: what has become of the words? It was much less agreeable in elaborate music, not only on the listener's ear but on the singer's voice. Emile Vuillermoz has left us a vivid description of Margarethe Siems's attempt to cope with the impossibly over-written line in the original version of Zerbinetta's Rondo, at the world premiere of *Ariadne auf Naxos* at Stuttgart in 1912:

> This indescribable florid romance where the unhappy Zerbinetta, her face contorted, her neck twisted, her eyes bulging, has to throw out a paradoxical number of high Cs, Ds, Es and F sharps for twenty five pages, a painful half hour that leaves you panting, your nerves shattered and your teeth on edge.[8]

The German Mozart revival is usually dated from Richard Strauss's inauguration of the Mozart Festivals at Munich in the late 1880s. This coincided with the heyday of the instrumental school of singing, and resulted in the spread of the German or Viennese method, which came to be accepted as 'the Mozart style' everywhere. It was, in fact, only the local German style of the late nineteenth century. This vocal method is still considered 'stylish' in Mozart today, although nobody would accept it for a minute in Verdi's operas; in the last years of the nineteenth century, it was simply the method used by German singers in every kind of music. Doubtless to Strauss the refinement of the instrumental singing technique seemed appropriate in eighteenth-century music, as indeed to some extent it is. The ladylike caution imposed on singers like Siems or Schumann by their inhibiting method, and the clarity of scale passages, even if sometimes achieved at the expense of correct intonation, might seem Mozartian to a none-too-demanding ear. But Mozart wrote for the voice in an Italianate fashion—in his day the only fashion in Vienna and Prague—and, quite the opposite of Strauss, had the instrumentalists copy the singers; we have only to think of the shapely 'singing' line in his violin and piano concertos. The German method applied to Mozart is not only unstylish and anachronistic, but it debilitates the music because the singer is not able to supply the needed emotional force. Mozart's vocal writing has this much in common with Wagner's; to be properly affecting it needs the spontaneous accents and intensity of the classical Italian school:

> Mozart may have reeled off his tunes by the hundred; but if he fitted the simplest of them to words, it never failed to embody in every accent and every phrase the full emotional content of the poet's lines. Alike as a piece of vocal music and as a vehicle for the expression of human feeling, it was complete, perfect in itself. The consequence is that it demands from the singer besides a certain warmth of expression, a depth of sentiment and even passion . . . He was a man of strong temperament, and every bar he wrote for the voice overflowed with the essence of his own nature.[9]

Something of the genuine Mozart tradition has survived for our scrutiny in recordings: in Patti's 'Batti, batti' (despite her collapse in the allegro when the accompanist has to finish a phrase without her) and Santley's 'Non più andrai', both singers are not only technically supreme so that while the freshness of their voices has inevitably faded with age, the purity, accuracy and finesse have not, but their interpretations have a 'warmth of expression, a depth of sentiment and even passion'[10] which is properly contained within the musical form and style. By comparison, the most acclaimed Mozart singing in the years between 1914 and 1925 confused a white with a pure tone, lacked a correctly supported legato and the characterisation either was contrived in an artificial fashion thought suitable for antique music, or else too greatly relied on those touches of personality which we have noted before in Italian singers; in an age which had little sense of style and not too much taste, not many of these mannerisms were inspired by the music. It is only fair to point out that if the Viennese-German school of singers—especially sopranos—were accepted as 'authentic' Mozartians all over the world, the Italian singers must shoulder the blame. With very few exceptions, they had abandoned the classical Italian style of the seventeenth and eighteenth centuries, and their verismo mannerisms were unthinkable in Mozart.

The Mozart Festivals were held each summer directly after Bayreuth. Although not actually conceived as correctives, they nevertheless provided an opportunity for pilgrims drunk on the lush harmonies and elaborate orchestrations to take the cure. They were not slow in doing so and revivals soon spread to other centres in Germany and elsewhere. Fifty years previously Mendelssohn had played a prominent role in re-establishing the greatness of Bach, around 1860 Berlioz revived Gluck's *Orphée* and *Alceste*; it was appropriate that Strauss should do the same for Mozart. By comparison with the complex, symphonic idiom of the post-Wagnerians, of whom Strauss was the most gifted, Mozart's purely vocal and classical style came as a refreshing treat. In the years before the First World War there was a gradual quickening of interest in antique music, a realisation that simplicity was not necessarily naivety and with it the first doubts as to the lasting value of all the new and sophisticated experiments. Though the comforting notion of progress, which had been at the root of nineteenth-century philosophy, was only put aside with reluctance and each season saw the introduction of a number of novelties, an increasing proportion of these failed to establish themselves. In the decade up to 1916, only two—*Elektra* and *Der Rosenkavalier*—remained prominently in the international repertory, compared with six in the previous ten years: *Bohème, Tosca, Andrea Chénier, Salome, Madama Butterfly* and *Pelléas et Mélisande*.

In London in 1920, after two depressing years, the Grand Opera season folded; when it came back four years later, it had changed into something different, more 'serious'—at least, in intention—and a good deal less entertaining. By then the repertory was composed overwhelmingly of revivals. Whereas about a century ago, in 1878, out of the twenty nine operas produced at Covent Garden, eleven were less than a quarter of a century old and even in 1902 the ratio was still seven out of twenty three, by 1928 only two of the nineteen works were contemporary pieces.

The increasing number of revivals, not only of Mozart but also of Gluck and Handel, and among nineteenth-century composers, certain of Verdi's operas, introduced a new and historical perspective into the repertory. For the singers this ranked second in significance only to the diversity of national styles, posing for them not only technical but also, so far as they can be separated, interpretative problems. From this period dates the general confusion in the use of the word 'style' in singing.

Until the beginning of this century, singers were principally occupied with music written by their contemporaries, or at any rate, by contemporaries of their teachers. The composer's and the interpreter's style were one. As early as the 1820s, a few English critics were shocked when Catalani sang cadenzas in Handel (and in church, too) similar to those which they approved of in Portogallo; by 1914, most critics had realised that what was appropriate to the music of Puccini and Giordano was not the right thing for the music of Gluck or Mozart. What is the correct style in 'old' music is a question that musicologists are still arguing about today. The recordings of the 1914–25 period show a fascinating diversity of methods in treating these problems. The 'stick to the printed score' school is already in evidence, but other singers are still very Victorian in their Mozart records. Many veer about; even some great prima donnas of very determined character sing appogiaturas, for example, in one Mozart aria but not in another.

There was undoubtedly a case for removing those sentimental manners better suited to the drawing room ballad than to the Mozart aria, thereby restoring to the music its rhythmic energy. However, the German notion that authentic style could be accomplished by purging the vocal line of all traditional devices—even the appoggiatura—without regard to their historical or musical validity, and resorting to a white tone and antiseptic style, arose out of a confusion between sentiment and sentimentality. If there was no place for the latter in Mozart's music, in his vocal writing Mozart demanded from the singer 'a depth of sentiment . . . even . . . passion',[11] as Klein pointed out.

In Italian music, particularly in the operas of Verdi, a similar 'purification' was going on under the baton of Toscanini, first at La Scala and later the Metropolitan. His attitude that tradition was no

more than yesterday's bad habits led inevitably to jettisoning the baby as well as the bathwater. As his latter-day recordings, particularly *La Traviata*, sugest, he seems either to have been unaware or not prepared to concede that to make its proper effect the music still relied for much of its expressiveness on the elegant devices of the old florid style. On his authority these were suppressed, but since he put nothing in their place—deliberately—the music was left bald, the singer's area of interpretation severely circumscribed with little room for much more than a literal reading of the score. Apart from robbing the work of much of its character and style, holding up the score as holy writ took no account of the fact that many of the markings Verdi made were themselves responses to the prevailing vocal style and traditions. Thus when he wrote 'senza le solite appoggiature' in *Rigoletto*, we may assume that in earlier works, there were places where he either wished the singers to provide them automatically or, at the least, he would not have objected had they done so. Even as late as *Aida* (1871), in the opening phrases of the final duet 'O terra addio', as Charles Osborne has noted,[12] the ear seems to require one; interestingly, in his operatic paraphrase of themes from *Aida* Liszt put one in. Since this was published some eight years after the opera's premiere, it is hard to believe that he did so on his own initiative, taking no account of the vocal practice of the day.

In Violetta's 'Ah! fors' è lui' from *Traviata*, it seems likely that those markings which are such a characteristic feature of the piece—staccato, marcato and the semi-quaver rests—were never meant to be treated literally but put there to remind the singers of the day (1853), whose technique was based in a portamento of the breath much as can be heard in the recordings of Patti and Battistini, that they should articulate the words with special clarity, separating them, so as to give them particular emphasis. This is what we hear in recordings made at the beginning of the century by Melba, Sembrich, Bellincioni, Lilli Lehmann and Tetrazzini; it is difficult to believe that they were, all of them—and their musical backgrounds were quite different—either capricious or simply careless in the same way. A literal reading encourages the singer to breathe between the words, which is ungrammatical; it is also ugly, and since it breaks up the line, unmusical. Like the overemphasis which we have already noted as a feature of the verismo style, so far from making the words more intelligible, it achieves the opposite effect.

The growing number of revivals and the proliferation of national styles were important factors in accelerating the classification of the various types of voices, a process which had been continuing steadily since the early years of the nineteenth century. By the outbreak of the First World War it was virtually complete and the categorisation established with which we are still familiar: Italian tenors divided into leggiero (Schipa), lyric (Gigli), lirico-spinto (Lauri-Volpi) and dramatic (Zenatello) voices. The Germans ranged from Mozart (Tauber) to Heldentenor (Melchior). The French even invented a special category for those like Martin whose voices had the character of a tenor but lacked the upward extension, calling it the baryton-martin (Périer and Crabbé). There were 'coloratura' (Galli-Curci and Ivogün), lyric (Dux and Vallin) and dramatic sopranos, among the last those who specialised, like Ponselle, in the Italian repertory and those, like Leider, who were principally renowned in the Wagnerian music dramas. In opera the mezzo-soprano had largely replaced the traditional contralto. There were now sub-classifications among the lower male voices: the baritones who could easily accomplish the high-lying tessitura of Verdi, Gounod and Massenet and those whose voices were pitched in the classical range, styled bass-baritone who, according to nationality, sang a wide variety of music from the oratorios of Handel and the operas of Mozart to Boris Godounov and Wotan. Of the basses, the basso cantante was the most typical, also the busiest, heard in supporting roles in most of the repertory works and showing an increasing disposition to poach leading roles, for example Don Giovanni from the classical baritone, within whose range it more properly falls, and Méphistophélès, which had been created by the baritone Jean-Baptiste Faure. Like the contralto, the basso profundo had become a *rara avis*, and the basso buffo was a stylistic rather than purely vocal discrimination; the range and quality of the singer's voice were less important than his dramatic aptitude, even physique. In general much of the classification was arbitrary and inconsistent from one country to another thus, for example, the Germans who sang Wotan and Boris Godounov (the roles have a similar tessitura) are usually referred to as bass-baritones, while the Russians are described as basses from Chaliapin onwards; though he never sang Wotan his repertory included a number of equivocal roles: Prince Igor, Eugene Onegin and Tonio in *Pagliacci*.

During the next forty years critics, composers, singing teachers and even the singers themselves tended to treat this not very systematic, merely convenient, guide as—de facto—immutable, like the laws of the Medes and Persians, the transgression of which was akin to breaking a law of nature. It is easy to sympathise with the singer's predicament. Faced with the increasing complexity of new works, the range of revivals and a greater variety of musical styles than ever before, he was at the mercy of conductors who were too often indifferent to or ignorant of the voice's limitations, and who regarded him at best as an unreliable instrumentalist. Out of self-preservation singers encouraged categorisation, if only to hide behind it. Unfortunately the art they professed to serve was not furthered by rigid specialisation. The lyric repertory, particularly the works of Rossini, Bellini and Donizetti, when shorn of dramatic intensity, quickly became meaningless, the style effete, and it was not improved by inserting the rhetorical devices of the verismo school into the line. It was at this time that the term 'coloratura' first gained general acceptance to describe a type of voice rather than a style of singing. Galli-Curci and Ivogün, two of the finest so-called coloraturas, attractive though their singing was, did not attempt, unlike their predecessors, any music more dramatic than Mimi's. History records that Patti's Valentine took her to the limits, Melba's Elsa wanted temperament and Tetrazzini's Aida could hardly have been as stunning as her Lucia, yet the dramatic accents of these roles gave to the singers' art an added perspective which, according to contemporary report, informed their interpretations of Gilda and Violetta. Next to that remarkable fragment of the Queen of the Night's second aria, when Mapleson caught Sembrich in full flood, the staccati like great balls of fire, Ivogün, for all her pretty vocalism, is rather small beer. If we did not know, it would be hard to tell that the Queen is hell-bent on revenge.

The absence of agility in all voices brought a general decline in accuracy and precision of execution. With the loss of interest in the works of the old Italian repertory, coloratura was discredited and the graces and accomplishments of the florid style cast aside. On the face of it agility was no longer a pre-requisite in the dramatic repertory and since it was only mastered by hours of solfeggio, a tedious practice, the facility was lost with more alacrity than it could be acquired; its absence, however, was easily discernible to the cultivated ear:

The vocal music of today is not embroidered with runs, trills, groups and other ornaments, as the operas of the late seventeenth century were, but it does contain thousands of progressions which can be executed with perfect smoothness and fluency by the agile voice, but by the untrained in coloratura only awkwardly and uncertainly.[13]

The two greatest dramatic sopranos of this period, Rosa Ponselle and Frieda Leider, were wonderful singers but they were not the virtuose that their predecessors, Lehmann and Nordica, had been; we cannot imagine either of them cavorting aloft with ease and brilliance as Lucia or Philine. Melchior's singing in Wagner was magnificent with overwhelming power and authority but it was without the suave line, finesse and command of nuance that had made Tamagno's Otello unique. Can one doubt that had he sung Mozart regularly, as Slezak had, the discipline would have refined his art? In the Italian repertory Martinelli, admirable artist though he was, never attempted Caruso's feat of reconciling Nemorino with Radamès. Gigli tried, but even his most uncritical admirers could not claim a complete victory for his Radamès, while as Nemorino, in spite of the sheer beauty of his voice, he was far indeed from the required elegant manner.

Up to 1914, for the general public the greatest opera singer of the moment—a Patti, a Melba, a Mei-Figner, a Calvé, a de Reszke, a Battistini, a Caruso— was automatically and quite simply the most exotic star of the entertainment world. The war was to change that. From the middle of the nineteenth century until the First World War, as a popular entertainment, opera was subjected to increasing competition from operetta, music hall and vaude-ville. Though competition was vigorous, it remained friendly and all managed to live in a state of harmony. Indeed, the harmony was such that there was possible a certain traffic of artists between them: Lina Cavalieri made her way up through variety and music hall to the opera; Eugenia Mantelli and Suzanne Adams went back down the same way. The idiom of the popular music of the day was not radically dissimilar from operatic music. It was still possible for a classically trained singer to have a foot in both camps; Caruso was quite as famous as a singer of Neapolitan songs and popular ballads as he was in the opera house.

The greatest holocaust that man had hitherto known rudely swept away the old society and its agreeable pastimes. Trench warfare made no fine discriminations; before the awful bombardment, officer and man were equal cannon fodder. From the New World, where generations of Europeans had fled, came the American troops, bringing with them a taste for entertainments more in tune with the new democratic spirit. This was the age of the cinema, which was creating its own idols—silent ones—to topple the diva from her traditional throne, while D. W. Griffiths was devising spectacles which could never be contained on any opera house stage. From America too, came a new music. The post-war world was enchanted by jazz with its heady tunes and syncopated rhythms. Opera seemed old-fashioned, the opera house with its diamond tiaras, serried tiers of boxes and dingy gallery, a metaphor for an outdated order: a polite and elegant but rigidly stratified society.

PART I

Revolution and Russian Singing

1. Chaliapin

The war was to make the most profound and lasting changes in Russia; the collapse of the Russian army led to revolution. In February 1917, less than four years after the splendid ceremonies celebrating its tercentenary, the Romanov dynasty was deposed. That October the fledgling republic was itself overturned by the Bolsheviks. An iron curtain did not descend at once and during the next ten years Russian artists continued to visit the west fairly regularly, but the glories of the Imperial Opera were at one with Nineveh and Tyre. A few of its artists, chief among them Sobinov and Nezhdanova, preferred to remain and serve the new regime but many, including some of the most distinguished, went abroad never to return. Even those who had once made common cause with progressive and socialist movements were hardly prepared for the harsh reality of the brave new world. The great bass FEODOR CHALIAPIN (1873–1938) spent a few years as an honoured but, in his opinion, insufficiently remunerated artist of the people and then left to recoup his fortune in the United States. The men of the revolution watched him go with mixed feelings; by then he had become an unmanageable embarassment, for such was his prestige that there was no way in which they could discipline him. At his last public appearance in Russia at the opening of the Third International Congress in Moscow in 1921:

> In front of eight or nine hundred international delegates and many thousands of Bolsheviks from Moscow, he sang in turn in French, German, Italian and English. 'As I am a nationalist,' he began, 'first of all, I shall sing in Russian.' At this everyone laughed. When the audience clamoured for more he replied, 'Comrades,' employing the word with infinite expression, 'what has become of discipline?' At this everyone laughed even more. Finally when he broke into the old song of the peasants in revolt, singing with passion and art, the entire hall took up the refrain and the

Communists gave him the kind of ovation that only Lenin gets. A veritable god among artists![1]

He was obliged to leave behind him all the valuable things he had accumulated in the affluent pre-war days, or almost all of them; he did manage to get away with eight priceless Gobelin tapestries. When an inexperienced Soviet customs officer found them in his luggage, Chaliapin ingeniously explained that they were just some backcloths for *Boris Godounov*.

After an absence of fourteen years he reappeared at the Metropolitan Opera House, New York. Though he had been singing for more than a quarter of a century, he was at the summit of his vocal and interpretative powers. In 1907 the critics had been impressed by his 'splendidly rotund voice',[2] but offended by the frank realism of his acting. This time with one accord they all acclaimed him:

> Last night nobility of acting was paired with a beautiful nobility of voice and vocal style, and his Boris stood out of the dramatic picture like one of the old time heroes of tragedy . . . He sang in Russian: and though it was possible even for those unfamiliar with the language to feel some of the intimacy which must exist between the original text and the music, the effect upon the Russians in the audience was akin to frenzy. All that we have heard of the greatness of his interpretation of the character of Boris was made plain. It was heart-breaking in its pathos, terrible in its vehemence and agony.[3]

Out of Pushkin's bloody regicide, Moussorgsky fashioned the greatest bass role in opera, a Russian Macbeth, an enormously demanding but equally rewarding role. And like Macbeth, while it is difficult to give a totally ineffective performance, to give a really memorable one is just as hard. As Krehbiel's review attests, Chaliapin's personality, his huge physical presence and magnificent singing, left an unforgettable impression on those who saw him in this role. No less remarkable were his Méphistophélès, Ivan the Terrible in Rimsky-

1 Feodor Chaliapin by himself

Korsakov's *Maid of Pskov*, Dosifey in *Khovansh-china*, Miller in Dargomizhsky's *Roussalka* and Don Quichotte (which was specially written for him); all of them very different from each other, each was a classic interpretation. Even in those roles, which in lesser hands might be considered small: Don Basilio, Colline and Khan Kontchak,

> one's eyes were drawn to him as to a magnet; there might be two or more principals on the stage and a chorus of sixty all singing their hearts out but one only saw Chaliapin. In the Polovtsian Dances in *Prince Igor*, the scene packed with chorus and dancers, most of the audience looked only at Khan Kontchak even though he was enthroned to one side, to give the ballet stage centre. I know because I too was magnetised, and watching him, hugged myself with delight.[4]

Like MacGregor, where he sat, that was the head of the table.

The gramophone cannot preserve a singer's physical presence, yet Chaliapin's art was so perfectly integrated, his singing so much an expression of the man himself, that his records almost achieve the impossible. Not surprisingly the histrionics in the Clock Scene and Death are tremendous but in the long phrases of Boris's Farewell, he creates an effect quite as potent solely through his singing. The timbre of the voice is characteristic, the tone limpid and correctly placed on the breath, the registers smoothly blended and like Battistini, his mastery of the head voice is complete. All of Chaliapin's technical skill was deployed for expressive purposes. For him speech and song were indissoluble; at its most intense speech turned into song and no mechanical adjustment was necessary; this is especially evident in the declamatory passages in the Clock Scene. The extraordinary dynamic range from a resonant forte through every shading to a hushed and—as we hear it in the famous live recordings from Covent Garden—perfectly audible pianissimo, was achieved entirely through intensity; never does he sing softly or loudly for its own sake; every effect has its cause. When he derided the empty virtuosity which took no account of words, he was merely echoing Tosi's complaint two centuries previously that singing which is instrumental in conception neglects the proper affections and disregards precisely that which makes the human voice unique: its ability to place words into the musical tone. Chaliapin's instincts, like his training, were classical (his teacher Dimitri Uzatov had studied with Camille Everard, a pupil of Garcia); for him beautiful singing was not merely smooth vocalism with some facility in the execution of fioritura, but a language of expression, the grammar of its effects responsive to the setting of the words. Just as Battistini had infused his singing with the more dramatic style of the music of the late nineteenth century and achieved it entirely by musical means, so Chaliapin sought to translate Italian bel canto into Russian opera and song. In Malashkin's 'O could I in song tell my sorrow' (for Rachmaninov no one could sing a love song as Chaliapin did), the flowing cantilena is full of nuances, the line punctuated ardently but not broken up; even when he pushes a note sharp deliberately, so as to stress a particular word or syllable, the tension is sustained. In his singing we can hear the traditional Italian devices modified, the messa di voce (of which he was an especial master), marcato, martellato and suoni ribattuti, to suit the Russian language and music. Although he rarely uses portamento in the Italian fashion, his singing is based in a portamento of the breath precisely as is Battistini's; it is implicit in all of his phrasing. His idiosyncratic treatment of mordents and gruppetti in French and Italian music has come in for a good deal of criticism, but, although it is unstylish, the use of the intrusive 'w' was not the result of a technical frailty but an attempt, albeit an unsuccessful one, to put new feeling into an old form. Even in Bellini's 'Vi ravviso', where he can hardly vie for smoothness of manner with Plançon, the interpretation, despite the eccentric style, is supremely expressive, especially the opening recitative 'Il mulino, il fonte . . .' In everything he did there was an extraordinary spontaneity and intensity, both highly prized features of bel canto.

He repeated his New York triumphs throughout the United States and also in Europe, when he visited Covent Garden for the first time in 1926, and reappeared at the Paris Opéra and La Scala, Milan. Wherever he went, he was greeted like the Tsar; he once remarked that had Nicolas let him play the role

there would have been no revolution. It was significant that the same New York critics who now hailed him as the Tsar had previously dismissed him as a mouzhik; in the intervening years a world war and the Russian Revolution had completely upturned the values of the Edwardian era; what had been thought unnecessarily crude and vulgar was now deemed noble and profoundly moving. No bass before or since has enjoyed such acclaim or such fees. He excused his rapacity to Raoul Gunsbourg pleading that he was not stingy, only grasping.[5] During these years he began another career as a recitalist, which was to occupy him increasingly in the remainder of his life. For Chaliapin the concert platform was an extension of the theatre and his recitals were dramatic events:

> Mr Chaliapin issues no programme of his own selections but announces before each song what it is going to be by the number it bears in the book of words in English translation, with which the audience is expected to provide itself. It is the same process as announcing hymns from the hymn book in church, but unlike the hymn book, the collection of Mr Chaliapin's words is sold at 25 cents.[6]

For the audience the uncertainty added immeasurably to the excitement: for the accompanist, as Ivor Newton and Gerald Moore recall, it was an occupational hazard. At a concert in Manchester with Gerald Moore in Schumann's 'Two Grenadiers'. 'Chaliapin thumped the lid of the piano to accelerate the tempo when he came to the Marseillaise section. In this song he even thrust his hand into the pocket of his dress suit at the illusion to Napoleon. Yet he did it so naturally that none of us smiled'.[7] Sometimes, when he thought the piano postlude an anticlimax, he would stride off, leaving the accompanist to finish as best he could in the face of a wildly cheering public. On other occasions, as at the end of Aleko's aria from Rachmaninov's opera, 'he would listen with such intensity that there would be no sound or movement in the audience until (the pianist) finally lifted the pedal at the end of the last bar'.[8]

Although Chaliapin was undoubtedly the dominating personality among the Russian singers, there was still active a large number of fine singers from pre-revolutionary days. One of the most popular of these was the baritone GEORGE BAKLANOV (1880–1938), the possessor of a dark and incisive voice, a great rumbustious giant of a man with a striking personality off stage as well as on. His skill in make-up was particularly admired: as Tonio when 'he conveyed by his appearance and facial mien the doltish, cruel and sensuous clown'[9] and Escamillo, in which he was no 'handsome dandy off a raisin box but a reticent, slightly sombre and deliberately mysterious matador'.[10] Upon completing his vocal studies in Milan with Vittorio Vanza, in 1903 he made his debut at the Kiev Opera in the title-role of Rubinstein's *Demon*. Within a couple of years he had secured an engagement in Moscow with Zimin's company, thereafter he moved on to the Bolshoi and the Marinsky where he continued to sing often until the Revolution. He made guest appearances in Paris at the Théâtre des Champs Elysées as Onegin, and at the Berlin Komische Oper, when his highly original and effective interpretations of Rigoletto and Scarpia created quite a stir. They did again at Covent Garden in the summer of 1910, and it was generally regretted that he had only been engaged for a handful of performances. The previous autumn Henry Russell booked him for the opening season of the Boston Opera. He made his debut on the first night in the role of Barnaba in *Gioconda* showing 'his vocal and pictorial aptitude for such a villain as the spy'.[11] Two days later as Amonasro in company with Boninsegna, Leliva and Mardones:

> [He] made the most unqualifiedly favourable impression of any of the newcomers. His voice is a baritone of beautiful quality, healthy, noble and easily and rationally produced. He sings with taste and understanding and last night acted with intelligence. He gives promise of proving one of the great baritones.[12]

2 George Baklanov as Vindex in Rubinstein's *Nero*

His other roles in Boston included Rigoletto, in which part he was much admired by the critic Hale who also thought his Escamillo 'the best here in many years, the first ... who comprehends the character of the Toreador Song, by singing the second verse directly to Carmen'.[13] He also sang Nilakantha, Valentin and Scarpia when he showed again 'he is one of the most talented ... members of the company. He has already accomplished much, and with his excellent voice, his temperament and his earnestness as an artist, should accomplish much more in the future'.[14] So he did, undertaking the title-role in an abridged version of Rachmaninov's *Miserly Knight* and, on tour, Telramund in an Italian *Lohengrin*. The following season came Tonio and Iago; both were warmly received. After Russell's departure from Boston, he appeared with the com-

pany organised by Max Rabinoff in 1915, when he moved over from Valentin to Méphistophélès, but in this he failed to please and his dramatic approach was considered exaggerated. Subsequently he sang Manfredo in Montemezzi's *L'Amore dei tre Re* and Gérard in *Andrea Chénier*, first in Boston and later on tour at the Lexington Theatre, New York. In spite of good notices, he was never invited to the Metropolitan, though he did sing with the company once on tour.

When war broke out in 1914 Baklanov was in Italy. To get back home he was obliged to travel through hostile Turkey. To do this and to avoid certain imprisonment or worse, he disguised himself as a woman. He must have looked, to say the least, a large lady, standing six feet three and weighing more than two hundred pounds; it says much for

3 Alexander Bragin as Eugene Onegin

Guido in Février's *Monna Vanna*, Golaud, Athanaël in *Thaïs*, Marc-Antoine in *Cléopâtre*, Simonson in Alfano's *Resurrection* and Manfredo in Montemezzi's *L'Amore dei tre Re*, all of them opposite Mary Garden. His finest achievements were Boris Godounov, which he succeeded to after Chaliapin's departure, and Wotan, when *Musical America* proclaimed him 'without doubt the best Wotan that ever stalked the Auditorium stage'.[15]

Baklanov's voice, as we hear it in recordings, was a full, dark, bass-baritone of fine quality, the vowels pure and the registers correctly blended over a wide range from the bass F to the G above middle C. A rapid vibrato was not, at least in his best years, obtrusive and he used it to considerable effect in moments of dramatic intensity. The Toreador's Song is done with splendid panache; an insinuating and at the same time slightly sinister interpretation. Although it is possible to feel that he overdoes it—too much rubato, and the marcato is roughly executed—he makes an undeniable effect in a repetitive piece, and it is not difficult to understand why he was so successful in a role that gives the singer few other opportunities. There is the same swagger, rhythmic vigour and brilliance in the Nuptial Hymn from Rubinstein's *Nero*. He shows himself a finer and more subtle artist in the air of Nilakantha from *Lakmé*, which is also sung in Russian. If it lacks the exemplary legato of Journet, the singing has considerable intensity and variety of colour and the tessitura lies perfectly in his range. In later years the voice, as we hear it in an electric recording of Prince Igor's 'No sleep, no rest', has lost its cutting edge and the vibrato loosened. Baklanov's best records confirm the high opinions of his contemporaries; his was an impressive talent even if, ultimately, more remarkable for histrionic skill than musical imagination.

The career of ALEXANDER BRAGIN (1881–) was hardly as successful and much of it, especially after the Revolution, was spent in provincial theatres, yet his records indicate that in his youth, at any rate, his accomplishments were representative of the high standards extant in Imperial Russia. The voice seems to have been a good-sized high baritone; on his earliest records the emission is smooth and the registers are blended up to a brilliant high A flat. In a swaggering rondo from Krotkov's *The Poet* he sings with spirit and plenty of rhythmic energy, sweeping through the high lying cantilena with ease and we can forgive an occasional tendency to shout. A much-abbreviated rendering of Tonio's Prologue (in Russian) reveals a wider

his skill in disguise that no curious Turk demanded to look under the yashmak. Once in Russia, he was conscripted and sent to the Austrian front. The climax of his military eminence took place at night when, to escape the incessant bombardment, he climbed a tree. Getting down again proved rather more difficult and by the time he managed it, it was dawn, and his comrades had long since retreated, leaving him stranded behind the enemy lines.

He must have found his way back somehow, for in the autumn of 1917 he made his debut with the Chicago Opera as Méphistophélès in *Faust* with Melba and Muratore; he was to remain with the company for nine seasons. During that time, as well as repeating many of his Boston triumphs, he added a variety of new roles from the French, Italian and Russian repertories. He was the Father in *Louise*, range of dynamics and the big melody is carried in an attractive and well-focussed tone. Bragin was a pupil of Glabely, a respected teacher of the day. Subsequently he went for further study in Vienna and Berlin before making his debut, like Baklanov, at the Kiev Opera, in 1899. After six years he was engaged at the Marinsky, where he remained a principal until 1911. For one season he also appeared in Moscow at the Bolshoi. His repertory included Germont, Rigoletto, Prince Igor, the Demon, the title-role in Don Giovanni, Figaro in *Le Nozze di Figaro*, and Yeletsky in the *Queen of Spades*. From 1911 he sang mostly in operetta, touring with various companies throughout Russia and making a particular reputation in Planquette's *Les Cloches de Corneville*. His voice by this time had begun to deteriorate, as a couple of duet recordings from the *Demon* and *Samson et Dalila* with Elizaveta Petrenko suggest; he can still bat out a top note when the occasion requires but the tone has become dull and spread, and the tendency to shout grown into a habit.

So far as is known the baritone IVAN GRIZOUNOV (1878–1919) did not sing outside Russia; we find no reference to his name in the various seasons of Russian opera given in London and Paris in the period immediately prior to the outbreak of the First World War. Most of his career was spent in Moscow. He was a principal with the Imperial Opera at the Bolshoi between 1904 and 1915, save for one season, 1908 to 1909, which he spent with Zimin's Opera. After 1915 he returned to Zimin's but by then he had lost his voice.

His is a typical Russian baritone, pleasantly vibratory and well schooled, the tone focused, the registers properly blended and with fine, ringing, high notes. In the aria of Abubeker from Cui's *Prisoner of the Caucasus* it cannot be said that his singing is imaginative; there is little variety of colour, nuance or dynamics but then Cui's music is not particularly inspiring.

Like so many other Russian singers of his day, we know comparatively little about IVAN IVANTSOV (*c.* 1880–). He spent the formative part of his career in the provinces but eventually emerged to sing with leading companies in Moscow and St Petersburg. During the last years of the Imperial regime he joined the Music Drama Theatre. His repertory ranged through principal roles in Russian opera as well as Silvio, Scarpia, Escamillo and Marcello. After the Revolution he fled Russia and made guest appearances in Germany. Subsequently he was a member of various emigré companies,

singing in Madrid and Barcelona and on tour in South America and the United States.

His voice as we hear it in Scarpia's 'Se la giurata fede', is a healthy-sounding dark baritone of good quality with notably well-produced high notes.

2. Smirnov

In the years before the Revolution the most outstanding lyric tenor in Russia after Sobinov was DIMITRI SMIRNOV (1881–1944). Unlike Sobinov, when the Revolution came Smirnov fled, making his abode first in Paris, then London and Athens, and finally ending up in Riga, Latvia. He declined repeated, and pressing, offers to return home. In 1940, however, events overtook him: at the time of the Ribbentrop-Molotov pact, the Baltic states, of which Latvia was one, were annexed by the Soviet Union; thus, whether he liked it or not, he found himself once again in Russia.

Smirnov was born in Moscow and educated at the Imperial School of Commerce. When he was twenty one he joined the private opera company of the

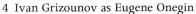
4 Ivan Grizounov as Eugene Onegin

and an unusually perceptive and knowledgeable critic, writing in 1909 noted that:

Smirnov possessed a strong lyric tenor of wide compass: a trifle harsh, but of good timbre. Having made an excellent job of the part of Rodolfo, he began to overrate his vocal potential, and even contrived to sing Raoul; but this feat won him no laurels, his performance being weak dramatically, as so often happens when the voice is strained. Smirnov's voice was beautifully produced and, paradoxically though it may seem, this very circumstance was harmful to the singer. Not being gifted with a sufficiently sensitive artistic intellect he used, first and foremost, to pick out in each role its superficial aspects . . . His temperament was shallow—one might even say superficial; his intuition was not notable for its delicacy; he never himself experienced sincere emotion, and he did not arouse it in the listener. Relying excessively on long fermate, diminuendi and melismate, he did not penetrate to the essence of the role but drifted on its surface . . . One strange quality of his voice [was] a minimal but persistent tremolo. Scarcely noticeable on short notes, on extended notes it consistently marred his singing.[1]

As in the case of so many of his compatriots Smirnov's first visit outside Russia was to Paris, when he was a soloist in one of the popular Concerts Russes.[5] The enterprising Raoul Gunsbourg heard him and snapped him up for Monte Carlo. During the next five years he was a regular and popular visitor, singing Almaviva, Faust in *Mefistofele* and the Prince in *Roussalka* with Chaliapin, Loris in *Fedora* with Marthe Chenal and Ruffo, Alfredo in *Traviata* with Hempel, Kurz and Lipkowska, with whom he also sang in *Roméo et Julietto*, *Rigoletto* and *La Bohème*. On 19 May 1908 he made his debut at the Paris Opéra as the Pretender in *Boris Godounov*, in company with Chaliapin, Altchevsky, Yuzhina and Kastorsky. It was one of the great operatic occasions of modern times; the opera, Chaliapin, his fellow soloists, the chorus and Bakst's costumes all created a sensation. Among the many prominent international personalities in the audience was Otto Kahn, Chairman of the Board of Directors of the Metropolitan, New York. Kahn was so impressed with Smirnov that he telegraphed Gatti-Casazza urging him to offer the tenor a contract.

Smirnov joined the Met in 1910 and sang there for two seasons, but like Bonci and Clément, both intelligent artists but with small and not particularly ingratiating voices, he failed to make an impression on a public which, in the heyday of

5 Ivan Ivantzov as Shaklovity in *Khovanshchina*

millionaire Savva Mamontov, at first singing in the chorus but within a comparatively short while graduating to small parts. Encouraged by his success, he decided to undertake a short but intensive course of vocal study under Pavlovskaya. When he returned to the stage, it was to the Bolshoi, as Bayan in Glinka's *Russlan and Ludmilla*, a performance which incidentally also introduced Rachmaninov as conductor. Until 1917 Smirnov sang regularly at both Imperial theatres in a variety of roles: Sinodal in the *Demon*, Doubrovsky in Napravnik's setting of Pushkin's unfinished novel of the same name, Rodolfo, the Duke, Vladimir in *Prince Igor*, Nadir in *Les Pêcheurs de perles*, Werther, the Hindu Guest in *Sadko*, Alfredo, Gerald, Tamino and Faust and he also appeared in Rachmaninov's *Francesca da Rimini* and Moniuszko's *Halka*. Notwithstanding his many successes his art was not admired without qualification. Sergei Levik, who was himself a singer

Caruso, cared for nothing but a big and sonorous tone. There being no Russian repertory he was obliged to compete directly with Caruso as the Duke in *Rigoletto* and share Alfredo with John McCormack, also in his debut season. The latter's sweeter voice, not to mention the vociferous presence in the audience of a large Irish contingent on his first appearance, assured him the popular success that was denied Smirnov. The critics too were indifferent, when not actually hostile; Henderson complained of his 'dead, flat and colourless'[2] Roméo. Smirnov sang one performance of Gérald in *Lakmé* for the Boston Opera, made a short tour of South America under the direction of Leopoldo Mugnone (the company also included a young and totally unknown soprano, Amelita Galli-Curci) and then returned home.

In Europe he continued his eventful progress, at the Monnaie with the Monte Carlo company in *Barbiere di Siviglia* and *Mefistofele*, again with Chaliapin; in Madrid, also in *Mefistofele*; and in the summer of 1914 Beecham introduced him to London, at Drury Lane, as Levko in Rimsky-Korsakov's *May Night*. *The Times* thought his voice 'pure and musical though not remarkably strong'.[3] In Paris Smirnov was a regular guest in seasons of Russian opera at the Théâtre du Châtelet and the Théâtre Sarah Bernhardt, where he sang in performances of *Prince Igor*, *Roussalka*, *Russian and Ludmila* and Serov's *Judith*. His good looks and fine stage presence delighted not only the public but some of his more susceptible colleagues: for Kouznetsova he was a favourite partner, while Litvinne, after appearing with him in *Roussalka* and *Judith*, dubbed him 'Prince Charming'. The one dissenting note came from the critic de Curzon, who thought his voice 'disagreeable'.[4] After the war he appeared only occasionally in opera: at Berlin, the Opéra-Comique, Geneva (where the size of his fee excited more comment than his singing), and again at Monte Carlo in 1924, when he sang in *Butterfly* and *La Foire de Sorotchintzi*. During these years he was mostly active as a concert and recital singer in western Europe, the United States and Japan. He was the first important emigré singer to revisit Russia, when he gave a number of concerts in 1926. A review of a Paris recital in 1923 suggests that his singing, virtues and vices alike, remained largely unaffected by time:

Before an extremely elegant audience *a priori* in raptures, the celebrated Smirnov showed off his graces. They are real ones. He is a virtuoso of bel canto,

6 Dimitri Smirnov as the Duke of Mantua

à la Rossini and à la Verdi. We already knew his voice, very well placed, full of charm and power, gifted with a remarkable evenness of timbre, in the high as well as the low notes. Now it swells and fills the hall, now it is nothing but a whisper . . . but Smirnov exaggerates. For him there is no piece that does not require its diminuendo, its formidable crescendo, its swooning. Prudently he limits himself to Puccini, Rossini and Massenet . . . What would he offer, one wonders, in a more refined, simple and grand style of music, in say Bach or Duparc?[5]

He was still singing a 'remarkable'[6] Gregori in *Boris Godounov* in a new production at the Théâtre des

Champs Elysées in January 1931, in which Chaliapin presented a 'revised' interpretation of his great role, as well as supervising the whole production.

Smirnov's many recordings reveal a characteristically Russian tenor voice of an appealing quality. Only rarely, *pace* Henderson, does he sound either dead or flat, and if there is little variety of colour in his singing, some of his technical accomplishments are remarkable. The only trouble is, as Levik observed, too often they seem to be displayed without any real cause. The records hardly substantiate the claim that he was a finer musician than Sobinov; it is true that his singing was more sensational but his effects were often at the expense of the music. The Duke's 'La donna è mobile' (in his first and Russian recording of this aria), with its impossibly drawn-out morendi, and the ridiculous ending of 'Donna non vidi mai', which he switches up an octave, hardly demonstrate sensitive musicianship. At his best his singing had considerable charm; Lohengrin's 'In fernem Land', for example, may sound odd in Russian but the declamation is a model—so clear and so poetically uttered. And though his manner is never very ardent, in Werther's 'Lied d'Ossian' the very deliberate and careful measuring of the words makes its own effect. The air from *La Foire de Sorotchintzi* was recorded soon after the performances at Monte Carlo and for that reason is sung in French; it is justly famous, an outstanding example of sustained mezza voce singing. 'Plus blanche' from *Les Huguenots* is altogether too dry-toned and literal, and the cadenza takes him to the limits of his resources; it is not difficult to hear why he made little impression in this music on an audience accustomed to Erschov's lambent and heroic tones. Alfredo's 'Dei miei bollenti' far better suited his voice; the recitative is done with a nice freedom and in the aria the rhythm delicately but firmly pointed. Many of the Russian pieces are outstanding: the aria of Doubrovsky (a noble bandit in the Ernani mould; the part was created by Figner) he delivers in an eloquent legato winding up to a finely poised high B natural. Kaschevarov's 'Tranquillity' and the arias from Kazachanko's *Pan Sotnik* and Gretchaninov's *Dobrynia Nikitch*, though not distinguished music, in Smirnov's renderings sound at their very best. He is less successful with Rachmaninov's Georgian love song; for all the advantage of being sung in the original the performance is neither as evocative nor as affectionately phrased as McCormack's and certainly not so accurate. Like the haunting air of Tsar Berendey from

Rimsky-Korsakov's *Snegourotchka*, which also disappoints, it dates from the twenties when his voice had lost its sheen and the vibrato had become obtrusive.

3. *Kouznetsova to Koshetz*

MARIA KOUZNETSOVA (1880–1966) was far the most brilliant and successful Russian soprano of her day. A woman of great physical beauty, an actress of charm and sensitivity and a first class singer, she was also a dancer, a film star and she even organised her own opera company. Born in Odessa, her father was a fashionable portrait painter who had earned his laurels at the Paris Exhibitions of 1889 and 1900. She was brought up in an artistic environment and when still only a girl she joined the class of a well known dancer, Alexander Petrovsky, at the Alexandra Theatre in St Petersburg. Later, when her voice had developed sufficiently, she switched to singing and became a pupil of the baritone Joachim Tartakov. Like Mary Garden whom she resembled in many ways her career began at the top: at the Marinsky Theatre where she made her debut in 1905 as Marguerite in *Faust*. She remained a principal with the company until the Revolution, appearing there often: as Juliette, Manon, Manon Lescaut, Thaïs, Elsa, Sieglinde, Violetta and Mimi and, in Russian opera, in Rimsky-Korsakov's *Snegourotchka*, *Pan Voyevoda* and *Legend of the Invisible City of Kitezh*; Glinka's *Russlan and Ludmilla* and *A Life for the Tsar*; Tchaikovsky's *Mazeppa*, *Queen of Spades*, *Eugene Onegin*, Napravnik's *Francesca da Rimini* and *Doubrovsky*, and Rubinstein's *Demon*.

In 1908 she made a highly successful debut at the Paris Opéra and began a career in France scarcely less distinguished than the one she already enjoyed in Russia. After Elsa, she sang Marguerite, Juliette, the title-role in Chabrier's *Gwendoline*, *Aida*, *Salome* and Fausta in Massenet's *Roma*. The French critics were swept off their feet by her art and, we may assume, not a little affected by her 'magnificent black hair, lustrous dark eyes and face so attractive that one dreams about it':[1] almost to a man they seem to have suspended their critical faculties and for some several years she could do no wrong. Of her Gwendoline Pougin wrote 'it is the perfect representation of a young girl, so loveable and so full of grace'.[2] For Henri de Curzon her Juliette 'in every gesture is always exactly what would become a young girl',[3] and he especially praised her use of a scarf as she bade Romeo a final 'Adieu' from the

7 Maria Kouznetsova as Jacqueline in *Fortunio*

of her figure. Singing away at the top of her voice, she danced as no one expected she could.

In the summer of 1909 she was invited to Covent Garden to sing Marguerite when 'her beautiful singing and rather unconventional treatment of the part were most acceptable'[4] and Mimi, a performance of 'great skill acted with rare pathos and power'.[5] In the following year she added Juliette and Manon Lescaut. Also in 1910 she expanded her Paris activities making her debut at the Opéra-Comique as Manon. In the course of the next few years she would be singing at the Opéra-Comique and the Opéra, often at both during the same week. By this time the honeymoon was over and the critics had become aware of certain failings in her art. In 1913 after a busy season at the Opéra when she sang Thaïs, Juliette and Marguerite:

> I recently went to hear this singer again, and I listened to her with the most scrupulous attention. If her voice, in its security, range and timbre pleased me as much as the first occasions on which I heard her, I must confess that in many passages the artist did not seem to me to realise all that one has the right to expect from a naturally superb organ. Mlle Kouznetsova, strong in her facility, neglects the nuances and contrasts that would give her voice a charm capable of doubling its beauty. Sure of her success, she does not want to work hard enough any more, and an artist must always be striving after perfection. She too often gives a free reign to her inspiration, which is not always a good counsellor.[6]

During these years she was active in concert and recitals, appearing frequently in programmes of 'ancient' music directed by her husband José Lassalle. Between 1912 and 1914 she was much admired at Monte Carlo. There, as well as Thaïs, Tosca and Aida, she was heard as Norma with Rousselière and Journet, Valentine in *Ugonotti* with Lipkowska and Martinelli, in Saint-Saëns's *Les Barbares*, Gunsbourg's *Venise*, and she created Fausta in Massenet's *Roma*, and a leading role in Massenet's *Cléopâtre* —'it was the most astonishing creation'.[7] In 1914 she sang in London again in *Prince Igor* during the second Beecham season of Russian opera at Drury Lane. *The Times* singled out the duet for Yaroslavna and Galitzky and praised 'the splendid characterisation and singing'[8] of Kouznetsova and Chaliapin. In Paris the same year she added another dimension to her art when she danced the role of Potiphar's wife in Richard Strauss's dramatic ballet *Josephslegende*. For the occasion she was superbly costumed by Bakst in pantaloons, a full length gown and a

balcony. No question of it, she was an artist to her fingertips; in Thaïs to her toes too, for she took every opportunity the role gave her to show off her terpsichorean skill. Her dancing, by all accounts and notwithstanding a classical training, was of the bare-footed lithesome school made fashionable by Isadora Duncan. It was to Isadora that she owed her use of the scarf; it was an important prop in many of her impersonations. In *Salome* with seven of them she had ample opportunity to demonstrate her skill and at the same time reveal the curvaceous outline headpiece bedizened with plumes and jewellery. Maybe all the paraphernalia impeded her movements, for she was not a success and she did not undertake the part in its London premiere.

In 1916 she made what were to be her only appearances in the United States, at the Chicago Opera in the local premiere of *Cléopâtre*. She caused something of a sensation, as a result of the way she was dressed, or rather undressed. *The Tribune* critic observed waspishly that she was clad so that 'voice teachers could assure themselves of her perfect diaphragmatic action'.[9] Unfortunately for Kouznetsova Chicago was Garden's town and Garden quickly decided to appropriate the role for herself; there was no room for both of them and Kouznetsova was never invited again. Back in Petrograd she was swept up in the events of the Revolution. Deciding to leave Russia for good, she sought asylum on board a Swedish freighter; so as to escape the regulation search before the ship was allowed to depart, she was obliged to disguise herself as a cabin boy. At the time she was thirty seven and her figure had never been ambiguous; she must have been greatly relieved when the Soviet police did not demand that the trunk she was hiding in should be opened up and the disguise was not put to the test.

In France, where she settled thereafter, she gave recitals of Russian music assisted by the tenor George Pozemkovsky, in which she both sang and danced. Marc-Samuel Rousseau wrote an opera, *Tarass Boulba* (based on Gogol's novel), especially for her. After the first performance at the Théâtre Lyrique in Paris in 1919, *Le Ménestrel* commented:

> she sang the exquisite prologue marvellously . . . and danced the mazurka in the last act in a manner to make one dizzy.[10]

In 1920 she was re-engaged at Covent Garden as Mimi, but she and Beecham did not get on and these were her last appearances in opera in London. In Paris throughout the 1920s she appeared in a variety of concerts and recitals, on several occasions with her son, the baritone Michel Benoit. She also starred in a season of operetta at the Théâtre Mogador in Kalman's *La Bayadère* and made several silent movies. She returned to Monte Carlo in 1924 for some performances of *Carmen* with Muratore. In 1929 with Benoit she organised a Russian opera company made up of emigré artists and gave seasons at the Théâtre des Champs Elysées in Paris, Barcelona, Madrid, Milan and at the Colon, Buenos Aires. The repertory included a number of works in

which she herself sang: *Prince Igor*, *The Fair at Sorotchintzi, Snegourotchka* and *The Legend of the Invisible City of Kitezh*. There was a tour of Japan as late as 1936 and the company remained active until the outbreak of the Second World War.

Kouznetsova made a few recordings for the G & T company in 1905, three series for Pathé in 1907, 1916 and 1920, and a small group of Odeons in the early electric period. It is unfortunate that the Pathés, the least successful technically, represent her at the height of her powers. They were made by the 'Hill and Dale' process which became obsolete in the early 1930s, with the result that for over thirty

8 Kouznetsova as Thaïs

years the records were virtually unplayable. There is little doubt that had she recorded for Victor or Columbia her reputation would today stand much higher. Hers was a lyric soprano of particularly fine quality, the tone pure and the diction always clear and musical. If it was not a large voice, the clean attack and brilliant high notes, to which a narrow and rapid vibrato gave an added shimmer, must have helped the voice to sound above the orchestra in parts like Aida and Salome, for which it might have been thought she would hardly have had the power. All of her records are characterised by sensitive musicianship and fine feeling. On a G & T, Violetta's 'Ah! fors' è lui' (sung in Russian), she contrives exactly the right spontaneous manner entirely through the music and without striving after effect. In the aria the rubato is nicely judged and the rhythm properly sustained. Only questionable is the ugly attack in the passage 'A quell'amor', brought on by the Russian language, and a trill in the cadenza which she does not properly resolve. In Manon's 'Gavotte', the French is impeccable and the singing better than most of her French contemporaries', the tone ingratiating and the graces delicately and expressively turned. Here, as in 'Adieu notre petite table', she achieves her effect by subtle vocal colouring and eloquent phrasing and without recourse to those so-called touches of personality, the coy and insinuating manner that too many interpreters of this role have offered in lieu of real characterisation. An air from *Tarass Boulba* is especially notable for a remarkable piece of unaccompanied singing which she tops off with a stunning pianissimo high B. Although she was passé by the time she made the electrics, the voice rather hoarse, and she can only suggest the high notes, she is still affecting in Lisa's aria from *The Queen of Spades*, in which incidentally she takes the optional ending on the low A, which Tchaikovsky had sanctioned for Mei-Figner. As with Garden, Kouznetsova's stage presence and reputation as an actress have tended to obscure the fact that she was also a singer of very considerable merit.

The career of MARIANNE TCHERKASSKAYA (1884–1919) lasted less than a dozen years, for she died when she was only thirty-five, but during that time she sang with notable success in Russia and abroad. Upon the completion of her studies at the St Petersburg Conservatory in 1906, she made her debut at the Marinsky Theatre where she remained a prominent member of the company until the October Revolution. Her repertory included principal roles in the lyric-dramatic repertory: Valen-

9 Marianne Tcherkasskaya as Lisa in *The Queen of Spades*

tine in *Les Huguenots*, Tatiana, Lisa, Elsa, Brünn-hilde and other Wagnerian parts. In December 1909 she sang on the opening night of the season at La Scala, as Brünnhilde in *Walchiria*, the cast also including Pasini-Vitale, Frascani and de Angelis. Two years later she was a member of a Russian company which gave a season of opera at the Théâtre des Champs Elysées in Paris: she was heard as Tatiana in *Eugene Onegin* with Bolchakov and Baklanov. At Monte Carlo in 1917 she sang Tamara in *The Demon* with Battistini.

Tcherkassaya made only a few records on the Russian Amour label, and these are now exceptionally rare. They reveal a full lyric dramatic soprano, characteristically Russian sounding, and with a particularly lovely quality. The high notes are strong and brilliant, and the registers correctly blended. There is the usual glottal Russian attack and though she sings with feeling and some expression, Gorislava's aria from Glinka's *Russlan and Ludmila* it is not an especially characterful interpretation.

Over the years all sorts of exaggerated claims have been made for the importance of singers whose records are superficially agreeable. This has been particularly the case with various Russian artists, of whose performances it is difficult to establish an accurate listing or to find reliable contemporary reports. A case in point is Marie Michailova, a singer whose career was of no great importance but whose small and pretty voice was phonogenic. Almost all or her recordings make an agreeable impression—at least on first hearing. They charm rather than assault the ear. Closer examination reveals a sketchy technique and no personality to compare with that of a contemporary of undoubted consequence, Antonida Nezhdanova. But for none have the claims been so extravagant as those made for NINA KOSHETZ (1894–1965); a great many, it would appear, made by herself.

In the first place even her date of birth is doubtful; was she really not yet nineteen when she made her operatic debut? And then there are so many different stories as to when and where and in what opera the event took place. According to one authority it was at the Bolshoi as Tatiana in *Eugene Onegin* in 1912 and that 'within a year she was being hailed as one of the Bolshoi's leading stars'.[11] Another gives the year as 1913 and claims that it was at the Marinsky in St Petersburg and that she sang Donna Anna. The facts are less sensational: she did sing one performance at the Marinsky, but only one, and that was not until the autumn of 1917; as for being a star of the Bolshoi, she never sang there at all. Her debut *was* as Tatiana, on 22 September 1913, but with Zimin's Opera; on the next night she sang Donna Anna. She remained a principal of the company for the rest of her Russian career, until the spring of 1919. If Zimin's was hardly the Bolshoi, it was an important and respected organisation giving more performances each season than its august rival. Like Mamontov, Zimin was chiefly concerned with popularising Russian operas and most foreign works were given in the vernacular. It was also a larger company than the Bolshoi; in the course of a season there might be six or seven different principals for the more popular roles. The singers were good, if not of the top rank. Few of their names mean much to us today; occasionally, however, Chaliapin and other stars of the Imperial theatres made guest appearances.

Koshetz's repertory was hardly the stuff of which stars are made. She sang Nedda, Tamara in Rubinstein's *Demon*, Lisa, Nastasia in Tchaikovsky's *Enchantress*, Germaine in *Les Cloches de Corneville*, Rachel in *La Juive*, Marina in *Boris Godounov*, Hermione in Goldmark's *A Winter's Tale*, also a variety of roles in lesser known operas. As a singer of songs, she enjoyed greater renown. She toured the provinces as one of the soloists with Koussevitsky's symphony orchestra; at the time the conductor was also active publishing music, commissioning new works from many leading composers including Rachmaninov, Scriabin and Prokofiev. Through his activities Koshetz came to introduce a number of songs by these and other composers. After the Revolution, in Paris and elsewhere, she was to make a feature of them in recitals—perhaps too much of one, for not many are significant works. The finest, the Six Songs Op. 38 by Rachmaninov, she sang on a few occasions in Russia during the autumn of 1916, with the composer at the piano. Apparently she had met Rachmaninov the previous year and, according to her, a professional relationship quickly developed into a romantic one, but for this we have only her word. It is true the Six Songs are all settings of love lyrics, but these had been suggested by another of Rachmaninov's female admirers, Marietta Shaginian (though their friendship was never more than platonic), to whom he had previously dedicated songs. What is certain is that from the summer of 1917 Rachmaninov and Koshetz did not meet for nearly twenty five years, and she admits that 'a cool formality characterised the few occasions on which they corresponded'.[12] All of which would be of small account were it not for the claim that has been made for her as the custodian of an authentic Rachmaninov performing tradition. This is based on some recordings, the only ones she made of his songs, in 1939, twenty two years after their last meeting when she was in very obvious vocal decadence. In other circumstances it would be only charitable to draw a veil over them.

The tasteful use of rubato and various interpretative devices not necessarily printed in the score is essential to make a stylish effect in the music of the late Romantic school. This is confirmed in gramophone recordings made by artists who created works, or were indisputably admired, by, among others, Massenet, Mahler, Puccini and Richard Strauss. With Rachmaninov we are doubly fortunate, for there exist recordings of him, as conductor and pianist, playing his own and other composers' music. What is immediately striking about them is the formal integrity of his readings: how, in spite of what may in our day seem daring, even colossal, liberties (we have only to think of the fortissimo re-entry in Chopin's Funeral March), these are never exhibitionistic or merely fatuous—they illuminate everything he touches. Though achieved through technical wizardry, this is a musical strength and is characterised by rhythmic control. The same can hardly be said for Koshetz's singing of his songs. To take one example, the well-known Georgian love song, an evocative setting of some equally evocative verses of Pushkin; this has been recorded many times but perhaps most eloquently by McCormack (Kreisler's obbligato is hardly less telling) and Ivan Kozlovsky. Next to either, Koshetz's is a halting, fumbling affair; she appears to have no conception of the song as a whole, dwelling whimsically on one note or another and letting the music slip away between them. The execution, especially of the haunting and difficult measures at the end, is only approximate. Small

10 Nina Koshetz as Nastasia in Tchaikovsky's *The En-chantress*

wonder that her accompanist was moved to complain that he only wanted to play what was in the music. It might be possible to overlook these failings if there were a particular intensity or subtle use of vocal colour; unfortunately the voice is no longer responsive, and she sings in a tuneless parlando throughout—was she really only forty-four? Ivan Kozlovsky was definitely over sixty when he made his recording of this song. His voice was never a thing of beauty in itself and there are those who find its plaintive timbre too much of an acquired taste, but with what skill and indescribable charm he sings this music, the rubato perfectly judged, and the ravishing morendos all used to telling effect and musical in themselves. Though the voice naturally has no great range of colour, so accomplished is he that it seems of infinite variety: here is the authentic Rachmaninov tradition.

After the Revolution Koshetz fled Russia and her career thereafter followed the usual emigré pattern. She sang in opera as a guest, chiefly in Russian works, appearing with the Chicago company in 1921 as Fata Morgana in the world premiere of Prokofiev's *L'Amour de trois oranges*, at the Paris Opéra as Marina in *Boris Godounov*, in Bordeaux as Yaroslavna and at the Colon, Buenos Aires, in 1924 for one season, where she also sang Lisa, Elena in *Mefistofele* and a single performance of Tosca in succession to Gilda dalla Rizza. Throughout the twenties she appeared with various emigré companies, mostly in France, but on occasion in the United States, Scandinavia and the Baltic states. By 1930 their novelty had worn off, as too had the freshness of the singers' voices and Koshetz's operatic career petered out. She remained active in the concert hall and recital room for a few more years, making good use of her Russian songs and contacts from pre-revolutionary days. She was one of the supporting artists when Medtner, Glazounov and Gretchaninov made their U.S. debuts. On these occasions, where she was concerned at least, critical opinion seems to have been qualified:

She sang best, and not unnaturally, the Russian songs, with the spirit native to them, a spirit with which she is obviously sympathetic, in many different manifestations. In these she was often deeply interesting and moving. Her voice seems to tend toward the mezzo quality and range. It is hardly notable for richness, colour or beauty; its upper tones are among its least agreeable ones . . . There was a tendency to flatness in those tones especially, and sometimes in others . . . Nor is the technique of high finish.[13]

Three earlier series of recordings have preserved her voice and art better. The first of them, and by far the finest, has only recently come to light through the researches of Vivian Liff. Sometime around the beginning of the First World War she visited the Beka studios. Only two titles have been traced so far: Tchaikovsky's Cradle Song (Rachmaninov transcribed it for the piano) and one of Tamara's arias from the *Demon*. These, not surprisingly, show the voice off at its freshest and loveliest, the tone pure, focussed and limpid on the breath, the high notes effortlessly produced—no question but that she is a soprano here. They also reveal a more artistic singer. There is none of that self-regarding and often meaningless use of pianissimo, nor the guttural attack and consequently throaty tone which she used to simulate feeling and to give her interpretations 'personality' and which over the years led to a general coarsening of her musicianship. Traces of this are already apparent in the group made for Brunswick about 1922. This includes Rimsky-Korsakov's 'Eastern Romance', a song also recorded to great effect by Alma Gluck and Rosa Ponselle. If Koshetz's is not as vocally remarkable as either of theirs, there is a nice touch at the end when she hums the vocalise. However, this is not as remarkable as has been suggested and it is instructive that she omits the final phrase which would have carried her up to the high C sharp. Moussorgsky's 'Humoresque' is a characteristic piece which Koshetz sings 'in a very realistic manner. Doubtless the manner the composer intended . . . It gives a certain non-musical effect'.[14] Lisa's aria disappoints; it is not a particularly eloquent reading and she communicates little sense of dramatic urgency. Among the electric group are Manuel Ponce's 'Estrellita', which although subsequently dedicated to Koshetz, was not originally written for her, and her most famous operatic recording, Yaroslavna's aria, which takes her down into the mezzo range. By 1931 when she recorded Litvinne's arrangement of Chopin's Etude Op. 10, No. 3, the voice has become throatier, the line less smooth and she bumps over the mordents.

In the latter part of her career Koshetz went to Hollywood and there became something of a character. She gave singing lessons to Marlene Dietrich, Ann Blyth and Carole Lombard. We catch a glimpse of her in the movies herself, looking like the fat woman at the fair. By then her principal hobbies were eating and drinking; she once claimed she drank everything except gasoline.[15] No doubt in part to satisfy her appetite and slake her thirst,

she opened her own restaurant. There she knocked up the blini in the back and afterwards, accompanying herself in numbers from Old Russia, 'knocked the customers in the aisles'—at any rate that was the intention, but it failed and by the early 1940s she had fallen on hard times. Rachmaninov, who moved to Hollywood at the beginning of the war, came to hear of her misfortunes and after nearly a quarter of a century, in a burst of sentimentality, renewed their friendship. He agreed to accompany her in recitals once again but it was too late, for she was quite voiceless. Curiously her records convey little of her personality and in 'Black Eyes', for which we might have thought her lifestyle gave her the ideal credentials, she is merely dull. In so repetitive a piece, to avoid monotony, the singer must suggest every drunken mood from manic to maudlin; Chaliapin does so wonderfully in a famous record, teasing our ears with his extraordinary range of dynamics and inflexions, so that we can hardly wait for the next verse; with Koshetz one is quite enough. In her youth she possessed a voice of particularly lovely quality and her singing was well-schooled, but she lacked artistic integrity and her lifestyle was hardly conducive to preserving her voice; in the course of time it corrupted her musicianship as well.

4. Two 'Coloraturas'

In the aftermath of the Russian Revolution escapology seems to have been the name of the game; at the time perhaps it was no game, but the stories told subsequently by various Russian singers of how they had been forced to make midnight flits in all sorts of operatic disguises suggests not so much real terror as the fevered imaginings of those who had imbibed too much from the world of romantic melodrama. LYDIA LIPKOWSKA (1880–1955), for example, so the story goes, was rescued in Odessa by a French naval officer who took her on board his cruiser dressed as an old peasant woman. If it sounds rather a conspicuous disguise, it seems to have worked for they eventually reached New York and safety. There lovely diva and noble captain were wed and she was then engaged to star in a revival of *The Merry Widow*.

Throughout her career Lipkowska had a taste for fantasy and enjoyed giving interviews to suggestible and no doubt cynical journalists with very different and equally unlikely accounts as to her early life. In fact she was born in Bessarabia, the daughter of a civil servant. Upon the completion of her formal studies at the St Petersburg Conservatory, in 1907 she made her debut at the Marinsky as Gilda. Two years later she appeared in Paris in a season of Russian opera at the Théâtre du Châtelet. Her debut was in the title-role of Rimsky-Korsakov's *Tsar's Bride*, with Petrenko, Chaliapin and Kastorsky. From the first she was a success:

> This young artist plays with a natural grace as expressive as it is simple. Hers is a voice of charming quality, sufficiently powerful and with an astonishing breath span which permits her to phrase with a rare flexibility.[1]

Afterwards she sang in *Russlan and Ludmila* with Zbrujeva and Smirnov. This led to an engagement at the Opéra-Comique. During three seasons she sang Lakmé, Violetta, Manon, Mimi and Rosina. Her North American debut was with the newly established Boston Opera of Henry Russell in the autumn of 1909. As at the Opéra-Comique her first role was Lakmé. She was a hit, but whether on account of her vocal or physical charms is not sure:

> She had but to clothe herself in oriental dress and ply the dextrous external routine in which she was trained; for the rest, her transparent personality, when once the music and the play stirred it, amply sufficed.[2]

Lipkowska remained in Boston for two seasons, her repertory embracing Violetta, Gilda, Lucia, Rosina, Mimi and Micaëla. Within a week of her Boston debut, as the result of a bi-lateral agreement on the exchange of artists, she made her debut at the Metropolitan as Violetta, but 'her light voice and pretty appearance did not satisfy yearnings for Sembrich'.[3] She was no better received as Gilda or Rosina, the latter at the New Theatre. She made a bigger impression in Chicago on tour with the Boston company when she appeared as Lucia, Lakmé and Violetta, sufficient to secure an engagement with the Chicago Opera in its inaugural season; she sang Lucia and Gilda. In the summer of 1911 she was engaged at Covent Garden as Mimi and Susanna in Wolf-Ferrari's *Segreto di Susanna*. She repeated both roles the following season and was also heard as Gilda and Violetta, but in these—in every way— she was overshadowed by Tetrazzini. At the Paris Opéra in 1913 she sang Gilda and Ophélie in a revival of Thomas's *Hamlet* with

Baklanov. For the occasion they relearned their roles in French, having sung them earlier the same year in an Italian revival at Monte Carlo. There she had also appeared in *Rigoletto*, *Traviata*, *Roméo et Juliette* and *Bohème*, all opposite Smirnov. She returned in 1914 to sing the Queen in a revival of *Ugonotti* with Kouznetsova and Martinelli, Oscar in *Ballo in Maschera* with Martinelli and Baklanov and in the same company took a leading role in the world premiere of Ponchielli's unfinished *I Mori di Valenza*, completed for the occasion by Cadore.

After the war she continued to appear in concert and recital, when her voice was still fresh and admired for its purity and refinement. Her programmes ran the gamut from songs by Purcell to Cyril Scott, including works by Glinka, Moussorgsky, Busser, Bruneau, Delibes, Bellini, Schumann and Schubert. She was a guest at the Opéra on occasion, in *Rigoletto* in 1926 opposite

11 Lydia Lipkowska as Rosina

Georges Thill and 'her voice was still pretty, light and pearly'.[4] As late as 1941 she sang Violetta at Odessa—it must have been under the Nazi occupation. In her last years she taught in Paris and finally Beirut; one of her pupils was the Roumanian soprano Virginia Zeani.

Lipkowska's voice was a light lyric soprano of wide compass and if her coloratura technique hardly rivalled Nezhdanova never mind Tetrazzini, the tone was notably pure and smooth. Her records reflect her wide-ranging musical taste. She was not, however, successful in everything. As a singer of brilliant music her manner is provincial and the execution sketchy. 'Bel raggio', though it shows off the fine quality of her upper range, all the way to a pure and sustained high E natural, finds her dwelling so often and, as it seems, so interminably on every good note in her voice that by the end the piece has lost all coherence and entirely falls apart. The *Roméo* Valse too, though the (scratch) orchestra sets off with a nice lilt, suffers from a lack of rhythmic impetus; she gives the impression that at any moment she might stop. A couple of Drigo's arrangements from Delibes's *Sylvia* and *Coppélia* being less ambitious are more successful, but this sort of thing is much better done by Galli-Curci. The duet 'Nega se puoi la luce' from *Amleto* with Baklanov is a souvenir of their performances at Monte Carlo; the voices blend well, especially in the sustained measures at the end. But it is in Russian opera that she comes into her own. A difficult and ungratefully written aria from Tchaikovsky's *Iolanta* she dashes off in fine style. Very lovely is Marfa's Mad Scene from Rimsky-Korsakov's *Tsar's Bride*. Here, where there is no need to sacrifice everything for brilliance, the voice takes on an added warmth and depth of tone. Two arias from *Snegourotchka* are done in affecting style; the quality is sweet as well as pure and she sustains the sad mood with many expressive touches. In the final scene, where the poor Snowmaiden melts away in the spring sunshine, there are some delicate glissandi and a couple of perfectly placed high B flats shaded away to pianissimo.

Unlike those of her more glamorous colleagues, the career of EUGENIA BRONSKAYA (1882–1953) continued without interruption at the Marinsky Theatre, or Kirov as it was later to become, through the Revolution until her retirement in 1923. For the following quarter of a century, she taught singing at the Leningrad Conservatory. Bronskaya was herself a pupil of Teresa Arkel in Milan, and there is in her recordings something of the same rather hard bril-

12 Eugenia Bronskaya as Rosina

liance that can be heard in those of another Arkel pupil, Lucette Korsoff. Bronskaya's debut took place at Tiflis in 1902. Between 1903 and 1905 she was a member of the company at the Kiev Opera, in the latter year securing an engagement at the Bolshoi. During the next five years she made guest appearances in the Italian provinces: Trieste, Florence, Venice, Bologna and subsequently at the Costanzi, Rome. In the autumn of 1909, Russell brought her to Boston, where she made her first appearance in a Sunday night concert. If we are to believe the critic H. T. Parker, she had already sung in New York:

> [She] proved to be no other than Mme Makarov, the coloratura soprano who was singing in September at the Academy of Music in New York. She is evidently experienced, but with a voice somewhat worn; still she keeps facility and glitter in showy music.[5]

Her first stage performance was as Micaëla; she was complimented for 'her practised skill',[6] but neither then nor later as Musetta, Gilda, Violetta, Marguerite in *Ugonotti* or Nedda did she make more than a routine impression. Her big moment came when at the last minute she undertook Lucia, stepping into the breach for an indisposed Lipkowska. Rather surprisingly it seems that she had never sung the part on stage, though she knew the set pieces. Her problem was to find her way from one of these to the next, which she managed by skilfully 'marking' the recitatives and with the conductor's collusion cutting out the second act up to the Sextet. For her service to the company, if not the opera, she was greeted with considerable affection by public and critics. Parker commended 'her skill in stage routine . . . resource in relating the voice to the orchestra', and went on to congratulate her for 'hardly a jar to illusion. It was gallantly done'.[7]

During her Boston engagement, with several other members of the company, including Boninsegna, Constantino and Mardones, Bronskaya made a number of recordings for Columbia. These had been arranged by Russell in his capacity as Columbia's consulting Director and provided splendid advertisement for his activities in Boston. In fact Bronskaya's voice is heard to better advantage on the Russian Amour label. She shows herself to have been a well-schooled singer with a good, but not first class, voice, rather colourless and tending to hardness in the upper range, where we can hear something of that wear to which Parker refers. She does not attempt the high E natural in the upward run at the end of a very much abbreviated version of the *Hamlet* Mad Scene, nor is the high C in the *Roméo* Valse a fortunate note; both of these selections are in Russian. She has a good legato style and the phrasing is affecting, though without any particularly characterful touches. In passage work the execution is not absolutely smooth nor is her trill clearly defined. She is adept in the use of a rapid, albeit unlovely, staccato, which she uses wherever the occasion allows, partly no doubt for reasons of effect but also, the suspicion arises, so as to avoid those figures in which she was less skilful. Violetta's 'Ah! fors' è lui' offers fewer opportunities for display and her singing here is neat and the tone secure, if a little tremulous. 'Sempre libera', however, brings out the shrill soubrette in some approximate coloratura—not recommended.

13 Elisaveta Petrenko as Marina in *Boris Godounov*

5. Contraltos

There was no Russian mezzo soprano or contralto active at this time whose voice was of such sheer power, or so well schooled, as that of Eugenia Zbrujeva. One of the best was ELISAVETA PETRENKO (1880–1951), the possessor of an attractive mezzo soprano extending to the high B flat, but less impressive in the lower range where there was a bald patch between the middle and chest registers. Although the quality was good, the emission was not ideally smooth, the tone slightly spread and there was a hint of that Slavic wobble that later came to infect so much Russian singing. She was a student at the St Petersburg Conservatory first with Iretskoy, and subsequently Mme Ferni-Giraldoni, the mother of the baritone Eugenio Giraldoni, whose vehement manner and rough voice production Petrenko's somewhat resembles. During that time she attended dancing classes conducted by the famous choreographer Michael Fokine, but any skill that she acquired, unlike Kouznetsova, she never displayed for its own sake; it was strictly subordinated to her work as a singer. Upon completion of her studies, she secured an engagement at the Marinsky where she appeared until 1915 in various small roles as well as Amneris, Dalila, Ljubasha in *Snegourotchka*, Vesna in *The Tsar's*

14 Vera Petrova-Zvanceva as Grounya in Serov's *The Power of Evil*

Bride, Carmen, Marina in *Boris Godounov* and Marta in *Khovanshchina*. In Paris 'she showed off a beautiful voice'[1] as Kontchakovna in *Prince Igor* in the Diaghilev season at the Théâtre des Champs Elysées in 1909. She sang in the same theatre in 1913, when her roles included the Nurse in *Boris Godounov* and Marta—'one can only praise the beauty of her voice and the warm passion of her singing'.[2] Following the outbreak of war she joined the ensemble of the Musical Drama Theatre in Petrograd. Later, after the Revolution, she moved to Moscow with the same company. From this period she was active as a teacher; in 1935 she was appointed Professor of Voice at the Leningrad Conservatory.

She makes a good colleague, as we hear in the duet 'Morire . . . Ah! tu dei vivere' from *Aida* (sung in Russian) with the Latvian tenor Eugene Witting, a reliable singer even if his voice is rather on the hard side. This is a competent performance sung with feeling and conviction but not without pro-

vincial mannerisms; throughout Petrenko appears to have misread staccato for marcato so that in the allegro agitato passage, 'Chi ti salva', on the repeated E flats, she attenuates the notes and by so doing robs the phrasing of its grandeur. Generally her phrasing is suggested rather than underpinned by a really firm legato and the attack is not always quite clean. In the Vengeance Duet from *Samson et Dalila* there is greater rhythmic incisiveness and at the end she neatly executes the downward run from the high B flat. She is at her most affecting in another duet, from Rubinstein's *Demon*, a more lyrical piece where her singing is better controlled and more expressive. In both of these, unfortunately, she has to cope with Alexander Bragin's hectoring manner and spread tone. A rare solo, Stephano's 'Que fais-tu?' surprises us by its neatness and general accomplishment.

The mezzo-soprano VERA PETROVA-ZVANCEVA (1875–1944) made a number of fine records but, as with so many other Russian artists of this period who did not travel outside their native country, full details of her career are now hard if not impossible to ascertain. It is known that she was attached to one of the leading Moscow theatres and in the season of 1911/12 was much appreciated there in the title-roles of *Carmen* and *Zazà*. The singer and writer Sergei Levik, to whom we are beholden for information concerning many important singers, considered her representative of what was then described as the modern Russian school. But though she was skilled in the delineation of character, her singing and acting were on a par and all of a piece.

Recordings give us some idea of her repertory: apart from excerpts from *Samson et Dalila*, *Carmen* and *Zazà*, there are solos from Rimsky-Korsakov's *Snegourotchka*, *Tsar's Bride* and *Sadko*, Massenet's *Sapho* and *Werther*, Serov's *Hostile Power*, Tchaikovsky's *Mazeppa* and *Maid of Orleans*, Moussorgsky's *Boris Godounov* and *Khovanshchina*, and *Trovatore*. The voice is an important sounding instrument with power and some brilliance but her singing is not notable for finesse in style or execution. The quality is typically Slavic, somewhat white and vibratory. Joan of Arc's Farewell to the Forests from the *Maid of Orleans* she sings in affecting style, but her phrasing is neither ideally smooth nor particularly distinguished and the high A at the end, though large, sounds forced.

KLAVDILA TUGARINOVA (1877–) was also a principal of the Marinsky Theatre, where she sang regularly between 1902 and 1917. Unlike Petrenko hers was a real contralto; warm and dark coloured

15 Klavdila Tugarinova as Vanya in *A Life for the Tsar*

with a light tremolo that she was able in some degree to intensify at will. Though it was hardly as imposing an instrument as Zbrujeva's, her singing—at least on records—has great fascination.

Her career, however, seems to have been strictly parochial, for we have no record of her having appeared outside Russia. At the Marinsky she sang Vanya in *A Life for the Tsar*, Siebel, Feodor in *Boris Godounov*, Olga in *Eugene Onegin* and the Countess in *The Queen of Spades*. Like Petrenko, when the Revolution came she preferred to stay in Russia, where she continued to sing for several more years. In her retirement she taught, first in Leningrad and later in Stalingrad. She was still living there at the time of the great battle, after which she disappeared without trace.

Records reveal a more accomplished singer than Petrenko; the registers are smoothly blended from the low G to high A flat, and the tone is pure and rounded. In Vanya's air from *A Life for the Tsar*, she relieves the melancholy mood with many graceful and well-turned inflexions; even in the lowest reaches the voice remains focussed and without a trace of plumminess. The Flower Song from *Faust*, taken down a whole tone, is a distinguished interpretation. In it she shows herself mistress of the portamento style and she uses the vibrato in her voice to suggest the youth's tremulous anticipation, yet without sacrificing the line. Each section of the piece is contrasted effectively, the phrasing eloquent and the line imaginatively nuanced.

PART II

The French Tradition in Decline

6. *Franz, Ansseau and Fontaine*

The finest of all the French voices that emerged in the years immediately prior to the outbreak of war was that of PAUL FRANZ (1876–1950). His was a superb heroic tenor. It was a naturally superior instrument to that of Dalmorès or Muratore, and though he did not have the remarkable brilliance of Escalaïs, Franz's singing was without either his or Affre's provincial style. His early years were spent working as a navvy for the French railways and he was past thirty when, after a period of study with tenor Louis Delaquerrière, in 1908 he took first prize in a singing competition organised by the magazine *Musica*. The following January he made his debut at Nantes, making such a good impression that within a month he had secured an engagement at the Opéra in the title-role of *Lohengrin*.

> His height, his build, also the size of his voice suit him to the great heroic roles . . . The voice is admirable, it is at once very large and of a charming delicacy, at times it even caresses. He has a good pronunciation, his phrasing is expansive, perhaps on occasion a little too much so . . . Above all he has that great quality, his is a natural voice; he sings without effort and without having to fake a brazen effect, for his is a clarion voice from bottom to top.[1]

In the course of the next few seasons he went on to Tannhäuser, Roméo, Sigurd, Siegmund, Radamès, Faust and Samson. Each of them was rapturously acclaimed by the public and drew scarcely less ecstatic notices from the critics. Not since Jean de Reszke had anything like it been heard, and where the effort had undoubtedly shortened de Reszke's career, Franz had, as well as the skill, the stamina to sustain such a repertory, season in and season out, for more than a quarter of a century. From Paris, in the summer of 1910, he journeyed to London and despite strong competition, from Dalmorès in particular, he established himself as the leading French tenor at Covent Garden until 1914. His first appearance was as Samson opposite that sedate seductress Louise Kirkby Lunn, and he repeated the role every season thereafter:

> A really convincing Samson had been secured in M. Franz who not only has the commanding appearance necessary for the part but whose voice is remarkable, robust and virile in quality. If he seemed a little too anxious to show its power constantly there were passages in the love scene which might have been taken more quietly with effect; yet his voice never failed him and the soliloquy in the prison was genuinely moving.[2]

He confirmed that 'the beautiful quality of his voice was admirably suited to the more lyrical parts'[3] as Faust. In subsequent years he was: an 'outstanding'[4] Roméo to Melba's Juliette, Radamès to Destinn's Aida, Julien in *Louise* with Edvina, an 'admirable'[5] Otello—in this, following in the tradition of Alvarez, he ranked with Slezak as the finest non-Italian Otello of his day. 'It effaces memories of a good many famous exponents since the year of grace 1889, and is an achievement for this artist, who happily is realising everything that the knowing ones prophesied for him.'[6] It was in the last successful revival of Meyerbeer's *Ugonotti* at Covent Garden in 1912 with Tetrazzini, Destinn, Donalda, Sammarco, Arimondi and Vanni Marcoux that he 'realised all prophecies concerning his greatness'.[7] As Raoul '[he] was in magnificent voice, and his singing of "Più bianca del vello" was a quite brilliant effort, if indeed that is the right word to describe singing so strong and so effortless.'[8]

In Paris, where he succeeded Van Dyck and Rousselière as the leading Heldentenor, he was involved in several major events; as well as singing Walter in *Les Maîtres Chanteurs*, Tristan and Siegfried, he was the first Parsifal at the Opéra in 1913. But Wagner was only part of it; Rodrigue in *Le*

16 Paul Franz as Roméo

Cid 'covered him in glory'; as Jean in *Le Prophète*
his presence and beautiful voice made a specially
strong impression. He was Jean in *Hérodiade*, Eléazar in *La Juive*, Paris in Saint-Saëns's *Hélène*, Faust
in Berlioz's *La Damnation de Faust*, Enée in *Les
Troyens* in which 'he was justly acclaimed in the air
in the third act',[9] and he took part in various
modern pieces: Dupont's *Antar* with Heldy,
d'Indy's *La Légende de Saint-Christophe*, Rabaud's
La Fille de Roland, Bruneau's *L'Attaque du moulin*
and, at Monte Carlo, Gunsbourg's *Lysistrata*. In
1915 he sang the role of Samson in a special
performance of Saint-Saëns's opera at La Scala.
Three years later he travelled to the Colon but,
thereafter, for the most part preferred to remain at
the Opéra. He made his last appearance there in 1938
at a gala dedicated to his students at the Paris
Conservatoire.

The high opinions of his contemporaries are
confirmed in Franz's recordings; he made a sizeable
quantity for the HMV, Pathé and Columbia companies between 1909 and 1932. It sounds a magnificent
dark tenor but never obscure, the tone is pure, the

words clearly, but not exaggeratedly, articulated.
In the middle range the voice has great solidity, at
the top the high notes are at once powerful and
brilliant, the tone focussed, the attack clean and
incisive. He makes an imposing effect in Sigurd's
'Un souvenir poignant' declaiming with great energy and passion—even introducing a little tremolando for effect—yet the phrasing remains firm and
smooth. In Roméo's 'Salut tombeau' there is something of the same grand and monumental manner,
but here he surprises us by his delicacy, range and
variety of expression, especially when he comes
upon Juliette: 'la voilà, c'est elle!' Two excerpts
from *Parsifal*, souvenirs of his performance at the
Opéra and sung in French, are rendered with a just
regard for the lyricism of the music and without
sacrificing a clear enunciation.

After Franz the finest tenor active in the French
repertory was the Belgian FERNAND ANSSEAU
(1890–1972). His, however, was a more lyrical
voice, the range and weight of tone somewhat
reminiscent of Dalmorès, many of whose roles he
assumed, but it had a greater brilliance especially in
the head register. Ansseau's background was musical; his father played the organ in the village
church of Boussu-Bois near Mons where he was
born. At the age of seventeen he was admitted to the
Brussels Conservatory and became a pupil of Demest. In the autumn of 1912 he was the tenor soloist
in a performance of Mozart's *Requiem*. The following summer he won first prize in a competition with
'Total Eclipse!' from Handel's *Samson*. His stage
debut took place at Dijon in the autumn of 1913 as
Jean in *Hérodiade*, which was to remain one of his
favourite roles. He stayed at Dijon for the next year
and a half, appearing as Don José, Sigurd, Faust,
Julien and in the local premiere of Saint-Saëns's *Les
Barbares*, in the part that had been created by
Charles Rousselière at the Paris Opéra.

After the war in the autumn of 1918, he joined the
company at the Monnaie, Brussels, which was to
remain the centre of his activities throughout the
rest of his career. There he expanded his repertory
with Des Grieux, Canio, Samson, the Duke, Radamès, Cavaradossi, Don Alvaro and Masaniello,
which he sang in the 1930 season to commemorate
the performance that had set off the Belgian revolution a century earlier. In the summer of 1919 he
was invited to Covent Garden and made a great
impression on his first appearance as Des Grieux to
Edvina's Manon, confirming this in *Faust* when
Melba was his Marguerite. The *Daily Telegraph*
wrote:

[Ansseau] combines in his voice in most delightful fashion all the attributes of a lyrical tenor with those of a French dramatic tenor. Not many nights ago he moved his audience to ecstasy by the sheer beauty of his singing in the Dream Song in *Manon*. Now, in *Faust*, he exhibited in an exalted degree precisely the same characteristics, yet even in his more dramatic moments M. Ansseau never loses by a hair's breadth the beautiful lyric quality of his voice, and whether worried by Méphistophélès, or enamoured by Marguerite, his singing was delightful.[10]

His debut at the Opéra-Comique was in 1920, in the title-role of Massenet's *Werther*. The following year he sang Orphée, the first time that a tenor had been heard in the French edition of the opera in Paris since Berlioz had altered it with the aid of Saint-Saëns to suit Pauline Viardot. A new adaptation had been made especially for the occasion by

17 Fernand Ansseau as Werther

Paul Vidal and included music from both the Paris and Vienna versions. The performances aroused great interest.

M. Ansseau is a remarkable tenor, whose voice of a superb quality possesses a fullness and flexibility which puts him in the first rank for the interpretation of those works which demand, above all, vocal effects. But as a tragic actor this admirable singer is still far from perfect, and his success, considerable and largely justified in passages of pure lyricism, would have been greater still if he had disclosed an emotion in any of these . . . Unfortunately, when he did, in the celebrated 'J'ai perdu mon Eurydice', this was exaggerated . . . It is to be hoped he will renew his efforts to improve himself as an actor . . .[11]

In the course of the following season Gunsbourg brought him to Monte Carlo where he sang Faust in Berlioz's *La Damnation de Faust*. Soon afterwards he was Alain in the first performances of Massenet's *Grisélidis* at the Opéra, creating a great effect with his rich and beautiful voice.

In 1923 he was engaged at the Chicago Opera, where he quickly established himself as the finest French tenor that the company had had since Muratore. He remained a principal through five seasons, to the roles mentioned above adding Hoffmann, Roméo, Don José, Avito in *L'Amore dei tre Re*, Prinzivalle in *Monna Vanna* and Dimitri in Alfano's *Résurrection*, the last three opposite Mary Garden. It was with Garden that he found himself in one of those predicaments of language which were not uncommon in that company. In *Tosca* he sang 'Recondita armonia' in Italian then, with the diva, the whole of the love duet in French—she preferred it that way. In Act Two he kept to the original since Vanni Marcoux would only sing in Italian. The height of absurdity came when Scarpia echoed Tosca's 'Combien?' with 'Quanto?', and then a few bars further along Garden herself elected to sing 'Vissi d'arte' in Italian. By the time she returned for Act Three, however, she had reverted to French; Ansseau obligingly followed suit.

He made his last appearances in Chicago and at Covent Garden, his powers largely undiminished, in 1928. For the next decade until his retirement in 1939, he sang only in France or Belgium, principally at the Opéra and the Monnaie in Brussels.

Ansseau recorded for HMV regularly in the decade after 1920. His was a full lyric dramatic tenor with plenty of thrust, the voice well placed on the breath, the high notes free and ringing. Although

'J'ai perdu mon Eurydice' is not his best record and there is some effort involved in managing the exacting tessitura, his execution is always clean and mostly accurate. His manner, however, voice production and use of certain devices such as the tremolando on Orphée's repeated cries of 'Eurydice' are neither particularly stylish nor convincing. He is far more in the vein with Jean's 'Ne pouvant reprimer' from Massenet's *Hérodiade*. Here, freed from vocal and interpretative constraints the voice takes on a greater warmth and amplitude of tone. This is, we feel, how it should go; the passion freely expressed but always within the line. There are several well-managed details, in particular the upward portamento to the final high A, most fitting in Massenet's music. He shows off his dynamic skill to build a considerable climax in the swelling phrases of Vasco's 'O Paradis' from *L'Africaine*; notwithstanding the cuts, it is one of the best renderings in the original.

Like Ansseau, another Belgian tenor CHARLES FONTAINE (1878–   ) was a pupil of Demest at the Brussels Conservatory. He was born in Antwerp and after making a successful debut there was invited to Covent Garden for the season of 1909, where his roles included Faust, Samson and Renaud in a solitary performance of Gluck's *Armide*. The engagement was, however, premature and the best notices he secured spoke well only of his acting. During the next two seasons he remained in relative obscurity in the French provinces. In 1911 he appeared for the first time in Paris, at the Opéra as Raoul in *Les Huguenots*, in which 'his powerful voice, the manner in which he deployed it, easy and vibrant'[12] made a suitable impression. In the course of the next three years he divided his time between Paris and appearances at various Belgian theatres. At Antwerp in 1914 with Yvonne Gall in *Roméo et Juliette*, he sang 'with a force that quite subjugated the crowds',[13] the same season at Liège he was Arnold in *Guillaume Tell* with another leading Belgian singer, the baritone Jean Noté. After the German invasion of Belgium in September he moved to Paris. At the end of the same year he made his debut at the Opéra-Comique as Don José, after which came: Dominique in *L'Attaque du moulin*, Gérald, Pinkerton, the title-role in *Le Jongleur de Notre Dame*, Des Grieux, Canio, Daniello in Leroux's *La Reine Fiammette*, Mylio in *Le Roi d'Ys*, Jean in *Sapho*, Cavaradossi, Rodolfo, Werther, Hoffmann, Armand in Massenet's *Thérèse*. He created Almerio in Février's *Gismonda* with Fanny Heldy and Henri Albers. By this time his singing seems to have much improved and *Le Ménestrel* picked out for special praise 'his beautiful voice and restrained playing'[14] in Fauré's *Pénélope*.

In the autumn of 1917 he sang in a special gala evening of excerpts from French opera at La Scala. In December 1918 he became a member of the Chicago Opera. During his first season in which, as a result of the presence of Mary Garden as principal prima donna, fourteen of the twenty nine works in the repertory were French, he shared the principal tenor roles with Lucien Muratore and John O'Sullivan. Although unable to produce the high notes that made the latter celebrated and without

18 Charles Fontaine in the title-role of Reyer's *Sigurd*

Muratore's charm of manner and good looks, he secured a repeat engagement the following season and appeared with Garden in *Carmen, Louise, Gismonda, Cléopâtre* and *Thaïs*. He took the role of Toliak in Gunsbourg's *Le Vieil Aigle* with Baklanov, and Pierre in Messager's *Madame Chrysanthème* with the Japanese soprano Tamaki Miura. When it was repeated on tour at the Lexington Theatre in New York, Aldrich noted that:

> [Fontaine] as Pierre showed an agreeable tenor voice, a little uneven in quality, and sometimes a little disposed to flat but with plenty of power, and his impersonation was vigorous and manly.[15]

He remained active through the 1920s in Paris and, the French provinces at Bordeaux, Nice (with Ritter-Ciampi in *Les Contes d'Hoffmann*) and elsewhere.

A comparison between Ansseau and Fontaine in 'O Paradis' reveals obvious similarities in voice production but Fontaine is a cruder singer; the intervals are not as clearly defined, the voice is rather throaty and when he piles on the pressure, the top notes become strained. Throughout there are signs of the disagreeable effects of the diphthonged French vowels, and he has a tendency to articulate the words at the expense of the quality of the tone. Next to Ansseau, or Franz, this is dry and lacking in sonority. When a less scrupulous delivery does not come amiss, in Sigurd's 'Esprits gardiens', he makes a brazen effect sweeping easily through the high tessitura.

7. A Quintet of Lyric Tenors

DAVID DEVRIES (1881–1936) was one of an outstanding trio of lyric tenors active at the Opéra-Comique at this time, and although not the eldest his career got under way first. He made his debut in 1904 at the Théâtre Montparnasse as Gérald in *Lakmé*. In the course of a long and distinguished career at the Comique he was heard as Almaviva, Don José, Toinet in *Le Chemineau*, Clément in *La Basoche*, Armand in Massenet's *Thérèse*, Alfredo, Jean in *Sapho*, the title-role in Rabaud's *Marouf*, Vincent in *Mireille*, Wilhelm in *Mignon* in which Ritter-Ciampi was Philine, Pedro in Laparra's *La Habanera*, Des Grieux, Werther, Julien, Pinkerton and Cavaradossi as well as principal roles in a variety of forgotten works. In

1909 at the Théâtre Gaîté-Lyrique he took the part of Georges Brown in a revival of Boieldieu's *La Dame blanche*: 'the role suits no one better than Devriès, the young tenor whose charming variety of nuances are used with so much art'.[1]

It was in the autumn of the same year that he ventured across the Atlantic. That great operatic warrior Oscar Hammerstein brought Devriès with a troupe of French artists to New York for his fourth season at the Manhattan Theatre. Three opening skirmishes with the Met had left victory in the balance; the critics and public were on Hammerstein's side but society dithered. Time being of the essence, he determined on delivering the coup de grâce, conceiving opéra-comique as the weapon with which to do it. Unfortunately it backfired; the public was not interested. In less than a month Hammerstein was obliged to abandon the venture and send the artists packing: first to Montreal and then when, in spite of the large French speaking population, that proved equally disastrous, back home. Failure or not, the experiment introduced to New York a number of fine singers, of whom Devriès was probably the most accomplished; at any rate Hammerstein thought so, for after the others had re-embarked, he was invited to stay on. As well as Ange Pitou in *La Fille de Madame Angot* and Sylvain in *Les Dragons de Villars* he sang, for the first time in his career, Pelléas and 'acquitted himself nobly'. He added Araquil in *La Navarraise*, Alain in *Grisélidis*, both with Garden, and when she was off somewhere else she graciously permitted Hammerstein to restore to Devriès the title-role in Massenet's *Le Jongleur de Notre Dame* (the role had been originally written for a tenor). The following summer, at the last minute, he repeated his Pelléas at Covent Garden and 'created an excellent impression with his round voice and good style'.[2] At Monte Carlo in 1913 Gunsbourg engaged him as Nicias in *Thaïs* with Kouznetsova and Renaud. Later the same year at the Casino, Nice, he created Paco in the world premiere of Manuel de Falla's *La Vie brève*.

Throughout his career Devriès was busy as a concert and recital singer. He appeared as soloist in all manner of pieces from Bach's *St Matthew Passion* to Berlioz's *La Damnation*. His recital programmes displayed his skill and knowledge of modern French music:

> M. Devriès is one of the most remarkable members of the company at the Opéra-Comique. As with so many of his colleagues he has wanted to show that his talent was not only a dramatic one and he has tackled the

concert platform. His success was complete. His voice is flexible and of good quality, managed with consummate artistry and is at the service of interpretative powers that are both intelligent and experienced. Franck, Fauré, Duparc, Pierné, Richepin, Hahn, Debussy, Rousseau, Laparra, Lévadé and Emile Nerini, who also accompanied him, were delivered with an exact sense of their style and a perfect diction enabled us to appreciate the smallest details of the work.[3]

Devriès was a singer of considerable technical skill, as we can hear in the 'Rêverie de Georges Browne from Boieldieu's *La Dame blanche*. In this and in 'Vainement ma bien aimée' from *Le Roi d'Ys*, his extraordinary facility in the management of the head voice and the grace of his delivery almost cause us to overlook the voice itself which is not a thing of loveliness, the tone dry with something of a bleat and verging on whiteness.

Two years after Devriès, FERNAND FRANCELL (1880–1966) made his debut at the Opéra-Comique as Vincent in Gounod's *Mireille*. The company remained the centre of his operatic activities for many years and he was heard in a variety of principal and supporting roles: Almaviva, Clément

19 David Devriès as Werther

Marot in *La Basoche*, Hoffmann, Georges Brown in *La Dame blanche* with Rose Heilbronner and Hippolyte Belhomme, Alfredo opposite Kouznetsova's Violetta, Pinkerton to the Butterfly of Marguerite Carré, Gérald, Tamino, in which he succeeded Edmond Clément, Des Grieux, Wilhelm in *Mignon* in a season at the Gaîté-Lyrique, the title-roles in Rabaud's *Marouf*, Méhul's *Joseph, Fra Diavolo* and *Le Jongleur de Notre Dame*. In a revival of *Don Juan* conducted by Reynaldo Hahn with Périer in the title role and Geneviève Vix as Donna Elvira,

> Francell merits special praise for the character with which he has endowed Don Ottavio: throughout he has reacted against the traditional sweet insignificance that discredits him and instead has possessed him with manliness and ardour . . .[4]

He created the title-roles in Messager's *Fortunio* and Nouguès's *Chiquito* among many and sang, at first performances at the Comique, Yamadori in *Madame Butterfly*, Ange Pitou in *La Fille de Madame Angot* and Paco in *La Vie brève*.

In 1914 he appeared at the Grand Hotel in Paris at a special gala of Monsigny's *Les Aveux indiscrets*, and three years later made a tour in South America, in the course of which he sang Des Grieux in some performances of *Manon* at the Colon, with Vallin, Crabbé and Journet. During the 1920s he was active in recitals and operetta, making a great effect at the Mogador in the title-role of Marcel Latte's *Monsieur l'Amour*. His recitals took him to many leading French resorts; he appeared regularly at Deauville, Cannes, Nice, Biarritz and Evian-les-Bains, where he was enthusiastically acclaimed:

> We have found still intact in M. Francell's art those qualities for which in the theatre he has deserved his considerable renown. They reside principally in an excellent enunciation and the very skilful way he presents to the best advantage a voice that has never been remarkable for quality or range.[5]

He also made a point of travelling extensively in the provinces; in 1926 for example, throughout Burgundy, appearing at: Besançon, Chalon-sur-Saône, Dôle, Bourges, Lons-le-Saunier, Oyonnax, Beaune, Dijon, Macon, Nevers and Montreau-les-Mines. On these occasions in a soirée entitled 'Madame, would you like to sing?' he introduced his programme with a little chat and sang various, particularly modern, compositions. These events were popular and by all accounts left a lastingly pleasant recol-

20 Fernand Francell as Wilhelm Meister in *Mignon*

slightly and sound uncomfortable. In part this follows from his obvious determination to keep the production open so as to pronounce the dipthonged French vowels clearly. Unfortunately, as W. J. Henderson pointed out, this involves sacrificing purity of tone and was part of the problem of keeping words and music in perfect balance. In Francell's singing there is not enough tone in which to hold the words, not so much because his is a small voice but because he over-articulates. This followed inevitably from his preoccupation with French art songs and operetta in which, for some critics and even composers, a clear pronunciation was considered more important than an attractive musical quality. That neither need be subservient to the other is clearly demonstrated in the recordings of a leading lyric tenor of the previous generation, Edmond Clément; whatever his other shortcomings, in this respect he is impeccable. His words are always clear but perfectly blended into the tone and never compromise it. By comparison Francell's enunciation is both affected and obtrusive, for it emasculates the tone and prevents any real variety of colour. In spite of his charm, after three or four of his recordings the listener becomes aware of a prevailing white quality and a monotony in his delivery.

Hardly had CHARLES FRIANT (1890–1947) taken first prize at the Paris Conservatory in the summer of 1914, than war broke out; it was not until the winter of 1919 that he made his debut in a season of opera at the Théâtre Lyrique. This introduced to Paris Massenet's last and posthumous opera *Cléopâtre* in which Maurice Renaud and Mary Garden—both of them by then rather middle-aged—played Anthony and Cleopatra. Friant took the comparatively small role of Spakos and in spite of the exalted company drew appreciative notices:

> His powerful voice of good quality was much applauded. Here is a young tenor of whom it is possible to expect much, especially if he improves his enunciation.[6]

He confirmed this good impression later the same season when he played opposite Maria Kouznetsova in Rousseau's *Tarass-Boulba*; his voice was thought 'enchanting'. In 1920 he secured a contract at the Opéra-Comique where he was to remain a much admired house singer for nearly twenty years. There he sang Werther, Don José, Armand in the 1936 revival of Lehár's *Frasquita* with Jenny

lection of Francell among audiences who rarely got the opportunity of hearing first class songs or singers. In 1925 he undertook a tour of the United States and there earned golden opinions. His recitals were mostly of French music but also included some classical airs and a Russian group, usually by Gretchaninov, Borodin and Tchaikovsky. One evening he was the supporting artist with Paderewski and on another Walter Damrosch accompanied him.

Two excerpts from Messager's *Fortunio* present Francell in a role that he created and hence are of considerable historical interest. His charming manner perfectly suits the music's sentimental style. Neither piece takes him out of his range and only at the top of 'Si voux croyez' does the voice tighten

Tourel, Pedro in Laparra's *La Habañera*, Jean in *Le Jongleur de Notre Dame* which he took for the last time in November 1939, Gérald, Marouf, Canio, Cavaradossi, Des Grieux, Basilio in *Les Noces de Figaro* and Jean in *Sapho*, a part which he also sang in summer seasons at Cannes and Deauville. At the Opéra-Comique he was Pedrillo in the first performance there of Mozart's *L'Enlèvement au serail* with Ritter-Ciampi and Lotte Schoene which Hahn conducted. He created principal roles in a variety of ephemera: Rousseau's *Le Bon Roi Dagobert* and *Le Hulla*, Erlanger's *La Forfaiture* (which reversed the usual practice by being based on a story derived from an American film), Lévadé's *La Peau de chagrin* (an adaptation of one of Balzac's less plausible novels), Duperrier's *Zadig*, and *Le Roi Candaule* of Bruneau in which his singing was praised, but he was thought without any histrionic skill.

In 1926 Gunsbourg invited him to Monte Carlo for a revival of Puccini's *La Rondine* with Yvonne Gall.

> His voice is warm and rich with exquisite subtle shadings and superb high notes which blended harmoniously with the magnificent voice of the beautiful Gall. His acting was correct and simple and he was an ideal personification of Ruggero.[7]

He sang regularly at seasons in Nice, Deauville and Cannes and on occasion in Brussels at the Monnaie, but his career does not seem to have extended outside the French-speaking countries.

Friant was not a great, nor even a very important, singer but he was a sensitive and refined artist and he made some very attractive and from our point of view important records—this in spite of an extremely throaty voice. Although it was of good quality, as his contemporaries noted, his voice was inflicted throughout its range with the type of pronounced tremolo that Garcia called a bleat. Many of his most admirable artistic intentions are confounded by it; in the upper range especially, and when under pressure, he often sounds as if he were going to choke. At the end of Gérald's 'Ah, viens dans la forêt' the final phrase, which takes him up to the high B natural, collapses on to the throat. The effort it costs him to get the voice out is only surpassed by that of trying to stop it; when he wants to relinquish a note at anything above a mezzo forte, he has to go into a glottal reverse. The effect of this is to spoil the line and give a general roughness to the execution, most noticeably in

21 Charles Friant   22 Louis Cazette

vigorous passages. Faults or no, Friant's records contain many admirable things. The opening recitative to Jean's apostrophe to Freedom from Massenet's *Le Jongleur de Notre Dame* is done with great delicacy and feeling and here the tone is not distorted in a misguided attempt to make the words clearer; his diction is always lucid and well pointed. Neither in the phrase 'Liberté, ma mie insoucieuse fée', nor in the opening measures of 'Fantaisie aux divins mensonges' from *Lakmé*, can he float the phrases with the required sweeping legato, but his powers of suggestion almost overcome the voice's intractability. Very fine is Vladimir's aria (in French) from *Le Prince Igor*, sung with a proper appreciation of the mood, the melody carefully prepared for both its appearances, and although he has problems in keeping a suave line, the soft high A at the end is more successful than elsewhere. In the electric period Friant recorded a number of selections from *Werther*. Students might well study his interpretation, if not his vocalism, for herein is the authentic Massenet style, full of expressive inflections, variety of dynamics and eloquent use of rubato while at the same time the orchestra, now out of the penumbra of the acoustic horn, richly supports rather than obliterates his performance. The ensemble is not perfect but the playing, especially of the strings, is full of intensity and feeling contrived by the frequent use of portamento and vibrato. It reminds us that the way of modern orchestras in this music is skeletal, rigid and mostly too loud.

LOUIS CAZETTE (1887–1922) died before he could fulfil his early promise. as a boy he was a church chorister and after his voice broke, at first, sang as a baritone. During his period of military service he took part in several concerts programming arias from *Le Roi de Lahore* and *Hérodiade*. At one of these Delpouget heard Cazette and recommended him to present himself at the auditions for the Paris Conservatoire, as a tenor. He was admitted to the class of Albert Saléza. Two years later, in 1914, 'with his charming tenor voice, natural grace, good taste and seriousness, he had no difficulty taking first prize'. Part of this was a contract at the Opéra-Comique, but only eight days later France declared war on Germany and he spent the next five years in the army. Eventually, in 1919, he made his debut as Le Noctambule in *Louise*, thereafter his roles included Fernando in *Così fan tutte*, Gérald, Pinkerton, Vincent, Wilhelm Meister, Des Grieux, Don Ottavio, in which his voice was much praised, and he created Tiberio in Février's *Gismonda*, Tebaldo in Moret's *Lorenzaccio* and Le Montreur d'ours in Lazzari's *Le Sauteriot*. Cazette died from blood poisoning: he cut his finger while repairing a bicycle puncture and developed tetanus.

His is a light-weight tenor and finely schooled, with its sweet timbre in half voice and pure quality very reminiscent of Clément. He sings the air of Alain from *Grisélidis* with eloquent affection, rising to a fine climax and there are many purely vocal graces in his treatment of the line that are conspicuously absent among his contemporaries. His early death would appear to have been a great loss for French singing.

We get a good idea of routine French standards from the records of RENE LAPELLETRIE (1884–). His career lasted almost forty years; to begin with he was a principal lyric tenor, mostly in provincial theatres, by the end he was a character singer at the Opéra-Comique. Upon the completion of his studies at the Geneva Conservatory under Leopold Kitten, he journeyed to Paris to make his debut in the 1908 season at the Trianon-Lyrique. During the next dozen or so years he went the rounds of the leading French houses. At Dijon he sang in Nouguès's *Quo Vadis?* and Dupont's *La Glu*; at Nice in 1911 he created the role of Leonard in Larmenjat's *Gina*; at Marseilles in 1912 he was heard in Saint-Saëns's *Proserpine* and Puccini's *La Fille du Far-West*. After 1911 he appeared regularly in the summer seasons at Vichy. In Paris that year he was Almaviva in *Le Barbier de Séville* with Maguenat and Nicot-Vauchelet. In 1913 he took the leading role in Weingartner's revival of Berlioz's *Benvenuto Cellini*. During the war he served in the army.

In 1919 he joined the Opéra-Comique, at first singing Werther, Don José, Hoffmann, Pinkerton, Julien, Des Grieux, Ulysse in Fauré's *Pénélope*, Rodolfo, Gérald, Alfredo, Mylio in *Le Roi d'Ys*, Faust and Lorenzo in Messager's *Béatrice* but by degrees moving down to Guillot in *Manon*, Spalanzani in *Les Contes d'Hoffmann*, Dancaire in *Carmen*, the Chief of the Bandits in *Don Quichotte* and Spoletta in *Tosca*.

It was a small and throaty light tenor with far too much vibrato. The early Odeon recordings show the voice at its best and he makes a reasonably agreeable impression with Tonio's 'Pour me rapprocher' from *La Fille du régiment* and in an unfamiliar piece from Thomas's *Le Songe d'une nuit d'été*. By the time he made the HMVs, the voice had lost any quality and his attempts at graceful music are most unfortunate. Almaviva's 'Ecco ridente' (in French) must be numbered among the worst performances on record; there is no shape, style or finish to the singing, he can do no more than suggest the fioritura and the high notes all sound strangled. A solo from Planquette's *Les Cloches de Corneville* suits him nicely for at best he is only equal to light music.

23 René Lapelletrie

24 Dinh Gilly as Wolfram in *Tannhäuser*

8. Baritones of the Opéra

The Algerian-born baritone DINH GILLY (1877–
1940), the possessor of an attractive, full voice, was
at one time or other a principal at the Paris Opéra,
the Metropolitan, Covent Garden and Monte Carlo.
He first went to Toulouse to study but after only a
few months left for Rome, where he joined one of
the classes of Antonio Cotogni. Cotogni was a
famous baritone in the generation next before
Battistini's, and he enjoyed a distinguished career
rivalled only by the successes of his pupils: Jean de
Reszke, Beniamino Gigli, Giacomo Lauri-Volpi,

Mario Basiola, Mariano Stabile and Benvenuto
Franci among many. From Rome Gilly travelled to
Paris and the Conservatoire, where he took first
prize in singing and shortly afterwards secured an
engagement at the Paris Opéra. He was a principal
there for five seasons until 1908, his roles including:
Gunter, Valentin, Silvio, Mercutio, Amonasro, di
Luna, Hidraot in *Armide*, the Herald in *Lohengrin*,
Wolfram, and Nevers in *Les Huguenots*. In 1909 he
journeyed to the United States and joined the
Metropolitan. His debut was in fact made at the
New Theatre, an extension of the company's activities. Ostensibly conceived to enlarge the repertory with smaller, more intimate pieces, in reality it
was nothing more than a riposte to mounting
competition from the Manhattan. It proved to be
quite as abortive as Hammerstein's experiment the
same season with opéra-comique. Gilly was Albert
in *Werther* with Clément and Farrar, and soon
established himself as an effective and useful, if not
front-ranking, member of the company. He was at
the Met for five seasons and during that time was
heard as di Luna with Slezak and Gadski, Valentin
with Caruso and Farrar, Merlier in *L'Attaque du
moulin* with Delna and Clément—this also at the
New Theatre—Amonasro (which he claimed was his
favourite role), and small parts in Gluck's *Armide*,
Charpentier's *Julien*, Puccini's *Fanciulla del West*,
Roméo et Juliette and *Rigoletto*; on more than one
occasion he was called upon to deputise for an ailing
Scotti, in *La Bohème*, *Manon Lescaut* and *Ugonotti*.

He might well have remained at the Met for the
rest of his career but at the outbreak of war he was
appearing in Vienna and as an enemy alien was
interned. At the time he had formed a romantic
relationship with the great Czech diva Emmy Destinn; when the news of Gilly's fate reached her, she
quit New York and rushed to join him. After
hostilities ceased in Europe in the autumn of 1918,
those between Destinn and Gilly broke out, where-
upon she determined to return to New York,
leaving Gilly in England. Though the relationship
was a stormy one and not productive, Destinn did
manage to teach Gilly enough Czech so they could
duet together in a couple of folk songs for the
record.

Gilly's Covent Garden career began in 1911. He
was thought an 'extremely impressive'[1] Amonasro
and 'an operatic artist of the first order' when he
undertook Rance in the London premiere of *Fanciulla del West* with Destinn and Caruso. In London
he repeated some of his New York repertory and
was also heard, in the course of eight seasons, as

Sharpless, Athanael—in which 'his great powers of earnestness, also tenderness in the Desert scene'[2] were especially remarked upon—Germont, Tonio, the High Priest in *Samson* and in 1920 he was acclaimed for his 'powerful'[3] Michele in another local premiere of Puccini's *Il Tabarro*. In the early twenties he sang in two seasons at the Monte Carlo Opera and in 1922 made his first appearances at the Opéra-Comique as Scarpia, thereafter adding Escamillo, Nilakantha, the four villains in *Les Contes d'Hoffmann* and Tonio. In London in 1921 and 1923 he appeared as Scarpia, a guest in seasons given by the Carl Rosa and British National Opera Company at Covent Garden, singing in English. Perhaps the experience confused him; at any rate when he took the role again, during the international season of 1924, *The Times* praised his interpretation, 'as polished as ever', but noted that 'he was not always sure of the words'.[4] From this time he made his home in London, continuing to sing in concert and on the radio for some time after his last season at Covent Garden in 1925. In those years he was a well-regarded singing teacher, his pupils including Edith Furmedge, who became his wife, Dora Labette, Dennis Noble and John Brownlee.

Gilly's short list of recordings includes the Czech songs mentioned above, standard pieces from the French repertory and classical airs by Caccini and Monteverdi. Aldrich describes him in a New York concert as soloist with the Schola Cantorum singing music by Purcell, Lully, Jean-Jacques Rousseau and others.

25 Louis Lestelly as Napoléon in Nouguès's *L'Aigle*

> [He sang] with robustness and sincerity and was successful even with the English words of the air from Purcell's opera (*King Arthur*),

as indeed he is in a recording of the *Pagliacci* Prologue in English. On records we hear a high baritone with an interesting and characteristic timbre. In Scindia's 'Promesse de mon avenir' there is evidence of fine schooling, especially in his management of the high-lying passages in mezza voce up to the high G flat where he shows how well the registers are blended. This is an attractive, suavely vocalised interpetation.

In an air from *Le coupe du roi de Thulé* by Eugène Diaz (a second class composer obviously indebted to Gounod), Gilly's polished phrasing, controlled intensity and suave line recall Maurice Renaud. By any standards this is distinguished singing and we can overlook the rapid tremolo and a certain throatiness in the tone.

Although not an artist of the very highest order LOUIS LESTELLY (1877–1936) made some agreeable records which show a high baritone voice of good quality and an accomplished singer. He made his debut in 1901 and appeared for some years thereafter in the provinces in France and Belgium, at Nice, Marseilles and Liège. In 1908 he joined the company at the Monnaie in Brussels. Two years later Higgins brought him to Covent Garden; he sang Valentin in *Faust* with Edvina, Franz and Vanni Marcoux and Nevers in *Ugonotti* with Tetrazzini and Destinn. At the Opéra he was a principal for six seasons after 1913 and was heard as: Nevers, Wolfram, Rigoletto, Valentin, Amonasro, Rance, Guillaume Tell, Alphonse in *La Favorite*, and the title-role in *Eugene Onegin*, as well as Amfortas in the local premiere of *Parsifal*. His career, however, did not last long and in 1920 he retired to teach singing in Paris.

Lestelly's was a nicely vibrant voice, a little throaty, but easily embracing high A flat, as we hear it at the end of Hérode's 'Demande au prisonnier', the quality warm and the tone rounded, but without any particular character or great variety of colour. He sings the slow measures of Henri VIII's 'Qui donc commande?' with sentiment and without exaggeration. In Nelusko's 'L'avoir tant adorée', the difficult intervals are skilfully done, and he shapes the phrases in the correct portamento style.

9. *Journet and the Basses*

MARCEL JOURNET (1867–1933) enjoyed a long and distinguished career in many of the world's leading opera houses. His was a full and noble bass voice which, in his youth, extended through a wide range from the low E to the G above middle C. As his records testify his singing was representative of the highest standards at the turn of the century; the tone was pure, the registers blended, the emission steady and he was not without skill in the management of florid music. On stage he looked well for he was a tall and big man and he filled out the principal bass roles to effect. For all this he never achieved greatness. He lived at a time when there were others who, though not all of them were generally so accomplished, excelled him in one or other aspect of their art. Thus, at the beginning of his career, Edouard de Reszke made a more imposing noise and his singing had greater character and authority, while Plançon's voice was of a finer grain and his art altogether more refined. Later on he had to contend with the personality and vocal imagination of Chaliapin, with whom he could not compare, while as an actor, especially in the contemporary French repertory, he was surpassed by Vanni Marcoux. Nevertheless his recordings, like those of Dufranne, reveal a singer of very considerable distinction whose art graced the stage for forty years.

Journet studied at the Paris Conservatoire under Obin, graduating in 1889. Two years later he sang the role of Balthazar in *La Favorite* at Béziers. From 1892 he sang regularly at the Monnaie. His international career proper began with an invitation to Covent Garden in 1897 where the bass roster already included Edouard de Reszke and Plançon. Their presence notwithstanding, Journet's engagement was renewed every season until 1907 and he came again in 1909, 1927 and 1928. At the time the theatre's director Maurice Grau was also presiding over the Met in New York, and in 1900 young Journet went west; there too, he reappeared re-

gularly until the end of the 1906/7 season. At both theatres he got through a considerable number of parts: Marcel and St Bris in *Les Huguenots*, the Landgrave in *Tannhäuser*, Méphistophélès in Gounod's *Faust*, Claudius in Ambroise Thomas's *Hamlet*, Jupiter and Vulcain in Gounod's *Philémon et Baucis*, Colline and Schaunard in *La Bohème*, Capulet and Frère Laurent in *Roméo et Juliette*, Leporello and the Commendatore in *Don Giovanni*, Sparafucile, the Kings in *Lohengrin* and *Le Roi d'Ys*, Escamillo and Zuniga in *Carmen*, Raimondo in *Lucia di Lammermoor*, Don Basilio, Comte des Grieux in *Manon*, Basinde in Missa's *Maguelone*, Alvise, Rodolfo in Catalani's *Loreley*, Fafner in *Rheingold*, Garrido in *La Navarraise*, the King and Ramfis in *Aida*, Ferrando in *Trovatore*, le Comte de Gormas in *Le Cid*, Don Pedro, the Grand Inquisitor and the Grand Brahmin in *L'Africaine*, Titurel and Gurnemanz in *Parsifal*, Myrtille and Olimpias in de Lara's *Messaline*, Lodovico in *Otello*, Oberthal and Zacharias in *Le Prophète*, Tom in *Ballo in Maschera*, Narr-Havas in Reyer's *Salammbô* and Plunkett in *Marta*. In 1915 and 1916 he sang with the Chicago Opera where he added to the above repertory Lothario in *Mignon*, Phanuel in Massenet's *Hérodiade* and Ennius, which he took in the local premiere of Massenet's *Cléopâtre*. While in Chicago he was involved in a curious incident. It seems that on the cold winter days when he was not singing, he used to lie in wait cat-like by the window of his hotel bedroom and when the half starved, almost frozen city pigeons settled on the ledge, grab hold of them. It was not until the hotel's plumbing seized up and masses of feathers were found down the lavatory that any one realised what he had been up to. What became of the carcasses is a mystery; since they were never found, it was assumed that he must have eaten them. The press made the story front page news; there was a great deal of poverty in Chicago at the time, but not even the poorest had been driven so far as to consider the city's verminous pigeons as fair game.

In 1916 he travelled to South America to take the part of the High Priest in some performances of *Samson et Dalila* at the Colon conducted by the composer. Journet returned for the next two seasons and again in 1923 and 1927. During those years he was heard as Rodolfo in *Sonnambula*, the Sultan in *Marouf*, the Archbishop in Messager's *Béatrice* and Wotan in a *Walchiria* in which he sang in French. From the time of the outbreak of the First World War he began to base the major part of every season in France. At the Opéra he sang in revivals of

26 Marcel Journet as Klingsor in *Parsifal*

Les Huguenots, Guillaume Tell, as a 'thunderous'[1] Walther, and Hans Sachs in *Les Maîtres Chanteurs*. He was Dosifey in the first performances there of Moussorgsky's *Khovanshchina*, in which,

> although he has not drawn the personality with all the dramatic imagination that one could have expected, yet he has shown the beautiful quality of his singing.[2]

As Benvenuto Cellini in the 1921 revival of Saint-Saëns's *Ascanio* comparisons were drawn with Lassalle in one of the latter's favourite roles. Journet was warmly praised for 'his admirable feeling, sincerity,

fine diction and supple voice with which he gave to the character a powerful authority'.[3] After 1916 he sang on a number of occasions at La Scala, as Alfonso in *Lucrezia Borgia*, Golaud in *Pelléas et Mélisande*, the Father in *Luisa*, Méphistophélès, Hans Sachs in *Maestri Cantori* and he created Simon Mago in the world premiere of Boito's *Nerone* in 1924; subsequently he sang this and other roles elsewhere in Italy. At Monte Carlo he was admired in a revival of Rameau's *Les Fêtes d'Hébé* and was heard as Oroveso, Scarpia and Gurnemanz. He remained active throughout the 1920s and gave his last performances less than a year before his death.

In 1932 he sang the role of Méphistophélès in a complete recording of *Faust* with the tenor César Vezzani. By then the voice had lost much of its quality but the high regard in which he was held by his contemporaries is more than supported by the evidence from records made in his prime. In Gounod's 'Sous les pieds' from *La Reine de Saba* he reveals a poised legato with lightly drawn portamenti; the execution, especially of the slurred quavers, is precise and accurate. The words are pronounced clearly yet without impeding the flow of mellow tone. Only the lower octave is rather weak but he makes no attempt to force it even when, as at the end, he sinks down to a thin but still focussed low E. His singing here has rather more expression than we might have expected, and he nicely contrasts the linking section using an incisive attack and then reintroduces the melody in suave and affecting style. He was a fine colleague and his voice blended well in duets, trios and ensembles, perhaps most eloquently with Caruso and Alda in 'Qual voluttà' from Verdi's *I Lombardi*. Though Journet's contribution is the least conspicuous, his backing sounds like some huge and articulate 'cello obbligato.

Few singers of this period have a more imposing and better-produced voice than the Belgian bass-baritone HECTOR DUFRANNE (1870–1951). His singing, though thoroughly French, belonged to the old school in which the language was not allowed to compromise vocal quality. He studied at the Brussels Conservatory under Demest and made his debut at the Monnaie in 1898. Two years later he arrived in Paris and appeared for the first time at the Opéra-Comique as Thoas in Gluck's *Iphigénie en Tauride*. He was to remain a prominent and much loved member of the company for nearly forty years. His wide repertory included Alfio, Nilakantha, Ourrias in *Mireille* with Adolphe Maréchal, Garrido in *La Navarraise*, Vulcain in Gounod's *Philémon et Baucis*, Karnac in *Le Roi d'Ys*, André Thorel in Massenet's *Thérèse*, a part which he created at Monte Carlo in 1907, Escamillo with Calvé and Clément, and the Dutchman in *Le Vaisseau fantôme*. He was also at the Opéra in 1909, succeeding Vanni Marcoux in the first performances of Février's *Monna Vanna*.

The fine role of Guido gave M. Dufranne the opportunity of displaying his beautiful voice, and expressing a full range of dramatic emotions with strength and flexibility. Though he does not create a personality so original, gripping and unforgettable as did M. Mar-

coux, he renders it with a simpler truth, one more suited to Guido's ingenuous character.[4]

At a time when both Paris houses were producing a number of novelties every season, Dufranne participated in several world premieres. He was the Bishop in Hahn's *La Carmélite*, which provided Calvé with an opportunity to do penance, as it were, for all her Carmens; apparently she did so with great success. He joined Geneviève Vix, Maggie Teyte, Suzanne Brohly and David Devriès in Hillemacher's *Circé*, Marguerite Carré, Lucien Fugère and Fernand Francell in Messager's *Fortunio*, and he was Judas in the first staging of Massenet's sacred music drama *Marie-Magdeleine* with Aino Ackté. It was his Golaud that brought him the wildest acclaim. He sang it on his only visit to Covent Garden in 1914. It led to his first American engagement at the Manhattan in the New York premiere of *Pelléas et Mélisande* with Garden, Périer and Gerville-Réache, all of whom had been in the world premiere; Dufranne's singing created quite a stir. Henderson especially was bowled over: 'he was one of the greatest artists who ever came here from France'.[5] Aldrich wrote:

27 Hector Dufranne as Golaud in *Pelléas et Mélisande*

Mr Dufranne has a baritone voice of resonance, of dark and rich colour; his enunciation is of exquisite perfection, his treatment of the phrase most musical, his declamation is of true eloquence. He is an actor of strong individuality and varied resources.[6]

In New York he repeated many of his Paris successes and added Valentin, Capulet, an 'admirable'[7] High Priest in *Samson*, the Father in *Louise*—though here he did not manage to efface recollections of Gilibert—'a truly noble' Jokanaan in a French *Salomé* (for the benefit of Garden), the Marquis in *Grisélidis*, the Prior in *Le Jongleur de Notre Dame* and Caoudal in *Sapho*, all of these with Garden. After the fall of Hammerstein he was a regular member of the Chicago Opera, missing only one season, until 1922. Here he extended his repertory further with Amonasro, Favart in Kienzl's *Le Ranz des vaches*, Klingsor, Lescaut, Albert, Father Peralta in Victor Herbert's *Natoma*, Chilon in Nouguès's *Quo Vadis?* with Teyte, Dalmorès and Clarence Whitehill, the three roles in *Les Contes d'Hoffman*, Pandolphe in *Cendrillon* with Teyte and Garden, Telramund, John in Goldmark's *Cricket on*

28 Paul Payan as Don Basilio in *Le Barbier de Séville*

the Hearth, Lothario in *Mignon*, Athanaël, Boniface in *Le Jongleur de Notre Dame* and 'a most sympathetic Yves (in Messager's *Madame Chrysanthème*) giving distinction by his singing, his fine diction, his skilful acting, to a part of no great prominence'.[8] While in Chicago he took the part of Tchelio in the world premiere of Prokofiev's *L'Amour de trois oranges*, the composer himself conducting. In 1923 in Paris at a soirée held at the hôtel of the Princesse de Polignac, he was Don Quichotte in the first performance of Manuel de Falla's *Les Tréaux de Maître Pierre*. His career continued almost until the outbreak of the Second World War and he gave his final performance at Vichy in 1939, appropriately enough as Golaud.

Records preserve a warm and mellow bass-baritone voice extending from G at the bottom of the bass clef to the G above middle C. The production is smooth and the tone forward on the breath. He sings the Comte des Grieux's ingratiating little homily to his son with a simple dignity, and perfectly realises the instruction 'presque déclamé' written over the passage 'La vertu qui fait du tapage . . .' In Athanaël's 'Voilà donc la terrible cité' he reminds us that Massenet's vocal line requires, as well as a clear pronunciation, a suave and lovely quality. If neither of these performances is notably refined or imaginative, in a number from Massé's *Les Noces de Jeanette* he reveals some virtuosity; not such as to rival Plançon, but a neatly turned trill and a few roulades at the end. He shows too the importance of a clean attack so as to execute accurately the marcato markings which help to give rhythmic energy. Only with a free and responsive voice, can the singer 'lead', otherwise he must let the conductor (more often the orchestra) carry him along.

By the standards of Journet or Dufranne PAUL PAYAN (1878–1959) was hardly a refined singer, yet his was an imposing bass voice with a wide range, the registers well blended, and his singing was not without some accomplishment. The major part of his career, from the time of his Paris debut in 1907, was spent at the Opéra-Comique with occasional appearances at various provincial French theatres. He sang a large number of comprimario roles in such operas as *Louise*, Saint-Saëns's *L'Ancêtre*, Magnard's *Bérénice*, Leroux's *Le Carillonneur*, de Severac's *Le Coeur du Moulin*, Laparra's *La Habañera*, Bloch's *Macbeth*, Rabaud's *Marouf*, Erlanger's *Aphrodite*, *La Basoche*, *Carmen*, *Hoffmann*, *Le Jongleur de Notre Dame*, Erlanger's *Le Juif polonais*, *Madame Butterfly*, *Tosca*, *Traviata*, *La Bohème*,

Werther and *Manon Lescaut*. Among leading parts he was heard as Lothario in *Mignon*, Vulcain in Gounod's *Philémon et Baucis*, the Commendatore, and Sarastro in *La Flûte enchantée*. He travelled to Chicago in 1921 and appeared there as the Old Hebrew in *Samson*, Frère Laurent in *Roméo et Juliette*, Zuniga in *Carmen* and the Prior in *Le Jongleur de Notre Dame*. Three years later at the Colon, Buenos Aires, he was heard as Comte des Grieux in *Manon Lescaut*. In 1928 he was engaged at Covent Garden but only for comprimario roles.

In Michel's couplets from Thomas's *Le Caïd* he can hardly vie with Plançon for accuracy or alacrity of execution and his is rather a rough and ready Drum Major, nevertheless he sings in the right spirit and cleanly enough. He makes a good fist at the roulades and even tries a trill, but since the voice has a pronounced vibrato, he does not succeed in establishing this very convincingly. The vibrato takes the edge off an eloquent and well-shaped legato in a charming number from Mompou's *Les Deux Reines*, 'Adieu mon beau navire', which is otherwise an attractive piece of singing, not notably refined, but affectionately phrased, the words pronounced limpidly and clearly on the breath without affectation or the dry and nasal tone we hear from so many of his contemporaries.

The authentic Massenet style can be heard in the charming duet for Cendrillon and Pandolphe, in which Payan is joined by Suzanne Brohly. The two voices make an agreeable effect, singing with warmth and breadth of tone.

29 Vanni Marcoux as Méphistophélès in *Faust*

10. Singing Actors

Jean-Emil Marcoux, one of France's greatest singing actors, is better known by his stage name VANNI MARCOUX (1877–1962). Vanni, an Italian diminutive for Giovanni, reminds us that he was born in Turin and that his mother was Italian. For all that he was a French artist, his training was French, from Frederic Boyer at the Paris Conservatoire, and it was in the French repertory, particularly contemporary works, that he enjoyed his greatest successes: as Guido in Février's *Monna Vanna*, Ramon in Laparra's *La Habañera*, Golaud in *Pelléas et Mélisande*, Athanaël in *Thaïs* and in the title roles of *Panurge* and *Don Quichotte*. He was also much admired as the Méphistophélès in Gounod's and Berlioz's *Faust*, Boris Godounov and Baron Ochs both in the vernacular, the four roles in *Les Contes d'Hoffmann*, Don Giovanni and even Iago and Scarpia; though the last two took him to the limits of his range, his histrionic skill compensating for occasional lapses 'into spoken dialogue'.[1]

His debut actually took place at Turin in 1894 as Sparafucile and it was not until 1899 that he made his first stage appearance in France, at Bayonne as Frère Laurent; thereafter he sang at a number of provincial theatres and later in Brussels. In 1905 he made his Covent Garden debut as an 'atrabilious'[2] Basilio and returned every season until 1912, doing duty with comprimario parts and as Sparafucile and Colline, then extending his experience with a number of principal roles. Although none of these seems to have brought forth much critical comment, they were all noticed: his 'excellent'[3] Marcello in *Ugonotti*, a 'sympathetic'[4] Arkel in the first London performances of *Pelléas et Mélisande*, and 'more than adequate'[5] Father in *Louise*. But these were formative years and it was not until he was engaged by Henry Russell for the Boston Opera that he established himself as a star. From his first appearance as Golaud he was greatly admired. There followed Méphistophélès in Gounod's *Faust* in which, if he could hardly rival Plançon as a singer, his dramatic conception was 'altogether more vivid, picturesque and varied'.[6] Taking his cue from Maurel he had discarded the traditional pantomime gear. Striking costumes were always a part of his stock in trade and in *Les Contes d'Hoffmann* on the opening night of the 1912 season he had exceptional opportunities for display:

As Coppélius he was a crabbed, fantastic figure, at once ridiculous and sinister. But it was as Dr Miracle, clad in a black robe, with white head and his supernatural height, that he made an unforgettable impression. This was, in fact, Death and the worm was his brother. Miracle danced a fiendish fandango and rattled his vials of poison in the face of the horror-struck Crespel. Nor must there be forgotten the manner in which this dark figure melted into a fearful shadow in one corner of the room, nor the sudden appearances and disappearances from the scene: through the windows, the walls, the doors, from nowhere he started out, and he disappeared as a shadow itself through the casement. And finally the figure which crept behind the unhappy Antonia while a voice as from her own soul hurried to her end.[7]

It seems that he was not satisfied with the effect, for in later performances 'he discarded the bald, pale head and enveloping robes . . . appearing as a mask of death with curling dark hair, in black riding dress with a cloak over his shoulders and shining boots'.[8] As an actor perhaps his most sensational achievement was Scarpia, 'the villain of melodrama,' 'the distinguished voluptuary and tyrant before whom all Rome trembled'.[9] Mary Garden was the Tosca at most performances and doubtless contributed no small part to the effect, even if at the climactic moment she was at the receiving end: in Act Two Vanni Marcoux launched at her in a rugger tackle, flung her back down on the sofa and then jumped on top, a position which puritan Boston found too explicit for its taste. Not surprisingly the critics had little space left to tell us about the singing.

Vanni Marcoux owed much of his success in the United States to Mary Garden. Her popularisation of the works of the modern French school provided

him with all sorts of dramatic opportunities, a fact that he seems to have been very well aware of. At the time of his arrival in Boston he was in the process of putting off his second wife and, according to press rumours, wondering whether the odds were on his making it third time lucky with Mary. She, however, declined the honour; his passion, like that of so many of the characters he played in their various stage relationships—Tosca and Scarpia, Thaïs and Athanael, Dulcinée and Don Quichotte, Mélisande and Golaud, Carmen and Escamillo—was destined to go unrequited. He followed her to Chicago in 1913 and returned regularly in the years between 1926 and 1931; he actually survived a season longer than Garden but the French repertory could not survive without her and thereafter there was no place for him.

Marcoux was an actor who sang. Even in Paris where he appeared regularly after 1914 and was a popular star, opinions of his voice and singing were hardly complimentary. André Mangeot praised his dramatic art and his enunciation of the French language but could not refrain from observing that:

He shows how true was Jacques Isnardon's remark that 'to say he who articulates clearly does not need a voice is not an absolute paradox'.[10]

It was an opinion held by most French critics. One called it 'an unresponsive voice' (une voix ingrate)[11] another, after expatiating at some length on his theatrical skill finished:

Let us not discuss the quality of his voice: on this point, everyone is agreed. Nor need we wrangle over his musicianship; on that point too, unanimity is easily reached.[12]

And abroad; in New York, Aldrich was impressed by his acting as Guido in *Monna Vanna* but complained of 'a somewhat recalcitrant'[13] voice.

After Guido he was most widely admired as Golaud, Boris Godounov and Don Quichotte. He took the role of Boris at La Scala in 1922 under Toscanini in succession to Sigismund Zaleski who was generally regarded as the finest exponent of Boris after Chaliapin (unfortunately he made no records). Later Marcoux appeared in a production at the Paris Opéra under Koussevitsky and in 1927 in Chicago. Again it was his acting that made the biggest impact.

30 Marcoux as Guido in Février's *Monna Vanna*

Just previous to the Tsar's death he practically had an epileptic fit—the entire body shaking, the jaw made stiff, the tongue paralysed, the eyes dead even though bewildered, the cheeks sagged and we saw a hideous figure, a face tortured with physical and mental ills, a man whose agony was frightful.[14]

One can only wonder how he managed to sing at all with the jaw stiff and the tongue paralysed. That the singing made less of an impression is confirmed in Emile Vuillermoz's review of the Paris *Boris Godo-unov*:

The overwhelming memory of Chaliapin led the management to seek out sensational solutions. Chaliapin is unique, a model that defies imitation. His superhuman voice, his authority, his simplicity . . . made him irresistible. It was decided to confer the succession on a creator of characters, a sculptor of masks, an artist who has specialised in picturesque creations, but whose vocal means are not his greatest gift. The mistake was serious. Boris must be sung, it must be sung with power, sonority and magnificence. It must be sung with a Tsar's voice. And this is more important than the more or less artificial mimings of delirium and remorse. Throwing chairs over, covering one's face and walking backwards, chasing off phantoms are all relatively easy tasks for which there is no need to call in a specialist . . . M. Vanni Marcoux, articulating forcefully, hammers, hacks and chops up the text and in so doing renders it irritatingly dry.[15]

This dryness was, records suggest, characteristic of his singing in all of his roles. As Don Giovanni, for example, he phrases the Serenade with some distinction—this was apparently the vocal high point of his performance—but the classical style of the music, as well as the dramatic circumstances, call for a pure and suave tone which he is unable to offer—'he has the air of a seducer but he has not the voice of one'.[16] As Don Quichotte, in the Death Scene, it has been suggested that this dryness is appropriate to the voice of a dying man. The argument is unstylish, for the singer, unlike the actor, must have regard not only for the dramatic situation but the convention: dying men do not sing. The illusion of death must be suggested without compromising the musical language of the composer; in Massenet's case the singer must match in his tones the melodic style, sentimental harmonies and sweet orchestration. Vanni Marcoux's carefully measured enunciation makes an effect but it is rather a literal, not to say literary, reading for the voice has more of the quality of speech than song. The line is smooth but it lacks the vocal poise and tension we can hear in the singing of Plançon and Journet. A comparison between recordings of the Death of Don Quichotte by Chaliapin and Vanni Marcoux is instructive. Chaliapin's treatment is altogether freer but it is not, therefore, less musical; rather the contrary, for all of its imaginative detail— the variety of colour, range of dynamics, use of tremolando—is supported by singing tone. He could not have done it any other way, for his technique was inextricably welded to a portamento of the breath and based in a pure legato; even in parlando the musical intervals are correctly marked and there is more tone here than in Vanni Marcoux's singing. Whether we agree or not with those critics who would deny that Vanni Marcoux had any voice at all, it certainly lacked a particular musical character—was it bass, baritone or even tenor? It could hardly be said of him, as Henderson did of Plançon, that 'he sang the modified vowels of his native language without abandoning that noble sonority of tone'.[17] Not surprisingly he sought to compensate for the deficiency with elaborate costumings and histrionics. The expressive range of his voice was limited; Mangeot describes him 'knees trembling but the voice as bland as if he were saying ''I'm going for a walk'' '.[18]

He appeared only infrequently in concert or recital; his was not the kind of art greatly appreciated without stage trappings. He recorded a number of songs of Paul Delmet; pleasant and agreeable in a sentimental vein, they suit his style. The words govern the shape of the vocal line and the music has not the melodic personality of, say, Denza or Tosti, whose songs to be shown off to their best advantage, need to be complimented by a lovely voice. An essay in the classical style, Martini's 'Plaisir d'amour', is less fortunate. This calls for precisely what Marcoux lacks: a beautiful limpid tone drawn cleanly on the breath, that makes possible the graces and at the same time perfectly balances vowel and consonant, we can hear it to perfection in Calvé's record of this song. He is not flattered by a 'close-miked' recording which lays bare his technique; especially in the middle range the voice is infected with a bleat which was surely not as obtrusive in real life. In the ascending phrase 'J'ai tout quitté pour l'ingrate Sylvie', though he intends a smooth legato, since the voice is not fully supported the registers separate and each note does not stand in the correct relationship with the next: his singing is not badly out of tune but the voice is not 'well-tempered'. Taken on its own terms it is a cultivated rendering, the enunciation very fine, but there is little or nothing in it of classical singing. From this distance in time, like period costumes in an old movie, it tells us less of the era to which it pretends than the one of which in fact it was a part: his delivery, perched uneasily between singing and crooning, is only a step away from the popular singers of his day.

Like Vanni Marcoux's the voice of JEAN AQUISTAPACE (1888–1952) was hardly remarkable for beauty or sonority of tone, but he was a skilful buffo and character singer. During the first two years of his career in the French provinces, he was already undertaking principal roles. At Lyons he was Boris and Don Quichotte in the local premieres of both operas. News of his successes soon reached

Paris and in 1913 he was invited to the Opéra-Comique, where his first appearance was as Scarpia; later he took the role of Ramon in a work from the theatre's staple diet, Gounod's *Mireille*. The same year he journeyed to London. His debut was as Colline in *La Bohème* with Melba, McCormack and Gilly and 'he made a favourable impression which we may hope will be strengthened later in a larger part'.[19] It was, when he appeared as Leporello. He was re-engaged for the following season, and repeated both parts, but as Figaro, in a generally unfortunate revival, 'he shows us his limitations a little by reminding one of his Leporello . . . still it is a thoroughly enjoyable and effective performance'.[20] He returned to Covent Garden in 1926 and sang Leporello again, in company with Leider, Lehmann and Schumann under the direction of Bruno Walter. These would appear to have been his only visits outside France. Paris remained the focus of his career and there he took part in several

31. Jean Aquistapace as Scarpia

important occasions. In 1922 he succeeded Vanni
Marcoux in the first French performances of *Boris
Godounov* at the Opéra; there too, when *Grisélidis*
moved up from the Comique, he sang the role of the
Devil.

He travelled extensively throughout France
and was an especially popular visitor at the
summer seasons in Cannes. He was Leporello in a
triumphant revival of *Don Juan* in 1920 under
Reynaldo Hahn with Ritter-Ciampi, Vallin and
Maurice Renaud, and when in some performances
Battistini replaced Renaud the opera was given in
the original. In 1921 in the role of the Doctor in
Gounod's *Le Médecin malgré lui* 'he created a per-
sonage of dry humour with farcical zest and he
deserved all the applause'.[21] His repertory also
included Papageno, the King in *Lohengrin*, Marco in
Monna Vanna and Le Vieux in Laparra's *La
Habañera*.

Aquistapace recorded for the Pathé company
a variety of excerpts from various operas,
including *Boris Godounov*, *Le Médecin malgré lui* and
Don Quichotte and also a number of songs by
Massenet, Flégier, Hahn and others. His voice
resembles Vanni Marcoux's; though it is somewhat
warmer and more attractive, there is a similar touch
of throatiness and a rapid tremolo which is more
apparent when he is singing above mezzo forte. His
diction is certainly clear but sounds rather precious.
He sacrifices purity of tone to the dipthonged
French vowels and there is little vocal colour. He
was a sensitive artist, as we can hear in Massenet's
'Pensée d'automne'; the phrasing has a considerable
variety of nuance and though the legato is not really
poised smoothly on the breath, it is an affecting
interpretation.

Like Aquistapace ALFRED MAGUENAT (*c.* 1880–
          ), though on occasion he ventured baritone
roles from the heroic repertory, seems to have been
preferred as a character and buffo singer. He sang
for the first time at the Opéra-Comique in 1908, as
the Baron in *Traviata*. Later his repertory included
Brétigny and Lescaut in *Manon*, the title-role in
Rossini's *Le Barbier de Séville*, Tonio, Alfio, the
Painter in *Louise*, Karnac in *Le Roi d'Ys*, Scarpia and
Pelléas, in which he was found inferior to Périer. In
1911 at Nice he created Sebastiano in the first
French performances of d'Albert's *Tiefland*. He sang
Figaro again in seasons at the Théâtre des Champs-
Elysées in 1911 with Nicot-Vauchelet and Renée
Lapelletrie. Three years later at the Gaîté-
Lyrique he took a leading role in a one-act
piece *Chacun pour soi* by Lamarjat.

32 Alfred Maguenat

Why does M. Maguenat whose acting has the right
kind of simple verve get so fussy in his singing? He
leaves one no time to discover whether he has a fine
voice or not.[22]

He visited Monte Carlo on more than one occasion
and was heard in *Parsifal*, *Ugonotti*, *Cléopâtre*, Saint-
Saëns's *Les Barbares* and Rameau's *Les Fêtes d'Hébé*.
For five seasons between 1915 and 1919 he was a
contract artist with the Chicago Opera. There he
sang Guido in *Monna Vanna*, Philoctète in Saint-
Saëns's *Déjanire*, Valentin, Mercutio in *Roméo et
Juliette*, Marc-Antoine in *Cléopâtre*, Cascart in *Zazà*,
Dapertutto in *Les Contes d'Hoffmann*, the Devil in
Grisélidis, the Khan in Gunsbourg's *Le Vieil Aigle*,
Nevers, Fréderic in *Lakmé*, Hérode in *Hérodiade*,
Ramiro in *L'Heure espagnole* and Zaccaria in
Février's *Gismonda*. He made his Covent Garden
debut as Pelléas in 1913, sang it again the following
year and was re-engaged in 1919 for performances

of *Roméo et Juliette*, *L'Heure espagnole*, *Manon Lescaut*, *Tosca* and as Thorel in Massenet's *Thérèse*, with the Welsh mezzo soprano Leila Megane. When Gilly became indisposed he stepped in as Rigoletto and Germont. He came again in 1920 singing Scarpia, Pelléas, and Athanael opposite Edvina; his last visit was in 1926 when it was noted that he sang 'a little more roughly than of old.'[23] In 1922 at the Opéra he sang Rigoletto, Ramiro and Hérode.

Maguenat's is a typical baritone in the French fashion, dry and gravelly in quality with a not very smooth or finished technique. He had a disagreeable way of stretching his voice up to the high notes. In the *Thaïs* Death Scene, with Marguerite Herleroy unequal to the big moments (the scented music demands some matching vocal quality) from Maguenat we hear only the words; the diphthonged French vowels so impede the progress of the tone it scarcely matters that he often only approximates sung pitches. The impossibly fussy diction will doubtless seem artistic to those who suppose that vocal quality is unimportant and that in French opera clarity of enunciation takes precedence over musical values. Nothing better exemplifies the decline in French singing than to compare him to Soulacroix in Bourgeois's delightful song 'La véritable Manola'. The text is abundantly clear in both versions but Soulacroix sings with elegance, limpidity and charm, the vocal graces finely etched and the words sit firmly in the tone. We shall find Maguenat least disagreeable when the fewest demands are made of him, for example in the passage 'Viens près de moi' from Nouguès's *Quo Vadis?*

The Belgian ARMAND CRABBE (1883–1947) was a singer of extraordinary versatility and a resourceful actor, though his was only a modest baryton-martin, a high and light-weight voice, the range of which enables the singer to accomplish certain tenor music as well as the less strenuous baritone repertory. In this Crabbé resembles Gabriel Soulacroix and Jean Périer and if he was scarcely as refined a singer as the former, his voice was better liked than Périer's. Crabbé sang in a great many of the world's leading opera houses in principal and comprimario parts, often in the same season. During his lengthy career he appeared in no less than eight different roles in *Les Contes d'Hoffmann*, undertook both Rigoletto and Pelléas and was perhaps the only artist who has ever sung Herod in Strauss's *Salome* and the same role in Massenet's *Hérodiade*. Like many of his compatriots he studied at the Brussels Conservatory with Desirée Demest. His debut was only a modest affair, as the Nightwatchman in *Les*

Maîtres Chanteurs. He remained at the Monnaie, a contract artist, for the next three years, but in this period he had already begun his travels. In 1906 he was engaged at Covent Garden, where his roles included Count Ceprano in *Rigoletto*, Le Moine Musicien in Massenet's *Le Jongleur de Notre Dame* and Valentin in *Faust*. He came again each summer until the outbreak of the First World War, taking various small roles as well as Alfio, Silvio, Abimelech in *Samson et Dalila*, Marcello and Ford in *Falstaff*. In the year following his first London engagement Hammerstein signed him up for the Manhattan. There in three seasons he got through Escamillo, Brander in *La Damnation de Faust*, Valentin, Ramon in *La Navarraise*, Silvio, Alfio, the First Philosopher and a Sculptor in *Louise*, Walitzin in Giordano's *Siberia*, the Doctor in *Pelléas et Mélisande* (in the New York premiere), Roucher in *Andrea Chénier*, Abimelech, Montano in *Otello*, Marcus in Blockx's *La Princesse d'Auberge*, Amonasro and, in various permutations of two or three in any one evening: Lindorf, Schlemil, Franz, Cochenille and Pitichinaccio in *Les Contes d'Hoffmann*.

Like Hector Dufranne and Gustave Huberdeau he moved on to Chicago, for four seasons between 1910 and 1914, enlarging his repertory with Fréderic in *Lakmé*, Melot in *Tristan*, the Father in *Hansel and Gretel*, Tonio, Hérode in *Hérodiade*, Picco in Victor Herbert's *Natoma* and in *Les Contes d'Hoffmann*, Coppélius, Dapertutto and Miracle. After 1914 he switched the axis of his career away from northern Europe and the United States to Italy, Spain and South America. In that year he made his La Scala debut in the title-role of *Rigoletto* with Finzi-Magrini as Gilda. Apparently the Milanese public, not for the first time, did not care for so French sounding a voice; nevertheless he reappeared in Milan in later years as Marcello in *La Bohème*, Lescaut in *Manon*, in the title-roles in *Gianni Schicchi* and Rabaud's *Maruf*, as Beckmesser in *Maestri Cantori* under Toscanini's direction with Favero, Pertile, Journet and Baccaloni and, again with Toscanini, he created the title-role in Giordano's *Il Re*. In Rome at the Costanzi he was Herod in Strauss's *Salome* opposite Geneviève Vix.

[They] sang in *Salome* with so profound an artistic and spiritual commitment that they could not shake it off for the next opera [Massenet's *Manon*]. There is an abyss between *Salome* and *Manon*, but for the two distinguished singers the distance was too short. . . . Crabbé acted the drunkard more than was necessary and jerked round the stage like a puppet on a string. By the way, why does not Signor Crabbé decide to give up singing in his amphibious baritone voice and settle once and for all on becoming a 'tenore drammatico'? I think that Zenatello's vocal transformation should have something to teach him. If only how to earn more money![24]

Apparently he did not heed the advice, for in South America he went on in the same vein as before with Gil in Wolf-Ferrari's *Le Secret de Suzanne*, Nevers in *Ugonotti*, Scarpia, Figaro in *Barbiere*, Hoël in *Dinorah*, Athanaël, the Devil in *Grisélidis*, Guido in *Monna Vanna*, Mercutio and Paquito in Granados's *Goyescas*. It was, however, in the title-role of *Marouf* that he came into his own. The part is equivocal, the tessitura provided throughout with alternatives so that either a low tenor or baritone can encompass the range.

> Signor Crabbé acted magnificently and his high, ringing and true voice rose triumphantly to the occasion. We should like to advise him, in brotherly fashion, to improve his diction, which is still very defective.[25]

Curiously, he did not appear very often in France. In 1922 he sang Beckmesser in *Maestri Cantori* with an Italian company under Serafin at the Théâtre des Champs Elysées, but it was not until 1926 that he

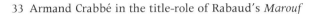

33 Armand Crabbé in the title-role of Rabaud's *Marouf*

made his debut at the Opéra-Comique, as Marouf, but thereafter he sang nothing else from the French repertory. He repeated his Beckmesser at the Opéra in 1933 and returned to London after an absence of more than a generation when he took the name part in *Gianni Schicchi* during the Coronation season of 1937. In the 1920s he organised a chamber opera group which toured in Spain and South America, giving performances of Pergolesi's *La Serva Padrona*, Paer's *Le Maître de chappelle*, Massé's *Les Noces de Jeanette* and Maurage's *Les Noces d'or*, a work for which he provided the libretto. He was something of a composer too and wrote a number of songs, one of which he recorded.

Crabbé made several series of recordings over a period of nearly a quarter of a century between 1908 and December 1932, and the voice changed little over the years. It is not a thing of beauty; the tone is dry and, especially in the middle range, a loose vibrato, on occasion spreading across more than a quarter of a tone, introduces warring harmonics that are musically disagreeable. He was an intelligent artist but his singing was mannered and his way of mouthing tones made his diction unclear. Mylio's Aubade from *Le Roi d'Ys*, here transposed, he sings with a nice lilt, but there is no attempt at a legato style and none of the sweetness of tone that the music ideally requires. As is so often the case with rattly voices, when he attempts a shake deliberately, as in the final cadence, the voice disobligingly refuses to budge. In Massenet's 'Ouvre tes yeux bleus' and 'Pensée d'automne', notwithstanding a comparatively narrow range of colour, the phrasing is sensitive to mood and feeling, though the voice is not fully responsive to his intentions. The lack of complete control and a want of finish in his singing are apparent in Fauré's 'Après un rêve'; the repeated vocalised triplets, a particular feature of the song, need to be executed with the utmost precision, while unfortunately Crabbé can only mumble over them. In the end it must be by achievement rather than intention that any singer is judged and there is little in his recordings to support the view that he was a refined musician. He is at his best in the air 'A travers le désert' from Rabaud's *Marouf* (sung in Italian). The opera enjoyed quite a vogue in the twenties, it was a kind of classical *Desert Song* in which, to judge from this excerpt, there was more desert than song; whatever may be thought of Crabbé as a Handel or Rossini singer, this sort of thing he does to the manner born. His fluency, versatility and unquestioned dramatic skill were important factors in

securing him a wide reputation; but in the nature of things, to encompass baritone roles of many different styles and vocal requirements, then to intersperse them with comprimario, and on occasion even tenor, roles cannot be managed without sacrificing the quality of the singing.

11. Contraltos

If none of the French mezzo sopranos and contraltos during these years enjoyed the wider acclaim of some of their German and Italian contemporaries, by no means all of them were inconsiderable. SUZANNE BROHLY (1882–1943) for example, though she spent virtually her entire career in Paris and never seems to have ventured outside France, was the possessor of a warm and full contralto voice and she made a number of pleasing recordings. She was a student at the Paris Conservatoire and in 1906 made her debut at the Opéra-Comique as La Vougne in Alexandre Georges's *Miarka*. She remained a principal of the company through more than a quarter of a century. At the Comique hers was an all-embracing accomplishment. She sang Carmen, Nicklausse in *Les Contes d'Hoffmann*, the Third Lady in *La Flûte enchantée*, Diane in *Iphigénie en Tauride*, Clytemnestre in *Iphigénie en Aulide*, Catherine in Erlanger's *Le Juif polonais*, the Mother in *Louise*, both Kate and Suzuki in *Madame Butterfly*, Geneviève in *Pelléas et Mélisande*, Mignon, Marthe in Massenet's *Marie-Magdeleine*, Pantasilée in Leroux's *La Reine Fiammette*, Hubertine in Bruneau's *L'Attaque du moulin*—in this she succeeded Marie Delna—Orphée which she 'sang with full and rounded tone, with much intensity and fine musicianship',[1] Thérèse in Massenet's opera of that name, Margared in Lalo's *Le Roi d'Ys* and Charlotte in *Werther*. She took part in several world premieres: Erlanger's *Aphrodite* with Mary Garden, Dukas's *Ariane et Barbe Bleue*, an adaptation of Maeterlinck's story in which Mme Georgette Maeterlinck-Leblanc declaimed Ariane, *Le Carilloneur* with the Comique's leading lady Marguerite Carré, *Circe* of Hillemacher and a number of other pieces whose names, together with their composers', have quite faded from memory. She made a particularly memorable impression in the 1908 production of Rimsky-Korsakov's *Snegourotchka* singing Lehl, and as the Grandmother in the first performances at the Comique of de Falla's *La Vie brève*, both of these again in the company of Marguerite Carré.

On records the registers of her voice sound properly equalised and if the emission, especially when she puts on the pressure, gets slightly tremulous and a little throaty, she is a sensitive and attractive artist. In 'Ah! pourquoi suis-je revenue?' from Masse's *Les Saisons*, her style nicely suits the charming manner of the music. But she was also capable of considerable feeling, even passion, as we can hear in Grisélidis's 'Il partit au printemps' from Massenet's opera. Here where the vocal line is more detailed, she phrases with some refinement and sensitivity, only questionable is an unsupported downward portamento in the recitative, which turns into a slide. The characteristic quality of her voice and expressive delivery are affecting in the Entrance of Marie-Madeleine 'O mes soeurs … c'est içi meme' from the sacred drama Massenet wrote for Pauline Viardot.

MARIE CHARBONNEL (1880–   ) was born in Lyons where she was a student at the local conservatory; there she secured first prize in piano,

34 Suzanne Brohly as Lehl in Rimsky-Korsakov's *Snegourotchka*

35 Marie Charbonnel as Carmen

voice and opera. In 1901 she made her debut at the Grand Theatre in her hometown as Fidès in *Le Prophète*. She remained with the company for the next six years appearing in a variety of operas: *Aida, Carmen, Orphée, Le Trouvère, Werther* and *Le Roi d'Ys*. In 1907 she was brought to the Paris Opéra to replace Kitty Lapeyrette in the local premiere of Wagner's *Ring*. She enjoyed a great success and was heard with the company thereafter as Amneris and Dalila. She joined the Opéra-Comique in the autumn of 1910 as Carmen, and subsequently sang Pygmalion in Masse's *Galathée*, the Mother in *Louise*, Mary in *Le Vaisseau fantôme* with Chenal and Renaud, Vanina in Saint-Saëns's *L'Ancêtre*, which she created at Monte Carlo in 1906, and she was heard in the world premieres of Magnard's *Bérénice* and Ernest Bloch's *Macbeth*. Throughout her career she sang widely in the French provinces, where her interpretation of Orphée was admired.

In Léonor's 'O mon Fernand' from *La Favorite*, the general quality and range of Charbonnel's voice remind us of Brohly. She phrases intelligently with appropriate vocal colouring, but the voice production suffers from too much loose vibrato. The tone is smoother and more limpid in Fidès's call for alms from *Le Prophète* 'Donnez, donnez', where the legato is expressively shaded and the interpretation eloquent.

Although JACQUELINE ROYER (1884–   ) sang at Covent Garden, the Colon and Monte Carlo,

the 'intended' moral that the only place safe from the temptations of Satan—where following Wilde's dictum everyone had long since given into them—was the rock of Monte Carlo.

When in 1916 at the age of eighty-one the venerable maître Camille Saint-Saëns decided to brave the perils of the Atlantic to accept an invitation to conduct his own *Samson et Dalila* at the Teatro Colon, Buenos Aires, he took Royer with him. As well as Dalila she sang Amneris, Gertrude in *Amleto* with Titta Ruffo, Mayabel in a local speciality, Buchardo's *Huemac*, Musidora in *Béatrice* and, also under Messager's direction, she was one of the soloists with Ninon Vallin and Marcel Journet in Franck's *Les Béatitudes*. Royer was the Principessa in the Covent Garden premiere in 1920 of Puccini's

36 Jacqueline Royer

she made only four gramophone records. She was engaged regularly between 1912 and 1922 at the Paris Opéra, where she was heard in *Lohengrin*, *La Favorite*, *Gioconda*, *Aida* and in various small roles in other works. At Monte Carlo she was especially admired. She made her debut as the Marquise de Prie in the Greek composer Samara's *Mademoiselle de Belle-Isle* with Cavalieri in the title role, Bassi and Renaud. In 1914 Gunsbourg produced Ponchielli's posthumous *I Mori di Valenza*, in which Royer sang in the company of Lipkowska, Martinelli and Baklanov. The following season she created Musidora in Messager's *Béatrice*; five years later she starred in one of Gunsbourg's own confections, *Satan*. In this poor Eve was blamed for everything from the Tower of Babel, Attila and the fall of Rome to Napoleon and the rise of Bolshevism. A leading French critic drew

Suor Angelica, making a fine effect with 'her rich contralto'; and repeated Geneviève in *Pelléas et Mélisande* which she had sung previously in the 1913 season.

At a Meyerbeer concert held in Paris in the autumn of 1920 she sang the Prison Scene from *Le Prophète* and with 'her beautiful voice demonstrated that she knew the tradition of this music'.[2] A recording of the first part 'O toi qui m'abandonnes' bears out that her intentions are at least stylish, but although hers was a substantial contralto voice, the singing is hardly polished enough for this music. The middle and lower range is slightly throaty and there is an ugly aspirate in the opening phrase—'ma-ha-bandonnes'—, she whoops through the wide-ranging intervals and at the end the cadenza is crudely done.

12. Five International Sopranos

The dark-eyed and beauteous MARIE-LOUISE
EDVINA (1880–1948), though not a great singer,
was a fine one. Born in Vancouver, Canada, as a
young woman she came to London, where in 1901
she married the Hon. Cecil Edwardes, a younger son
of Lord Kensington. She spent the first few years of
her career in musical comedy. Sir Seymour Hicks in
My Missus and Me tells of his chagrin after he fired
her to find her name on the Covent Garden roster of
artists. Her operatic studies began in Paris with Jean
de Reszke but she returned to London to make her
debut as Marguerite in *Faust* in the 1908 season at
Covent Garden. Whether it is true that the engagement had been secured, as was rumoured at the
time, through her husband's social contacts, no
uxorious machinations could account for her immediate popular and critical success and subsequent re-engagement every season until the
beginning of the war. However, there is little doubt
that as a close friend of Harry Higgins, then
Chairman of the Opera Syndicate, she was able to
use her influence to help secure the engagements of
those whom she approved; it was she who urged
Higgins to invite Rosa Raisa to Covent Garden in
1914. It seems too that she was quite as successful as
Melba, perhaps more so, in keeping out anyone who
might have threatened her position. And it was an
enviable one; she had carved out her own empire.
At Covent Garden she was the first Louise, Thaïs,
Maliella in Wolf-Ferrari's *Gioielli della Madonna*,
Fiora in Montemezzi's *L'Amore dei tre Re* and
Francesca in Zandonai's *Francesca da Rimini*; not
since Patti had any artist been so dignified. She also
created the Dubarry in Camussi's opera of that
name, with Martinelli and Sammarco, but in this she
'revealed a lack of body in the tone, as well as giving
an impression by her facial expression that the
favourite was short-sighted'.[1] Her other roles included a 'fairly successful'[2] Desdemona—'her rendering of the Willow Song in the last act was very
good',[3] Tosca, where her voice was thought too light
and she had not the elemental passion to make the
murder of Scarpia convincing, and Mélisande,
which found the most favour:

> [she] looked the part to perfection and realised the
> pathos and tender wistfulness of the unhappy Mél-
> isande, as well as singing the difficult music with
> complete appreciation of its requirements.[3]

In Paris at the Opéra-Comique in 1910 she sang

Louise, Tosca and Manon. Two years later Russell
brought her to Boston where her sympathetic
personality, good looks and 'limpid and even voice,
with its pure, sensuous quality, held great charm,
even though produced in the 'open' French manner'.[4] Hale thought her Antonia in *Les Contes
d'Hoffmann* 'ideal', her Louise 'as interesting as her
Tosca was commonplace'.[6] She stayed with the
company two seasons then moved to Chicago repeating Louise, Fiora and Maliella. After the war she
reappeared in opera at the Monnaie, Brussels, as
Mélisande, Louise and Thaïs, in which she was
especially admired. She was at Covent Garden again
in the 1919 and 1920 seasons and for the last time in
1924. Two years later she left to take the leading role
in a musical comedy *Hearts and Diamonds*, produced at the Strand Theatre, London. Following her

37 Marie-Louise Edvina

second marriage she retired to the Riviera and there opened an antique shop.

Edvina made only six titles, in 1919, when she was still in good voice. They show a pure, vibrant lyric soprano of lovely quality and well-schooled. In the most attractive of them, 'Depuis le jour', we can hear the 'clearness of her voice and the easy way she produced it'[7] which commended her to *The Times* critic when she sang Louise for the first time at Covent Garden in 1909. She manages the difficult floating line, forte and piano passages alike, smoothly and with complete security; only the final high B is a little hard and sour. Something of the 'charming simplicity and freshness'[8] had gone out of her interpretation by then, and her habit of using the words to nudge the line is too mannered to convey genuine feeling.

38 Marthe Chenal as Camille in Pierné's *On ne badine pas avec l'amour*

Edvina's career ended in musical comedy; that of MARTHE CHENAL (1881–1947) began in variety. When she failed to secure admission to the Paris Conservatoire in 1901 she went straight out and got a job at the Moulin Rouge, for she too was a lovely looking woman with a fine figure. When she tried again a few years later, she was accepted immediately—perhaps the judges had remembered their spectacles. After a year's study with Martini, the teacher of Alvarez, she graduated with first prize, part of which was an engagement at the Paris Opéra in 1905. She made a fine impression as Brunehild in Reyer's *Sigurd*. Two years later in 1908 came her debut at the Opéra-Comique as Chrysis in Erlanger's *Aphrodite*. Thereafter she sang regularly at both theatres. She created Camille in Pierné's *On ne badine pas avec l'amour*, La Reine Tudo in Bruneau's *Le Roi Candaule*—in which she was greatly praised—the title-role in Silver's *La Mégère apprivoisée*, La Reine in de Lara's *Les Trois Mousquetaires*, Zoraya in Erlanger's *La Sorcière*, and she was Mlle Lange in the first performances of *La Fille de Madame Angot* at the Opéra-Comique. Her other roles included Tosca, Carmen, Salomé in Massenet's *Hérodiade*, Donna Anna, Fany in Massenet's *Sapho*, Monna Vanna in Février's opera—'so tragic, so beautiful'—Senta in *Le Vaisseau fantôme*, the title-role in de Lara's *Sanga* and Margared in Lalo's *Le Roi d'Ys*, which she sang on the occasion of the centenary of the composer's birth. She enjoyed a great success in a revival of Suppé's *Boccaccio* at the Théâtre des Champs Elysées in 1921. Throughout her career she was a guest at many of the leading French and Belgian provincial theatres, where she was much admired. On occasion, however, she overdid it. In *Carmen* at Liège in 1914, the audience was scandalised when she rolled up her skirts to show off her legs and then in the dances proceeded to grind her hips. At Cannes too, she was taken to task for 'lack of sincerity'.[9] She was a regular visitor at Monte Carlo between 1908 and 1910, where she was heard as Margherita and Elena in Boito's *Mefistofele* with Smirnov and Chaliapin, Tosca with Anselmi, Dinh Gilly and Pini-Corsi and Fedora with Smirnov and Ruffo. In all of her successes her glamorous stage presence was an important factor. Opinions on her voice were often divided; after the premiere of *La Mégère apprivoisée* in 1922, André Mangeot noted how much more convincing she was in the Shrew's music with her 'shrill and strident'[10] voice than after she had been tamed. Occasionally she ventured into the concert hall. When shorn of the stage trappings, her faults were laid bare:

39 Geneviève Vix as Manon

With Mme Chenal everything is an approximation for cheap effect. Her lack of technique, and doubtless also lack of culture, prevents her either suiting her interpretation to the work, or from achieving the maximum of expression, which only comes from perfect vocal flexibility. 'Non mi dir' and Bach's 'Mein gläubiges Herz' suffered from a lack of previous understanding with the orchestra, as Mlle Chenal had not wanted to agree to a rehearsal which was most willingly granted by her partner (Jacques Thibaud), who had, doubtless, no need of one. However, the three songs 'Chanson pour le petit cheval' by de Severac and 'L'Esclave' and 'Marine' by Lalo, somewhat reconciled her with the public. She sang them with that charming colour and caressing expression which is one of her most seductive features.[11]

Chenal made a short list of recordings for Pathé including arias from *Sigurd*, *Carmen*, *Werther* and *Tosca*. Among the song titles is 'La Marseillaise' which she sang on several occasions during the First World War in Vidal's patriotic tableau *Sur le front*. 'Dis-moi, Venus?' from *La Belle Hélène* shows her voice off in a part in which she would have looked superb. She sings Offenbach's music with élan and character and is adept in using the chest register for effect. The voice seems to be no more than of routine quality, the tone far from smooth, with a tendency to become shrill under pressure, and thin and dry in the middle range.

According to Lauri-Volpi 'the spirit and charm of the French were in the emerald eyes of GENEVIEVE VIX (1879–1939), in her face a little long but of infinite expression, in her body slim and lithe'.[12] From this we may assume that as with other leading French sopranos of this time, her good looks counted for much.

Hers was the conventional route to success, via the Paris Conservatoire to a debut at the Opéra-Comique in 1906 as Louise. Her repertory there was a large one: Chrysis in Erlanger's *Aphrodite*, Santuzza, Carmen, Antonia, Manon, Tosca, Violetta, Mimi, Gismonda in Février's opera of that name, Prince Charming in Massenet's *Cendrillon*, and Donna Elvira in a *Don Juan* conducted by Reynaldo Hahn. She created the title-roles in Franco Leoni's *Francesca da Rimini* and Hillemacher's *Circé*, in which the rest of the cast included Maggie Teyte, Suzanne Brohly, David Devriès and Hector Dufranne. She was also the first La Tisbe in Bruneau's *Angelo, Tyran de Padoue*, which derives from the same Victor Hugo melodrama that Boito had previously fashioned into *Gioconda* for Ponchielli, and she was the first Concepcion in Ravel's *L'Heure espagnole*. In this last part Emile Vuillermoz remembers 'with what incandescence she created a clock seller so attentive to the chimes of the hour of the muleteer'.[13]

She was engaged at the Colon, Buenos Aires, for the 1915 season as Carmen, Manon and, following the precedent of Mary Garden—for it was originally written for a tenor—Jean in *Le Jongleur de Notre Dame*. Two years later she sang it in Chicago; Garden was in Europe at the time. Vix was also heard as Fany in Massenet's *Sapho*, Marguerite and Manon. It was as Manon that she made her New York debut in the company's post-season tour and she was much admired. In 1920, after some performances of *Thaïs* and *Manon* at Barcelona and Lisbon she returned to South America appearing in a season

40 Yvonne Gall

drine courtesan 'neither conductor nor prompt existed for her. It was she who imparted the rhythm and even, where she felt it appropriate, altered the text'.[15] In Monte Carlo again in 1923, Gunsbourg presented her in *Pagliacci* and *La Navarraise*, and two years later in *L'Heure espagnole* and *Pelléas et Mélisande*. In 1924 after a season in Havana she made her rentrée at the Paris Opéra as Thaïs, but by this time the effects of the many unsuitable roles she sang so often, particularly Salome and Tosca, had begun to show up in her singing. 'The tiresome vocal accidents of which she was a victim proved that this role is no longer for her.'[16] She sang at the Costanzi again in 1925 as Louise, with Journet, and in *Salome* at Bordeaux, but when she asked to be allowed to take formal leave of her public at the Opéra-Comique, the scene of so many of her greatest triumphs, the management declined. In her retirement she taught in Paris.

Recordings suggest Vix's voice was small, the tone fluttery, slightly pinched and infantile sounding. She would appear to have been a better singer than Chenal, more assured technically, for in spite of the persistent tremolo, the voice sits securely on the breath and her phrasing is often eloquent. In Santuzza's 'Voi lo sapete', here rendered as 'Vous le savez', she sings with considerable intensity yet still containing passion within the vocal line; just occasionally her rather consonantal delivery catches in the tone. In Charlotte's 'Air des carmes' she is genuinely affecting, though she has not the extraordinary presence of Supervia, whose singing hers in other ways resembles.

By no means all of the leading French critics were deaf to the importance of a beautiful and sonorous voice. In a review of a recital given by YVONNE GALL (1885–1972) in 1926, *Le Ménestrel* noted that:

All who have heard this artist at the Opéra are unanimous in praising her clean and flexible emission, powerful without ever being hard; she is one of our best dramatic singers today . . . We have grown too much accustomed to saying that it is not necessary to have any voice in order to sing. Listen to Ravel's 'Chansons Grecques' or Milhaud's 'Poèmes juifs' sung by one of our skilful 'diseuses' or by Mlle Yvonne Gall, and you will spot the difference; how these songs bloom when they are sung as well as articulated. Hearing the first singer, one could think this artist is delicious; listening to the second, one exclaims: how lovely this music is![17]

After graduating from the Paris Conservatoire Gall made her debut as a Rhinemaiden in the first

of operas at Rio de Janeiro: *Thaïs, Manon, Carmen, Pelléas et Mélisande* and *Le Jongleur de Notre Dame*. In all of them 'she had a veritable triumph with her beautiful voice and expressive playing'.[14] The year after, at Monte Carlo, she took a leading role in the world premiere of Auguste Chapuis's *Les Demoiselles de Saint-Cyr* with Dinh Gilly. At the Costanzi, Rome, in 1921 her Salome, Thaïs and Manon were received with enthusiasm, though there were complaints when she sang everything in French. In Spain in 1922, at the Teatro Real, Madrid, the King came to all her performances and led the applause from the Royal Box. She sang Tosca, Manon and Salome, in which she did the Dance of the Seven Veils herself, and Thaïs. As the Alexan-

performance of *Le Crépuscule des Dieux* at the Opéra
in 1908. Her first leading role was Mathilde in
Guillaume Tell with Escalaïs. She returned many
times in later years and took part in a number of
novelties; with Altchevsky in Bachelet's *Scemo* in
1914, and five years later with Chenal and Kouznetsova in Alberic Magnard's *Guercoeur*. It was
not until after the war that she became a principal at
the Opéra-Comique. Her first appearance was at a
benefit, as Marguerite in Act Five of *Faust*. In
due course she sang Tosca, Louise, Manon, Antonia,
Ariane in Dukas's *Ariane et Barbe-Bleu*, Donna Anna
—in which she was praised for accuracy and good
taste—Juliette and Daphne in Henri Busser's *Les
Noces Corinthiennes*. In 1918 she was invited to the
Colon, Buenos Aires, where she was heard as Thaïs,
Juliette and Salome in Massenet's *Hérodiade*. In the
autumn of the same year she journeyed north to
Chicago making her debut as Thaïs; this was at the
beginning of the season and before Mary Garden
had made her rentrée and repossessed herself of
those roles which she regarded as her particular
preserve. Gall, like Geneviève Vix the previous
year, had been called in to undertake whatever the
great lady was unwilling (or unable) to sing. She was
'a fine'[18] Marguerite, 'pleasingly Gallic' as Juliette,
and took the role of Concepcion in the first American performances of Ravel's *L'Heure espagnole*, a
part she repeated later on in New York when the
company visited the Lexington Theatre. Aldrich
observed that 'she presented a face and figure
sufficient to account for the masculine interest
shown in her'.[19] Afterwards came Mathilde in
Guillaume Tell, Manon, Salomé in *Hérodiade*, Tosca
in which she greatly pleased, especially her subtle
stagecraft: 'she placed the candles at Scarpia's head
. . . she did it with face averted and with a quiver of
shrinking',[20] Isaura in Marinuzzi's *Jacquerie* and
Zina in *Le Vieil Aigle*.

   Le Vieil Aigle was the work of Raoul Gunsbourg,
the remarkable Russian impresario who for more
than a half century presided over the fortunes of the
Monte Carlo Opera. It says something for his prestige abroad that although the sum total of his
musical training amounted to whatever had been
dinned into him whilst playing in a band in the
Russian Army, he was able to get the piece mounted
in Cologne, Brussels, Moscow and Barcelona, as well
as Chicago. The only assistance he enjoyed was from
Léon Jehin with the orchestration; Jehin conducted
the world premiere at Monte Carlo in 1909, with a
cast including Chaliapin, Rousselière and Marguerite Carré. In 1923 Gunsbourg brought Gall to

41 Fanny Heldy in Gunsbourg's *Ivan the Terrible*

Monte Carlo for *Thaïs*, a French *Tristan* with Paul
Franz, and the title-role in another of his own chef
d'oeuvres, *Lysistrata*. She returned three years later
for a revival of *La Rondine* with Charles Friant.

   Gall was a prolific recording artist. In 1912 she
was the Juliette in a complete recording of Gounod's
opera with Affre, Albers, Belhomme and Journet.
Between 1917 and 1928, for the Pathé company, she
recorded a variety of songs and arias from Mozart
and Schubert to Busser and Stephen Foster; these
represent her at the height of her vocal powers. An
electric group for Columbia preserve much of her

artistry. Her voice was a bright sounding, good sized lyric soprano, typically French, the production slightly tremulous and not without some hardness in the upper range, while the chest register is rather dull and thin. In general the quality of the voice is attractive and characteristic, and only occasionally does she over articulate the French language at the expense of purity of tone. Among her best records are two unfamiliar Gounod numbers, 'Plus grand dans son obscurité' from *La Reine de Saba* and 'Nuit resplendissante' from *Cinq-Mars*. Though the voice lacks sensuousness, and her legato style is not ideally smooth—nor expansive enough when Gounod brings in the big tune—in the music from the Queen of Sheba especially, she accomplishes the wide ranging tessitura with ease, the top of the voice has an appropriately brilliant edge on the tone and her singing plenty of dramatic energy. She captures the right mood in an electric recording of Marguerite's 'D'amour l'ardente flamme' from Berlioz's *La Damnation de Faust*, but the voice is beginning to sound worn in the middle register and the singing, which was never notable for a fine finish, is not sufficiently accurate; in the tricky Gluck-like central section, some of the intervals are aspirated.

The most internationally renowned of the 'French' sopranos in the inter-war years was the Belgian FANNY HELDY (1888–1973). In Paris she was a popular idol; so frequently did she appear at the Opéra over so many years that the star's dressing room almost became her personal property and retained her decorations long after she had retired.

Following a period of study at the Liège Conservatoire she made her stage debut at the Théâtre de la Monnaie, Brussels, in 1913 in another of Raoul Gunsbourg's creations, *Ivan the Terrible* (which by all accounts it was, but that is another matter). Heldy remained a contract artist there for the next two years and sang for the first time many of the roles which she was subsequently to adorn in the world's greatest theatres. In 1914 she made her first visit outside Belgium to appear in Victor Buffin's *Kaatje* at Monte Carlo. From time to time she made guest appearances at the Liège Opéra, and appeared in concerts, once with her great compatriot the violinist Eugene Ysaye. For the occasion, in Mozart's 'L'amerò sarò costante', Ysaye provided both obbligato and cadenza. In 1917 after spending two seasons in Vichy and Aix-les-Bains she moved to Paris and the Opéra-Comique, making her first appearance as Violetta, going on to Gismonda, Rosina, Butterfly, Tosca, Mimi, Manon, the three

heroines in *Hoffmann* and Orlanda in Leroux's *La Reine Fiammette*. This last part she sang first in 1919 and again in 1935, by which time she was dividing her time between the two Paris houses. Her debut at the Opéra took place in 1921 and, by all accounts, her soprano voice was still growing in size and brilliance. Over the years she sang Juliette, Marguerite, Thaïs, Salomé in Massenet's *Hérodiade*, Violetta, Elsa, Rosina in the first performances of *Le Barbier de Séville* at the Opéra and Concepcion in *L'Heure espagnole*. In this last part Vuillermoz thought her 'more gracious than ardent . . . but she sang like a great artist'.[21] At the Opéra she took a leading role in the world premiere of Gabriel Dupont's *Antar* with Paul Franz, and created Portia in Reynaldo Hahn's *Le Marchand de Venise* to the Shylock of André Pernet.

She returned to Monte Carlo in 1922 to appear in Bruneau's *Le Jardin du Paradis*:

> She sang the role of Arabella with her habitual qualities, sonorous voice, a little strident at the top, excellent enunciation and she looks well on stage. But she plays everything exaggeratedly which gives to her singing a provinciality lacking in distinction.[22]

Subsequently she was heard in *Roméo et Juliette*, *Thaïs*, *Manon*, *L'Heure espagnole*, *Les Contes d'Hoffmann*, Gunsbourg's *Venise* and, in 1937, during her last season, she took the title-role in the world premiere of Honneger's *L'Aiglon*, an operatic adaptation of the play Edmond Rostand had written for Sarah Bernhardt. Toscanini invited Heldy to La Scala, an honour accorded few French singers of her generation. In 1923 she sang Louise with Pertile and Journet, and two years later, again with Toscanini, returned for some performances of *Pelléas et Mélisande*. She came to London in the season of 1926 as Manon. Ernest Newman complained of some hardness and nasal tone,[23] but as Concepcion he thought 'her youth and freshness delightful'.[24] She returned in 1928 but on that occasion she was unwell and sang only one performance of Louise. In the intervening years she made her only trip to South America where she was heard as Louise, Thaïs and Manon at the Colon, Buenos Aires.

Heldy made a number of acoustic recordings for Pathé, including a complete *Manon*, and a group of electrics for HMV. The Pathés show off her voice at its best. It was a more important sounding instrument than any of her contemporaries', a high soprano, very Gallic, and with more than a trace of vinegar in the head register. She sings proficiently, but as we hear for example in Violetta's 'Ah! fors' è lui', hardly accurately. The cutting edge on her tone was helpful in projecting the voice over a full orchestra, especially in roles like Tosca and Butterfly. On records, however, it is not pleasing. Like many of her contemporaries she gives an impression of trying to make too much of her voice and by so doing sacrifices sweetness and purity of tone. Perhaps her most attractive recording is the Air of the Oasis from Gabriel Dupont's *Antar*. The music, with its 'oriental' gestures showing that Dupont knew his *Thaïs* and *Sadko* is agreeable, atmospheric stuff and it gives Heldy the opportunity to show off some soft high notes and sing easily and attractively without forcing the tone.

13. Lyric Sopranos at the Opéra-Comique

Neither Aline Vallandri nor Marguerite Merentié were singers of the front rank but both made recordings which are very attractive, more so in some cases than those of their more celebrated contemporaries. MARGUERITE MERENTIE (1880–), had the darker and more dramatic voice. She went directly from the Paris Conservatoire to the Opéra, making her debut in 1905 as Chimène in *Le Cid*. Thereafter she undertook other roles associated with Félia Litvinne, including Armide and Valentine in *Les Huguenots*. At the Opéra she sang the title-role in Reyer's *Salammbô* and created Ariane in Massenet's opera of that name. In 1909 she joined the Opéra-Comique. Her first appearance was as Carmen, a part she was later to sing in the first complete recording of the opera made by Pathé. At the Opéra-Comique she was heard as Berenice in Magnard's opera of the same name, Toinette in Leroux's *Le Chemineau*, Fany in Massenet's *Sapho*, Tosca, Charlotte and Mlle Lange in *La Fille de Mme Angot*. From the beginning there were reservations about her singing; of her Ariane in Dukas's *Ariane et Barbe-Bleu*, *Le Courrier Musical* commented:

> Mme Merentié possesses a warm voice, well placed, but she spoils her singing with an annoying habit of sliding from one note to the next which after a while becomes very tiresome for her listeners. As a result the accent is weakened and the phrase debilitated.[1]

In 1909 she made her La Scala debut in the title-role of Leroux's *Théodora* but the premiere was a fiasco; the Milanese public detested the music and

there were no subsequent performances. In 1912 at the Théâtre Gaîté-Lyrique she appeared in the title-role of de Lara's *Naïl*. Her good looks and fine voice were thought to give suitable expression to Naïl's passion but there were complaints, in particular over 'her habit of strangling the voice in the throat as if she had just swallowed a fishbone'.[2]

Merentié's recordings do not suggest a throaty voice; the tone is pure throughout its range and the registers fully equalised. For the kind of repertory she sang there is a certain lack of weight and authority but in 'La fine grâce', some pages from Massenet's *Ariane*, the voice sounds most agreeable, the high notes are warm and fully rounded. Throughout she enunciates clearly and without making a meal of the consonants.

ALINE VALLANDRI (1878–1952) was a pupil of Jacques Isnardon. She made her debut at the Opéra-Comique as Mireille in 1904 and sang there regularly throughout the rest of her career. Her

42 Marguerite Merentié

43 Aline Vallandri as Marguerite

repertory included L'Ensoleillad in *Chérubin*, Dor-abella, L'Errante in *La Légende du Point d'Argentan*, Hilda in Février's *Le Roi aveugle*, Micaëla, Donna Elvira, Pamina, Lola in *Cavalleria Rusticana*, Gismonda, Grisélidis, Lakmé, Louise, Manon, Philine, Susanna, Eurydice in Gluck's *Orphée* with, at various times, Caron, Raveau and Ansseau, Orlanda in *La Reine Fiammette*, Rosenn in *Le Roi d'Ys*, Tosca, Violetta and Jeanne in Godard's *La Vivandière*. At Monte Carlo in 1907 she was Donna Elvira in company with Renaud, Pini-Corsi, Litvinne and Maggie Teyte. She sang Mélisande and Manon at the Monnaie, Brussels, in 1911 and in the same year visited London. Oscar Hammerstein engaged her for his last ill-fated operatic venture at the London Opera House, later the Stoll Theatre, Kingsway. Vallandri appeared in Nouguès's *Quo Vadis?* in which 'her acting and singing deserve sincere praise'.[3] As Adalgisa she showed 'sincere feeling'[4] though she did not sing with 'complete success'.[5] She was 'a pleasing and capable Marguerite'[6] and in the title-roles of *Louise* and *Le Jongleur de Notre Dame* 'she proved herself an excellent artist and capable singer'.[7] She continued to appear in opera

and concert during the 1920s in France and abroad: in 1921 she sang Louise in Cologne.

Vallandri has left us a souvenir of her performances in Nouguès's *Quo Vadis?* 'Des fleurs de ce jardin'. It is heavily scented, vapid music after the fashion of Massenet, with a fiddle obbligato sliding too persistently through all the intervals. One can understand why Hammerstein sought to inject a little life into the proceedings with a couple of lions on the stage, but apparently even they did not save the show—perhaps the music sent them to sleep. Vallandri's voice is a pretty, well-placed instrument, slightly tremulous but secure and sweet in the upper range. An air from Massenet's *Grisélidis*, another of her roles at the Opéra-Comique, does not suggest any great variety of expression or personality but she sings agreeably and she was a capable artist.

Another attractive soprano from the Opéra-Comique, ZINA BROZIA (1880–   ), was born in Arles in the south of France, and studied with Elena Teodorini. She made her debut as Marguerite in *Faust* at the Théâtre de la Monnaie in Brussels. For four years she was a member of the company at the Opéra-Comique between 1905 and 1909. After her debut as Violetta, she sang Gilda, Manon and Seso in the world premiere of Erlanger's *Aphrodite*, the title role being taken by Garden. In 1907 Gunsbourg invited her to Monte Carlo, originally pencilling her in for Dubel in Saint-Saëns's *Le Timbre d'Argent*, Donna Elvira, and Thamyris in the premiere of Leroux's *Théodora*. In the event she sang none of them, making her debut as Elena in *Mefistofele*, and thereafter appearing as Elisabeth in Verdi's *Don Carlos*. Neither part could possibly have suited her lightweight lyric soprano; not surprisingly, she did not return. She was a guest at the Monnaie, Brussels, and in 1908 at the Teatro Regio, Parma, as Butterfly and Manon. In 1911 Russell brought her to Boston at the instigation of one of his European directors, the French banker Max Léon. The exact nature of Léon's admiration is not certain; it may have been that he had a genuine regard for her vocal art but, as the Boston critics made plain, her attractions as a coquette were considerable. If she touched a sympathetic chord with Léon, in Boston she did not leave much of an impression:

She conceived the character [of Thaïs] as a 'petite femme', aimiable, amorous, vexed as a child when the Monk did not at once fall at her feet, easily persuaded to abandon the world when assured that she would be beautiful for ever. She did not rely on undue bareness to excite admiration and compel applause.[8]

44 Zina Brozia as Marguerite

From Boston she returned to France. In 1914 at the Gaîté Lyrique she sang Salomé in Massenet's *Hérodiade* and took part in Bianchini's *Radda*, a one-act piece after a drama by Gorki. In the latter she was partnered by Cesar Vezzani and her interpretation 'did not lack fire or character'.[9] A recording of Thaïs's 'L'amour est une vertu rare' reveals a small voice moving easily in the upper range, of an appealing quality with a light tremolo. It is a pretty rendering but quite lacking in authority.

14. A Trio of Concert Singers

The career of GABRIELLE RITTER-CIAMPI (1886–1974) was mostly a local affair. She sang only on occasion outside France and she never established herself as a front-ranking international artist. Her records, however, are often delightful and display considerable musical and technical gifts. Hers was a light-weight lyric soprano with something of the quality of a mezzo in the middle register. At the top the voice extended at least to the high D and if the highest notes were rather thin, they were without the shrillness of so many of her compatriots. To an extent this may have been the influence of her father's Italian ancestry and perhaps also of his teaching; Ezio Ciampi, who had a

tenor voice, taught in Paris for many years in his retirement.

Following the example of a maternal uncle, the pianist Theodore Ritter, she at first elected to study piano at the Paris Conservatoire. It was not until she was sixteen and had already made some appearances as a concert pianist that her voice began to develop and she decided to become a singer. Her first engagement was at the Trianon-Lyrique in Paris in 1917 as Violetta. Two years later she appeared at the Opéra-Comique in *Les Noces de Figaro* and according to *Le Ménestrel* she was 'a perfect Countess'.[1] Over the next decade she established an enviable reputation as a Mozart singer. She sang Fiordiligi in the first performances of *Così fan tutte* at the Opéra-Comique under the direction of André Messager and 'displayed her prodigious skill rising to the highest summits of the art of singing'.[2] in 1921 at the Opéra she undertook Constanze in *L'Enlèvement au Serail* and enjoyed a great triumph; sixteen years later she repeated the part when the work was introduced at the Opéra-Comique; Reynaldo Hahn conducted on both occasions. She was Donna Elvira in Mozart seasons at Cannes, Deauville and elsewhere; these were organised by Hahn and the Don was usually Renaud. In 1923 at the Opéra she added Pamina in a revival of *La flûte enchantée*. It was as a Mozart singer that she was heard on visits to Belgium and Germany and at the Salzburg Festival in 1932.

Her operatic repertory also included Louise, Marguerite, Manon, the Marschallin in *Le Chevalier à la rose* (she took this role at Monte Carlo in 1926 with Lubin and Vanni Marcoux), all three parts in *Les Contes d'Hoffmann*, Philine, Telaise in Rameau's *Castor et Pollux* (this in a revival at the Opéra when she was praised for her stylistic as well as vocal mastery), Eurydice to the Orphée of Alice Raveau, Rosina, Gilda and Violetta. She sang the last two in a summer season at Cannes in 1920 in company with the sixty-three-year-old Battistini, and

> gave the impression of being a new Patti. She truly revived the charm of music written especially for the voice, to it she added a new life and vitality.[3]

Ritter-Ciampi sang regularly in concerts and recitals and was greatly admired. Her programmes ranged through classical airs by Bononcini, Jomelli, Pasquini, Pergolesi, Caccini and Paisiello to modern French songs by Rabaud, Duparc, Dupont, Chausson and Chabrier. At Brussels in 1922 she took part in a recital of 'Musique Ancienne' with a small group of instrumentalists directed from the harp-sichord by Wanda Landowska. Her career continued until after the Second World War. As late as 1949 she created the role of Dona Irene in Hahn's *Le Oui de jeunes filles* at the Opéra-Comique.

Apart from a few electrics for Polydor, her recordings were made for the Pathé company. The list includes items from most of the operas she sang in but there are no *arie antiche* and except for one song each by Erlanger and Busser, the latter with the interesting title 'Jazz dans la nuit', no modern French songs either. Instead Pathé presented her in waltzes by Strauss and Arditi, popular operatic arias of Puccini and variations by Rode, originally for the violin, and by Massé on the Carneval of Venice. In brilliant music, though her voice is pleasing and she sings effortlessly and with some grace, her execution is generally rather approximate. If the timbre of her voice, especially in the middle range, has some of Patti's warmth, it is also throaty, which Patti's definitely was not, and there

46 Berthe Auguez
de Montalant

is none of the fine finish to be heard in the recordings of the older singer. She pleases far more where she can show off the purity of tone in the upper register without having to indulge in flights of fioritura. There is some contrivance in the difficult tessitura of Pamina's 'Ah! l'ingrat', but the radiant tone and fine phrasing make this a most appealing rendering. Admirable too, is 'L'amerò sarò constante' where the cadenza does not make excessive demands of her. In general her singing is not notable for any great variety of expression. In the duet for Rosina and Figaro, here 'Je suis donc', there is little characterisation. Her execution, though not really accurate, sounds wonderfully fluent next to the dry baryton-martin of André Baugé who is completely unequal to its demands. In that kind of company she *is* a Patti and since standards are relative, doubtless she sounded so on many such occasions to her contemporaries.

One of France's most beloved concert artists BERTHE AUGUEZ DE MONTALANT (1868–   ) was born in Baltimore but from the time of her marriage, to a singer by the name of Numa Auguez, she settled in Paris. Her career began before the turn of the century and she remained active well into the 1920s:

> singing always with incomparable charm and that rare purity of taste that distinguishes her from so many superficial singers.[4]

Her appearances at the Conservatoire, with the Concerts Colonne, Lamoureux and Pasdeloup were regular events every season. She was the soprano soloist in Gounod's *Gallia*, Berlioz's *Roméo et Juliette* and *La Damnation de Faust*, Franck's *Les Béatitudes*, Saint-Saëns's *Le Déluge*, Rossini's *Stabat Mater*, Pierné's *Les Enfants à Bethléem* and many others. She travelled widely throughout the French pro-

45 Gabrielle Ritter-Ciampi

vinces and made tours abroad to Belgium, Germany and Austria.

Much of her charm of manner and the pure quality of the voice survives in recordings. In 'La Romance de la Lettre' from Grisar's *Les Porcherons* she sounds very French and we must believe that her name indicates French ancestry. The registers are fully equalised, a very light vibrato is never displeasing and only rarely does an edge creep into the highest notes. She is at her very best in Inez's 'Adieu mon beau rivage' from Meyerbeer's *L'Africaine*, a most affecting rendition in which her intonation is pre-eminently correct in the exposed line with its difficult intervals.

There once was a Carmen . . .

> who wore a long robe covered in spangles. Her splendid body was not hidden by this indiscreet drapery. Her arms and shoulders were bare. Alma, gypsy, daughter of the East, princess of the harem, Byzantine empress, or Moorish dancer? All these were suggested by the fantastic and seductive costume. In a tavern where gypsy women met soldiers she evoked the apparition of a woman of Mantegna or Botticelli, degraded, vile, who gave the idea of a shameless creature that had not entirely lost the gracefulness of her original rank.[5]

This was the exotique actress-diseuse GEORGETTE LEBLANC-MAETERLINCK (1860–1941)—in fact, she had no legal claim to the second half of the name for she was never more than mistress of the famous Belgian poet and dramatist. At their retreat, St Wandrille, she played Lady Macbeth (in his translation) moving from room to room in the castle and—weather permitting—in the park and grounds, the audience trailing after her. She had ambitions to sing too. In 1893 at the Opéra-Comique she created Françoise in Bruneau's *L'Attaque du moulin*. Thereafter she was Thaïs, La Navarraise and Ariane in Dukas's setting of Maeterlinck's *Ariane et Barbe-bleue*. But the management resisted the poet's attempts to impose her as Mélisande and Monna Vanna; her voice and singing were matters for dispute, and she was passed over in favour of Mary Garden and Lucienne Bréval. Russell brought her to Boston in 1911 and she played and sang Mélisande in the original drama and in the opera. Her extraordinary stage manners and the precise nature of her relationship with Maeterlinck appear to have excited more interest than her singing.

> Miss Leblanc makes light of her voice. She maltreats it, threshes it, subjects it to inhuman inflections. Her singing is not musical, her interpretations lack the naivety necessary to true dramatic power. Nevertheless she is one of the most emotional interpreters of our time. Thanks to her, Antioch and Alexandria, corrupt and adorable cities, live again for an hour.[6]

In the twenties, after Maeterlinck had married a nymphette while her back was turned she consoled herself with what she styled 'auditions lyriques mimes' or 'interpretative recitals'. Draped in a low-cut creation and glittering with costume jewellery she would alternatively declaim and sing, her posturing 'plainly modelled after illuminated borders of medieval missals'. On these occasions, it was claimed, she even made Schubert sound erotic. On record, in Lully's 'Bois epais', there is nothing of that. The voice is a little tremulous but the quality by no means disagreeable and her delivery without affectation, even if the singing is sloppy and hardly classical.

47 Georgette Leblanc-Maeterlinck as Thaïs

PART III

The Heyday of Verismo

15. The 'Duse' of Song

With audiences in many parts of the world, for her colleagues and the critics CLAUDIA MUZIO (1889–1936) was the most admired Italian soprano of her day. Hers was not a voice of remarkable size and her singing lacked the brilliance and the refinements which would have been pre-requisite a generation or so previously, but there was in her performances a compelling sincerity that made a deep impression on those who saw her. Her physical presence played an important part in this. When John McCormack sang Faust opposite her Margherita in the 1914 Covent Garden revival of *Mefistofele*, he immediately recognised 'the charming girl with beautiful liquid brown eyes and ringlets down her back'[1] whom he had met five years before, when she was back-stage with her father at the San Carlo, Naples. Since then, as photographs show, she had grown into a dark-eyed classical beauty, with an intensity of expression that reminded her contemporaries of the great Italian actress Eleonora Duse. Her singing was equally affecting; it still moves us in her best recordings. Muzio's style was a complete expression of the taste of her times, in this resembling Bellincioni—but with a voice of finer quality. She represented the verismo at its zenith, yet her effects, at least in her best years, were without calculated artifice and she altogether eschewed the ranting and raving that so many of her colleagues tried to pass off as genuine temperament but which today stand revealed as sensationalist and unmusical.

This was, in part at any rate, the result of her upbringing; like Patti she had been raised in the theatre, but whereas the elder diva's family were all musicians, the dominating figure in Muzio's background, her father, was in turn stage manager at the San Carlo, Covent Garden and the Metropolitan successively. From her earliest childhood she had delighted in helping him. By the time her voice had developed sufficiently for her to begin her vocal studies, she was already thoroughly conversant with the stage business in many of the operas that she would later appear in to such effect in the world's greatest theatres.

Her first teacher was Annetta Casaloni who had created Maddalena in *Rigoletto* at the Fenice, Venice in 1851; subsequently she took lessons from Callery-Viviani in Milan. Her debut took place at Arezzo in January 1910 in the title-role of Massenet's *Manon*. Soon afterwards she was engaged at Messina where she appeared opposite the youthful Tito Schipa in *Traviata* and *Rigoletto* (these were her only performances of Gilda), and at Catanzaro where she was Manon in Puccini's opera. From the beginning she enjoyed enthusiastic notices from a press by no means predisposed in favour of debutantes. Of her Manon Lescaut, the *Orfeo* critic wrote:

> Signorina Muzio reveals herself an artist not lacking in worth, especially for the limpidity of her voice, the head register and general extension of her range,[2]

though he complained that her acting was somewhat exaggerated. In the course of three seasons she sang Marguerite, Nedda, 'a delicious Musetta, especially in her second act aria',[3] an 'ideal'[4] Desdemona, Violetta, the title-role in Mascagni's *Isabeau*, Susanna in Wolf-Ferrari's *Segreto di Susanna* and she was even advertised as Freia in *l'Oro del Reno* for the first night of the 1912/13 season at the San Carlo; in the event the part was taken by another singer.

Within four years of her debut she was invited to La Scala. Her first appearance was as Desdemona opposite the Egyptian tenor Icilio Calleja; she had sung the role at the Dal Verme, Milan, the previous year, when the *Corriere della Sera* had found her 'affected and lacking in expression'.[5] Her other roles were Mariella in Smareglia's *L'Abisso* and Fiora in *L'Amore dei tre Re*. It was not until the latter, according to Carlo Gatti, that she moved 'from the subordinate position she had occupied during the season to take her place among interpreters of the highest rank'.[6] It was to become one of her favourite roles, an impersonation only surpassed by those of Bori and Garden. For whatever reasons her first season at La Scala failed to establish her with the public and it was more than a dozen years before she returned as Violetta in 1926;

48 Claudia Muzio as Tosca

she came again the following year and for two performances of *Traviata* in 1930. This was the sum total of her appearances in Italy's leading theatre. She was never a 'creatura della Scala' as Storchio and Burzio had been before her and her career there hardly equalled those of her contemporaries dalla Rizza, Pampanini and Cobelli.

In the summer of 1914 she sang in London for the first time, stopping in Paris on the way to make a guest appearance at the Théâtre des Champs Elysées with the Boston Opera as Nedda in *Pagliacci* with Ferrari-Fontana and Ancona. At Covent Garden *The Times* thought her interpretation of Manon Lescaut 'in many ways an interesting one with a voice of considerable richness' even if she wanted 'charm' and 'spontaneity'.[7] She made a bigger impression replacing Edvina as Tosca opposite Caruso, an interpretation 'thoroughly and fervently Italian in every detail both of voice and infinite variety of gesture, and it was truly wonderful';[8] she was the first Italian Tosca heard at Covent Garden. Afterwards came Desdemona in succession to Melba, Margherita with Raisa as Elena, and Alice in *Falstaff*, in which, though 'she lacked authority',[9] she was deemed 'charming'.[10] Altogether the press thought her 'a fortunate discovery',[11] nevertheless she was not re-engaged after the war and did not sing in London again.

In 1916 she was called to the Metropolitan to fill the vacancy caused by the indisposition of Bori. Her debut was in *Tosca* and as in London she was supported by Caruso and Scotti.

> Every circumstance was . . . favourable for the first appearance of the new singer, on whom a great share of interest centred. In many ways she justified the interest. She is young and beautiful. It is possible to feel enthusiasm over her acting, which is composed, animated, intelligent and tasteful. She had dramatic feeling and an individuality governs her work. Of her voice . . . it was to be noticed . . . that she was always willing to sacrifice display to the need of colouring a phrase to suit the dramatic intention of the moment . . . Miss Muzio established the fact that her voice is of fresh and agreeable quality and that she governs it artistically. There were times when a certain hardness was noticeable and the lower range was not always full and warm . . .[12]

Henderson thought her 'a good lyric soprano, [the voice] full and vibrant in quality . . . but prone to become shrill when pinched'.[13] During six seasons she sang a variety of lyric and spinto roles, by no means all of which had figured in Bori's repertory.

She was Aida on thirty six different occasions earning reviews from 'brilliant'[14] to 'mediocre',[15] Nedda, Leonora in *Trovatore*, Fiora though her 'physique [was] not considered suitable for the childish heroine',[16] Tatiana, Manon Lescaut, Loreley, Mimi, Santuzza and a 'handsome'[17] Berthe in *Le Prophète*. She created Giorgetta in the world premiere of Puccini's *Tabarro* and was particularly admired as Maddalena in the first performances of *Andrea Chénier* at the Met. Yet, in spite of her 'invaluable power to interest an audience'[18] and 'her fine and communicative enthusiasm',[19] as Kolodin points out '[she] did not take the press by storm'[20] nor was she ever a great popular favourite with audiences in the way of Farrar and Bori. Perhaps, as Henderson suggested, being cast in a number of roles 'for which she was not qualified, retarded somewhat the natural development of her talents'.[21] Certainly increasing competition in later seasons, after the debuts of Ponselle and Easton and the return of Destinn, made this apparent, particularly as Aida, Santuzza and Leonora, in which she was without the sheer vocal resources of her colleagues. Unfortunately too, such parts as Mimi, Manon Lescaut and Violetta, which especially suited her, she sang rarely if at all for they were the property of Alda, Farrar and Galli-Curci. Her position was not improved after Bori's triumphant come-back in 1921 but the last straw was the sensational debut of Jeritza and in particular the furore she created as Tosca, one of the few parts in which until then Muzio had had relatively little competition. Before sailing for Europe in the spring of 1922 she announced that she had signed a contract to appear the following winter in Chicago. She did return to the Met once again but not until 1934 when she was at the end of her career and then she sang only two performances.

From 1919 Muzio appeared regularly at the Colon, Buenos Aires, where she added to her repertory: Madame Sans-Gêne, Leonora in *Forza del Destino*, Norma, Monna Vanna, La Wally, Elsa, the Marschallin (this on tour at Rio), Fiamma in Respighi's opera of that name and finally the title-role in Refice's *Cecilia*, which she created in Rome in 1934. For almost a decade Chicago and Buenos Aires were the principal centres of her career. Between the two she sandwiched in short seasons in Italy. In Chicago she sang most of her famous roles and shared Tosca, Fiora and Monna Vanna with Garden and Aida, Santuzza and Leonora in *Trovatore* with Raisa. In the company's hierarchy she ranked after Garden sharing second place with Raisa. She was adored by the public, while the critics, as with Garden, were content to dilate on her interpretative skill without detailing her vocal shortcomings. In Buenos Aires her position was supreme. In a theatre which was traditionally dominated by Italian interests and where the verismo style had held sway since the early years of the century, she even essayed Norma. Though she had neither voice nor technique for the role, she was able to make an effect on a public content for Norma to sound as if it were the work of Catalani or Refice. Wisely she never ventured it in Chicago, where it was a part of the exclusive dominion of Raisa, whose voice, as one Argentinian critic noted, was 'more genuine and suitable for the role'.[22] After leaving Chicago in 1932 she spent an increasing part of each season in Italy, especially at the Rome Opera, where she was especially loved, and it was in Rome that she died at the early age of forty seven in the spring of 1936.

Muzio's great personal beauty, the unique and characteristic quality of her voice—once heard it is not soon forgotten—the unquestioned sincerity of her style and manner, her lonely and unhappy private life with its broken romances that led to an early death, are the stuff of which legends are compounded. They deeply affected her contemporaries, and over the passage of years her reputation seems actually to have grown, even in those centres where she appeared comparatively infrequently or not at all. Undoubtedly the principal factor in this has been the almost continuous availability of a small but remarkably successful group of recordings she made in the last years of her life. This is not without its sad irony, for she actually paid to make them. There are those who affect to find in them, notwithstanding her failing powers, the best of Muzio. Undoubtedly they are her most characteristic performances, as we should expect from a singer in her early forties. They represent her art in maturity and from the best of them we can still hear much of that 'fine and communicative enthusiasm' of which Henderson wrote. Yet familiarity and closer examination reveal not only vocal decadence but a certain musical slovenliness, even coarseness; in particular 'Casta Diva' and 'Ah! non credea' are hardly more than sketches. As is apparent from her earliest recordings, she had neither the control nor finish on her technique to create a stylish effect in this music. By 1934, instead of a gracefully nuanced legato informed by the breath, and the imaginative and purely musical detail such as we can still hear in the singing of Patti, Melba, Sembrich, Nordica and others, she offers a kind of generalised emotion and curiously mannered enunciation. It is often affecting in some of the music she sang, for example Refice's *Cecilia*, but for Bellini it is at once too fussy and not detailed enough. In his music it is hardly possible to exaggerate the importance of a clean and accurate execution. Detail is of the essence of the style; the fioritura, in particular, is neither window dressing nor singers' vanity. Thus in Norma's 'Casta Diva'—a prayer to the moon—it is not being too fanciful to hear in the descending chromatic runs a musical metaphor for the moonlight slanting through the leaves of the oak trees. To make the proper effect these must be sung with both delicacy and precision.

The arias from *Trovatore* and *La Forza del Destino* still please for their soft and rounded high notes, which make an agreeable change from some of the shrill agitations of her contemporaries. Although the shortness of breath, also to be heard in the pieces from *Norma* and *Sonnambula*, may be attributable in part to the heart disease from which she was suffering, acoustic records suggest that the voice was never fully supported. In 'Amami, Alfredo' made in 1911, though her singing is at its freshest and free of mannerisms, she has not the necessary expansion for the big phrases and is obliged to snatch breaths. Of all her late recordings 'Addio del passato' most clearly defines the limitations of her art and also of her voice. The way in which she rationalises her failing powers demonstrates plainly enough how much her priorities reflect the taste of the day. Her reading of the letter is most dramatic and done after the fashion of a tragedy queen in deepest parlando. It is true that Verdi has written 'con voce bassa' but he added 'senza suono' and it is surely wrong that the speaker should so dominate the accompaniment; rather should she take her cue from it and let the voice rise and fall in line with the melodic cadence. Certainly Muzio's does not seem basically a musical approach when at the end, as Violetta's anguish intensifies and speech is heightened into song, instead of moving imperceptibly from one to the other without any obvious laryngeal adjustment (as Maria Callas does perfectly in a live recording from La Scala), she engages vocal gears so abruptly that it sounds as if someone else has started to sing. In the aria she equates the symptoms of her own heart condition with those of Violetta's consumption, thus turning her breathlessness to dramatic advantage. Unfortunately she exaggerates it so greatly that we should hardly be surprised if Violetta expired before the end. What is only

implicit in Verdi's music, she makes explicit, and by so doing she is obliged to alter note values; in particular, by attenuating precisely those notes which are marked to be stressed, she shifts the rhythmic accent in such a way as to give a chopped up and jerky effect to the phrasing when the opposite is intended. Her interpretation is a document, not so much of style as of her own mannerisms: the glottal attack, sudden, often dislocated, pianissimi, the rough way of relinquishing notes—the high As, for example, she lets go with something like a yelp—and her extraordinary enunciation.

Of them all it is the last which is the most mannered and upon repeated hearing becomes most tiresome. She has a way of holding the tones in the mouth and almost chewing out the words with the result that most of the vowel sounds are, to some degree, impure and distorted, 'a' and 'o' especially, but she is not consistent, and they vary considerably. Since there is virtually no trace of this idiosyncrasy in her two early HMV recordings and it is much less apparent on the Pathé and Edisons, it was probably, at least in its origins, a deliberate affectation, an attempt to translate into opera the pretentious delivery of some stage actors and actresses of that time, the 'birignao'. By 1934 it had become a bad habit and there are countless instances of it on her Columbia records; often, as it seems, for no apparent reason. In the opening phrases of Tosca's Prayer 'Vissi d'arte, vissi d'amore, non feci mai male ad anima viva!', 'd'arte' becomes 'duartoy', 'non' almost 'nun' and the 'a' in 'viva' modified to 'e'. The consonants are also affected; 't' changes to 'd' and even on occasions disappears altogether. None of this can be blamed on the recordings which are exceptionally good for their age; the only criticism that could be made of them is that being closely recorded they expose her faults all too clearly.

Her mannerisms were undoubtedly informed by genuine feeling and for many of her audiences they came to be enjoyed in themselves; record collectors too have come to love them, and indeed it could be said that she was loved for, rather than despite, them. The fact remains, however, that by the end of her career the mannerisms had taken over, and taken the edge off the finish of the music with the result that there is a sameness, a lack of characteristic detail in her interpretations; on records Violetta, Margherita, Maddalena and Cecilia all seem to be dying from the same excess of neurotic temperament. And it was not only on records that she became self-indulgent. Even when she was young, so we are told, she often came off stage in a complete daze; once, during a performance of *Andrea Chénier* at the Met, after she had finished the aria in Act Two she actually fainted away. All of which suits her legend, but Noel Coward's dictum is worth recalling: it is the actor's business to indulge his audience, not himself. If that applies in the legitimate theatre, how much more appropriate it is to opera, where the discipline of the music demands that at all times the singer shall be in complete control.

The 'Hill and Dale' recordings made for Pathé and Edison preserve her voice and art in a fresher condition; her musicianship too is less affected. The Entrance of *Adriana Lecouvreur* begins with a bit of declamation from Racine's *Andromaque* and in the aria, though lacking the grand manner, she sings in affecting style with a lovely vocal quality. 'Son pochi fiori' from Mascagni's *L'Amico Fritz* suits her to a tee, the tessitura lying perfectly within her range. She manages the soft high phrases with particular ease; in general she seems more relaxed in lyrical music. Here, presumably because she never sang the role on stage, she uses an alternate concert ending. Neither did she sing *Zazà*, for though the opera was in the Met's repertory while she was under contract, it was a part of Farrar's exclusive preserve. A recording of the passage 'Dir che ci sono al mondo' sounds as though the role would have suited her. If it fails to make its full effect, this is Edison's, not Muzio's fault. In this scene in the opera a little girl plays Cherubini's 'Ave Maria' on the piano on stage, while Zazà ruminates on the wickedness of the world, accompanied by the full orchestra in the pit; virtue and vice, as it were, in counterpoint. By using a piano reduction, the effect is nullified.

Any discussion of Muzio's records must at least mention some of the song titles. There are many, from Pergolesi and Rossini, in which she is rather short on classical graces and frequently has recourse to a helpful aspirate, to Sanderson's 'Until' and from Victor Herbert's *Orange Blossoms*, 'A kiss in the dark'. In all of them the sweetness of her voice and sympathetic manner are most appealing. She had an especial partiality for the songs by the voice-teacher and composer Buzzi-Peccia; 'Mal d'amore' shows off her singing at its most warm and affecting and without any lapses in taste. Even in later years when she found it difficult to put aside the mask of tragedy, in his 'Colombetta' there is suddenly revealed a delightful sense of humour of which we should scarcely have thought her capable.

16. Raisa and some Dramatic Sopranos

The careers of Claudia Muzio and ROSA RAISA (1893–1963) ran on parallel lines for some years; both of them were guests in Paris with Russell's company in the spring of 1914, thereafter travelling on to Covent Garden, both were prominent members of the Chicago Opera for many years and both sang with great success in South America. Raisa's career also began in Italy; though Polish by birth, like Arkel, Krusceniski and Ruszkowska she identified herself from the beginning with the Italian repertory and for our purposes may be considered an Italian singer. She studied at the Naples Conservatory with Barbara Marchisio. Barbara, the elder of the Marchisio sisters, was a contralto; with Carlotta in the title roles she had appeared in notable revivals of *Norma* and *Semiramide* at La Scala. So great was the sisters' success in the latter work that Rossini was cajoled into producing a revised French version, *Sémiramis*, especially for them to star in at the Paris Opéra (in the event, it seems to have been largely the work of Count Carafa). Raisa never sang Semiramide but she was a successful Norma in Chicago and South America and if her interpretation was hardly a classic, it ranked with Ponselle's as the best of its day. Upon the completion of her studies in 1912, she made her first public appearance in a concert at the Accademia di Santa Cecilia in Rome. The programme included Cavalieri's *Rappresentazione di Anima e Corpo* and excerpts from Monteverdi's *Orfeo*, in both of which she was supported by Giuseppe Kaschmann. Her voice made a big impression and the critics prophesied a great future. She confirmed their good opinions at her stage debut as Leonora in *Oberto* during the Verdi centenary celebrations at Parma:

> To make her debut at the Teatro Regio, and moreover on such an occasion, was considered risky but Raisa won a triumphant success. She possesses a magnificent voice, rich in sonorous and powerful notes of beautiful timbre; she is very successful in impetuous and accented passages, eminently dramatic and her phrasing is also correct. She cannot yet show off her dramatic talent, for she is still awkward, and her singing is not animated by that artistic fire which makes the greatest singers of the lyric theatre live in our memory; but she will be splendidly successful.[1]

Two months later she arrived in Chicago and began there a career that was to last more than a generation. Her first appearance was as Aida show-ing off 'a voice matched by no other in volume or intensity'.[2] Her other roles included Queen Isabella in Franchetti's *Cristoforo Colombo* with Bassi and Ruffo, Mimi to Giorgini's Rodolfo and a Flower Maiden in *Parsifal*. At the end of the season she travelled to Latin America where we read of her fulfilling an impromptu engagement: one night the famous Mexican bandit Pancho Villa held up the opera train and ordered the company off; at Villa's insistence (apparently he was a music lover), Raisa obliged with several arias. It is pleasant to imagine that one of these was 'Tacea la notte' and that Pancho himself, seizing a guitar (they grow on trees in Mexico), joined in with Manrico's serenade 'Deserto sulla terra'. At all events Raisa's singing must have done the trick, for only a short time later she was at the Théâtre des Champs Elysées as Amelia and Nedda. It was Aida again for her first night at Covent Garden:

> . . . her performance seemed to gain the immediate sympathy of the audience. It was not so much on account of any peculiar qualities of the voice that she gained one's interest, though her voice is an adequate and serviceable one and is perhaps something more in its upper register, but rather because of an in-dividuality of style which appeared in her moulding of certain phrases, many of them quiet ones and not always the most telling ones in the music . . . Some-times she disappointed the expectation she had raised. A phrase was not quite smoothly taken, or her voice got lost beneath the orchestra or the other voices; but she always had a definite conception of what she wanted to do, and when she reached it, as she did completely in the beautiful aria that begins her scene in the third act, it was worth doing, her soft ending of that aria was one of the most beautiful things in the performance, although Signor Caruso and Madame Kirkby Lunn were parts of that perfor-mance.[3]

In the autumn of 1914 after repeating her Aida at the Costanzi, Rome, she took the title role in Zandonai's *Francesca da Rimini*. She sang both these parts in her first season at the Colon the following year, together with Santuzza and the Marschallin with dalla Rizza and Galli-Curci. There, in 1916, she was Lida in one of the first modern revivals of Verdi's *Battaglia di Legnano*, Amelia, Valentine in *Ugonotti* and Alice in *Falstaff*. In December the same year she made her Scala debut as Lida, subsequently joining dal Monte, Pertile and Danise in perfor-mances of *Francesca da Rimini*. She was a guest at La Scala again in 1924, when she was admired as Asteria in the long awaited world premiere of Boito's *Nerone*. She repeated the role the following season and was heard as Alice and the *Trovatore* Leonora, all under the direction of Toscanini. Her greatest triumph came in 1926 when she created Turandot:

> [Raisa] has a voice of the widest range and power (even if a little hard). Her part Puccini has written in an altitudinous tessitura often obliging the singer to pronounce words in the least appropriate register. Yet Raisa surmounts the difficulties and pleases with the smoothness of her phrasing, her perfect intonation and her dramatic fervour.[4]

49 Rosa Raisa as Suor Angelica

In her final visit to La Scala in 1932 she took part in yet another world premiere, that of Zandonai's *Una Partita*; she created the part of the Contessa Manuela.

Her career in South America continued in 1918 when she added Donna Anna and Norma to her previous achievements. In the latter she was especially admired and she sang it again at the Coliseo in 1921 with Gigli as Pollione. She returned to the Colon in 1932 for *Norma*, *Aida*, *Turandot* and Leonora in *Trovatore*. In Europe she made guest appearances at the San Carlo, the Rome Opera and in the summer of 1933 sang Valentine opposite Lauri-Volpi's Raoul in *Ugonotti* at the Verona Arena. The major part of her activities, however, was centred in Chicago with occasional sorties to the west coast and to New York. There she was first heard in opera at the Lexington Theatre in 1918 as Maliella in Wolf-Ferrari's *Gioielli della Madonna*. Henderson praised her voice 'full and rich and of large power . . . so genuinely beautiful that it cannot fail to give pleasure'.[5] In Chicago hers was an all-embracing accomplishment: Aida, Santuzza, Maddalena, Alice, Francesca, the title-role in Mascagni's *Isabeau* (a re-working of the Lady Godiva legend in which Raisa created quite a sensation jumping from the horse and rushing off stage seemingly nude; in fact she was wearing a body stocking), Valentine, Maliella, Tosca, Leonora in *Trovatore* and *La Forza del Destino*, Gioconda, Basiliola in Montemezzi's *La Nave*, Norma, Suor Angelica, Turandot, Desdemona, Elisabeth in *Tannhäuser*, Minnie, Rachel in *La Juive*, Conchita in Zandonai's opera of that name, Selika in *Africana*, the Marschallin, Amelia, Butterfly, Toinette in Harling's *The Light from St Agnes*, Donna Anna, Rosalinde in an English version of *Die Fledermaus* and Silvana in Respighi's *La Fiamma*. Her last performance, in *La Juive*, took place in December 1936 more than twenty three years after her debut. Her career in Chicago ranked second only to Garden's and actually surpassed hers in duration by more than two years.

All her recordings confirm the opinions of her contemporaries that hers was an imposing and—especially at the top—powerful voice, the range extending from bottom A to the high D flat. It was not, however, as even as Ponselle's, and the registers were not fully equalised. On the early Pathés there is an ugly break when she carries the chest register up to G, even A flat. After a period of study with Sembrich, by the time she came to make the Vocalions and Brunswicks, she had largely corrected this. The middle register remained through-out her career comparatively weak, and to compensate for this she had a tendency to use too forceful an attack. On the best of her records she has a good legato style, the voice is firm, the emission smooth and as we can hear in 'O patria mia', she is skilled in the use of mezza voce. This is a fine piece of singing even if the high C is thin and disappoints. Yet, as in so many of her recordings, something is missing. In the passage 'I sacri nomi' for example, there is want of rhythmic vitality; the voice sounds 'fixed', lacking in responsiveness and this adversely affects her intonation. Her coloratura technique—though not brilliant—is mostly accurate, save for a tendency to aspirate lightly certain intervals, and in Margherita's 'L'altra notte' she even shows off a serviceable trill. This is a fine interpretation, among the best versions on record. She sings with warmth, eloquence and more feeling than elsewhere. Generally, however, she relied on the power and quality of her voice to make their own effect and her interpretations are not remarkable for any dramatic or musical personality. In the Act Four duet from *Trovatore* for the Count and Leonora, with her husband Giacomo Rimini, the execution is clean and she trips neatly through the difficult passages of slurred semi-quavers, but the impression is of a cosy matrimonial sing-along (it was a popular encore at their joint recitals), and neither singer communicates any dramatic urgency. The four Victor titles were made towards the end of her career, and in them she adopts rather slow and stately tempi but her singing has not the intensity to make them convincing; the voice, however, remains imposing, especially in the chest register where the tone seems more voluptuous.

Although the Polish soprano ELENA RUSZKOWSKA (1878–1948) sang in Vienna, at La Scala and extensively throughout Italy, Poland always remained the focal point of her career. She studied there with Valery Wysocki, a busy teacher of the day whose other pupils included Adamo Didur, Janina Korolewicz-Wayda and Salomea Krusceniski. Her debut took place at Lemberg in 1900 as Lady Harriet in Flotow's *Martha*. In less than a year she secured an engagement at the Warsaw Opera. She was to remain a great favourite with audiences there for more than a quarter of a century until her retirement in 1928. Her repertory ranged through leading lyric dramatic soprano roles of the Italian and Polish repertory as well as certain Wagnerian parts, and she was greatly admired as Valentine in *Les Huguenots*. In 1905 she sang at the Vienna Imperial Opera as Lisa in the *Queen of Spades*

and *Aida*, which was to become one of her favourite
roles. Two years later she was invited to La Scala,
where she appeared as Gutrune in *Il Crepuscuolo
degli Dei* with Litvinne, Giraud and Bellantoni,
Elena in *Mefistofele* with Chaliapin and Alda, and
Iguamota in Franchetti's *Cristoforo Colombo* with
Amato, de Angelis and Mazzoleni, all three operas
conducted by Toscanini. She returned to Milan in
1911 for some performances of *Aida* and as Leonora
in *Trovatore* at the Dal Verme. Her Aida in particular
was a great success with both the public who
greeted her 'with warm and insistent applause'[6] and
the critics who wrote of her 'artistry of the first
order'.[7] She had a similar success with it the same
season at Trieste and at La Scala in 1913.

In the years up to 1915 she appeared at many
leading Italian theatres. In Turin in 1912 she sang
Iguamota to the Cristoforo Colombo of Giraldoni.
The following year she was Elisabetta in a revival of
Verdi's *Don Carlo* with Frascani, Scampini and de
Luca; it was the year of the hundredth anniversary
of Verdi's birth and she took part in special concerts: at Ravenna with Danise, and in Trieste, where
she was a soloist in the Trio from *Lombardi*. The
same year at Bologna she appeared as Kundry in one
of the first Italian performances of *Parsifal* with
Giuseppe Borgatti in the title role. The next season
she returned and added Selika to her repertory with
de Muro as Vasco and Viglione-Borghese as Nelusko. She also sang at Parma and at Padua as Amelia
in *Ballo in Maschera*.

The voice, as we hear it in Leonora's 'La Vergine
degli angeli' from *Forza del Destino*, is a brilliant
lyric dramatic soprano, the quality finer than either
Krusceniski or Korolewicz-Wayda, and she is a more
sensitive and imaginative artist. Although the production has a rather pronounced tremolo, and occasionally her intonation is not perfect, this is rarely
disturbing and the voice sits limpid and secure on
the breath. She phrases tenderly, moving with ease
and radiant tone in the higher range, without
making any obvious adjustment for the soft notes or
recourse to the teutonic clutch. It would be difficult
to imagine a better performance, the voice soaring
above the chorus to a beautifully poised soft high B
at the end; a musical as well as a most effective
interpolation. She made a number of excerpts from
Tosca and *Aida* mostly of concerted music and,
unfortunately, not in the best company. It is a great
pity, for her singing of Aida's music especially is
distinguished. In 'Là tra foreste' for example, the
phrasing is replete with poetic accents and subtle
use of rubato, she carefully observes all the ex-

50 Elsa Ruszkowska as Elisabetta in Verdi's *Don Carlo*

pressive markings, and the triplets are clearly
articulated and rhythmically precise. In a vocal
arrangement of Chopin's Nocturne in E flat, Op. 9,
we hear the same virtues and the tone has a
haunting quality. There are two recordings of this,
one of them slightly abbreviated. Both were made in
the late twenties when she was almost at the end of
her career, but the singing is still beautiful and, like
her art, uncorrupted by the years. A performance of
the 'Inflammatus' from Rossini's *Stabat Mater* is
sung brilliantly and only the passage of rising trills
rather defeats her as it does Austral; she includes a
third and final high C that Rossini sanctioned for
Clara Novello at a performance in Bergamo when he
was present and which Donizetti conducted.

51 Maria Labia as Mimì

too who brought her out in a concert tour of Italy in 1902; she sang in Milan, Verona and Padua. In 1903 she went to Russia and the following year to Sweden, where she made an especially good impression. As a result she was given a contract at the Stockholm Opera. She made her debut as Mimi and was later heard as Margherita in *Mefistofele*, Santuzza and Nedda. In 1906 she moved to Berlin where she took the title-role in *Carmen*, Martha in d'Albert's *Tiefland* and Tosca in the first German language performances of the opera. It was as Tosca, with Zenatello and Renaud, that New York first heard her during Hammerstein's 1908 season at the Manhattan. She was enthusiastically received for her dramatic skill but as a singer she could not compare to Ternina or Eames:

> Her voice, not large in volume, was best in its middle register, the tones having much color; but the top notes seemed hard and somewhat constricted. As an actress she displayed more ability and temperament than was usual on the opera stage.[8]

Her other roles included Santuzza, Desdemona and Carmen, in which she appeared on the opening night of Hammerstein's Philadelphia Opera House with Dalmorès and de Segurola. Though she looked well her interpretation was thought tame and wanting in character. In Philadelphia she also sang Nedda and, on tour with the company in Boston, Mimi with Constantino and Sammarco. This was her only season in the United States and she left for Europe immediately thereafter, singing Salome in Berlin, making guest appearances in Vienna and in 1912 at Kiev, with a company of Italian singers including Olimpia Boronat. In the autumn of that year and after an absence of nearly a decade she returned to Italy to make her La Scala debut as Salome. The event was preceded by too much publicity and she failed to please. In Paris, she was more successful when she took the role at the Opéra with Dalmorès and Noté under Messager and she was 'praised for her magnificent voice and acting of a rare dramatic force'.[9]

The events of the war effectively put paid to her international career and in 1916 she was obliged to return home. Her reception was a warm one: since she was coming from Berlin and was fluent in German when she arrived at the frontier, the Italian military authorities quite persuaded themselves they had found an operatic Mata Hari; it was with some difficulty that she escaped the firing squad. The later part of her career was based in Italy. In

Ruszkowska travelled to Italy to make her reputation, MARIA LABIA (1880–1953), upon the completion of her studies, sang in Sweden, Germany and Russia and did not establish herself in her native country until after the First World War. She was the younger daughter of an impoverished Venetian aristocrat. Her elder sister Fausta was also a soprano but her career followed a more conventional route in the Italian provinces, with appearances at La Scala and the Costanzi, Rome, chiefly in Wagnerian roles; a small group of recordings made when her powers were on the wane does not indicate more than a routine artist.

It was Maria's mother who nurtured her talent and was her only singing teacher. It was her mother

52 Adelina Agostinelli as Margherita in *Mefistofele*

Madame Sans-Gêne there in Giordano's opera. She was still singing Carmen as late as 1933, and Felice in seasons at Berne, Lausanne and Zürich in 1936. In her retirement she taught singing in Warsaw and Rome and finally at her own villa on Lake Garda.

It is easy to believe from her records that her wide reputation was not based solely on her singing. The voice was of a naturally attractive quality, and when she confines herself to, say, Tosti's 'Seconda Mattinata' (not as good as the prima), which makes no heroic demands of her, the singing is expressive and charming. But even in Ciampi's 'Tre giorni son che Nina', where she gets rather tearful and broadens out the style as if it were by Puccini, the tone becomes fluttery, the high notes strident and the line is not sufficiently smooth. In a couple of souvenirs of her Berlin Tosca, 'Vissi d'arte' and 'Non la sospiri', granted that the German translation, especially of the latter, is no aid to a good legato, it can hardly be blamed for the whiney tone and the hard and constricted top notes which sound very much as described by the New York critic above. In both these excerpts the voice is not well supported and she tends to sing flat.

Although they travelled to many of the world's leading theatres and were often warmly welcomed, neither Maria Labia nor ADELINA AGOSTINELLI (1882–1954) were front ranking artists. Agostinelli studied in Milan with Giuseppe Quirolli, whom she subsequently married. She made her debut at Pavia in 1903 in the title-role of Giordano's *Fedora*. During the next four years we find her singing in the Italian provinces, then in 1907 Hammerstein engaged her for his second season at the Manhattan. Her first appearance was in *Faust* with Bassi, Crabbé and Didur; she quickly 'proved herself to be a serviceable soprano'.[10] In the course of a two year engagement she sang Aida, Nedda, Stefania in Giordano's *Siberia*, Santuzza, Valentine and Leonora in *Trovatore*, all of them with Zenatello and Sammarco. She made the best impression as Amelia in *Ballo in Maschera* at Philadelphia; the *Evening Bulletin* acclaimed her 'facility and brilliance, her tones being firm, pure and of crystalline clearness'.[11] In the summer of 1910 she went to South America, to the Colon, Buenos Aires. She was both Margherita and Elena in *Mefistofele* with Didur, Mimi to the Rodolfo of Anselmi and Nedda with Rousselière and Ruffo. She came again the next year to take the title-role in *Thaïs*, Minnie in the local premiere of *Fanciulla del West* with Ferrari-Fontana and Ruffo and Elisabetta in Verdi's *Don Carlo*. When in the autumn of 1910 she made her Scala debut as Maria in *Simon*

1918, at the Costanzi, Rome, she sang Tosca and Giorgetta in the European premiere of Puccini's *Tabarro*. She took the role again in Turin and at the Colon, where her repertory also included Manon Lescaut, and she shared Tosca with Muzio and Mazzoleni. At Trieste in 1921 she was Carolina in a revival of *Matrimonio Segreto* and Felice in Wolf-Ferrari's *Quattro Rusteghi*. She repeated Felice at La Scala in 1922, 1923 and 1925 and with Stracciari as Napoleone she was the first, and to date the only,

Boccanegra with Battistini, *Musica* wrote of 'her beautiful voice, round, strong and ringing'.[12] The same season she was the Scala's first Marschallin with Bori and Pavel Ludikar and created Speranza in the world premiere of Filiasi's *Fior di Neve*; 'her execution of the part was magnificent'.[13] The following year she sang Eva in *Maestri Cantori* with Bonini, de Luca, Krismer and Ludikar, but opinion was less enthusiastic about her Isabeau.

En route to London in the summer of 1912, Agostinelli stopped in Paris to take the role of Margherita in two gala performances of Boito's *Mefistofele* with Chaliapin and Smirnov.

> The romanza of Margherita 'L'altra notte . . .' which opens the third act was a splendid success for Agostinelli, who has a mellow voice, vibrant and cultivated with all the refinements and graces.[14]

At Covent Garden as Manon Lescaut she 'did not succeed in making a very strong impression at first.'[15] *The Times* thought her voice not always steady and that occasionally she was over-powered by the orchestra. Her Mimi was better received, but she was not a popular success and was never invited again. From the time of the First World War her appearances were mostly confined to provincial theatres. In the 1920s she settled in Buenos Aires and taught there for some years.

Agostinelli's records reveal a particularly attractive, slightly tremulous, lyric soprano, not a large voice but the quality is unusually sweet and pure. 'Addio del passato' is affectingly sung, her 'Vissi d'arte' hardly an outpouring of tone in the manner of Destinn but the phrasing is sensitive, the diction pellucid and she rises to a nicely shaded and, for once, unforced climax. Her restraint was admirable and, to some extent, from necessity, for she sounds as if some of the roles she undertook were too dramatic for her resources.

ESTER MAZZOLENI (1882–1981) is the odd diva out; though she was very much of her time, and her art is stamped with the familiar hallmarks of the verismo style and with a particularly strong vibrato, her identification with an earlier repertory and the dramatic roles of Cherubini, Spontini, Meyerbeer and Verdi, places her firmly in the tradition of Boninsegna and Russ. For a short period, at any rate, she was more successful than either.

Although born in Dalmatia, at the time a part of Austro-Hungary, her family was Italian. An uncle, the tenor Francesco Mazzoleni, sang the role of Oronte in Verdi's *Lombardi* at La Scala in 1857; this was one of the operas in which Mazzoleni herself later took part. At first she wanted to study art and it was not until after she had moved to Italy that she changed her mind. Upon the completion of her vocal training she made her debut in 1906 at the Costanzi, Rome, as Leonora in *Trovatore*; the same season also heard her as Rachel in *Ebrea* and Freia in *L'Oro del Reno*. From Rome she moved to Bari where she sang in *Aida*, *Ballo in Maschera*, Giordano's *Siberia* and Virgilio's *Jana*. In only a year she was at La Scala. Her first appearance was as Queen Isabella in Franchetti's *Cristoforo Colombo*; the part of Iguamota was taken by another debutante, Elena Ruszkowska. During the next two years her repertory included Leonora in *Forza del Destino*, Giulia in *Vestale* (which she also sang with the Scala company on a visit to the Paris Opéra), Elena in *Vespri Siciliani*, Francesca in Mancinelli's *Paolo e Francesca*, Medea in the first performances of Cherubini's opera at La Scala (with the Lachner recitatives), and Selika in *Africana*. In 1916 after an

53 Ester Mazzoleni in the title-role of Catalani's
Dejanice

absence of six years she returned to take the role of Amazilly in a revival of Spontini's *Fernando Cortez*, Elvira in *Ernani* with Battistini and the title-role in *Lucrezia Borgia*. From La Scala she proceeded to the San Carlo for *Africana* with Mario Gilion and Ruffo, *Gioconda* with Grassi and Stracciari, and *Tristano e Isotta* and *Norma* both opposite Ferrari-Fontana:

> Ester Mazzoleni was an exceptional Norma. From the first notes of her recitative with a long, finely spun high A to the last phrases of the third act, she gradually built up an impression of which it is not possible to find a more suitable adjective than laudable. She impressed in turn with the richness of her voice, her command of the stage and her beautiful singing . . . 'Casta Diva', the duets with Pollione and Adalgisa and above all the plea to her father: 'Deh! non volerli vittime', sung in a fil di voce, raised an enthusiasm without equal at the San Carlo for many years.[16]

Mazzoleni appeared at most of the leading Italian theatres: at the Fenice, Venice, as Elisabetta in *Don Carlo*, Valentine, Norma and Lucrezia Borgia; at the Regio, Turin, as Gioconda, Damara in Waldi's *Figlia del Re*, the title-role in Catalani's *Dejanice* and *Traviata* with Pertile and Noto; at Bologna as Giselda in *Lombardi* with Garbin (the Trio had to be encored at each performance), Norma and Lucrezia Borgia; at Palermo in *Gioconda* and *Traviata*, and at the Dal Verme, Milan, as Leonora in *Trovatore*, Loreley in Catalani's opera of that name and Aida. She took the last part with Maria Gay and Zenatello in the augural performances of opera at the Verona Arena in the summer of 1913. Outside Italy she sang only occasionally: at the Paris Opéra, the Liceo, Barcelona, the Teatro Real, Madrid and in Budapest. She made two visits to the Colon: in 1910 she was heard as Gioconda, Isabella and Giulia, nine years later she repeated Gioconda and added Suor Angelica in the opera's local premiere, Tosca and Lucrezia Borgia. The last was with Gigli who has left us a vivid description of the sensation she created on opening night when Lucrezia finally reveals to the dying Gennaro that he is her own son. Her stage manners, it would appear, were quite as vehement as her way of singing; she took hold of Gigli's head so roughly that his wig came away in her hand. Losing her balance she went reeling back across the stage, still holding on to the wig and singing away at the top of her voice: 'Figlio mio! Figlio mio!'

Mazzoleni's recordings date from early in her career, but the voice sounds fully mature. So much so, in fact, that it is hard to believe that she was still only in her twenties. She makes an important sound, big and brilliant. It is larger though less attractive than Russ's, rougher than Boninsegna's, but she had more temperament. Of all her immediate predecessors she reminds us most of Burzio, but if she is not so extravagant, neither does she so fascinate us. It is an interesting comment on what then passed for a classical style that a singer with so vibrant a method and so little conception of legato should have been selected to intone the suave and stately measures of Spontini; her rough manner quite debilitates Giulia's 'Tu che invoco'. A snippet from Act Four of Verdi's *Vespri Siciliani* 'Arrigo, ah parli a un core', provokes a more sympathetic response. The emotion is better contained and the phrasing, if not inspired, well-shaped; in the cadenza she alters the line so as to avoid having to descend to the impossible low F sharp. Here, when she is not ploughing into it, the quality of the voice is by no means disagreeable. Something of her Norma is preserved in the passage 'Teneri figli' and the duet 'In mia man' with Zenatello. As we should expect it is singing very much in the contemporary Italian style but there is a warmth of feeling and variety of expression despite the abandoned manner that enable us to appreciate how potent an interpretation it was in the theatre; as in the excerpt from *Vespri Siciliani*, here she has a surer sense of line and the fioritura is surprisingly clear, though not always accurate. She comes into her own in *Gioconda*, giving free rein to the chest voice and contrasting the registers to great effect, but she cannot resist the temptation to overdo it and in the duet 'Dal carcere m'hai tratto' she pushes so hard that collapse seems not far off.

17. *Verismo Sopranos*

The careers of Tina Poli-Randaccio, Carmen Melis, Juanita Caracciolo and Gilda dalla Rizza were based in Italy, where they were mostly associated with what could still be described with some degree of accuracy as contemporary works. TINA POLI-RANDACCIO (1877–1956) was the heavyweight, the possessor of a full lyric dramatic soprano of fine quality and considerable power, especially in the chest register. A pupil of Ortisi in Pesaro, she made her debut in 1902 at Bergamo as Amelia in *Ballo in Maschera*. For the first half dozen or so years of her career she was constantly on the move; we read of her taking part in seasons at Messina, Barcelona, Rio de Janeiro, Oporto, Bucharest and Mexico City. At that time her repertory embraced Aida, Valentine, Lucrezia Borgia, Elisabetta in *Don Carlo* and Elvira in *Ernani*, as well as Gioconda and Santuzza. It was after hearing her in the latter part that Mascagni engaged her for the leading role in his opera *Amica* in a tour throughout Italy which he himself directed. Henceforth she was to become increasingly preoccupied with the operas of the modern school. After making her Scala debut as Brünnhilde in *Sigfrido* in the autumn of 1910, she was invited back to create Minnie in the first performances of Puccini's *Fanciulla del West* at La Scala. There had been a great deal of jockeying among the warring divas for the honour, but Poli-Randaccio laid the strongest claim, having already sung the role with conspicuous success at Lucca, the San Carlo, Naples, with Martinelli and Viglione-Borghese, and in Paris,

54 Tina Poli-Randaccio in the title-role of Mascagni's *Parisina*

where she and Melis had shared two gala evenings at the Opéra with Caruso. *Fanciulla del West* was a great success at La Scala (as indeed it was at first in most centres), being given thirteen times, and Poli-Randaccio's 'exuberant dramatic temperament, full of voice of good timbre, delighted with its vibrant colour'.[1] She confirmed the impression she made in Milan when she joined Edoardo di Giovanni (Edward Johnson) in the Rome premiere soon afterwards. The role was to remain a favourite of hers for the rest of her career and she sang it all over Italy and often, as at the San Carlo, on several occasions.

In the 1913/14 season at La Scala she took the title-role in Mascagni's *Parisina* with Lázaro and Galeffi, Gisca in Smareglia's *L'Abisso* and Vannina in Alfano's *L'Ombra di Don Giovanni*. At the Carcano, Milan, in 1914, she was Tosca with Garbin and Viglione-Borghese, a part she repeated the following June at the Colon, where she was also heard as Santuzza and Gioconda. In the latter, according to Lauri-Volpi, she created a tremendous effect with her masculine-sounding low notes; it was one of her favourite roles.[2] In 1920 alone she sang it in Barcelona, Rome and Palermo and she was unquestionably its greatest exponent for more than a decade. In the summer of 1920 she made her only appearances in England when she succeeded Edvina and dalla Rizza at Covent Garden in *Tosca*.

> She made a decidedly successful first appearance . . . [Her] voice has a rich and emotional quality which is often very telling in the part. It has the defect of unevenness and of losing its purity in moments of intensity and she is, perhaps, too anxious to get intensity at every point. But very few singers succeed in reserving their energies sufficiently for the climaxes, and something must be allowed to the natural anxiety of a first performance to create an immediate impression.[3]

She remained active in Italy throughout the 1920s, returning to the Scala to create another new role: Madama di Challant in Carmine Guarano's opera. In 1922 at Bologna she sang Valentine in *Ugonotti* with Ada Sari and John O'Sullivan; in 1924 at the Fenice she was Aida with Gay and Zenatello, conducted by Mascagni. She continued to sing Minnie until 1933, the last time at the Adriano, Rome; and in the following year at Bologna, when she was fifty seven, she took the title-role in *Turandot*.

The opinion of *The Times* critic is certainly borne out in her records: the voice has a rich and emotional quality which is often very telling. The registers are fully developed, but as with so many of her contemporaries she cannot always resist the temptation to hoist the chest too high. The very strong but by no means regular vibrato (much less so than Mazzoleni's), is to a great extent self-induced, most strongly apparent in moments of intensity but when not required, to some extent, she is able to suppress it. In this, as in much else, her style is very much of its period. As we can hear in Minnie's 'Laggiù nel Soledad', the singing has character with a variety of colour and expression but it lacks refinement and there is the usual over-emphatic delivery. For all that, she can still surprise us; after a squally climax comes a sudden tenderly turned phrase. Her recording of Suòr Angelica's 'Senza Mamma' is perhaps the most stylish on record. It is true that she is without the suave emission and secure legato that others offer but hers is a vivid and suitably melodramatic reading, phrased eloquently with a nice use of portamento. Though detail was not her strong suit, she reveals here a deeper musical sensitivity than many of her contemporaries, differentiating effectively between the various sections of the piece—how movingly she launches the melody 'ora che sei un angelo del cielo'—and without sacrificing its overall integrity. At the end there is a fine sustained soft high A.

Few sopranos of the period had a more imposing vocal pedigree than CARMEN MELIS (1885–1967); she studied with Antonio Cotogni and Jean de Reszke, yet her singing on record, notwithstanding a fine voice, is quite without the suavity of tone and classical repose that we might have imagined. She was hailed by her contemporaries as a singing actress and her entire career was spent in the service of contemporary opera, especially those which gave her full opportunity for dramatic display. Her art was not notable for restraint and hers was the kind of overwhelming commitment hardly conducive to vocal longevity, a fact that she came to recognise too late. In her retirement, when she taught singing she confessed to her pupils that if she were allowed her career over again, she would be careful not to make the same mistakes. In effect: do what I say, not what I did; not the best example to follow. Her most outstanding pupil, Renata Tebaldi, was chiefly remarkable for the natural beauty of her voice.

Melis was born in Sardinia and made her first stage appearance at Novara in the 1905/6 season in the title-roles of *Iris* and *Tosca*. The following year she sang at Ferrara and the Costanzi, Rome: Butterfly, Mimi and Thaïs. In 1907 she visited Russia and Poland, where she was the first Thaïs at the Warsaw Opera. Two years later Hammerstein brought her to the Manhattan in succession to Agostinelli and Labia. Her debut was as Tosca with Zenatello and Renaud, an impersonation redolent of the Latin temperament'.[4] There was plenty of it too in her Mimi and Santuzza, but she got back a bit more of it than she had bargained for from an unlikely quarter when she begged McCormack to put a little spunk into his Turiddu. Taking her at her word, at the end of the big duet he flung her from him with such force, she went crashing into the wings. She came limping back on stage, but she was not seriously hurt.

55 Carmen Melis as Louise

From the Manhattan she moved to Boston and sang there in three successive seasons: Elena in *Mefistofele* with Sibiriakov and Alda, 'a finely tempered'[5] Desdemona to Zenatello's Otello, Tosca in company with Jadlowker and Baklanov (which must have afforded quite a study in jarring styles), Santuzza with McCormack again (by this time presumably she had forgiven him), and Manon Lescaut. In all of these she made a strong impression as much for her 'opulent, dark Italian good looks'[6] as for the quality of her singing. Parker's chain of adjectives for her Tosca: 'hot and gusty, alternatively affectionate and jealous, playful and piqued, self-doubting and resolute'[7] is hardly appropriate to a discussion of her voice. Her other roles in Boston included Nedda, Butterfly, Minnie in *Fanciulla del West*, Ricke in Franchetti's *Germania*, all with Zenatello, Thaïs and Maliella in Wolf-Ferrari's *Gioielli della Madonna*. In this part she made a great impression at Covent Garden in 1913:

> She plays the part to the full and gives us all its romance and savagery, its blind longing for every unknown experience. As a dramatic performance nothing could be more complete. As a musical one there was something missing, her voice was apt to sound curiously pale by comparison with the vividness of her personality. There were a few moments of uncertain intonation ... Mme Melis's singing was generally true and had great range of expression, varying from moments of intense excitement, such as the one in the second act where she rushes out, the voice rising to the top C instead of the expected B, to the quiet dream-like tone which she used at the end of the same act while she decked herself in the jewels. What one missed was the power of conveying fervour without effort. Her voice seemed to want natural warmth of quality ...[8]

Later in 1913 she travelled to San Francisco in a touring company directed by Leoncavallo and starred in two of his operas: *Zingari* and *Zazà*. The following year she sang Fedora at the San Carlo with de Lucia. In the 1915/16 season she returned to the United States for a season at the Chicago Opera, where she was heard in several of her familiar roles and also Aida and the title-role in Saint-Saëns's *Déjanire* with de Cisneros and Muratore. On a visit to the Colon in 1917 she sang the Marschallin in *Cavaliere della rosa* with Giraldoni as Ochs and dalla Rizza in the title-role, Manon Lescaut with Caruso, Tosca and Sieglinde in *Walchiria* with Journet as a French Wotan. Her Scala debut fol-

lowed at the end of the year, as Driada in Victor de Sabata's *Il Macigno* with Lappas. She reappeared there in 1924 to create Ginevra in Giordano's *La Cena delle Beffe* with Lázaro and Franci under Toscanini. In Rome she was heard as the Marschallin, Musetta and in the title-role of Brogi's *Isabella Orsini*. She returned to Covent Garden in 1929 as Musetta and Tosca and in the same year took the latter part in a complete recording of the opera.

Melis's voice was more lyrical than Poli-Randaccio's with a fine and affecting quality, though her manners differ profoundly from those of other de Reszke pupils—Lucille Marcel, Rachel Morton and Edvina for example—yet the conception of beautiful tone is common to them all. In Manon's 'Adieu notre petite table' and 'N'est-ce plus ma main?' (both are in Italian), her highly emotional way is part of the Italian Massenet tradition. She brings to bear all the devices of verismo: the dolent and fluttery tone, sudden lurches in the line, exaggerated and pinched sounding subito pianos, and a quantity of aspirates and sobs. Yet for all the lack of discipline and the cavalier way with note values, the singing has genuine charm and it could be argued that the warm and expansive tone of her voice conveys more of the sweet and fragrant style of the music than the vinegary vocalism of many French sopranos. Massenet, following Gounod, was part of the Italo-French tradition and a mastery of his idiom depends equally on a full vocal response to his melodies as to the setting of the words; it is no coincidence that his two best operas, *Manon* and *Werther*, have remained almost consistently as popular south of the Alps as in the French speaking world. Fedora's 'O grandi occhi' is not a piece notable for its musical distinction but Melis's voice is here at its loveliest and her ardent and expressive phrasing—she is more restrained than elsewhere—puts the best complexion on it. A couple of pages from forgotten ephemera, Virgilio's *Jana* and Parelli's *Hermes*, made at the beginning of her career, are attractively turned though less characteristic and the bottom of the voice sounds immature. Both are typical of the period; the latter is the more appealing but neither indicates buried treasure.

JUANITA CARACCIOLO (1890–1924) was at the very point of accomplishing great things when she died at the untimely age of thirty four. She had recently sung at La Scala and the Colon, in both houses to much acclaim. A group of recordings show off an attractive voice and her singing, though representative of her time, was not without delicacy and sensitivity. She was born into a musical family, her father being the director of a touring operetta company. It is said that she was named after the heroine of Suppé's operetta; at the time it was enjoying a considerable vogue and greatly assisted her father's fortunes. Family encouragement and a career in opera followed: she studied in Milan with Clelia Sangiorgi and made her debut at Genoa as Nedda in 1907. She first began to attract wider attention during a season of Italian opera at the Teatro Khediviale in Cairo, where she seems to have sustained almost the entire repertory. She was much 'applauded'[9] as Margherita in Boito's *Mefistofele*, acclaimed an 'ideal'[10] Manon, a 'marvellous'[11] Butterfly and she was also Elsa in *Lohengrin*, Carmela in Giordano's *Mese Mariano*, Alice in *Falstaff* and she took the title-role in Samara's *Rhea*. While in Egypt she married the director of the opera orchestra, Giacomo Armani.

56 Juanita Caracciolo
as Madama Butterfly

Back in Italy she was at the Dal Verme as Butterfly and at Cremona Sieglinde in *Walchiria* with Cesare Formichi as Wotan. By the end of the war she had graduated to leading theatres: at Palermo during the 1919 season she sang Manon with Dino Borgioli (both were obliged to give frequent encores during the performances), Mimi in which she was complimented for her 'exceptional singing and for a stupendous dramatic interpretation and Susanna in Wolf-Ferrari's *Segreto di Susanna* with Ernesto Badini. With Badini later the same year at Pesaro she created Giovanna in Zandonai's *La Via della Finestra*; in this too she earned golden opinions. In the summer of 1920 came an invitation to South America: to Rio where as well as Butterfly she sang the Marschallin in performances of *Cavaliere della Rosa* conducted by Richard Strauss, and Buenos Aires, appearing as Thaïs, Sieglinde, Butterfly, Margherita and Manon. In Italy that year, at the Pergola, Florence, she took the title-roles in *Iris* and *Lodoletta* and at Trieste Manon opposite Lauri-Volpi. In the autumn of 1921 Toscanini introduced her at La Scala in *Mefistofele* with Merli and de Angelis, thereafter she sang Eva in *Maestri Cantori* with Merli, Journet and Pinza also conducted by Toscanini. She repeated both parts the following season and added *Manon* with Pertile and the title-role in Charpentier's *Luisa* in succession to Heldy with Pertile and Pinza. These would appear to have been her last engagements.

In a short list of recordings we hear a bright, lyrical and pure voice, the tone limpid and secure but with a typical narrow and rapid tremolo apparent throughout its range. 'Flammen, per-

donami' from Mascagni's *Lodoletta* is a touching interpretation, the phrasing delicately inflected and her singing is largely free of the coarseness and stridence of many of her colleagues.

GILDA DALLA RIZZA (1882–1975) was the archetypal verismo soprano. Though she did sing a little Wagner and some Verdi, chiefly *Traviata*, her repertory was drawn principally from contemporary works. She was a noted Octavian and was Italy's first Arabella at Genoa in 1936 and she took the role of Salud in the Scala premiere of de Falla's *La Vita Breve* during the 1933–4 season. However, her great reputation in Italy and South America was earned in the operas of Mascagni, Giordano, Montemezzi, Zandonai and above all Puccini—she was his 'cara dolce Gilda'. A reference, we must presume, to her disposition, for certainly her voice, an agitating and shrill soprano, was anything but sweet. Lauri-Volpi's description of it is confirmed in almost all of her recordings:

> The voice, characterised by guttural and nasal inflexions, imperfect technically, responded to the demands made of it by the actress, who employed it rather to express the emotions than for purely musical effects.[12]

She studied at Bologna with Ricci, and later with Orefice, and made her debut there in 1912 as Charlotte in *Werther*. Within a year we find her name prominently placed on the cartello of the Costanzi, Rome, where she appeared in two novelties: Tommasini's *Uguale Fortuna* and Guasco's *Leggenda delle sette torri*, as well as the title-roles of Mascagni's *Isabeau* and Puccini's *Fanciulla del West*. Throughout her career she remained a great favourite in Rome, subsequently singing Margherita and Elena in *Mefistofele*, Giulietta in

57 Gilda dalla Rizza in the title-role of Zandonai's
Francesca da Rimini

Aires; she was to return eight times during the next eighteen years. Here she expanded her repertory with Maddalena in *Andrea Chénier*, Stefania in Giordano's *Siberia*, Alice, Butterfly, Jaele in Pizzetti's *Debora e Jaele* and Lodoletta in Mascagni's adaptation of Ouida's *Two Little Wooden Shoes*. In the autumn of the same year came her first engagement at La Scala. After Jaroslavna in *Le Prince Igor* she was heard as Maddalena, Isabeau, Tosca, Violetta, Manon Lescaut and Louise, the last three conducted by Toscanini. The critics and public were divided in their degree of enthusiasm:

> Gilda dalla Rizza has had a moderate success with the public but superlative praise from the newspapers. In our opinion her singing lacks sincerity and conviction; but her unusual technical skill enables her to get out of her voice the maximum that it has to give. She is an artist who gives pleasure in roles in which dramatic accents and fullness of tone are not required; thus Lauretta suits her and Tosca does not. She is an intelligent and diligent interpreter, and her voice has a wide extension and she sings in tune. However [she] never completely conquers the audience. We believe that this is due to her indistinct pronunciation and the throaty tones which she probably affects to enrich the colour of her voice.[13]

In the summer of 1920 she visited Covent Garden to take part in what amounted to a Puccini festival. After creating Lauretta and Suor Angelica in the local premiere of the *Trittico*, she sang Mimi, Tosca, Manon Lescaut and Butterfly. In the last part . . .

> Her girlish presence and dainty treatment of the character evidently caught the fancy of the audience. It is something to get a Butterfly who can carry the name without obvious absurdity, but Madame Butterfly must not be a vocal butterfly. Mlle dalla Rizza hovers over her notes, sways from one side to the other, never remains securely poised. By the end of the second act one began to long for a phrase of clean, true and unemotional singing.[14]

Zandonai's *Giulietta e Romeo* and in the same composer's *Francesca da Rimini*, both with Miguel Fleta, Octavian to Carmen Melis's Marschallin, Mariella in Mascagni's *Piccolo Marat*, Magda in *La Rondine* (which part she had created at Monte Carlo in 1917) and Lauretta in *Gianni Schicchi* and Suor Angelica in the first Italian performance of the *Trittico*. During 1913 she was a guest at Turin in *Traviata* with de Luca, and she also sang in Manon Lescaut and Catalani's *La Falce*. During the summer of 1915 she made her first visit to the Colon, Buenos

At Monte Carlo she was a big star singing every season from 1917 to 1939. Her final appearance was as Suor Angelica in a special commemorative performance at Vicenza in 1942. In her retirement she lived in Venice and taught at the Conservatoire Benedetto Marcello.

Her records are not attractive. The voice production is vibratory and rough, and not secure on the breath. There is an edge on it that would have given it presence in a big auditorium. Her enunciation, like Muzio's, is affected, and often unclear, for which she was much criticised. She has a way of mouthing the words and so compromising the purity of the vowels; the habit grew over the years. The consonants too are hard and obtrusive, especially the rolled *r*s, and in the middle range keep getting caught in the tone, with the result that even in her earliest recordings the voice already sounds dry and too mature. She was Toscanini's favourite Violetta and sang the part (very much) under his baton on several occasions at La Scala. It is no accident that her recording of this music, like Albanese's, is something of a frog-march and utterly charmless. Almost all the traditional interpretative devices have been suppressed: there is hardly any portamento, little rubato, she misinterprets the marcato markings, as for example on the word 'misterioso', so they come out as if they were staccato, and of her florid singing it would be polite to say as little as possible. She is on surer ground with Maddalena's 'La mamma morta' and in the rather slow and deliberate delivery establishes that it is a racconto, but the voice is without the colour or warmth to give a proper expansion to the climax, where she snips out a few of the high notes so as to make the going easier before the top B. 'In quelle trine morbide' and 'Vissi d'arte' are given a straightforward treatment and, within the limits of her technique, managed well enough; but there is no real differentiation between them. Her reputation is more easily explained in Isabeau's 'Questo mio bianco manto', where her agitating and intense style are appropriate. In a complete *Fedora* made in 1931, when she was not yet forty, she sounds as if she were sixty. The exaggeratedly consonantal delivery has made the voice cracked and old before its time. The general outlines of the role she communicates with fervour but there must have been something in her stage presence which compensated for the lack of any individual character in her interpretations or imaginative detail in the musicianship.

18. Galli-Curci and the 'Coloraturas'

In the whole course of our survey it would be hard to find a singer with a more phenomenal career than that of AMELITA GALLI-CURCI (1882–1963). It began inconsequentially in the Italian provinces at Trani in 1906 when she took the role of Gilda in *Rigoletto*. For a decade thereafter she busied herself in the old-fashioned repertory as Gilda, Violetta,

Rosina, Lucia, Elvira in *I Puritani*, Amina, Linda, Dinorah and the Queen in *Ugonotti*, at first in the Italian provinces, with various touring companies in Egypt, Spain, Russia, South America, and eventually at the Dal Verme, Milan, the San Carlo, Naples, and the Costanzi, Rome. During those years, wherever she went, although she was no conventional beauty, her engaging vocal manners, grace, and her acting with 'a certain infantile ingenuousness'[1]

58 Amelita Galli-Curci as Gilda

brought her generally complimentary notices and enthusiastic audiences. But with a repertory mostly over fifty years old, it was not surprising that she was unable to sweep all before her as Patti had. A whole procession of Gildas, Lucias and Violettas had passed by, a public weaned on verismo wanted to hear them only if they were charged with something of the quality of contemporary music. For this, however, Galli-Curci had neither sufficient voice nor temperament and she was unable to vie with Storchio, or even Finzi-Magrini. The critic of *Orfeo*, commenting on her first engagement at the San Carlo, Naples, in 1911 as Amina, gives us a good idea of the impression she made during her early career:

> The protagonist has a delicate, pleasing voice; well-schooled in florid music and extending to the almost flute like notes of E and F in alt. Applauded after her first entrance aria, after the duets, the ensembles and the rondo finale, Signora Galli-Curci pleased equally in the tenderness and carefully considered sentiment with which she imbued Amina's moving melodies.[2]

No doubt had she remained in Italy, her days of relative obscurity would have been numbered; a voice of such fine quality could not fail to be properly appreciated in any country, and yet it is unlikely that she would ever have created the furore in Italy that she did in the United States. The Italian public was infatuated with the melodramas of Mascagni, Leoncavallo, Puccini, Cilea and Zandonai in which it preferred to find its heroines.

It was in the middle of the First World War that Galli-Curci found herself stranded in South America: after the sinking of the *Lusitania*, with the high seas full of German U-boats, there was a considerable risk involved in trying to get back to Europe. Instead she determined to make an exploratory trip northwards, to the United States. Circumstances were propitious, though not at first. In New York it appears that she gave an audition for Gatti-Casazza 'but her inclination to sing flat was uncommonly evident'[3] and she did not secure an engagement; in any case, with Hempel and Barrientos firmly ensconced, there was no room for her. She travelled on to Chicago and sang for Campanini. Although not greatly impressed, he offered her two trial performances: one Gilda and one Lucia. If these were successful, he promised, more would surely follow. It was only at the dress rehearsal of *Rigoletto* that he realised what had so providentially fallen into his lap; after 'Caro nome' and without waiting for

public confirmation, he went back-stage and booked her for the rest of the season, upping her salary from $500 to $1000 for each appearance. At the performance, as Edward Moore remembers:

> We who went to the Auditorium that Saturday afternoon, were in an entirely calm, unhopeful mood, expecting to hear just another performance of *Rigoletto*. For one scene and ten or fifteen minutes of the next, that was all it was . . . [Then] a figure appeared from the door into the garden on the left hand side of the stage, an oval, mediaeval face with large nose and an ivory pallor, a gracious winsome manner, a throat out of which poured the most entrancing tones the generation had ever heard. The audience promptly rose; it shouted, screamed, stamped, stood on its figurative head, and otherwise demeaned itself as no staid, sophisticated Saturday afternoon audience ever did before or since. Galli-Curci was made not only for Chicago but for the United States . . . This is the magic that happens occasionally in music and, when it happens, compensates for a lot of boredom. You cannot explain it. It just happens. Some of the best trained, best equipped, most intelligent musicians never find it, in fact, most of them never do. The technique of musicianship has little or nothing to do with it.[4]

Thereafter throughout her great years Galli-Curci's career was almost entirely in America; she did not sing in opera outside the United States and made only concert appearances in England and Japan. As her manager Charles Wagner tells us, following her success no time was lost in planning 'a campaign of exploitation'.[5]

> We had at least one condition greatly in our favour. The public just about to plunge deeply into a frightening and horrible war, was in the mood for a new thrill that would give them pleasure and take their minds from this tragic prospect for a few hours. Galli-Curci could supply that needed relief . . . I felt confidence from the start and my press work in her campaign rang the bell consistently. Dressing her in old-fashioned gowns added considerably to her early popularity. The Mona Lisa story was well timed—appearing just when the famous masterpiece had been stolen and was on all the front pages. Then, when a dear old lady in Columbus, Ohio, who had heard Jenny Lind, told me how much Galli-Curci reminded her of the 'Swedish Nightingale', I was inspired to give out the story of that celebrated singer of the past century. Papers were delighted to print it and the public gobbled it up . . . These were only initial efforts. I knew my limitations, and after the

preliminary releases Madame had to float herself on her ability as a songbird. And she delivered in grand style.[6]

Galli-Curci's great international reputation was entirely the result of her gramophone recordings, which followed inevitably from her Chicago triumph. Until then no other soprano, even Michailova, Huguet and Gluck, for example, who had all made highly successful recordings, had established her name so completely throughout the opera-going world. Hers was a supremely phonogenic voice, small, but with 'that delicately lovely, that cream velvet, that entrancing quality'. It had none of the powerful brilliance that made the voices of Melba and Sembrich so difficult to contain on wax, and unlike Tetrazzini the registers were evenly blended. They were not, however, fully equalised, for the chest register was comparatively backward and sat less securely on the breath, which became increasingly evident with the passage of time. She not only made records, she broke them too: 'Una voce poco fà' was an all time best-seller. Listening to it today, it is easy to hear why: the tone is soft and mellow, the voice delightfully fresh. One critic noted, 'she is no paragon of technical perfection',[7] but her spontaneously charming and tasteful manner, the delicate staccati and a beautifully controlled sforzando and morendo on the high C make the whole effect entrancing. By all accounts Rosina was her best role; it suited her personality and even when the voice had begun to fade, which it did very quickly, her interpretation never failed to delight audiences.

In Chicago she was heard as Violetta, Juliette, Dinorah, Lakmé, Linda, Mimi, Annetta in *Crispino e la Comare*, Amina, Norina, Butterfly and Manon. It was with the Chicago company that she made her first appearance in New York at the Lexington Theatre as Dinorah in January 1918; her success was complete—it was Chicago all over again. Henderson was ecstatic, a rare thing for him:

> She is an artist of brilliant abilities. Her voice is singularly smooth, deep coloured and flexible. It is a pure flute voice . . . capable of much warmth and tender expression.[8]

Thereafter came Gilda, Lucia, Rosina and Violetta, all of which were 'beautifully vocalised'[9] though dramatically her Gilda was disappointing.[10] After her last Violetta, when between seven and ten thousand people had clamoured for only two thousand five hundred seats, she received more than forty curtain calls! To get the audience home the broadest hint had to be dropped; eventually a piano was wheeled on and the diva accompanied herself in 'Home sweet home'. As in Chicago her timing was perfection:

> The town, amid war privations and alarms, has made a series of gala days over a new prima donna's appearances . . . She was well advised in choosing a forgotten *Dinorah* of Meyerbeer for her debut; in no other was there more opportunity for her wistful, winsome charm or playful acting . . . Her success has been won in all modesty, on her merits as the completest and most beautiful voice of any woman singer of the present time. Her amazing appeal to the public is based, not on 'stunts' or vocal acrobatics, but on a higher artistic conscience in all she does; on the moving and spiritual thrill of the simplest beauty; on the moral value of art unspoiled, such as hers, at the present period of a world at war.[11]

By the time she returned the following year, the war had been won and the critical euphoria subsided; as Kolodin puts it 'the marriage of opinion among press and public was greatly strained'.[12] When she reappeared as Linda 'though she sang its florid measures with ease and skill, critical ears found the voice dulled by overuse in a year of great activity, and the tendency to flat rather disconcerting'.[13] It was perhaps inevitable that her New York career thereafter, so far as the critics were concerned, was subject to diminishing returns, though she remained a popular favourite and she usually sang to full if not capacity houses. In 1920 as Amina she was considered 'not close to the vocalist she had been two years before'.[14] The next year she moved to the Met and was granted the honour of opening the season, the first after Caruso's death. Henderson still found it 'one of the most beautiful voices this public ever heard'[15] and she had no difficulty making herself heard in a far larger auditorium than the Lexington. But the gilt had gone off and he went on:

> [in the first scene] . . . her singing was not that of a great operatic star. She was frequently below the pitch and some of her phrasing was not in accordance with her own former methods. In the scene with Alfredo she gave the illusion of a much flattered demi-mondaine in a fit of ill-temper. There was altogether too much staccati in both 'Ah! fors è lui' and 'Sempre libera'. But the audience regarded her efforts—quite palpable even to the strangely impulsive drawing aside of her lips—with warm applause.[16]

Aldrich wrote in a similar vein:

> [Her impersonation] has ingenious [sic] charm, a youthful freshness; it is not notable for vivid emotional power . . . her singing was generally such as to command admiration. Her coloratura has never been remarkable for brilliancy or the finest finish; nor was it last evening. She was a pleasing representative of the heroine, but not one who could be compared with some of the great singers who have been heard in the part in years gone by.[17]

At the Met her career echoed that of Chicago and the only novelty was the Queen of Shemakhan in *Le Coq d'or*. She continued to sing in opera at Chicago until 1924 when she left in a huff over being kept to the letter of her contract. The management declined to switch for opening night from *Lakmé* to *Dinorah*; by that time E natural was a chancy note and in *Dinorah* she needed to go no higher than D flat. She returned to the Met regularly each season until 1930 but usually in the same pieces and only for a limited number of performances. By the end Henderson noted 'the small volume of tone and a dispiriting want of brilliance'.[18] Her first London appearances in concert in 1924 were made too late and the Albert Hall was too large; probably no singer in recent times with so great a reputation was so disappointing.

The comparatively rapid decline in her powers, to which gramophone records testify in abundance, and in particular the frequent lapses of intonation, were subsequently ascribed to a goitre which she claimed had troubled her for more than fifteen years and led to an operation in 1935. But this cannot have been the whole story, for even in 1912 we read of her 'as being none too observant in matters of intonation'.[19] The goitre doubtless exacerbated the problem, but her method was far from correct. Hers was a natural voice, fresh and responsive in her youth but fragile and without proper support. It soon tired, the placing slipped, especially in the later part of her career the whole of the lower range sounds dropped. As Henderson and Aldrich noted, the singing lacked brilliance; the only ornaments she accomplished with real finesse were staccati. Passage work, though not aspirated, was never clear, she could not manage triplets cleanly or accurately and 'never in her life was she even within bowing distance of Tetrazzini's carefree, bewildering vocal gestures'.[20]

Galli-Curci made many lovely records. The best of them are usually those that make the least demands of her florid technique. When the going gets hard, as in Dinorah's Shadow Song and the *Mignon* Polonaise, her execution is more of a sketch than a full realisation and she not only lacks Tetrazzini's stunning brilliance but she is without her rhythmic brio. Nevertheless, the fresh, limpid tone and spontaneous delivery of the early records compensate for much. No wonder she was an international best-seller, for her records, with all their failings, come as a welcome relief to the ear after those of—for example—her German contemporaries with their eternal cautious squeezing. Tosi would doubtless have raised his eyebrows at some of her florid essays, but surely he would have forgiven much for her spontaneity—one of the great classical virtues. We, too, can be indulgent to her; is there any other famous soprano on record who so often and so obviously sings out of tune and yet does it so endearingly? She reminds us of Busoni's famous rebuke to Egon Petri, then one of his pupils, when he took him to hear Eugen d'Albert play. Every time d'Albert played a wrong note, which was rather often, for he was long past his prime, Petri made a whistling sound under his breath. He had been doing this for some time when, at the end

59 Galli-Curci as Violetta

of a piece, Busoni turned and said smilingly: 'Don't you wish you could play wrong notes like that?' The best of Galli-Curci's operatic records include the Bell Song where the bells are beautifully done and there is none of the hard-boiled manner we are familiar with from so many French sopranos; 'Charmant oiseau' from David's *La Perle du Brésil* which, though not brilliant in the way of Tetrazzini or Calvé, is sung with great charm, and Amina's 'Come per me sereno', when her voice has naturally the girlish purity which so many divas in this role, from Pasta to Callas, have had to affect. It is a pity that she spoils 'Sovra il sen' by bumping through all the semi-quavers. It should not be thought, however, that there was anything careless in her approach to recording; on the contrary, few great singers took greater pains. Many of her best records were only achieved after four or five different attempts. The famous 'Una voce poco fà', the published version, is in fact the eighth take. She was equally thorough in rehearsal, as Marguerite d'Alvarez recalls:

> I was amazed to hear Madame Galli-Curci repeating a phrase ten times to make it perfect: I stood outside her suite in admiration of her tenacity.[21]

She told Carl van Vechten she knew that she sang out of tune but assured him that it was beyond her powers to correct it. As a recital artist she was not notably subtle, and in many of the songs she recorded her singing is rather bland, but when a lovely vocal quality is of the first importance, as in Massenet's 'Crépuscule' she makes a bewitching effect.

Like Frieda Hempel, the Spanish soprano MARIA BARRIENTOS (1883–1946), though she made her name as a 'coloratura', redeemed herself in the eyes of contemporary critics who had come to frown upon the trivialities of Rossini, Bellini and Donizetti, by going on to gain a great reputation as a singer of songs, from *arie antiche* to the works of her compatriots Granados, de Falla and Nin.

> The *Revue Musicale* has a ruling to dedicate its concert criticism to musical works rather than performers: we are compelled to depart from this ruling thanks to the exceptional quality of the performers and the riches of the programmes of the concerts . . . Maria Barrientos, the undisputed star of the operatic stage, revealed the greatest gifts of the classical singer during these concerts. The fluidity of her voice, as agile as the flute or the violin that accompanies her, her marvellous accuracy of pitch, the purity of timbre in her vocalises,

60 Maria Barrientos as Linda di Chamounix

and the passion with which she sometimes colours her singing, particularly in the Catalan popular songs, makes certain naïveties in her pronunciation seem all the more trivial.[22]

Her records hardly suggest a singer with so refined and accomplished a technique. But it was enough that she had discarded the traditional drawing-room ballads and prima donna waltzes in favour of Bach, Handel, Paisiello and Mozart. As with Hempel, the critics were quite prepared to accept her at her own valuation as a mistress of the classical style—for at the time few of them had any clear idea of what that was. The mere act of associating herself with serious music made her a serious musician; if serious then must she not also be good? Good she was, but not exceptional; as the New York critics were sharper in noting, her singing lacked the finish necessary in classical music. Paradoxically, there is a finer musicianship in Patti's recording of 'Kathleen Mavourneen', Melba's 'Songs my mother taught me', Tetrazzini's 'Aprile' or Sembrich's 'Lass with a delicate air'—more of the classical virtues too—than is displayed in any of Barrientos's records.

She gained admission to the Barcelona Conservatory at the remarkable age of six, in order to study the 'cello. It was not until she was fifteen years old and her voice had developed that she commenced her vocal studies under Francesco Bonet. Within a year she made her debut at the Teatro Novedades as Inez in *Africana*. During the next few years she travelled to Italy to sing at the Costanzi, Rome, and at the Lirico, Milan, where her Lakmé was much admired. In 1903 she appeared at Covent Garden, succeeding Erika Wedekind as Rosina with Pini-Corsi, Bonci and Ruffo. The following year at La Scala she sang Dinorah and Rosina, but the biggest impression she made was on the young intendant Giulio Gatti-Casazza. He proposed and she accepted; but when her fancy turned elsewhere, she jilted him. It was not surprising that her contract was not renewed. She married soon after, and for some years contented herself with playing the role of wife. In the summer of 1911 she returned to the stage at the Colon, Buenos Aires. She sang there in five seasons in the course of the next decade and was a great favourite as Gilda, Lucia, Amina, Rosina, Elvira in *Puritani*, Violetta, Leïla in *Pescatori di perle*, Lakmé, Ophélie, Adina, Dinorah and the Queen in *Ugonotti*, in company with many of the greatest singers of her day: Anselmi, Bonci, Constantino, Caruso, Borgioli, Martinelli, Schipa, Ruffo, Stracciari, Galeffi, Didur and Journet.

In 1912 she returned to Italy to sing Lucia at the Costanzi and was praised for 'insinuating a new emotional force, even into the fioritura, which deeply moves us'. In the same year she travelled to Budapest to take the part of Gilda opposite Baklanov's Rigoletto and was active in the concert hall at Deauville, Nice and Ostend. The following year at the Théâtre des Champs Elysées she was heard as Rosina and Lucia and by her skill reminded the critics of years gone by, when such vocal art was in less short supply. In the course of a journey to Alicante with members of her own touring company the boat was shipwrecked off the coast of Ibiza. They were rescued by the local inhabitants but, since the island had no telegraph, had to wait more than four days before a passing ship heeded their distress signals. She reappeared in Spain regularly throughout her career. In 1914 she provided funds for a singing prize in her name at Barcelona. The first winner was the tenor Antonio Cortis. The same year she sang as soloist with the Orfeo Catalá in London:

> . . . the choir had the great advantage of the assistance of Signora Maria Barrientos, a coloratura soprano of conspicuous ability. Although not always precisely in tune, her execution and control were remarkable. She could apparently do what she liked with the high D.[23]

She was engaged at the Metropolitan for the 1915 season. By that time Gatti and she were good friends, doubtless after seven years of marriage to Alda he was able to look back on his brief courtship of Barrientos with some affection. Alda was less charitable:

> She was not at all pretty and made tremendous grimaces as she sang; but she was a very chic little person.[24]

She remained there through five seasons sharing the lyric coloratura repertory with Hempel. Her debut was as Lucia, when Aldrich gives us the most complete critical examination of her art:

> It is a voice of light and fine spun texture and great delicacy; it showed little power. The quality is agreeable, frequently very charming, although it is not always, especially in the higher tones, of the finest purity and smoothness. Mme Barrientos has . . . a free and spontaneous utterance in coloratura. This coloratura was sometimes not of the highest finish. There was occasionally a lack of pure legato in passages where pure legato is indispensable. Her staccati were marked by much precision. [In the Mad Scene] she made no attempt to gain dramatically incisive power, but sought her effects in a subtler way by extreme delicacy and a fine chiselling of phrase, matching her pose and gesture. Her highest tones sung pianissimo, had an exquisite quality. One of her most noteworthy accomplishments is . . . the 'messa di voce', which used as she used it, is of striking effect.[25]

Her New York repertory included Rosina, Amina, Gilda, Lakmé, Lady Harriet, the Queen of Shemakhan in Rimsky-Korsakov's *Le Coq d'or* and the title-role in Gounod's *Mireille*, in which she left 'an agreeable impression within a limited dynamic range'.[26] From the time of Galli-Curci's New York debut the position of Hempel and Barrientos became increasingly difficult; the former was having

61 Graziella Pareto as Ophélie in *Hamlet*

The voice on records is pure even if the timbre is rather thin and hard, especially when she attempts to impose any dramatic accents. Her singing has an easy alacrity but, as Aldrich noted, it is not always of the highest finish, particularly in more difficult passages. Her account of Elvira's Polonaise from *Puritani* is proficient if rather brittle, but neither here nor in the Mad Scene, where she shapes the phrases with some feeling, is there any particular character or fascination in her singing. At times the intonation is not quite precise, and the voice production slightly tight. At the end of Zerlina's 'Or son sola' from *Fra Diavolo*, where her spirited manner is more fitting, she needs a few aspirates to help her, as it were, to rough out the brilliant concluding measures 'Al suon del tambourin'. In general her peculiarly Spanish style did not translate easily; in Caballero's 'El cabo primero', a typical Zarzuela number, we find a warmth and affecting quality in the lower range, a variety of nuance, swelling and diminishing of tones, which amply compensate for the occasional shrillness in moments of intensity when she is inclined to pin the voice too ruthlessly against the hard palate.

The second of this group of Spanish sopranos GRAZIELLA PARETO (1889–1975), like Barrientos, was from Barcelona. She took her first singing lessons there before proceeding to Milan to study with Melchiorre Vidal, one of the greatest teachers of the day, whose pupils included Gayarré, Valero, Vignas and Storchio. Like Barrientos too, Pareto was still very young when she made her debut as Micaëla at the Liceo in 1906. During the next two years she sang Amina, Gilda, Lucia and Ophélie at various theatres in Spain and Italy. It was as Ophélie that she made her first appearance in Rome in 1909 opposite the Hamlet of Titta Ruffo. She sang it with him again shortly after at the Colon, in the same season when she was heard as Gilda, and, with Bonci, as Adina and Rosina. She returned for further performances the following summer. In 1911 she married the composer Gabriele Sibella, after which she sang Rosina at the Costanzi; over this there was a division of opinion. According to *Orfeo*:

[She] sang with delicate voice and admirable art, reaping unanimous warm applause.[28]

Musica, however, was less enthusiastic. . .

[She] did her best in the difficult role of Rosina; her voice is inadequate in the lower and medium registers, but takes the high notes with ease, and is of excellent

trouble with her high notes and the latter lacked the voice with which to compete. Wisely they both withdrew and it was perhaps no coincidence that they chose that time to move their careers away from the operatic stage to the recital room. Barrientos settled in Paris where, as we have already noted, her art was ecstatically praised. The passage from *Revue Musicale* quoted above refers to a series of concerts in which she appeared at the Théâtre des Champs Elysées in 1922, organised by Wanda Landowska; the programmes included modern and classical works and Barrientos was supported by flute and violin as well as the harpsichord. A couple of years later in a recital of Spanish music she would appear to have quite overshadowed her accompanist, the composer Nin, but then, as Marc Pincherle put it, 'who would not think it a glory to be overshadowed by Mme Barrientos'.[27] Occasionally she returned to the stage; in 1924, in the intimate circumstances of the Monte Carlo Opera, she sang Baucis in Gounod's *Philémon et Baucis*.

timbre and audacious in the florid passages. Her acting was nearly always too ingenuous and occasionally even awkward and cold.[29]

At Trieste in 1913 when she sang Gilda and Juliette, though she was praised for 'a first class voice, superbly trained and which she uses with mastery', it was thought 'too slender, and more suitable for the concert hall than the stage'.[30] In the same season she was heard in Stockholm, Budapest, Kiev and at the Théâtre des Champs Elysées as Lucia. During the war years she busied herself in Italy and Spain as Rosina, Amina, Lakmé, Gilda which she sang at La Scala in company with Lázaro and Galeffi, and Violetta at the San Carlo 'singing with passion, grace and elegance'.[31] At Monte Carlo in 1915 she was Nedda and Lucia with Caruso, the following season Carolina in a revival of *Matrimonio Segreto* and Amina and Mimi and in 1918 Rosina in Paisiello's *Barbiere di Siviglia* and Gilda and Violetta with Battistini. At Covent Garden in 1920 her reception was mixed. Many agreed with Beecham, who conducted her appearances in *Les Pêcheurs de perles*, that she was 'one of the most accomplished [singers] of our age'.[32] The *Daily Telegraph* wrote of the 'singularly clear, delicate and appealing quality'[33] of her voice. For *The Times* on the other hand she was a 'disappointment'.

> Her light voice, easily obscured by the orchestra except on the highest notes, and with only a very moderate command of technical agility, is not the right kind at all. She created little impression except among that part of the audience which is always ready to cheer for the top note.[34]

As Norina, the same critic found her 'graceful. . .but without character'. Only over her *Traviata* was there a consensus:

> Pareto played and sang Violetta. She sang with her face and hands and acted with her voice; and it is the power of doing this that can cheat us into the belief that opera is a higher form of art than either the stage or the symphony.[35]

She was at Monte Carlo again in 1921 with McCormack in *Barbiere di Siviglia* and Smirnov in *Rigoletto*. Afterwards she travelled west to make her U.S. debut at Ravinia Park, Chicago, where her roles included Susanna in Wolf-Ferrari's *Segreto di Susanna*, Lady Harriet in *Marta*, Violetta and Lucia. Her first appearance at the Auditorium Theatre was as Amina with Tito Schipa in January 1924.

At the time the Chicago company was on the look-out for a replacement for Galli-Curci and Pareto stayed two seasons; she was Rosina with Schipa, Rimini and Chaliapin, Lakmé, Lady Harriet and Violetta. In 1925 in Europe again she returned to the Liceo, Barcelona, and in the winter to London for a concert at the Albert Hall. In 1926, after an absence of sixteen years she was re-engaged at the Colon. Following her second marriage the same year she sang only infrequently. Of her later performances the most important were as Carolina at the 1931 Salzburg Festival.

On records Pareto's voice seems rather small but it is of great sweetness and sympathetic character. The registers are evenly blended through a wide range to the high F, though the highest notes are rather hard and piercing. 'Sovra il sen' is quite as fresh and virginal sounding as Galli-Curci's version, and she manages the elaborate semiquaver passages more smoothly even if they are not clearly defined. Here, as in most of her florid singing, the manner is somewhat tentative and lacking in brilliance. 'Ah! non giunge', appropriately, awakens in her some rhythmic energy and the voice climbs easily to the F at the end. In both these pieces her ornaments are largely unfamiliar yet stylish. Occasionally at the top of the stave, her intonation is not quite perfect, which is apparent too in some staccato passages in a subdued rendering of 'Caro nome'. It will appeal to those who suppose that a piece written in a brilliant style does not require brilliance, and that Gilda ought really to sound as if she were singing to herself. Later recordings include the duet 'Dite alla giovane' with Matteo Dragoni, who makes a decent Germont. Here her voice seems to have matured and there is a greater depth of feeling and warmth of tone but without any loss of purity. Her phrasing is graceful and tender, and though not memorable explains why she was so highly regarded as Violetta. Norina's 'Quel guardo' ranks with Bori's and is one of the best interpretations of this music on record; she sings with charm and takes what little coloratura there is easily in her stride. Of her song recordings, 'O Bimba bimbetta' by Sibella is enchanting.

It is the fate of the last of this trio of Spanish coloraturas, ELVIRA DE HIDALGO (1888–1980), to be best remembered as the teacher of Maria Callas. In fact, de Hidalgo enjoyed a considerable career in Spain, Italy, South America and even journeyed to London and New York. She too was a pupil of Vidal, and like Pareto and Barrientos—it seems to have been characteristic of many Spanish sopranos of this period—made a precocious debut: at the age of sixteen in 1908 as Rosina at the San Carlo. She was an instant success. Word quickly reached the ears of Raoul Gunsbourg at Monte Carlo, who lost no time in engaging her to replace Kurz in one of his gala performances of *Barbiere di Siviglia*, at the Théâtre Sarah Bernhardt in Paris. At such an age, in company with Smirnov, Ancona, Pini-Corsi and Chaliapin, hers was an extraordinary triumph. She repeated the role at Monte Carlo the following year and again in 1911 and 1912. During those seasons she was also heard as Linda, Amina and in Nerini's *L'Epreuve dernière*. After engagements in Prague, and Cairo, Gatti brought her to the Met. There he hoped to use her as bait to lure back some of the customers he had lost to the Manhattan since Tetrazzini's debut, but it was a vain hope. He was no more successful with de Hidalgo than Conried had been with Ellen Beach Yaw two years previously. Her youth and charm were much appreciated but as Henderson remarked acidly 'old frequenters of the Met (do not consider) the institution a nursery for little girls'.[36] She sang two Rosinas, one Amina and then returned whence she had come. The following season she was at Loreto in company with Bonci as Adina in *Elisir d'Amore*, and at the Pergola in Florence as Linda and a 'delicious' Zerlina to the Don of Battistini. In 1911 at the Costanzi, Rome, she repeated her Rosina with Carpi, Ruffo and de Angelis. *Orfeo* wrote:

> La de Hidalgo was deservedly applauded for her skill in picchettati and flautati, although her voice is neither secure nor pure in the high notes.[37]

Her La Scala debut in 1916 was also as Rosina in the centenary production with Stracciari and Pini-Corsi. This was her only role at La Scala. She sang it there again in 1921. In Rome in 1915 she was a member of the company at the Teatro Quirino under the direction of Mascagni; her roles included Philine to the Mignon of Besanzoni and Dinorah with Battistini. In the course of the next decade she travelled throughout Italy; Genoa, Pistoia, Bari and Verona, in *Barbiere*, *La Figlia del Reggimento*, *Lakmé*, *La Figlia di Madame Angot* and *Lucia di Lammermoor*. In 1922 she sang Gilda, Violetta and Rosina at the Colon, Buenos Aires, in the latter with Montesanto and Lauri-Volpi, who was making one of his rare appearances as Almaviva. In January 1924 she was a guest artist with the British National Opera Company at Covent Garden in *Rigoletto*, performances given in Italian as a curtain

raiser to the return of Grand Opera that summer. At the end of the year she went again to New York for one Gilda and one Rosina and returned the following season for a solitary Lucia. In Chicago she sang one Lakmé, and two Rosinas in 1924. Though her greater experience was noted, so too was the loss in vocal quality. In Europe her career continued well into the 1930s, at Helsinki, Corfu and Athens. Eventually after her retirement she joined the staff at the Athens Conservatory, moving on to Ankara after the war where one of her pupils was the Turkish soprano Leyla Gencer.

In her operatic recordings, the *Mireille* Valse (sung in Italian), for example, she reminds us of her countrywoman Maria Galvany. Though she can hardly rival the latter's astounding facility in staccato, the tone is pinched against the hard palate to much the same disagreeable effect. It is an

62 Elvira de Hidalgo as Rosina

uningratiating performance, by no means accurately sung, and without any character. In Spanish music, in Zarzuelas, where something quite different is demanded and she is in her element, she changes into a vivid and infectious personality singing with great gusto and wit. The voice is not of top quality and in the Spanish way there are plenty of aspirates, but the Cancion Española from *El Principe Carneval* is a captivating record. What sounds like part of the chorus from the local theatre has been brought round to join in the reprise; after some preliminary 'Olés' and a couple of 'ahems' (in Spanish) from de Hidalgo calling everyone to order, they're off! It may be that everything was more carefully rehearsed than it seems, but in any case the effect is quite irresistible.

19. Bori

Unlike her countrywomen, LUCREZIA BORI (1887–1960) was a lyric soprano and her career was not associated with brilliant music. Although in her early years she was a notable Violetta, her effects were expressed through beauty of tone, a suave vocal style and affecting delivery. As W. J. Henderson put it: 'Verdi's florid expression of Violetta's desire to keep free from the shackles of love was beyond her'.[1] She once tried Gilda but the part was too high. At the other end of her range she sang Margherita in *Mefistofele* and the title-role in Mascagni's *Iris* but though, particularly in the latter, 'she disclosed unexpected power in the enactment of tragedy,'[2] both roles were uncomfortable for the voice and were in part instrumental in bringing about a vocal crisis which obliged her to retire from the stage for six years, during two of which she did not even raise her voice above a whisper. Her restraint was rewarded for she was able to return to the stage in 1920 the instrument, as records attest, unaffected.

Lucrezia Bori was the *nome d'arte* of Lucrezia Borja and she was in fact descended from one of the branches of the family of Alessandro, Cesare and the other Lucrezia. She was born in Valencia and at the age of six, so it is said, she could sing Arditi's 'Il Bacio'. After some tuition at the Valencia Conservatory, she travelled with her father to Milan and there became a pupil of Vidal. Her debut took place at the Teatro Adriano, Rome, in 1908 as Micaela. In the course of the next two seasons, in the Italian provinces, she sang Nedda, Mimi, Violetta, Manon and Butterfly, on one of these occasions in a

company that included the Portuguese bass Andrès de Segurola. He remembered her lovely voice and engaging personality, so that when the Met came to Paris for a season at the Théâtre du Châtelet in 1910 and Lina Cavalieri failed to appear for two performances of *Manon Lescaut*, he persuaded Gatti to take the unknown Spanish soprano instead. Bori had the Parisian public at her feet and the loss of the beauteous and bejewelled Cavalieri passed unlamented. Gatti lost no time in booking her for New York but he had to wait until after her debut at La Scala. This took place in January 1911 as Carolina in Cimarosa's *Matrimonio Segreto*; Richard Strauss was present on the occasion and urged the management to give her the role of Octavian in the first Milan performances of *Cavaliere della Rosa* which took place soon after. Since the part lay uncomfortably in Bori's voice he even agreed to make some alterations to suit her. Later she sang Juliette in Gounod's *Romeo e Giulietta* with Sobinov.

After some appearances at the San Carlo, Naples, where she was admired in the title-role of *Madama Butterfly*, she made the first of three visits to South America in the summer of 1911 during which she sang Carolina, Mimi, Butterfly, Manon Lescaut, Margherita in *Mefistofele*, Manon, Gilda, Norina, Nannetta, Juliette, the Goosegirl in Humperdinck's *Figli di Re*, Zerlina in *Don Giovanni* and Alma in Lopez Buchardo's *Il Sogno d'Alma*. At La Scala that autumn she repeated Carolina and was heard as the Goosegirl and Frau Fluth in Nicolai's *Vispe comari di Windsor*. Her debut at the Met took place on the opening night of the 1912 season, in the title-role of *Manon Lescaut*. It had not been planned that way, but when Hempel fell ill and there was no one available to replace her as the Queen in *Ugonotti*, Gatti switched operas. At first, understandably, Bori was nervous and the voice did not ride the clamourous orchestra under Polacco's direction, but as the evening went on;

> She surprised the audience, critical and uncritical alike, by the real fineness of her vocal art—by an exquisite exhibition of legato singing, by exquisite diction, impeccable intonation and moving pathos.[3]

It was the beginning of a love affair with New York audiences that was to last, notwithstanding the enforced separation of six years, until her farewell in 1936. Her other roles that first season included Nedda, Antonia in *Les Contes d'Hoffmann*, Mimi and Norina; it was in the last that she delighted most. It was, wrote Henderson, an impersonation that had 'brilliance of style . . . understanding . . . and communicative temperament'.[4] In the autumn of 1913 she was chosen to take part in the Verdi centenary celebrations at Busseto, where she sang Violetta with Garbin and Amato, and Nannetta in *Falstaff*; she took the latter part again, also under Toscanini, at La Scala. In New York the next season she expanded her repertory with Lucinda in Wolf-Ferrari's *L'Amore medico*, Fiora in *L'Amore dei tre Re* in which 'her voice has never sounded more beautiful',[5] Micaëla, Ah-Yoe in Leoni's gruesome *L'Oracolo* and the title-role in *Iris*.

At the end of the 1915 season she underwent an operation for the removal of a nodule from her vocal cords. It was not until 1919 that she recovered her voice and was able to sing in public again. In her own words 'all of a sudden, there it was'.[6] Wisely she chose to make her return to the stage in the small auditorium of the Monte Carlo Opera, as Zerlina in *Don Giovanni*. She made her New York rentrée at the Metropolitan in 1921 as Mimi. The occasion was a highly charged one for singer and audience alike; everyone wished her well but there was consider-

able apprehension. In the event, a completely genuine success made hers the most triumphant comeback since Jenny Lind's return to the stage after a long retirement caused by premature wear of the voice. Lind had been saved by Garcia, but Bori won her way back by good medical advice and her own common sense.

> Now, Miss Bori's voice was never one of the great voices that have been heard on the stage of the Metropolitan. It was agreeable, expressive, admirably used—the vehicle of some really artistic singing; and it once more has all these qualities . . . Within her range, which is not, naturally, one of the widest, she was, and will unquestionably continue to be, one of the most delightful and artistic members of the company.[7]

The second part of her career was spent almost entirely in the United States, chiefly at the Metropolitan but with occasional excursions out of town, notably to Ravinia Park, Chicago, where she sang for several years. To her earlier repertory, in the course of the next fifteen years she also added the title-role of Wolf-Ferrari's *Segreto di Susanna*, in which Henderson found her voice after her rest 'more mellow, sonorous and smooth' without that 'slightly acid quality'[8] that had been noticeable previously; the title-role in Rimsky-Korsakov's *Snegourotchka*; Violetta; Manon, in which she was particularly acclaimed; Juliette, but here she could not entirely banish memories of Melba, Eames and Sembrich; Suzel in *L'Amico Fritz*; Mélisande—she was probably the first singer to attempt and succeed in a delineation that owed nothing to Garden— Mistress Ford; Giulietta in *Les Contes d'Hoffmann*; 'a beautiful, petulant and roguish'[9] Concepcion in *L'Heure espagnole*; Salud in *La Vida Breve*; an entirely winning and lovely Mignon; Magda in *La Rondine*; Despina in *Così fan tutte* and the Duchess of Towers in Deems Taylor's *Peter Ibbetson*. She was one of the most highly respected and greatly loved singers in the history of the Metropolitan Opera and in her retirement she was appointed to the Board of Directors, the first singer to be so honoured.

Her voice is an attractive, warm lyric soprano, the registers smoothly blended and the range extending to high C; occasionally a hard edge creeps into the tone in the upper range. It would be easy to ascribe this to her vocal crisis except that it is just as discernible in recordings made before this had taken place. Her singing is finely schooled and she

63 Lucrezia Bori in the title-role of Rimsky-Korsakov's *Snegourotchka*

64 Giuseppe de Luca, Lucrezia Bori, Ezio Pinza and
Giovanni Martinelli

has an excellent conception of legato, even though it is not ideally limpid. Everything she does is affecting and, within the limits set by nature on an instrument of no great size, the range and variety of colour are considerable. Her coloratura is serviceable and sufficient to grace an outstanding performance of 'Quel guardo' from *Don Pasquale*, full of wit and charm; utterly delicious is her repeated enunciation of the word 'Conosco'—a knowing Norina, indeed. Her charm is entirely spontaneous, touching everything she does but never ladled out; it is not used—as many of her colleagues in the inter-war period used it—as a ploy to try to disguise a lack of voice or insufficient technique. She sings the two arias of Suzel from *L'Amico Fritz* with a tender and expressively inflected line. Muzio made a fine recording of the first but there is a certain refinement in Bori's delivery, an elegance which is entirely her own. She makes an eloquent advocate of this music and also of the pretty aria 'O gioia o nube leggiera' from *Segreto di Susanna*, where the flute snakes round the voice—a metaphor for cigarette smoke. These contrast wonderfully with her dainty and piquant English in Thomas Moore's arrangement of the traditional air 'When love is kind'; her voice is not quite so firm and the graces not quite so neatly accomplished as they are in a version by Alma Gluck, but again Bori has the finer taste, and more imaginative musicianship. She was a good colleague and does her best to support Miguel Fleta in the famous Cherry Duet from *L'Amico Fritz*, but is altogether more courteously and lovingly treated by McCormack's Alfredo in 'Parigi, o cara'. This is a model of duet singing; the voices, perfectly balanced, complement each other in the exchanges and blend exquisitely in the concerted music.

20. Italian contraltos

The contralto GABRIELLA BESANZONI (1888–1962) followed in the grand Italian tradition of Sofia Scalchi, Giulia Ravogli and Guerrina Fabbri. Hers was a rich and dark instrument, full in the lowest register, smooth and rich in the middle and brilliant at the top, though here she had not the weight of tone suitable for some of the higher mezzo-soprano roles. Upon the completion of her studies with Alessandro Maggi and Hilde Brizzi in 1911, she made a most successful debut at Viterbo as Adalgisa.

[Hers] is a mezzo soprano with a lovely, ample, sonorous quality of perfect and secure intonation. She conquered the public with the charm of her tender, winning voice which, especially in the middle and lower range, is capable of infinitely evocative musical effects.[1]

Within a few months she had secured an engagement at the Costanzi, where she sang Afra in *La Wally*, the Musico in *Manon Lescaut* and Azucena. During the next few seasons she sang widely throughout Italy: at Trieste as Lola in *Cavalleria Rusticana*, in Genoa as Ulrica, at the Adriano, Rome, as Cieca, the same part in Turin with Mazzoleni and Stracciari, at Viareggio as Leonora in *Favorita* and at the Costanzi again in *Aida*, *Norma*, *Carmen* and *La Forza del Destino* with Battistini. In 1915 at the Teatro Quirino in Rome under Mascagni's direction she took the title-role in *Mignon*.

Her debut at the Met as Amneris took place in 1919 but she remained only one season and was not a success.

With the exception of a few really impressive low notes, which are indeed baritone-like in quality, and a fairly good middle register, her high tones are shrill and inharmonious. . . [her singing was] far below the standard set by some of our American contraltos, such as Louise Homer.[2]

Later she sang Dalila, Marina in *Boris Godounov* and Preziosilla where there are hardly great opportunities for display. But when the opportunity came, as Isabella in the first Met performances of Rossini's *Italiana in Algeri*, she demonstrated that 'her skill for florid music was limited' and. . .

Neither the quality of her voice nor the dexterity of her vocal art in her solos was wholly satisfactory; yet she showed skill and humour in the comedy, even if

65 Gabriella Besanzoni

not the lightest touch, as an imperious and resourceful lady thoroughly mistress of the situation.[3]

The following season she sang in Mexico City and Havana with Caruso in *Aida* and *Samson et Dalila*. Her first visit to the Colon, Buenos Aires, was in 1918 and she returned five times until her final appearances as Carmen in 1935; she was also heard there as Dalila, Mignon, Amneris, Leonora, Santuzza, Adalgisa, Isabella and Orfeo. At La Scala in 1923 under the direction of Toscanini, she took the part of Amneris with Franci, Pertile and Pinza and succeeded Anitua as Orfeo with Alfani-Tellini and Paikin; later she sang Carmen, and Mignon in 1933. She continued to sing in Italy and abroad right through the thirties. She was a guest at the Berlin Opera, and made her farewell appearances at Caracalla during the summer of 1938.

The full splendour of her tones can be heard in any one of a small group of solo recordings. In beauty of timbre few contraltos have been her equal. She is not the most dramatic of Azucenas in 'Stride la vampa' but her slow and deliberate tempo makes its effect. She sings, for the most part, cleanly and with more freedom than we are accustomed to, and includes a passable trill. The music of Dalila suits her suave legato and stately manner and with her statuesque looks it is easy to understand why she was so successful in this role. After the Italian fashion, she is very much the femme fatale but as Carmen, in an almost complete recording, she shows that she knew how to lighten the voice and sing with some delicacy and grace. Her account of Cieca's 'Voce di donna' from *La Gioconda* is one of the finest on record and the music lies perfectly in her voice. She sings with a nicely nuanced line and then, through a beautifully graded mezza voce in 'A te questa rosario', builds to a voluptuous climax in the 'con espansione' passage.

If her voice was less remarkable than Besanzoni's, the range and variety of skills of the Mexican mezzo-soprano FANNY ANITUA (1887–1968) were by any standards remarkable. She sang Erda, the Queen in Thomas's *Amleto*, Rosina and Marina in *Boris Godounov*. She studied first in Mexico City with Leonor de Samaniego and later in Paris with Aristide Frances Chitti. Her first appearance in Italy was at the Teatro Nazionale, Rome, in 1909 as Orfeo. After only a little more than a year she was at La Scala, where she returned on a number of occasions until 1925; her debut was as Erda in *Sigfrido* with Poli-Randaccio, Borgatti and Bellantoni, conducted by Serafin. Thereafter she sang Climene in a revival of Pacini's *Saffo*, Etra in the premiere of Pizzetti's *Fedra*, Kontchakovna in *Le Prince Igor*, Azucena, Ulrica and Orfeo. From La Scala in the summer of 1911 she journeyed to South America and began a career at the Colon that lasted more than a quarter of a century. Her repertory ranged through: Azucena, Pantalis in *Mefistofele*, Olga in *Eugene Onegin*, Dalila, Brangäne, Amneris, Fricka in *Walchiria*, Etra, the Queen in *Amleto*, Dame Quickly and Rosina. Although the latter part was adapted, and transposed, by sopranos, the mezzo tradition had never been broken and Anitua followed Mantelli and Fabbri as

a noted exponent of the part and also of the title-role in *Cenerentola*. She was the Rosina in the first modern uncut performances given at Pesaro as part of the *Barbiere* centenary celebrations with Macnez, Galeffi, Kaschmann and de Angelis. The performances were repeated to great acclaim at the Argentina, Rome, the venue of the premiere, with the Pesaro cast except that Carpi replaced Macnez.

In 1920 again at Pesaro, she sang the title-role in a revival of Rossini's *Cenerentola*.

No amount of praise could do justice to the artistic merits of Fanny Anitua. A superb singing actress with perfect diction, a unique and inimitable interpreter of the Rossini repertory, she has a voice of unhampered resonance reaching to the highest notes and descending to the lowest, which sound like delicate organ pipes. Particular to her singing are the rare qualities of agility in fioriture and picchettati—qualities rare, above all, in this type of ample and robust mezzo soprano.[4]

As Fabbri had done a generation previously, Anitua made a progress through Italy in the role; she sang it at Parma, Reggio Emilia, Asti, Bologna and at the Argentina, Rome. At Turin she created the Principessa in the local premiere of Puccini's *Suor Angelica*; at Palermo she was a 'stupendous'[5] Giglietta in Mascagni's *Isabeau*, at Bologna she sang Ortrud and Emilia in *Otello*. Her Amneris was heard at the

66 Fanny Anitua

67 Luisa Bertana

singing more suavely and more artistically, but this evidence does not suggest that she was anything better than a routine artist.

Though the Argentinian mezzo soprano LUISA BERTANA (1898–1933) was not a front-ranking artist, her records show her to have been a singer of more than average competence. In her short but extremely busy career she sustained leading as well as comprimario roles during eight seasons at La Scala, where she was brought by Toscanini. She was at the Colon, Buenos Aires, every year but one from the time of her debut as Preziosilla in 1921 until her untimely death in 1933. In a dozen or so years her roles included: Theodore and Marina in *Boris Godounov*, Maddalena in *Rigoletto*, Brangäne, Meg in *Falstaff*, Rubbria in the world premiere of *Nerone*, Marta in the first production of *Khovanshchina* at La Scala, La Vierge Erigone in *Le Martyre de Saint-Sebastien* of Debussy, Geneviève, Cieca, Gutrune, Mara in *Debora e Jaele*, La Abuela in *La Vida breve*, the Musico in *Manon Lescaut*, Amneris, Madelon in *Andrea Chénier*, Azucena, Adalgisa, Afra in *La Wally*, Una madre in Pizzetti's *Fra Gherardo*, Siebel, Lola, Ortrud, La Bruja in Respighi's *La Campana sommersa*, Eboli and Beppe in *L'Amico Fritz*.

In the folk song 'Mi ranchito viejo', her voice is a colourful, rather vibratory, light-weight mezzo soprano. She sings with some character and affection.

Fenice, Venice, in company with Scampini, Boninsegna and Galeffi under Mascagni, and on a visit to Spain at the Teatro Reale, Madrid, in 1916. Her only U.S. appearances were at San Francisco in 1913 in a company organised by Leoncavallo to exhibit his operas.

Anitua sings in a complete recording of *Carmen* and Amneris in excerpts from *Aida*, otherwise the list she made is a short one and not especially characteristic, for there is no Rossini. Hers is a well-rounded mezzo voice with a wide range, but the lengths to which her repertory went have rubbed much of the bloom off it. In 'Re dell'abisso' from *Ballo in Maschera* she sounds hoarse and uses too much vibrato. Her interpretation wants authority and a sense of drama. The quality of the voice is heard to better advantage when she is not forcing it. In the Mexican song 'La Golondrina' the tone is more agreeable but the piece does not appear to awaken in her any memories, and she just plods along at the same tempo with a few regulation ritards, and scarcely any variation in the dynamic level. A short excerpt from *La Favorita* shows her

21. Lyric Tenors

Few tenors enjoy a greater reputation among collectors of old records than TITO SCHIPA (1889–1965). If we play almost any of the large number he made over a period of nearly forty years, it is easy to hear why. His was not a big, wide-ranging or beautiful voice—rather the contrary. In many roles, especially in later years, 'he only just got by',[1] as Edward Johnson put it. The skill with which he presented limited natural resources to their best advantage to give full expression to his attractive personality makes him unique. In this period he was principally an opera singer and it is as such that we shall be considering him here; later he gained an equal reputation as a singer of songs.

Schipa was from Lecce, a town in the province of Puglia, where he commenced his musical studies under Alceste Gerunda; these studies included

68 Tito Schipa

Pareto in a revival of Paisiello's *Barbiere di Siviglia*. As with de Lucia it is interesting to note that the critics of the period seem to have preferred him in the later music:

> The tenor Schipa, whom we recall as an excellent Des Grieux, did not seem up to standard either in *Rigoletto* or *Barbiere di Siviglia*. Schipa's voice is cold in quality and colourless; he belongs to the category of so-called virtuosi; he indulges in falsetto notes and interminable smorzature [dying away]; his singing is all saccharine and self-indulgences and we look in vain for severity and accuracy of execution. We point out that an abuse of a white half voice is not in the correct style of our old operas. In the time of Rossini and Verdi, the mezza voce was understood to need a certain amount of sonority.[2]

Schipa's North American career began after the war when he was engaged for the Chicago Opera in 1919. The following year, with the company on its annual visit to New York, he made his debut at the Lexington Theatre as Elvino with Galli-Curci. The critics, if not enraptured, were certainly appreciative; Henderson wrote of a voice though 'a little reedy. . . yet very pleasing in quality'.[3] His success aroused the curiosity of at least one colleague; Caruso, who almost never went to the opera when he was not singing, took his wife to hear Schipa. They sat in the back of a box, and after Schipa had finished the first bars of recitative, Caruso turned and whispered 'We go now'. 'Go?' asked his wife, 'don't you like him?' 'Oh, yes,' came the reply, 'but there's nothing to worry about!'

Throughout the 1920s Schipa was principally in the United States; at Chicago, in the summer at Ravinia Park, and on tour in various American cities. In 1927 he reappeared at the Colon, Buenos Aires, but it was not until 1929 that he sang once more in Italy. During these years his repertory included: Gérald, Almaviva, Ernesto, Alfredo, Fra Diavolo, Lionel in *Marta*, Fritz in *L'Amico Fritz*, Roméo, Edgardo, Des Grieux in *Manon*, Carlo in *Linda di Chamounix*, Elvino, Ottavio and Nemorino. It was in this last role that he eventually appeared at the Met but that was not until 1932.

Most reference books and record sleeve notes describe Schipa as a master of bel canto. Certainly his management of the voice on many of his recordings creates a beautiful effect, but if the term is not to be so debased as to have no useful currency left, then he was never, not even at the beginning of his career, a bel canto singer. Though one of the exceptions at a time when Italian singers were not

piano and composition as well as singing. In due course, with financial support from the Bishop of Lecce, he travelled to Milan and became a pupil of Emilio Piccoli. In 1910 he made a successful debut at Vercelli as Alfredo in *Traviata*. During the next three seasons he sang widely in the Italian provinces in various operas: *Zazà*, *Mefistofele*, *Adriana Lecouvreur*, *Mignon*, *Werther*, *Barbiere di Siviglia*, *Don Pasquale*, *Cavalleria Rusticana*, *Traviata* and *Rigoletto*, the last two at Messina with a young soprano whom he was later to appear with in some of the world's greatest theatres: Claudia Muzio. In 1912 he gave his first performances in Milan, at the Teatro dal Verme, as Cavaradossi and Alfredo. The following year he visited South America for the first time, singing at the Colon: Elvino, Ernesto, Alfredo and Gérald in *Lakmé* with Barrientos. His Scala debut followed in the autumn of 1915 in the unlikely role of Vladimir in *Le Prince Igor*, after which he was heard as Des Grieux in *Manon*. Two years later at Monte Carlo he created Ruggero in the world premiere of *La Rondine* opposite Gilda dalla Rizza and returned the following season to appear with noted for their fine art or irreproachable taste, nevertheless his good manners reflect the era in which he lived quite as much as do the bad ones of some of his contemporaries. Bel canto is more than merely beautiful singing, it is a language of expression with its own grammar of affecting devices. Even the art of de Lucia, Bonci and Anselmi only retained certain aspects of bel canto and those modified by the often unvocal demands of the latter-day repertory. Schipa's recordings show how there has been a subtle but decisive shift in interpretative emphasis in less than a generation; we have already had occasion to note it. His singing does not have, as theirs does in varying degrees, the poised tone informed by the breath, and an underlying tension in the legato—a musical, not muscular one. Although his manner is graceful, his singing style is virtually graceless; since there is no tension in the line, there is nothing to relieve with the devices of bel canto: gruppetti, mordents, trills and so forth. Thus, unlike the singers cited above, he virtually never sings any ornaments other than those explicitly notated, and those he rarely executes with the chiselled perfection that would have been expected not long before. To take one example: in the duet from Act One of *La Traviata*, 'Un di felice eterea, mi balenasti innante', on the last word there is a turn written in the score, A, G sharp, A, B flat, A. He manages it smoothly, but does not, like de Lucia, articulate each note with perfect clarity, and we do not quite hear the second A. It is precisely by the mastery of such detail that the bel canto style is recognisable.

Notwithstanding his artistic restraint and good taste, in the music of Rossini, Bellini and Donizetti his style was decadent, ultimately more rhetorical than musical, for it is through his pronunciation of the text rather than beauty of tone or the vocal imagination of bel canto that he charms us. There is no longer in his singing the classical balance between words and tone; the words predominate. And this was not simply because it was a small voice and the tone lacked sonority. The same could be said of his colleague Richard Tauber, but although Tauber's diction—at least in German—is of exemplary clarity, it is his musicianship and singing, even the questionable vocal mannerisms, that impress us most and are so characteristic. Despite his German origins and idiosyncratic method, Tauber retains certain practices of bel canto, in his conception of line and particularly the way he so often graces it with improvised gruppetti and mordents. Neither he nor Schipa would have been

remotely acceptable as bel canto singers at a time when everyone sang in the 'old Italian' fashion and there was no need of such a term as 'bel canto', but surprisingly there is more of the spirit of the style preserved in Tauber's singing, even in Lehár's 'Dein ist mein ganzes Herz', than in Schipa's Mozart or Scarlatti, for all his endearing qualities.

Where Schipa came into his own was in that music which during his career was then so often delivered in a crude and vehement manner, allegedly to serve realistic purposes. In Turiddu's Siciliana he shows how it is possible to convey ardour and do so without screaming. His rendering of 'Che gelida manina', which is transposed down a semi-tone, is not entirely comfortable at either end of the range, but it is fresh-sounding and romantic; the idea of Rodolfo as a poet no longer seems quite so absurd. The youthful quality is similarly affecting in Fenton's 'Dal labbro'; the recording was made soon after he took the role under Toscanini's direction at the Dal Verme, Milan. Cavaradossi's music by all accounts taxed him considerably yet he sang it, at least in his early years and in small theatres, more often than we should have expected. In both of the famous arias he is able to make a fine effect by his clearly measured and controlled enunciation. In all of these, however, the voice is sometimes a little shaky and there are occasional aspirates in the line; in the song titles, where the demands are less exacting, his musicianship as well

69 Fernando Carpi

as his singing is much more relaxed. One of the best, Richard Barthélemy's 'Pesca d'amore', displays the full range of his charm, the rhythm delicately teased and the line drawn out in a long *fil di voce*; this introduces a purely vocal dimension into his art which is not often heard elsewhere and at the end there is even a graceful turn. In the head register, pianissimo, he could focus the tone finely and move easily in a tessitura that would have been far too high for him in full voice; by so doing the voice itself acquires a sweeter quality, only the A vowel remains rather open and dry sounding. As we shall see later on, it was in the idiom of the light music of his day, particularly after the invention of the microphone and the popular Italian songs shed their operatic manners, that his art reached its highest expression. Here there was no need for the kind of vocal compromises that he was obliged to make even in his most successful operatic interpretations and he sings with a spontaneity and freedom from constraint that would have been impossible in the theatre. It is not so strange then that when Joan Crawford, for one of her films, decided to extend the range of her talents and sing them a song, she went to Schipa for lessons.

Recordings of the voice of FERNANDO CARPI (1876–1959), with its narrow and rapid tremolo, remind us more of de Lucia or Bonci and the lyric tenors of the old Italian school than Schipa and Gigli. Carpi made his debut in 1898 at Lecce, Schipa's home town, in Gounod's *Faust*. In 1906 he was engaged for the autumn season at Covent Garden, as Faust, the Duke, Cavaradossi and Alfredo with Melba and Sammarco. He returned the following summer, for Faust, Turiddu and Pinkerton, and again that autumn for performances of *Traviata*, in which he appeared opposite Tetrazzini in her memorable debut, and later with her in *Rigoletto* and *Lucia di Lammermoor*. Though he never sang at La Scala, he was regularly at the San Carlo, Naples, and in Rome where his roles included Des Grieux in *Manon*, Walther in *Maestri Cantori*, Fernando in *La Favorita* and Almaviva. At the Costanzi in 1911 in company with de Hidalgo, Ruffo, Schottler and de Angelis,

[He] sang his difficult role persuasively, with exquisite art and deep feeling. He was such a Count Almaviva as we have not heard for years. . . the beauty of the voice is equalled by the study of the character, his ability is such as to overcome with masterful ease the difficulties with which the part is strewn. He sang everything in the original key. . .[4]

At the Teatro Sao Carlos in Lisbon, as Carlo in *Linda di Chamounix* with Rosina Storchio, he made such a good impression that the King himself deigned to accompany Carpi at a private recital. In 1916, he replaced Umberto Macnez when the special centenary production of the *Barbiere di Siviglia* was brought from Pesaro to the Argentina in Rome. The revival was given in an uncut version, so it was claimed, and even included an orchestral introduction to Act Two. About this there is some mystery; apparently it was based on the melody from the last act ensemble 'Di si felice' but since all trace of it has subsequently disappeared, we do not know whether it was in fact by Rossini or run up for the occasion by the editor, Zanelli. Also included was the brilliant aria for Almaviva 'Cessa di più resistere', part of which Rossini later worked into Cenerentola's Rondo Finale.

In the autumn of the same year Carpi made his U.S. debut at the Met in *Traviata* with Hempel. In the course of three seasons he seems to have provided solid service, as Almaviva, Edgardo and Tonio in a revival of *Figlia del Reggimento* in which he was part of an 'able cast (that) gave handsome support to the brilliant vocalisation of Hempel'.[5] His New York career, however, came and went without making much effect. After his retirement in 1923 he became a teacher, first in Prague and later as far afield as Saigon.

Carpi's singing lacks individuality. Although the voice is a good one with a wide range, the quality is rather nondescript; but he is an honest musician and a singer of very real skill, whose records come as a refreshing treat after those of his colleagues who traded so shamelessly on their personality and mannerisms to disguise obvious technical shortcomings. His is not the suavest rendering of Ernesto's 'Sogno soave e casto' but it is accomplished singing; despite the tremolo and a slight touch of throatiness the tone is secure in the high-lying tessitura and he sings in the original key. He reveals a fine command of line and a long breath span which he uses to shade the voice away in some delicate and expressive morendi. In the duet 'All' idea' with Stracciari, though he has not the quicksilver brilliance of de Lucia any more than Stracciari can compare for humorous unction with Pini-Corsi, neither singer need bow anywhere else. Here, where the line is lower, there is a touch of metal in Carpi's voice and at the bottom the roulades are full, clear, and never degenerate into the kind of asthmatic suggestions we so often hear. It is an outstanding piece of duet singing; both singers perfectly in harmony, with the correct ritards yet rhythmically alert, and though Stracciari's technique is not quite as finished as Carpi's, their skill in fioritura is affecting in itself. They show how this is not a tiresome convention of Rossini's to be bungled through as best one may, but a device that when properly executed, creates a brilliant musical, and hence dramatic effect.

22. Tradition and the Italian Tenor

Far and away the most celebrated Italian tenor of this period, whose career spanned more than forty years, was BENIAMINO GIGLI (1890–1957). Others—notably Pertile, Lauri-Volpi, Martinelli Schipa—were as much admired by opera-goers and generally more respected by the critics, but the wider public which had acclaimed Caruso in his later years felt no singer could challenge Gigli's supremacy. His name was a household word even among those who had never been inside an opera house, his records were best-sellers, and his concert appearances occasions for display of the kind of extravagant rapture which was increasingly coming to be reserved for motion picture idols and crooners.

Gigli's origins, like Caruso's, were humble and he gained early musical experience in a church choir. It was at Macerata when he was still a treble that he made his first stage appearance as Angelica in Alessandro Billi's *La Fuga di Angelica*. There followed a difficult period—the only one throughout his career—when his voice broke, but after winning a prize he secured admission to the Accademia di Santa Cecilia in Rome, where he studied first under Cotogni and then Rosati. In the spring of 1913 at a pupils' concert he sang in the duet 'Sola qui resto' from Massenet's *Re di Lahore*, and 'roused the enthusiasm'[1] of the audience with the aria 'Dei canti il suon si perde' from Reyer's *Sigurd*. In the course of the next year he appeared in several private musicales and in three public concerts at the Accademia. His stage debut took place in 1914 at Rovigo in *Gioconda* with Poli-Randaccio: 'the young debutant sustained the part of Enzo marvellously, the limpid voice promising many glories to come'.[2] And they were not slow in coming; in 1916 he sang Faust in *Mefistofele* at the San Carlo, the following year at the Costanzi, Rome, and in the autumn of 1918 it was his debut role in a series of performances at La Scala under Toscanini, given soon after the death of Boito. This was indeed a swift and triumphant progress, embracing appearances at Palermo,

Bologna, Bergamo, Verona, Leghorn and other leading provincial cities in *Mefistofele, Cavalleria Rusticana, Tosca, Manon, Iris, L'Amico Fritz, Lucia di Lammermoor, La Favorita, Lodoletta, Rigoletto, La Rondine* and *Adriana Lecouvreur*.

He was greeted with the same enthusiasm on his first visit to the Colon, Buenos Aires in the summer of 1919, where he sang Cavaradossi to the Toscas of Muzio, Mazzoleni and Labia, Faust in *Mefistofele*, Enzo, Gennaro in *Lucrezia Borgia* and Rodolfo. He returned to South America the following year, appearing at the Coliseo, Buenos Aires and in Rio de Janeiro and Sao Paolo, and this time as well as *Gioconda, Tosca,* and *Bohème,* he was also heard in *Norma, Lohengrin, Loreley, Iris* and *Francesca da Rimini.* That autumn he proceeded northwards to the Metropolitan where once again his first appearance was as Faust.

> Here's an Italian tenor, by no means a beginner, but with many of the inclinations and manners of his kind, such as a persistent disposition to sing to the audience, to the neglect of Margherita or whomever else the dramatic situation requires him to address; also to cultivate the high note and make whatever there is to be made out of it in the way of applause. But he has a voice of really fine quality, which he does not force, still fresh and possessed of colour; and he sings not without finish and style. He was evidently at home in the part, and indicated assurance and experience on the stage, though his action rarely rose above the safely conventional.[3]

Gigli remained a member of the company at the Metropolitan through the next decade, expanding his repertory with the title-role in the first Met performances of *Andrea Chénier*, which had been intended for Caruso, Avito in *L'Amore dei tre Re*, Alfredo in *Traviata*, which he sang on the opening night of the first post-Caruso season with Galli-Curci, Pinkerton, Vasco in *L'Africana*, Roméo in Gounod's *Roméo et Juliette*, Lionel in *Marta*, Baldo in Ricciitelli's *I Compagnacci*, Fenton, Loris in *Fedora*, Giannetto in *La Cena delle Beffe*, Wilhelm Meister in *Mignon*, Des Grieux in *Manon Lescaut*, Don Ottavio, Nemorino and Elvino in *Sonnambula*. Although the bulk of each season was spent in New York, he travelled to the west coast and continued to sing in South America until 1928, the year in which he was heard as Riccardo in *Ballo in Maschera* for the first time. Every summer he sang in concerts in Italy and appeared at the Verona Arena in 1929 as Lionel in *Marta*.

By the end of the 1920s Gigli had established

70 Beniamino Gigli

fruits of prosperity, and ought now to shoulder a corresponding share of the burdens of deficit. Most of the artists accepted the inevitable, for they were in no position to do otherwise; opera companies elsewhere in the United States, would take their cue from the Metropolitan. The position of Gigli, however, was unique; as the Met's highest paid singer—over a period of five years his contract guaranteed him earnings in the region of a quarter of a million dollars—he could not afford the loss of face involved in accepting the proposed cut of half of it and, unlike his colleagues, since he had another string to his bow, he could afford not to accept it.

After quitting the Met he turned to the concert hall, partly in order to recoup his fortune but also because it was there that he could give fullest expression to his style; Gigli's instincts were basically those of a popular singer. In the period until the end of the war, as Caruso had demonstrated, it was still possible for an opera singer to be equally successful with popular songs and ballads; the musical idioms were similar, and no awkward vocal or stylistic adjustments were necessary to accomodate both. In the 1920s, however, the two began to grow increasingly apart. The shattering impact of jazz and the invention of the microphone led to a dramatic development of popular music, which the gramophone carried to all corners of the civilised world; meanwhile opera was becoming more 'intellectual', and modern classical music more incomprehensible to the layman. The popular songs that Gigli sang on radio, record and in recital encouraged him to adopt a vulgarity of style that corrupted all his work; critics protested when he introduced the mannerisms of his popular successes into his operatic performances. In the pursuit of realistic effects they were no more than an extension of the language of verismo, and had opera developed on similar lines there would have been no conflict. But the twenties coincided with the end of verismo and the drying up of that well of instantly appealing melody that had sustained the popularity of Italian opera for so long; after the death of Puccini, except for a gesture or two by Zandonai and Pizzetti, it was exhausted. While popular music under fresh influences gained a new dynamism, opera, or at least the repertory of the world's major opera houses, settled for retrospection and a period of revivals. During the first three or four seasons of Gigli's career something like half of the roles he sang were from works of comparatively recent origin. During his years at the Met, only five out of his twenty-eight roles were

himself unequivocally as the Met's leading tenor and, after Chaliapin and Ruffo had left, also its biggest box-office draw. His departure from the company in 1932 is not only a convenient point at which to pause and take stock of his career but appropriately it coincides with the end of a period in which opera reached its greatest popularity in the United States. This had happened in Europe in the years immediately before the First World War; afterwards economic and social changes effectively put paid to Paris and London as international opera centres. Throughout the twenties, a time of burgeoning prosperity in the United States, opera remained both a focus for social ambitions and a popular entertainment for thousands who still hankered after a taste of the culture from which they or their ancestors had sprung. In spite of the rapidly growing popularity of jazz music and moving pictures, the Met's position was unassailable until the depression. But when that came it revealed just how precarious were the theatre's finances; for all classes of patrons, opera was one of the first of their economies. The management, faced with bankruptcy, had no choice but to make drastic cuts in expenditure. What more natural than that it should turn to the artists who had enjoyed part of the modern compositions, and in rather more than half the rest his style clashed with the composer's, despite the beauty of his voice. Critics complained, conceiving it as their solemn duty to educate Gigli's taste, reflecting the German notion of high seriousness in Art. Henceforth the opera house was to become a temple of enlightenment rather than a theatre for entertainment; in such a place Gigli's shameless courting of the gallery 'like a picturesque beggar appealing for alms'⁴ was little short of blasphemy. He remained unrepentant, like all popular musicians; as an entertainer he was concerned with keeping in tune with the taste of the general public, and what the critics wrote was beside the point. Apart from questions of money, by spending less time in opera he was able to broaden the base of his activities in extensive concert tours and keep his appeal fresh and vigorous. He continued thus until he was past sixty, his voice still in good condition, and unlike most of his contemporaries, his communicative skill and popularity with audiences still as great as it ever was.

The earliest recordings he made in 1918 and 1919 give us a good idea of the effect of his singing at the time of his debut. The voice is a perfect example of a lyric tenor, the production pre-eminently smooth and steady, with no faulty or affected vibrato. The range extends to the high C and even in forte passages he gives the impression of singing well within his means. The registers are fully developed and his mastery of mezza voce is complete; this is one of the most exacting accomplishments requiring perfect breath control and usually more support than in forte singing. With Gigli, however, the voice is naturally so responsive that he seems just to let it float on the breath, giving an irresistibly lazy grace to his singing (later he abused it and it degenerated into crooning). This is especially apparent in 'Cielo e mar' and one can well believe that such a performance would arouse the enthusiasm of any audience. There are several of those mannerisms in embryo which later on were to become so tiresome: the sobbing marcato and aspirates, in some measure deliberately introduced for effect. It is a romantic piece of singing, the tone truly radiant, and he surmounts all technical obstacles with masterful ease. There is the same fine quality, and an expressive and well controlled line in Loris's 'Amor ti vieta', building up to a fine high A. One can readily hear why he liked the role of Faust in *Mefistofele*; both solos and two duets show how the music lay perfectly in his voice and he had no difficulty with the high tessitura. His

interpretation of Turiddu has always been famous and he recorded it much later on in full under the composer, but he does not make in that the same effect with 'Mamma quel vino è generoso'. Here it is both better sung, more eloquent and characterful even if the tone is unrelievedly maudlin. His partner in the Act One duet from *Bohème* is routine but Gigli's singing throughout is fresh and ardent and at the end he joins her with a fine piano high C.

HIPOLITO LAZARO'S (1887–1974) first stage appearances were in Zarzuelas but it was not long before the fine quality of his voice and his easy management of brilliant high notes brought him to the attention of the management at the Teatro Novedades in Barcelona, and in 1910 he made his debut there in the exacting role of Fernando in *La Favorita*. Soon afterwards he sang Cavaradossi at Valencia, but these experiences must have made him aware of the need for further schooling for later that year he left for Milan and a period of intensive study under Enrico Colli. His Italian debut took place at Ferrara in 1911 as the Duke in *Rigoletto*. Afterwards he travelled to England and sang in concerts in Manchester and London, for some reason under a *nome di teatro*, and made some recordings for HMV. Apparently he was displeased with the results and convinced that the company had deliberately tampered with them so that he would be no competition for their great star Caruso. In fact the records present his voice much as we hear it in later years.

His Italian career continued at Udine and Treviso in *Gioconda*, and at Genoa in Petrella's *I Promessi sposi* and Mascagni's *Isabeau*. As a result of the great success he enjoyed in the latter, in the role of Folco, he was summoned to La Scala at the end of 1913 to create Ugo in the world premiere of another work by Mascagni, *Parisina*. It marked the beginning of a close friendship between singer and composer: at Leghorn that season he sang Folco fifteen times. At the same time he remained busy in the standard repertory. In Rome he was heard as Cavaradossi, Faust and Enzo, when 'he compensated for the strain in his loud notes by his heavenly mezza voce'.⁵

Lázaro obstinately persists in a repertory unsuited to him. He has lost a great deal of those sweet sfumature [shadings], which were once all his own; the middle and lower notes are about to disappear, and the high notes, once taken so easily, are now forced.⁶

In 1915 he made the first of two visits to the Colon, Buenos Aires, extending his repertory with Ro-

71 Hipólito Lázaro in the title-role of Mascagni's *Il Piccolo Marat*

sang Turiddu, Rodolfo and Danielo in Leroux's *La Reine Fiammette* with Farrar. Henderson thought his 'one of the best voices'. In 1917 in Havana with a touring company it was the high notes again which brought audiences to their feet. In Rome in 1921 he took the title-role in another Mascagni premiere, *Il Piccolo Marat*. Thereafter he was heard in revivals of *Iris* and *Rigoletto*. Throughout the 1920s he sang regularly in Spain and with various companies in Central and South America. On these occasions, whenever he could get away with it, at the beginning of an aria he would rush to the front of the stage, and, striking an attitude, turn to the audience as if to say: 'Pay attention, now you are going to hear the greatest tenor in the world'. It was not a gesture calculated to endear him to colleagues. He sang at the Colon again in 1922 in three Mascagni operas, *Il Piccolo Marat*, *Iris* and *Isabeau*, and was also heard as Paolo in *Francesca da Rimini*, Lázaro in Breton's *La Dolores* and Nemorino in *Elisir d'Amore*. Two years later at La Scala he created Giannetto in the world premiere of Giordano's *La Cena delle beffe* in a cast of 'singing actors' that also included Carmen Melis and Benvenuto Franci. He was a guest at the Verona Arena in the summers of 1921 and 1929 and continued to appear regularly throughout the 1930s in Spain in both opera and Zarzuelas. He sang at the Liceo, Barcelona, as late as 1941 and for a short time in 1936 was the company director. His final stage performances were at the scene of some of his great triumphs, at Havana in 1950.

Lázaro's recording career lasted nearly thirty years and even at the end he could still bat out a top note to set the gallery on its ears; though they are not always a pleasure to listen to. His is a very throaty voice with a tremulous bleat and only when he steps up the breath pressure can he get the voice forward. In 'O Paradiso' and 'Bianca al par', both of which start at a low level of intensity, we have to turn up the volume level to hear clearly and then at the climax turn it down again when the disproportionately loud high notes overweight the line. Those who advised him against staking everything on brilliant high notes and a repertory essentially too dramatic for the voice were right. He did not lose his voice, but over a period of years it became increasingly thick-sounding and intractable. Thus, where the tessitura should have suited him perfectly, in Nadir's 'Mi par d'udir ancora', instead of a limpid tone, the voice moves stiffly and he can only negotiate the difficult intervals and graces with a liberal helping of aspirates. Here, as in the Duke's

dolfo, Paolo in Zandonai's *Francesca da Rimini*, Turiddu, des Grieux in *Manon* and Dick Johnson in Puccini's *Fanciulla del West*.

At the Metropolitan between 1917 and 1920, although his art had neither charm nor finesse and he lacked the personality of a great star, he was effective in roles requiring an easy execution in high tessitura and brilliant top notes. As the Duke he made a fine effect capping the Act One duet with a high D flat, and his Edgardo and Arturo, both opposite Barrientos, were 'neatly sung'. He also

'Questa o quella', though he tries to be elegant, the rough attack and his way of swerving up to high notes spoil the attempt. The opening measures of the duet 'Vieni fra queste braccie' from *Puritani* afford him opportunity for the display of his forceful D; his manner is always that of a provincial singer more anxious to show off his voice than show off the music. Recordings of pieces from those works which he either created or was closely connected with—*Isabeau*, *Il Piccolo Marat* and *La Cena delle beffe*—have some historic interest for us today.

The reputation of the Spanish tenor MIGUEL FLETA (1893–1938) rests far more on his gramophone records than on the achievements of a short career. His was a lyric tenor of fine and unusual quality and at his best his singing has a certain fascination. Ambition, however, encouraged him to undertake a repertory for which he lacked the vocal resources or technique and, as a result of a generally self-indulgent life style, after a comparatively short time his singing had become little more than a collection of mannerisms. These are present to some degree in all of his later recordings, perhaps most characteristically displayed in Freire's 'Ay, ay, ay' where he seems to be parodying himself in the preposterously drawn out and wobbly morendi.

He was a student at the Madrid Conservatory and then a pupil of Luisa Pierrich, to whom for a time he was later married. His debut took place in 1919 at the Teatro Comunale, Trieste, as Paolo in *Francesca da Rimini* of Zandonai, a composer with whose music he felt a special affinity. During the next couple of seasons he sang extensively in Spain and Italy, usually in *Aida*, *Rigoletto* or *Carmen*. In Rome in 1921 at the Costanzi, he made his first appearance in a 'shabby performance'[7] of *Aida* but his Radamès was distinguished:

> He sang with enthusiasm (a little overdone in the last act) showing a sympathetic voice, ringing and voluminous, full of colour and magnificent filatura, based on clear and impeccable diction. Fleta (a very young Spanish artist) will have a rapid and brilliant career.[8]

In the same season he also sang Don José with Besanzoni and created Romeo in Zandonai's *Giulietta e Romeo* with Gilda dalla Rizza. The following year he travelled to South America for the first time, to the Colon, Buenos Aires, returning in 1923, 1924 and 1927; his repertory included the Duke, Radamès, Cavaradossi, Don José, Paolo, Romeo, Pedro in Filiasi's *Fior di neve*, Des Grieux in Massenet's

72 Miguel Fleta as Don José

Manon, Turiddu, Alfredo, Andrea Chénier and Lohengrin. In the 1923/4 season he was brought to La Scala for some performances of *Rigoletto* and *Carmen*. As the Duke, however, his idiosyncratic way with the rhythm was clearly not to the liking of Toscanini. Nevertheless in 1926 he was chosen to create Calaf in the world premiere of Puccini's *Turandot*. In this, as Carlo Gatti records, he was impressive with his fine stage craft and the fact that the voice showed no sign of flagging in the demanding tessitura. But he never sang it again and, in the opinion of those who were also present at the Met premiere, the role better suited Lauri-Volpi. Fleta's career at the Met began in a performance of *Tosca* in the autumn of 1923. At first he seems to have been well enough liked, even though his extravagant way with 'E lucevan le stelle' failed to draw attention away from Jeritza. He went on to sing

Hoffmann, the Duke, Rodolfo, Canio, Radamès, Don José and Andrea Chénier, but the competition was too much for him. At the time the Met's roster of Italian tenors included Gigli, Martinelli and Lauri-Volpi, and Fleta left precipitately in the middle of his second season. His departure was hardly noticed, much less lamented, but the Met's lawyers gave chase and made certain that he never sang in the United States again.

In Europe, too, his difficult professional behaviour and bad living were steadily ruining his career. It was impossible to predict what he might do: at a performance of *Carmen* after he had spun out the Flower Song to great effect, in the middle of the scene a piano was trundled on and he proceeded to give an impromptu recital of popular songs. The audience was enraptured; what Carmen, the conductor or the orchestra felt is not on record. It is hardly surprising that after 1928 he appeared only in Spain and principally in Zarzuela, where no one seems to have cared much what he did. Lauri-Volpi heard him in a concert at the very end when he was still not yet forty; the voice 'faint, collapsed, a tattered remnant'.[9] It was the sad irony of Fleta's career, which eventually condemned him to poverty and an early death, that although his life was tragic, the very lack of self-discipline which killed him made it possible for him to convey genuine tragic feeling through his art.

Fleta's voice was undoubtedly a fine one but it is possible to believe that even in his earliest records it was already past its best. The characteristic and naturally affecting quality is apparent from the first bars of the Flower Song, but so too is an incipient wobble, and the voice does not move steadily on the breath; it is not possible for him to shape the phrases smoothly. The performance has vocal colour and expression and a certain intensity which would be more convincing if it were not for his habit of lingering on this or that high—not too high—note, to show off his skill in morendi. He does not succeed in making these either dramatically or musically plausible. At the end, after a nasty wrenched high B flat, there is a display of emotion of the kind calculated to wreak havoc on the susceptible emotions of provincial audiences; it cuts little ice today. By the time he made the first electrics, among them Lohengrin's Farewell to the Swan (in Salvatore Marchesi's Italian text), the rot has well and truly set in. The registers have started to separate; the opening phrases are crooned in a none-too-well supported mezza voce and when he switches into full voice the tone thickens and on almost

every note there is a pronounced and irregular wobble. As an interpretation it cannot compare to Pertile's, never mind Borgatti's; instead of a clean declamation he substitutes a tearful and exaggerated marcato and the expansive rubato makes de Lucia seem quite virtuous by comparison. In a souvenir of the Met's production of Mascagni's *L'Amico Fritz*, the Cherry Duet, he starts well—if not quite steadily—but as soon as he has to sing out, the spread tone quite obscures Lucrezia Bori's lovely singing.

At any time there are singers who, though their vocal endowment is not of the first rank, nevertheless sing better than some of their more talented colleagues. Such a one was GIULIO CRIMI (1885–1939). Born in Catania he studied there under Maestro Aderno. His debut was at Treviso in 1912 as Giuseppe in *La Wally*. In the course of the next two years he appeared at Palermo as Dick Johnson in *Fanciulla del West* and Des Grieux in *Manon Lescaut*, at the Dal Verme, Milan, as Radamès and at Bologna as Avito in the local premiere of *L'Amore dei tre Re*.

The tenor Crimi overcame all the ungrateful difficulties of the part with security and revealed praise-

73 Giulio Crimi as Vasco in *L'Africana*

worthy intentions, with regard to phrasing and accent … Nonetheless, he must correct certain incorrect emissions and avoid singing in a rather open manner, which spoils the beauty of the timbre of his robust voice.[10]

In 1914 at the Théâtre des Champs Elysées in Paris as Des Grieux, 'his superb voice created a sensation';[11] this was with Russell's company. He then proceeded to London, appearing at Covent Garden in *Manon Lescaut* and *L'Amore dei tre Re* in which he was described as a 'fervent'[12] Avito. The same season in Rome at the Costanzi, he sang Radamès in *Aida*. At the beginning of 1916 he made his debut at La Scala in a revival of Verdi's *La Battaglia di Legnano* in company with Rosa Raisa and Giuseppe Danise. He took the part again that summer on his first visit to the Colon. Thereafter he sang the title-roles in *Andrea Chénier* and Buchardo's *Huemac*, and Canio and Radamès. In the autumn he moved to Chicago, where in the course of two years he appeared in *Aida*, *Andrea Chénier*, *Cavalleria Rusticana*, *Isabeau*, *Traviata*, *La Bohème*, *Tosca*, *Francesca da Rimini*, *Lucia* and *Gioielli della Madonna*. At the Metropolitan, for four seasons until 1922, his roles included Radamès, Cavaradossi, Don José, Rodolfo, Alfredo, Manrico, Edgardo, Des Grieux in *Manon Lescaut*, Turiddu, Dufresne in *Zazà*, Canio, Pinkerton, Don Alvaro in *La Forza del Destino*, Andrea Chénier, Araquil in *La Navarraise*, and he created Rinuccio in *Gianni Schicchi* and Luigi in *Tabarro* at the world premiere of Puccini's *Trittico*. From the Met he returned to Chicago for another couple of years, and added to his previous achievements Manrico, Don Alvaro, Dick Johnson and Faust in *Mefistofele*. On his reappearances at the Colon in 1921 and 1924 his repertory included only one novelty, Walther, in Catalani's *Loreley*. He spent the last years of his career in Italy again and enjoyed a success in Rome at the Costanzi in 1924 as Vasco, in a revival of Meyerbeer's *L'Africana*. After 1926 he taught in Rome, one of his pupils being the baritone Tito Gobbi.

It is an attractive but unremarkable voice, the production smooth, and he makes an agreeable effect in duets: with Raisa in 'O terra addio' and Marguerite d'Alvarez in 'Ai nostri monti'. Caruso's influence is strong in his singing and was perhaps not altogether a happy one; Crimi has not the support to float the phrases, as Caruso does, in such full tone, with the result that the portamenti slip off the breath, and he has a habit of attacking a note a little on the flat side, which is particularly apparent

in the closing measure of *Trovatore*. His 'Spirto gentil' is a dutiful piece of singing, solidly, even stolidly, sung; but it sounds like Giordano rather than Donizetti; the music of Dufresne from *Zazà* finds a surer response stylistically.

The career of the Greek tenor ULYSSES LAPPAS (1881–1971), though not of the first class, took him to a number of the world's leading theatres. It began at Athens where he was a pupil at the Conservatory; he made his debut at the Royal Theatre in 1913. Shortly afterwards he decided to go to Italy for a period of renewed study. In 1916 he sang Enzo at Bologna, displaying his 'beautiful mezza voce'[12] even if it was not always used with perfect skill. The same year he was at the Dal Verme, Milan, as Dick Johnson and Julien in Charpentier's *Luisa*. This proved a stepping stone to La Scala where he appeared the following season as Ibetto in the world

74 Ulysses Lappas as Marco Gratico in Montemezzi's
La Nave

premiere of Victor de Sabata's *Il Macigno* with
Carmen Melis and Danise. In 1918 he was engaged
for performances of *Pagliacci* and *Fanciulla del West*
at Parma, and *Gioconda* at Pisa. Subsequently he
returned, a fully mature artist, to sing in Athens. In
1919 he journeyed to London to Covent Garden and
was heard as Cavaradossi 'displaying a resonant
voice and pleasing style of singing',[13] Pinkerton and
a 'full-blooded'[14] Canio, which he repeated the year
after. That year too, he was a guest at the Cairo
Opera. In the spring of 1922 he was engaged at the
Chicago Opera for one performance each of *Fanciulla del West* and *Louise*. Three years later in
London after he had 'made a good deal'[15] of the role
of Pinkerton he was Loris in a production of *Fedora*
staged especially for Jeritza. His last appearances at
Covent Garden in 1933 were in an unfortunate
revival of Verdi's *Don Carlo*. He sang in Chicago
again in 1928 in *Aida* with Eva Turner, *Carmen* and
Pagliacci. At La Scala in 1927 he was Canio and in
1934 created the title-role in Lattauda's *Don Giovanni*. He continued to sing in Athens fairly regularly
and made his final appearance there as late as 1952.

Though conditioned greatly by Italian opera, his
style is subtly mutated by a different language and
tradition. It has a particular character of its own. His
is a big and brassy tenor, rather throaty with a
pronounced tremolo, which is less apparent when
he sings softly. As we can hear in Illica's paraphrase
of the real André Chénier's lines 'Come un bel dì di
maggio', he was a good artist and a sensitive
musician. Though he cannot launch the opening
phrases with a real legato, his tender and affectionate manner go far in compensation. He shows,
too, a sensitivity to the music's shape and rhythm.
A couple of Greek songs are attractive. In the first
with its strumming accompaniment the voice is
smoother than elsewhere and the lower range firm
and well-focussed. The second is slightly more
conventional, it could almost be Italian, and he
shapes the phrases affectionately.

23. Four Dramatic Tenors

The contrast between the size of BERNARDO DE
MURO (1881–1955)—he stood only just five feet
tall—and the size of his voice—at his La Scala debut
the pealing high notes set the rafters ringing—never
ceased to astound those who heard him in person.
His small but compact build was then typical in the
poverty-stricken rural districts of Sardinia where
he came from. It was there, he tells us in his

75 Bernardo de Muro as Folco in Mascagni's *Isabeau*

autobiography, that he first discovered his voice,
singing to the birds in the fields. Possibly it was the
wide open spaces of the country or perhaps the
birds' indifference to his serenading and his strenuous attempts to capture their attention that
helped to develop the voice so remarkably. At any
rate, it was not until after a successful concert with a
local operetta company that he determined on a
professional career and decided to try his fortunes
in Rome. He won a place in a competition against
forty-two other entrants at the Accademia di Santa

Cecilia. After studying with Martini he made his debut at the Costanzi in 1910 as Turiddu in *Cavalleria Rusticana*. It was quite an event:

> The tenor . . . an unknown, was a revelation, producing splendid high notes and singing with ample and impassioned accent . . . He sings with a happy abundance of means and modulates pleasingly at times. The voice, beautiful, warm and vigorous, is at ease and secure in all registers. In short [he] was the surprise and . . . the success of the evening.[1]

Within two years and after engagements at Bari, Lecce and Rimini as Pinkerton, Ruy Blas in Marchetti's opera and Osaka in *Iris*, he was brought to La Scala to sing Folco in the first performances there of Mascagni's *Isabeau*. The role was to become his favourite, the one in which he appeared most often and most successfully throughout the rest of his career. The critics compared his voice to Tamagno's, the way he 'threw out the high notes with such sureness'.[2] In the course of the next couple of seasons he was Tucha in Rimsky-Korsakov's *Pskovitana* with Chaliapin as Ivan the Terrible, Don Carlo, in which he seems to have been one of the few admirable things in a revival that was otherwise a fiasco, Turiddu and Don José.

In 1913 after appearing at the Teatro Malibran, Venice, in *Carmen* with Conchita Supervia and Mariano Stabile, he proceeded to South America and sang in a season at the Teatro Coliseo, Buenos Aires. He made a good impression on the public with his calling card Folco, but the critics were less enthusiastic and declined to compare him to Tamagno. Though acknowledging his 'powerful voice of beautiful colour'[3] and the way 'he declaims and phrases with vigour',[4] they accused him of vocal profligacy 'singing too open too frequently, forcing the middle with natural detriment to the top register',[5] 'a bad presage for the future, constituting a danger to the purity of timbre'.[6] The following year after performances of *Carmen* and *Isabeau* in Rome, he took part in a revival of *L'Africana* at Bologna with Ruszkowska. In the summer of 1915 his first season at the Colon, Buenos Aires, coincided with the return of Caruso and he was overshadowed. His roles included Osaka, Dick Johnson, Turiddu, Vasco, Don José and he shared Radamès with Caruso. Though generally well received, he does not seem to have sustained his early promise and was never invited again, though he sang at the Coliseo once more in 1920.

In Europe after the war he appeared in seasons at Madrid and Barcelona where his interpretation of Andrea Chénier was greatly admired. He sang this role too at Monte Carlo in 1923. During the next decade in Italy, at the San Carlo and Costanzi and in many provincial theatres, he was usually heard as Andrea Chénier, Folco or Manrico. His Radamès too was a popular impersonation, especially when at the end of Act Three on the final phrase 'Io resto a te' sustaining an infinitely prolonged high A, he would perambulate round the stage past Ramfis and, holding up his sword as if it were Excalibur, offer it to the gallery. From the mid-twenties the effects of his forceful way of singing began to undermine his technique, the voice would no longer stand up to the punishment, and he lacked the stamina to carry off the big roles without vocal mishaps. He continued to be active but usually in the provinces or with touring companies. In 1925 at the Yankee Stadium, Philadelphia, he took part in an *Aida* calculated to put the Caracalla performances in the shade; as well as a military band, full ballet and troops of extras, there was an entire zoo of camels, elephants and other animals. In the circumstances it was surprising that the Yankees were not recruited to give an exhibition game in the Triumphal Scene. De Muro's last appearance in opera in Europe was at Caracalla in 1938 as his beloved Folco. In his later years he lived in the United States, where he emerged once again for an open-air performance of *Carmen* at the Polo Grounds, New York, in 1944, when he was sixty two.

The voice we hear on records is an outstanding heroic tenor, big and important-sounding; unlike so many of his contemporaries the emission is smooth and the registers correctly blended. Though he cannot manage Manrico's Serenade 'Deserto sulla terra' with the skill and vocal poise of Tamagno—the short D on the first syllable of 'Deserto' is not clearly defined—he creates a great impression. So too in 'Di quella pira' (in the key of B) where the strongly-coloured vowels give some bite to the tone, and the rhythm is incisively marked. His faults too are prominently on display: the slurred semiquavers characteristic of this music are either bumped over, or aspirated. He has a tendency to oversing in the upper range where the tone is too open, with the result that the voice tires slightly before the end, and the final high B on 'all 'armi', though approached boldly enough in a great sweeping portamento, is not carried off without a sense of strain. We can hear what happened to the top notes in the final duet from *Andrea Chénier* made in 1923;

by then he is obliged to take cover under the soprano Oltrabella—the top B flat has become wobbly and difficult to sustain. It is in the music of Giordano and Mascagni that his singing is at its most expressive. He puts himself into the top league with the 'Improvviso', a piece that has inspired many great tenors, but his interpretation is second to none. Though the line is not as perfectly measured as it is in Martinelli's record, nor has he Caruso's glorious legato, de Muro's voice is more naturally suited to the music than either of theirs, and there are many subtleties and shades of expression to hear. He shows that he knew how to sing softly and there is almost a radiance in the tone in the opening measures, and the grand way he takes the B flat is certainly shattering. The excerpts from *Isabeau* show us the correct style in this music, how, in fact, we must believe, Mascagni expected the singer to make his effects. The opera may seem the merest trumpery today but it deeply affected his contemporaries and undoubtedly awoke in de Muro a complete response, for which reason he called his life story *When I was Folco*.[7]

76 Edoardo Ferrari-Fontana as Canio

The Italian tradition in Wagner remained vigorous in Italy, Spain and South America throughout this period, and one of its finest exponents—albeit only for a short time—was the tenor EDOARDO FERRARI-FONTANA (1878–1936). As a young man he had a chequered career; at first in Rome he studied medicine, then shifted to the diplomatic service, and it was not until after a spell as a secretary at the Italian Embassy in Montevideo that he decided to join a touring operetta company. With it he sang small parts in Brazil and the Argentine, returning to Italy for a season at the Dal Verme, Milan. The experience encouraged him to settle on a career in the opera. He made his debut at the Regio, Turin, in 1909, jumping in at the deep end as Tristan. He was an immediate success and stayed on for some performances in the title-role of Mascagni's *Guglielmo Ratcliff*. His next Wagnerian role was Tannhäuser at Bologna with Elsa Bland and Stracciari.

He was a revelation. His warm, powerful, secure, brilliant and colourful voice is most suited to bringing the name part into prominence [and] after the Narration, he was awarded an enthusiastic ovation.[8]

During the next couple of years he showed off his Tristan at Turin, Verona, the Dal Verme and the San Carlo, Naples. In the Italian repertory he was heard as Pollione in *Norma*, Licinio in *La Vestale* and in the title-role of *Don Sebastiano*, in his Rome debut at the Costanzi in company with Virginia Guerrini and Battistini. In the summer of 1911 he was chosen to create Dick Johnson in the local premiere of Puccini's *Fanciulla del West* at the Colon, Buenos Aires, where his other roles included Tristan and Tannhäuser and, the year after, Siegfried in *Crepuscolo degli Dei*.

Ferrari-Fontana's stage presence, seems to have recalled for older opera-goers something of the romantic charm of de Reszke; he was very popular with his female colleagues, one of whom—Margarethe Matzenauer—he married. It was while he was with her in New York in the winter of 1911/12 that the opportunity came to make his American debut. Carl Burrian, having departed for Europe suddenly, left the Boston Opera without a Tristan. The director Henry Russell persuaded Ferrari-Fontana to take over the part at very short notice. He further persuaded him to relearn it in German. Though the flesh was willing—the reward offered was considerable—the spirit was unable, and after he had battled through two acts, the management let him finish in Italian. He stayed at

Boston for two seasons, where he also sang Canio, Turiddu, Gennaro in *Gioielli della Madonna* of Wolf-Ferrari and Samson. In the spring of 1913 he returned to La Scala to create the part of Avito in the world premiere of Montemezzi's *L'Amore dei tre Re*, which he repeated the following season with Tristan. Avito was probably the most successful of all his impersonations, and subsequently he sang it at Boston, in Paris, Chicago and at the Metropolitan in New York.

> He made an immediate success, not only by his fine and impassioned acting—acting of genuine tragic temperament and of finished skill—but still more on account of his remarkably beautiful tenor voice. He is a true tenore robusto, with not only power but also fullness, richness, and warmth of tone, splendid resonance and penetration, especially in his upper ranges. Mr Fontana sings with admirable art, with style, in a manner that makes his voice count for its utmost. He would seem to be a valuable acquisition [and] if his future appearances bear out the promise he offered in his first one . . . his work will be watched with interest and pleasure.[9]

Strangely, though he was under contract for two seasons, he sang no other part. He returned to the Colon in 1920 for some more performances of *Tristano* and Siegmund in *Walchiria* but thereafter his career seems to have fizzled out.

He only made a short list of recordings but they all repay careful listening. The voice was of an unusual and attractive quality; there was a slight movement in it, the tone was pure and the production free and limpid. Notwithstanding the opinions of his contemporaries, it does not sound heroic-sized, perhaps it was the telling projection that made it seem so in the theatre; the balance between words and tone is of a classical perfection. Otello's 'Niun mi tema' follows in the tradition of Borgatti, expressively, almost delicately, but not effetely sung, the phrasing and declamation full of light and shade, and still firmly placed in the vocal line. Though he has not the rich and full tone to sweep grandly through the Flower Song (done in very Italian French), it is nevertheless a beautifully composed piece of singing, the phrasing eloquently drawn and with a subtle and effective use of rubato. From the lightly and cleanly attacked opening F to a climactic high B flat full of sentiment, there are none of the lurchings and sobbings of the verismo. We hear how well the registers are blended; instead of weighting the passage notes he gives

them a heady focus so as to help them project surely and brilliantly. Canio's 'Vesti la giubba' is perhaps the only Italian performance on records which owes nothing, save the traditional sob in the last phrase, to the example of Caruso. It is a distinguished performance in which, following alternatives in an early edition of the score, on the phrases 'Bah, se' tu forse un uom!' and 'Tramuta in lazzi lo spasmo ed il pianto', he moves from sung tone to parlando smoothly and effectively.

The Hispano-Egyptian tenor ICILIO CALLEJA (1882–1941) was born in Corfu and educated in Paris where he took a degree in law. Thereafter, however, he determined on a career in opera and travelled to Italy for instruction. In 1906 he sang in an audition for Toscanini who was greatly impressed with his splendid if unformed talent, and secured him an engagement at La Scala the following season as Giuseppe in Catalani's *La Wally*; Svengali-like, Toscanini taught him the part by rote. It was a successful debut and Calleja was much applauded in a 'difficult and heavy role'.[10] He returned the following season, when at the last moment he was called on to sing Don Alvaro in a revival of *Forza del Destino* which the maestro was also conducting. The premiere was a fiasco and there were no repetitions. Calleja sang badly; mainly, it seems, because he did not know the role, so possibly Toscanini had been less than thorough in preparing him. Every time he opened his mouth the gallery jeered and whistled; Toscanini was so furious he stalked off the podium and declined to finish the performance. The incident does not seem to have had any lasting effect on Calleja's career, for subsequently he appeared extensively throughout Italy: at Ferrara, Modena, Bari, Rome, Bologna, Palermo, Leghorn, Udine, Florence and Genoa, usually as Samson, Otello or Radamès, but also in Romani's *Zulma*, Franchetti's *Germania*, Wolf-Ferrari's *Gioielli della Madonna*, *Norma*, *Andrea Chénier* and *Ballo in Maschera*.

He took part in a season of Italian opera at Cairo and in the autumn of 1911 joined a touring company singing all over the United States, from New York to San Francisco, in Puccini's *Girl of the Golden West*. This led to an engagement with the Chicago Opera the following year, where he sang Canio, Radamès and Gennaro in *Gioielli della Madonna*. In Italy again he re-established his reputation at La Scala in a revival of *Otello* under Serafin's direction in the autumn of 1913; he was greatly praised for his skill as an actor and the fine quality of his singing. Soon afterwards he created Hanno in Smareglia's *L'Abisso* in company with Poli-Randaccio and

Muzio. In the 1916 season he sang Otello at the San Carlo and the Costanzi, Rome, with rather mixed reviews.

> He has some powerful high notes but it is not enough to shout and still less to speak Otello, there is a greater need to sing it. And moreover Calleja's voice seems unequal, lacking smoothness and disagreeably thick. The same inequality is apparent too in his acting, happy and appropriate at certain points; inexpressive and grotesque at others.[11]

He sang Radamès at La Scala, and though not greatly admired, returned in 1916 for a revival of Spontini's *Fernando Cortez* in which he took the title-role opposite Mazzoleni under Panizza. In the later part of his career after the war he sang Wagnerian roles in Italian, including Tristan at the Dal Verme, Milan, Bergamo and Reggio Emilia, and Siegmund at Turin and the Fenice, Venice.

As his contemporaries noted and records con-

77 Icilio Calleja as Otello

firm, it was a big and brilliant voice, especially at the top and he sings more smoothly than some reviews suggest. A souvenir of his Dick Johnson, 'Let her believe that I have gained my freedom', he belts out to fine effect though the tone is a bit tight, probably from the effort of trying to keep the English comprehensible, which he manages rather too successfully, revealing an accent out of a music hall turn. If it is hardly a subtle rendering—it seems appropriate that he should have sung it with the Savage Company—it is in its own way quite memorable.

After the death of Caruso in 1921 many tenors vied to take his place at the Metropolitan. As time passed it became obvious that none had succeeded, but undoubtedly the two leading contenders were Gigli and GIOVANNI MARTINELLI (1885–1969). Largely speaking it was Gigli who assumed the lyrical repertory, while Martinelli was heard in the more dramatic roles which Caruso had been associated with, particularly in the later part of his career: Samson, Don Alvaro, Jean in *Le Prophète* and Eléazar in *La Juive*. Martinelli's career at the Met began in the autumn of 1913 and, unlike Gigli's, lasted through the crunch of the early thirties, season in and season out with only one missed until his farewell in 1946. He continued to appear in opera on occasion thereafter: in 1950 as Samson at Philadelphia and as late as 1967 when he sang—and he still could—the Emperor in *Turandot* at Seattle; he was eighty-one.

He was born in the little town of Montagnana in the Veneto. Even today the population only just tops ten thousand, yet only a fortnight later another famous tenor first saw the light of day there: Aureliano Pertile. It was during Martinelli's period of military service when he played the clarinet in the regimental band that his voice began to attract attention. The bandmaster organised a benefit concert, and with additional assistance from friends he was able to travel to Milan to study with Mandolini. Within a month of appearing as the tenor soloist in Rossini's *Stabat Mater* in December 1910 he sang the title-role in *Ernani* at the Dal Verme. Thereafter his climb to the top was rapid, much of it achieved as Dick Johnson in *Fanciulla del West*; in just two years he sang it at Brescia, Monte Carlo, the San Carlo, the Costanzi, Rome, in succession to Bassi, and at Genoa when the composer was present, and as a result he was engaged to make his debut in its first performances at La Scala. Rather surprisingly, for he seems to have been a success, he never sang there again.

In the summer of 1912 he began his international career at Covent Garden as Cavaradossi and made a very favourable first impression:

He has that rare gift, a true tenor voice. It remains the finest tenor voice heard in England for years. Its quality is luscious, ringing, musical and delightful to hear. The moment he had finished the first cadence of importance the house rose at him. Later ... he confirmed and augmented this impression. Deficiencies as an actor and a tendency to give out all his voice in insignificant passages are his present defects; but they cannot discount his voice.[12]

Thereafter came Gennaro in *Gioielli della Madonna*, Radamès, Des Grieux and Dick Johnson, in all of which he was enthusiastically received; the principal reservation was over his habit of trying 'to pile climax upon climax [when] his mezza voce can be so telling that he might often use it and hold the full power in reserve with advantage'.[13] He came again the year after and in 1914 and 1919, during which time he added Pinkerton, Canio, Riccardo in *Ballo in Maschera*, Faust, Rodolfo, Duca di Brissac in Camussi's *Dubarry* and Paolo in Zandonai's *Francesca da Rimini*. It was observed that he had worked an improvement on his previous form; as Rodolfo with Melba he had never sung with 'finer finish or more beauty of tone'.[14] His limitations too were more clearly apparent; as Paolo 'there was nothing poetic about him, and if his singing was supposed to be the attraction in the eyes of Francesca, then it is a matter of wonder that she ever thought anything about him'.[15]

His initial reception at the Met was qualified:

His is a splendid, clear, resonant organ; much could be done with it were intelligence, taste, feeling, a sense of nuance and the value of changing timbre called to its aid. But his strongest conviction seemed to be that force meant feeling, and that there was no emotion that

78 Giovanni Martinelli

could not be best expressed by explosion. He would try to blow up a ship of the line when telling of the joys of being a poet or the stirring of a new love. And so he grew tiresome early in the evening . . .[16]

Henderson described the voice as 'of unusually beautiful quality',[17] Aldrich was impressed but felt that his tendency to 'force his voice somewhat . . . resulted happily for neither quality nor pitch'.[18] Nevertheless he immediately established himself in the front rank of the company's tenors, and in the course of time his art acquired greater refinement, though his habit of forcing the voice grew with the years. Florence Easton describes singing with him: 'He had the close-all-passages-and-push method. All the same he had a good high C. In the Butterfly duet I really thought that sometimes he was going to explode'.[19] Marguerite d'Alvarez remembered him looking:

> like a handsome ram in a biblical picture, he had an eternal smile and was very loveable, but I did not admire his way of singing. It was so strained I felt his vocal cords must be made of steel and he swung on them like a fox terrier on a bone.[20]

From this time his career was based almost entirely in the United States, save for his visits to London and three seasons at Monte Carlo in 1914 when he was heard in *Aida, Tosca* and *Ugonotti* with Kouznetsova, *Fanciulla del West, Ballo in Maschera, Trovatore* and in the world premiere of Ponchielli's posthumous *I Mori di Valenza*. In the course of thirty two years at the Met he sang thirty six roles: Radamès, Don José, Canio, Manrico, Faust, Pinkerton, Cavaradossi, Rodolfo, Eléazar, Otello, Huon in *Oberon* (in English), Don Alvaro, Edgardo, Gérald, Lefèbvre in Giordano's *Madame Sans-Gêne*, Samson, Gabriele Adorno in *Simon Boccanegra*, Ernani, Avito in *L'Amore dei tre Re*, des Grieux in *Manon Lescaut*, Vasco, Gennaro in *Gioielli della Madonna*, Enzo, Paolo in *Francesca da Rimini*, Arnold in *Gugliemo Tell*, Loris in *Fedora*, Dick Johnson, Dufresne in *Zazà*, Don Carlo, Lensky in *Eugene Onegin*, Heinrich in Respighi's *La Campana sommersa*, Andrea Chénier, Pollione, Fernando in Granados's *Goyescas*, Riccardo and Jean in *Le Prophète*. Outside New York he sang with the Boston Opera in 1913 and on tour with it the following spring in a season at the Théâtre des Champs Elysées, Paris; at San Francisco between 1923 and 1939; and in Chicago from 1937 to 1947. It was in Chicago that he once ventured Tristan opposite

Flagstad's Isolde in 1939. By any standards his was an impressive accomplishment.

After an absence of more than fifteen years in 1929 he reappeared in Italy at the Dal Verme, Milan, and the Teatro dell'Opera, Rome, but he was not a success:

> His voice disappointed the almost frenetic expectations of the public, who found it too darkened, hooty and fixed-sounding.[21]

Apart from some performances of Radamès at Bari in 1934 he never sang in Italy again. In London when he returned in 1937 he was heard as Radamès, Cavaradossi, Don José, Calaf and Otello. In spite of obvious vocal decline (he was by now fifty one), he was greeted like a conquering hero, particularly as Otello:

> The score asks that when Otello utters his first word 'Esultate' we should be at once dominated by a man of elemental force. Martinelli has not this to give. But in compensation there is so much in the way of pure singing and sensitive art and tone and phrasing equally beautiful that his Otello earns a place in the history of opera. He represented a slight, nervous, aristocratic Otello. Nine-tenths of the score justified his conception and in the marvellous music of the first duet with Desdemona the ideal expression was obtained.[22]

So far as the British public was concerned it was a fitting swan song and he left in the memory of those who saw him an imperishable recollection.

Martinelli made a large number of recordings from the early years of his career until almost the time of his death and these, plus various off-the-air transcriptions, mostly from the Met, provide a full documentation of his career. His was an outstanding lirico-spinto tenor voice, the emission smooth and the registers correctly blended up to a fine high C. A remarkable breath span gave his phrasing a nobility and grandeur that was characteristic and time never robbed him of it. Unfortunately, as his contemporaries noted and as is apparent to some degree in almost all his recordings, he forced; not in the way of a crude vocalist who can do nothing else nor, as for example in the Fleta manner, from an excess of uncontrolled temperament, but he used too much breath pressure. The result of this was to make the voice tight and over the years intractable; though it survived all the strain, it lost the quality and the tone became thin and fixed-sounding—it was the 'voce fissa' that the Italian public so disliked in his singing in his later years. It was, they claimed, the result of imitating Caruso. There is little doubt he tried to; so did virtually every tenor of the day in one way or another, for the great man's example was irresistible. But though Caruso also used far more breath pressure than any singer had before him, in order to make that big and full tone so beloved of his audiences, he did not sing beyond his means and even in his last years, as he proved in Nemorino's music, the voice remained easy on the breath. Caruso's method was only superficially unorthodox; his effects were achieved by a mastery of the breath just as they had been in Tosi's day, and he left the vocal mechanism free to follow its natural movement. Martinelli's voice, however, as we can hear even in the Edison recordings, was already slightly tight in the upper middle range; there is reason to believe that in part this arose from a conscious effort by him to focus the tone. In an interview in his retirement he tells how throughout his career he was concerned to 'keep the voice collected' so that it should not spread in the passage notes E to F sharp above middle C. In this he succeeded admirably, but since the voice did not float freely when he turned on the pressure, tightness followed inevitably.

It adversely affected every aspect of his singing. He had a fine conception of legato but the execution was imperfect; instead of letting the voice flow poised on the breath, he squeezed it out like toothpaste; for a musical tension he substituted a muscular one. Especially in later years, as we can hear in complete performances of *Aida*, *Simon Boccanegra* and *Otello*, the unrelenting intensity becomes monotonous and wearisome. In life, however, his personality was full of variety and energy, and those who had the good fortune to know him in his old age will not quickly forget the grace and charm of his manners, yet these two characteristics are conspicuously absent from his art; the voice was not responsive enough to reflect them. He makes a thrilling impact in a vigorous piece like 'Di quella pira' with its strongly marked rhythm, but the more elegant patterns of 'Questa o quella' or 'Di tu se fedele' require a grace of style and flexibility which were simply beyond his technique. In his early years he could sing persuasively, as we hear him in Ernani's Romance; he sang the role with great success at the Metropolitan. The tone is not exactly limpid but he draws a fine line, phrases sensitively and sings with ardour and also restraint. Don Alvaro's 'O tu che in seno', made twelve years later, is more effortful but there is much to admire in the splendidly solid tone and eloquent use of upward

portamento to sculpt the phrases. Although the voice lacks any romantic quality and the singing is not imaginatively graced, there is nevertheless a sincerity and manliness about the interpretation.

Martinelli has been much admired as a Verdi stylist, it would be more accurate to describe him as a Verdi specialist; his singing might have pleased Verdi but it would certainly have sounded strange to him. It is not at all in the same fashion of Tamagno, Patti, Maurel, Bellincioni and other artists whom Verdi is known to have admired, and from whose recordings we can glean something of the prevailing interpretative style in the composer's later years. Next to any of theirs his singing is bald, literal, lacking their purely musical imagination and graceful style, which was based on an affecting use of rubato, portamento, morendo and other traditional expressive devices, nor is there in his shaping of the line any of their play of colour and nuance. By comparison with the over-effusive manner of many of his contemporaries, who imposed on Verdi's music accents more suited to Puccini or Mascagni, Martinelli's respectful attitude to the score may seem praiseworthy, but it is not therefore stylish. It took no account of the fact, as we have already noted, that especially in Verdi's earlier period, though the score contains the music, it does not—it could not possibly—contain the whole of it; Verdi's vocal writing, both what he included and what he left out, was conditioned by the practices of the day. By expurgating most of the traditional devices, as Martinelli does, his singing reflects not Verdi's (or even his own) style but that of Toscanini. Though his Verdi singing was without the bad manners of Gigli, equally it lacked the good ones of Tamagno. Instead of harking back, as some enthusiasts have claimed, to the nineteenth century, his singing anticipates the modern, so-called objective approach.

The modernity of Martinelli's style is apparent in other aspects of his singing. He is almost the first Italian tenor of any importance to depart in his pronunciation from the traditional balance between tone and words. His enunciation on records is always in some degree obtrusive, and especially later on comes increasingly to sound like an elocution lesson. In view of the many years he spent singing to audiences who understood little Italian, one cannot help wondering whether perhaps he was not unconsciously emulating the Cockney on a day-trip to Paris, who when he was not understood started to shout. Its origins at any rate lay in his tight and thin vocal production; there simply was not space in the tone sufficient to blend the words in. As with some modern singers he used the words as a means of levering up the voice, particularly the hard consonants and the exaggeratedly rolled *rs*. His careful articulation gave a fine thrust in recitative but in cantabile music it is apparent how much it was achieved at the expense of beauty of tone; the vowels are not of equal weight or purity— they never are in a fixed voice—and, especially in the upper middle range, he is obliged to modify them so much, particularly 'e', that they become obscure. In the United States, over the years, his prenunciation actually came to be regarded as a model, and its influence is particularly apparent in Richard Tucker's exaggerated style.

24. Principal Baritones

GIUSEPPE DE LUCA (1876–1950) was in Havana in the summer of 1915 when an invitation came from Gatti-Casazza to join the Metropolitan. At the time de Luca was an established baritone of considerable repute. He had sung with success in Italy, Spain, South America, Poland, Russia, England and Austria. His was a wide ranging achievement but, perhaps because of his more generously endowed colleagues: Pacini, Ancona, Giraldoni, Sammarco, Amato, Stracciari and Ruffo, though he sang a number of heroic roles, it was as a character and buffo singer that he was chiefly renowned. He created Michonnet in *Adriana Lecouvreur* at the Lirico, Milan, in 1902 and two years later at La Scala, Sharpless and Gleby in Giordano's *Siberia*, there he was also Alberich in *L'Oro del Reno*, Hoël in *Dinorah*, the Devil in Massenet's *Griselda*, Malatesta, Wolfram, Beckmesser, Escamillo, Méphistophélès in *Dannazione di Faust*, Valentino in Bruggemann's *Margherita*, Gualtiero in Franchetti's *Notte di Leggenda* and Figaro in both Mozart and Rossini's operas. It was as Figaro in *Barbiere* that he made his Met bow:

> His voice has an excellent quality and resonance, though he showed last evening an unnecessary tendency to force it. He has the volubility and the volatile spirit, and an intelligence and comic power that made his performance acceptable and that gave his part the value it should have in the whole . . . [But] the chief point of distinction in the performance was Mme Frieda Hempel.[1]

From that time New York became de Luca's artistic home and it was not until the Second World War that he returned to sing in opera in Italy. At the Met he undertook more than fifty roles in the course of twenty seasons. Whatever initial reservations the critics had, time and circumstances set aside. His professionalism, reliability, skill in characterisation, fine singing and careful husbanding of a not first class voice, earned increasingly favourable reviews. He created Paquiro in Granados's *Goyescas* and the name part in *Gianni Schicchi*. Aldrich thought he 'has done nothing better than his insouciant and humorous impersonation of the adventurous cobbler Marouf' in the local premiere of Rabaud's opera, his Taddeo in the first performances of *Italiana in Algeri* at the Met was pronounced 'an admirable impersonation full of drollery',[2] as Guglielmo in *Così fan tutte* he was 'delightful in his beautiful singing of the music, as in the unctious humour of the action',[3] there was 'warm enthusiasm'[4] for his elder Bruschino in Rossini's *Il Signor Bruschino*, while his Nickelmann in Respighi's *La Campana sommersa* 'was a masterpiece of comic grotesquerie'.[5] His repertory also included Ping in *Turandot*, Scindia in *Le Roi de Lahore*, Cinna in *Vestale*, Antonio in *Linda di Chamounix*, Sancho in *Don Quichotte*, Eugene Onegin, Lescaut in *Manon Lescaut*, Zurga in *Les Pêcheurs de perles*, Plunkett in *Marta*, Enrico in *Lucia*, Riccardo in *Puritani*, Valentin, Mercutio in *Roméo et Juliette*, Belcore, Hoël in *Dinorah*, the High Priest in *Samson et Dalila*, Nelusko in *Africana*, Malatesta in *Don Pasquale* and Miracle, Dapertutto and Coppelius in *Les Contes d'Hoffmann*. He appeared less often in verismo opera, as Scarpia, Cascart in *Zazà*, Gérard in *Andrea Chénier*, Kyoto in *Iris*, Gianotto in *Lodoletta* and de Siriex in *Fedora*. It was a parade any artist would have been proud of and this is by no means all of it.

De Luca's arrival at the Met was timely. Hitherto most of the leading Italian baritone roles had been sustained by Scotti and Amato. But by 1915 the former was in his fiftieth year and had begun to specialise in parts in which his great histrionic skill could compensate for a fading voice. The full burden of the repertory fell on Amato. The results of this were painfully obvious in his singing by the end of the war. In 1921 he withdrew, leaving de Luca in command of the field. As a result de Luca came to make important contributions to a number of Verdi revivals, several of which we can still hear something of through his recordings: Don Carlo in *Forza del Destino*, Rodrigo in *Don Carlo*, Carlo Quinto in *Ernani* and Miller in *Luisa Miller*; and each season, almost without exception, he was heard as Rigoletto, Germont and Amonasro. A number of lesser singers were active at the time, including Mario Laurenti and Renato Zanelli, who provided dutiful service but failed to establish themselves; Zanelli, indeed, eventually became a tenor. Until after the death of Caruso and the need to find a new superstar, the Met had demurred at paying Titta Ruffo the fee of a tenor, but though he was eventually engaged in 1921, and appeared fairly regularly thereafter, he only did make a handful of appearances each season. The one new Italian baritone to be engaged, who came to share much of de Luca's repertory, was Giuseppe Danise. He was a competent artist with a sturdy, if rather thick sounding and wobbly, voice and not to be compared with the best of his predecessors. So it was by a combination of good luck and shortage of the genuine article de Luca was able to lay claim to many leading roles and gain an ascendancy where formerly he could not endure the competition.

Especially in later years there were reservations about his lack of voice but even in the thirties he continued to play principal parts in all the Verdi revivals until Lawrence Tibbett came into his maturity with Simon Boccanegra in 1932. De Luca officially retired in 1935 but returned in 1940 for a review of his favourite roles. By then he was the grand old man and could do no wrong. A couple of souvenirs of his Rigoletto and Figaro, duets with Lily Pons, recorded at about this time, reveal what sentiment disguised in the reviews, that the voice was very frayed and though he was acclaimed for his skill in bel canto, the roulades he offers in 'Dunque io son' are either simplified or blurred with aspirates and would not have passed for the real thing a quarter of a century previously when there was a genuine appreciation of florid music. It is instructive that de Luca was only spoken of as a bel canto singer at the end of his career, when most commentators had forgotten what the term meant.

He belonged to that fine company of singers who made the first successful electric recordings for Victor; one that boasted Galli-Curci, Rethberg, Ponselle, Martinelli and Pinza. They represented much of the best singing of the day, and of them all de Luca was perhaps the most accomplished technically, which is not really surprising for he was the eldest and a pupil of Venceslao Persichini, the teacher of Battistini. At its best his range extended easily to the high A. The production throughout was limpid and although the quality was nondescript, the perfect blending of the registers gave to the top especially, a heady re-

sonance that showed the voice off to its best advantage. We can hear this in the nicely weighted high G flats in Hoël's air from Meyerbeer's *Dinorah*, something too of his excellent sense of line, and he knew how to prepare a phrase. The voice was hardly a brazen thing to compare with Ruffo's but by the judicious management of dynamics, he was able to sound a fine dramatic climax, as for example in Rigoletto's 'Cortigiani', even if ideally the voice lacks the sonority for this music. He has the good manners of the old school in duets with Caruso from *L'Elisir d'Amore* and *La Forza del Destino*, making a worthy companion, singing strongly but always considerately. With Martinelli both artists are effective in the Friendship Duet from *Don Carlo*, a souvenir of their performances at the Met; however, as a piece of duet singing, it is not as successful as Caruso and Scotti's, for the voices do not blend so well. With Galli-Curci, de Luca is a model of rectitude; it would be hard to find another recording of 'Piangi, fanciulla' sung so smoothly and touchingly, in which the Rigoletto for once actually sounds sympathetic, as if he meant the words he was singing.

Though de Luca remained a matchless buffo artist, in the hey-day of his career at the Met he made few recordings from that repertory. 'Largo al factotum' is well done but it is not until we see him in action in a short clip of film made in the late twenties, that we get any real idea of the effect he made as Figaro. The rich humour seems to have come as much from his ebullient personality and physical presence than from anything he put into his singing, for others have sung it more brilliantly. The fioritura is not always perfectly clean and especially in later years when the lower part of the voice had dried out and become rather throaty, he was not above taking advantage of a few helpful aspirates; coloratura seems not to have been an intrinsic part of his technique in the way that it was with Kaschmann, Ancona, Battistini, Scotti or even Ruffo, and over the years it got rusty. By the time he made electrical recordings he was past fifty: much of the old skill was still there but although the voice remained secure, the tone had begun to spread and sound rattly, as we hear in 'Il balen'. The gruppetti, a characteristic feature of the piece, are all neatly turned and his artistic intentions admirable, yet incipient unsteadiness is obvious, especially in the lower range—in the opening phrase, for example—while at the climax the voice has noticeably lost quality. Decadence is apparent when we compare the first part of the Death of Rodrigo from *Don Carlo*, made in 1921, with the second recorded eight years later. The two, however, add up to a fine interpretation; the singing has an appropriate simplicity of delivery and, as always, de Luca's enunciation is a model, without vehemence or exaggeration; in the final phrases he sounds the note of resignation perfectly.

But for all its virtues, its admirable restraint and lack of the extravagant gestures of verismo, this is Verdi singing of the twenties. There is little in it of the wealth of fascinating detail that survives in recordings left by singers closer to Verdi's own day. A whole grammar of effects which informed their singing and nourished the vocal line—bel canto, if the term means anything at all—is simply not there. Play Battistini's recording of this music and we hear the difference at once. That great artist's complete mastery of the breath, where not a wisp of it is wasted and all of it converted into sung tone, enables him to treat the music with a far greater freedom than de Luca and yet at the same time make a more musical effect. It gives a spontaneity to the attack, coherency to the phrasing and variety of colour to the line, so that the whole piece (or as much of it as he recorded) is set out with architectural clarity; Battistini shows off Verdi through his own prodigious technique. In the grave cantilena 'Io morrò' he gives a demonstration of the portamento style and by his exquisite skill in the art of messa di voce, is able to express in the musical line alone, the ebb and flow of vitality of the dying Rodrigo. What effect could be more ravishing vocally and apt dramatically than the sudden pianissimo on the F, in the phrase 'Ah! di me non ti scordar' (Ah! do not forget me)? It is this touch of purely vocal imagination that was common to the great singers of the nineteenth century, a part of the language of effects of the real Verdi style and which, for all its many admirable qualities, there is no trace of in de Luca's singing.

The lengthy career of RICCARDO STRACCIARI (1875–1955) began in the chorus of a touring operetta company, but it was not long before his sturdy baritone attracted the attention of his colleagues, and he was advised to seek professional training. After completing a course of study at the Bologna Conservatory, he made his debut in 1899 in Lorenzo Perosi's oratorio *La Risurrezione di Cristo*. In the course of the next year or so he sang in opera at Rovigo, Reggio Emilia, Trieste and Mantua, and abroad in Egypt and Chile. His first stage appearance at Bologna in Mascagni's *Le Maschere* led to an engagement at the São Carlos,

Lisbon, in Franchetti's *Germania*, *Africana*, *Traviata* and *Aida*. In the 1903/4 season he was a member of the company at Genoa singing Méphistophélès in Berlioz's *Faust*, Gleby in Giordano's *Siberia*, de Siriex in *Fedora* and the Devil in Massenet's *Griselda*. It was as Amonasro that he made his Scala debut in the autumn of 1904; thereafter came Vincenzo in *La Wally*, Hermann in *Loreley*, Yeletsky in *Dama di picche*, Germont and Simonson in Alfano's *La Risurrezione*. In 1905 he toured Italy in Mascagni's *Amica* and at the end of the year was engaged for the autumn season at Covent Garden as Amonasro, di Luna, Lescaut in *Manon Lescaut*, Rigoletto and Germont. In a company that included not only Sammarco but also Battistini, returning after many years' absence, it was not surprising that Stracciari caused no stir, and he never sang at Covent Garden again. The competition was stiff at the Met when he arrived there the following year. There were complaints of a tremolo and general monotony; 'he does not give great evidence of

79 Riccardo Stracciari

natural gifts,'[6] and 'he is not an artist of the calibre of Caruso, Plançon, Sembrich, Fremstad, Gadski and others of the Metropolitan company'.[7] His New York repertory included Germont, Amonasro, Enrico in *Lucia*, Marcello, Sharpless, Tonio and other of his usual roles.

In the next decade he confined his appearances to Italy and the Italian operatic empire. At the Colon in 1913 he added Gil in Wolf-Ferrari's *Segreto di Susanna* and Renato in *Ballo in Maschera* to his growing repertory. In Italy he was heard as Barnaba, Napoleone in Giordano's *Madame Sans-Gêne*, Wolfram in *Tannhäuser*, in which he was especially admired, Scarpia, Carlo Quinto in *Ernani*, Antonio in *Linda di Chamounix* and Alfonso in *La Favorita* with Bonci and de Angelis. Of this last in Rome in 1911 *Orfeo* wrote:

> Stracciari's accents were of rare sweetness and his tone full and pure. In the aria 'A tanto amor' the great artist showed how it is possible for a powerful voice to be modulated with exquisite subtlety and the singing to be suffused with melancholy and irony. At the end of the performance Toto Cotogni rendered homage to him, embraced him and proclaimed him a singer worthy of the best Italian tradition.[8]

But his most admired impersonations were Figaro and Rigoletto. He sang them everywhere, throughout the provinces of Italy, and after he resumed his travelling again, throughout the world. He appeared in them both in a season at Havana in 1917 and then that autumn in Chicago when he returned to the United States. There he also took part in revivals of *Ernani*, *Forza del Destino*, *Linda di Chamounix* and *Crispino e la Comare*, the last two being staged for Galli-Curci; it was opposite her that he appeared in *Rigoletto* and *Barbiere di Siviglia*. At La Scala where his career continued until 1924, both roles were part of a repertory that also included Cinna in *La Vestale*, Enrico in *Lucia*, Napoleone and Gérard in *Andrea Chénier*. It is reported that he sang Figaro almost a thousand times in his career; even allowing for exaggeration there is little doubt he sang it more often than any of his contemporaries. His last appearances in the role were after the Second World War when he was over seventy years old.

Stracciari's was not so splendid a voice as Ruffo's, not as mellow or as beautifully used as Battistini's and not as characteristic as Amato's but it was a first class instrument, a fine ringing baritone, admirably produced and easy up to the high A flat. Like de Luca's, Stracciari's career went on a long time and he continued to represent all the fine accomplishments of his day at a time when these were in increasingly short supply; his voice was still, even in his mid fifties, in excellent condition. He was not an especially subtle or imaginative artist but he shows in Nelusko's 'Figlia di Regi' from *L'Africana* that he knew how to discriminate effectively between the opening section with its difficult marcato passage from the swelling legato of 'O Brahma, o Dio possente'. There is too, sensitivity and fine feeling in his phrasing of Hamlet's 'Come il romito fior' and he was as assured in comedy as he was in tragedy; Figaro's 'Largo al factotum', any one of the several versions he made, is a brilliant piece of bravura and he and Carpi manage the passage work of 'All'idea di quel metallo' accurately with rhythmic spirit and a strong sense of character. As a verismo singer he makes his effects without the vehemence of Sammarco and with more expression than Giraldoni in, for example, the music of Worms from Franchetti's *Germania*, in both 'Ferito prigonier' and the Death Scene. Much in his complete recordings of *Rigoletto* and *Barbiere*, though made when he was over fifty, remains unsurpassed after half a century. In particular, his singing of Figaro's recitatives is a textbook lesson in style, rich in humour, every appogiatura in place and he moves from spoken to sung tone with complete spontaneity of utterance. In a group of English and American popular ballads he surprises us with his clear diction—they are sung in the original—and sympathetic style. He made a great number of records and there are hardly any of them that do not exemplify the basic virtues of fine singing, while his interpretations are always strongly felt and effective.

DOMENICO VIGLIONE-BORGHESE (1877–1957), was the possessor of a powerful baritone voice, second in weight and sonority only to that of Ruffo. He studied under Leonese at Pesaro and made his debut in 1899 at Lodi, in the same role as Ruffo, the Herald in *Lohengrin*. This led to other engagements at small provincial theatres but after a year or so, dissatisfied with his progress, he emigrated to the United States and worked as a navvy on the railways in California. He did not give up singing, however, and in 1905 Caruso heard him and gave him an introduction to a touring company, then visiting San Francisco, organised by Tetrazzini. Viglione-Borghese sang with it for two seasons in Mexico and other Latin American countries. In 1907 he returned to Italy and created something of a sensation with the sheer power of his singing as Amonasro at Parma. That difficult citadel once

80 Domenico Viglione-Borghese as Gérard in *Andrea Chénier*

tophélès in Berlioz's *Faust*, Falstaff, Michele in *Tabarro* and Gianni Schicchi.

He sang at La Scala in *Africana* and *Rhea* in 1910 and returned subsequently for *Tristano* and in 1930 as Rance and Alfio. Abroad he appeared at Barcelona and Madrid, and in 1919 at the Colon, Buenos Aires, as Herman in Catalani's *Loreley*, Scarpia, Barnaba, Michele, Amonasro, Marcello and Napoleone in Giordano's *Madame Sans-Gêne*. At the Paris Opéra in 1912 he replaced Ruffo in the second of two gala performances of *Fanciulla del West* with Caruso. His career continued throughout the thirties and he made his final appearances in 1940 in Rome.

It is a big and imposing voice, not used with any particular skill or finesse but nimble enough to get round the Meyerbeerian vocal figures in Barnaba's 'Pescator, affonda l'esca'. The high notes are especially noteworthy but in the middle range the tone is slightly spread. 'Anima santa', the air of Wolf from Puccini's *Villi*, suits his forthright, unsubtle but impressive delivery. Viglione-Borghese may not have aped Ruffo, for the two were contemporaries, but he was the first of that stream of provincial baritones that followed afterwards, who had the advantage of great natural resources but who neglected much that would have made their art equally impressive.

The career of RENATO ZANELLI (1892–1935) was complicated by his switch mid-stream from the baritone to the tenor repertory. Chilean by birth, his father's family was Italian and he was educated in Switzerland. At first he sang as an amateur for he was occupied in the lucrative nitrate business. It was only after he had taken part in a concert in Santiago and a teacher present, Angelo Querzé, advised him to abandon mining nitrates and instead mine the gold in his throat, that he began to study singing in earnest. After three years he made his debut as Valentin in *Faust*, subsequently singing di Luna and Tonio. The experience was not discouraging but it made him aware of the need for further study and he departed for the United States, to work with Andrés de Segurola. In the autumn of 1919 he secured a contract at the Metropolitan and made his debut as Amonasro. He was not, however, a success:

> Zanelli has a good 'voix de salon', but entirely inadequate for the heavy roles for which he has been featured.[9]

He remained with the company for four seasons singing Don Carlo in *Forza del Destino*, Tonio, King

stormed, his Italian career was secure.

He appeared at almost all the most important theatres, at the Costanzi, Argentina and Adriano, Rome, the Dal Verme and Carcano, Milan, the San Carlo, Naples, Bologna, Palermo, Turin, Brescia, La Spezia, Cremona, Treviso, Florence and Genoa. He sang the big parts: Rigoletto, Barnaba, Rance—in which he was especially admired—Cristoforo Colombo in Franchetti's opera of the same name, Rafaele in *Gioielli della Madonna*, Gellner in *La Wally*, Amonasro, Posa, di Luna, Scarpia and Iago. He took part in various novelties—Leoncavallo's *Maja*, Wolf-Ferrari's *Segreto di Susanna*, Mancinelli's *Ero e Leandro* and *Paolo e Francesca*, Samara's *Rhea*, Canonica's *Sposa di Corinto* and Bianchi's *Ghismonda*. Other roles included Kurvenal in *Tristano e Isotta*, Amfortas in *Parsifal*, Méphis-

81 Renato Zanelli as Tristan

Venice. It was the conductor Mugnone who introduced him to *Otello*. He sang it for the first time at Turin in 1926, two years later at Parma he was at last recognised as an artist of ranking importance and a great Otello. Thereafter he sang the role widely throughout Italy, and at Santiago, Buenos Aires, Lisbon, Monte Carlo and Covent Garden.

> The chief event of the evening was the first appearance of Signor Renato Zanelli whose singing of the famous passage culminating in 'Della gloria d'Otello e questa al fin' provoked an outbreak of noisy applause from the gallery. Quite apart from vocal success in those moments in which a tenor is given exceptional opportunity to excel Zanelli was able to create a powerful impression through his consistent dramatic treatment of the part. It took him a little time to get used to his surroundings, and his first duet with Desdemona was not quite in tune, but from Act Two onwards his singing was equal to his acting.[10]

He returned to Covent Garden in the same role in 1930. Elsewhere he sang Tristan, Lohengrin and Siegmund, all of them in Italian, the title-role in Pizzetti's *Lo Straniero*, Faust in Mefistofele, Andrea Chénier, Pollione, Cavaradossi, Manrico and Dick Johnson in *Fanciulla del West*.

Zanelli made acoustic records as a baritone and electric records as a tenor. In the first of these it is hard to reconcile the splendid, warm and full baritone we hear with descriptions of a 'voix de salon'. And certainly the voice was naturally a baritone. Though he made a greater reputation as a tenor and his interpretation of Otello is finely wrought, full of passion and intensity, the effort it cost him to move in the higher tessitura is always obvious. As a baritone it sounds as if he took Ruffo as a model, which may account for a tendency to attack notes from below, a bad habit which grew on him in his tenor days. His singing generally has a firm line and his artistic intentions are admirable as in Alfonso's 'A tanto amor' from *La Favorita*. The legato is smoothly poised, expressively shaded and though there is a trace of sentimentality in the rather self-conscious sweet tone and slightly exaggerated treatment of marcato markings, this is a distinguished performance. His singing had genuine charm, in Tirindelli's 'O Primavera' with the careful shading of each stanza and variety of inflexions. Cascart's 'Zazà, piccola zingara' is not quite in the class of Ruffo or Schwarz but it rises to an effulgent climax and without doing injury to the vocal line.

The Spanish baritone EMILIO SAGI-BARBA

Dodon in *Le Coq d'or* and Valentin, but in none of these does he seem to have made any impression. He also appeared at Ravinia Park and was a member of the Scotti Grand Opera Company and, in concert, sang under Charles Wagner's management. By 1923, when it was apparent that his career was getting nowhere, with his brother, the baritone Carlo Morelli, he departed for Italy determined to re-study as a tenor.

He made his second debut at the San Carlo, Naples, in 1924 as Raoul in *Ugonotti*, afterwards singing Alfredo in some performances of *Traviata* at

(1875–1949) sang only rarely in opera but he was one of the leading Zarzuela singers of his day. He deserves a place here for the fine quality of his singing, his musicianship and splendid comic sense. He spent the major part of his career in Spain but did make occasional appearances with various touring companies in Latin America.

His is a light-weight baritone with a characteristically Spanish tremolo, the tone somewhat throaty but not unattractive and always secure and well-focussed. His records include Rigoletto's 'Cortigiani' (in Spanish); though lacking the vocal stature of the greatest interpreters of the role, it is strongly declaimed, the phrasing smoothly moulded and he cleverly intensifies his tremolo for emotional effect. Schumann's 'Widmung' sounds a little odd in Spanish and will not appeal to those who must have their Lieder in the original but his singing has its own charm, a caressing line and eloquent use of vocal colour. His execution of mordents and gruppetti is done with notable finesse; crushed in the typical Spanish style and properly subordinate. He is incontrovertibly a master in a brilliant patter song from Mazza's *La Campanone*; after the fashion of the Maestri di Cappella of Cimarosa and Paer, the singer imitates the various instruments of the orchestra. He throws off the words with the deft skill and unction of the finest Italian buffo singers and like them improvises a few extra effects for good measure; this is a tradition now virtually extinct. Its disappearance accounts for the gradual decline in popularity of an opera like Rossini's *Barbiere*.

25. Mardones

Those who heard JOSE MARDONES (1869–1932) in person recall him as the possessor of one of the greatest voices of his day. The critical adjectives 'imposing', 'grand', 'impressive', followed him throughout a long career. Born in Fontecchia, Spain, he studied at the Madrid Conservatory and thereafter made his first stage appearances in South America, singing at Rio and Buenos Aires. In 1908 he was engaged in Lisbon at the Sao Carlos Theatre and the following year given a contract for the new Boston Opera by Henry Russell; he was with the company throughout its short history. He provided 'serviceable' impersonations as Ramfis, Colline, Mefistofele, Don Basilio, Marcel in *Ugonotti*, Wallace in *Fanciulla del West*, Sparafucile, Lodovico in *Otello*, the Father in Laparra's *La Habañera*, Escamillo, Alvise, Abimelech in *Samson et Dalila*, the Doctor in *Pelléas et Mélisande*, Stapps in Franchetti's *Germania*, Raimondo in *Lucia*, the Commendatore, Méphistophélès, and with the Rabinoff company he added Archibaldo in *L'Amore dei tre Re*. In 1917 he moved to the Met, where he was a leading member of the company for nine seasons. To his Boston accomplishments he added Zacharias in *Le Prophète*, Giorgio in *Puritani*, Padre Guardiano in *Forza del Destino*, Pimen in *Boris Godounov*, the Old Hebrew in *Samson et Dalila*, Rudolph in Catalani's *Loreley*, Walter Furst in *Guillaume Tell*, Indra in *Le Roi de Lahore* and in Spontini's *La Vestale* as the ...

> inevitable high priest of the operatic temples of all climes and ages, [he] did his best for Pontifex Maximus.[1]

Not enough, it would appear, for the management at any rate, since the following year we find his name replaced on the roster of artists by that of Ezio Pinza. He returned to Spain where he was active almost until the time of his death.

The voice on records sounds large and is sonorous throughout a range of more than two octaves to an easy high F sharp. In Zaccaria's 'Del futuro nel buio' from *Nabucco* he has the right authority and sings cleanly, but we may agree with Lauri-Volpi that there is no characterisation, personality or depth in his interpretations. He represents the best kind of house singer; his versatility was equal to pretty well anything that was given him, but the singing has no subtlety or detail and is quite unmemorable. In later years the tone became increasingly cavernous and his intonation vague.

82 Emilio Sagi-Barba   83 José Mardones as Ramfis

PART IV

Singers from the English-speaking World

26. Alda and Mason

By the 1920s the great prima donnas of Victorian days belonged to the distant past, as remote from the modern world as the Cretaceous age. They had been in decline, unable to adapt themselves to shifting circumstances, for a long while, but it was the enormous upheaval of the First World War that threw aside the society where they flourished and finally caused their extinction—well, almost—for one dinosaur did survive, FRANCES ALDA (1883–1952). In her retirement she wrote a spirited volume of memoirs *Men, Women and Tenors*, which makes a good read, but the portrait she paints of herself, a pilgrim in Babylon, tenacious, loyal, honest, industrious, her only weakness a disposition to be candid, if it were true, would have made her into the most insufferable prig. In fact, like another and more famous autobiography, Richard Wagner's 'Mein Leben', it is chiefly remarkable for what it does not tell. For nearly twenty years, married to the general manager Giulio Gatti-Casazza, Alda was Queen of the Metropolitan where she wielded enormous influence. She did this more circumspectly than Melba had at Covent Garden, without trying to keep out those whom she did not like or was jealous of—she was shrewd enough to realise that she had not the talent to get away with it. She preferred to concentrate on her own preferment and keep herself in roles, for many of which, as events transpired, she was not really suited.

Born in New Zealand, she was brought up in Australia; her father was British, her mother part German, part French. Her mother's family were theatrical people and one of her sisters, Frances Saville, a pupil of Marchesi, had a successful career in Vienna and at the Metropolitan. As a girl Alda sang in the chorus of a Gilbert and Sullivan company, but did not begin her studies seriously until she came to Paris to work with Marchesi. She made a successful debut at the Opéra-Comique as Manon in 1904. For the next three years she sang at the Monnaie, Brussels: Manon, Marguerite, the title-roles in Massenet's *Chérubin* and Messager's *Madame Chrysanthème*, Salomé in *Hérodiade*, Marguerite in Berlioz's *Faust*, the Countess in *Le Nozze di Figaro*, Violetta, Ophélie and the Queen in *Les Huguenots*. The last two she did not appear in very often and, as she tells us herself, the high Ds in the Queen's aria were beyond her range. In 1906 she was brought in to deputise for an ailing Melba in *Faust* at Covent Garden and then sang Gilda with Caruso and Battistini. Battistini was with her again soon afterwards in *Rigoletto* at Parma. Her debut at La Scala in 1908 was as Louise in the Milan premiere of Charpentier's opera, two months later she was Margherita in some performances of Boito's *Mefistofele* with Chaliapin. It was in Milan that she first encountered Gatti-Casazza who was then Director at La Scala; it was not long before he was proposing marriage. His move to New York was already in the wind, and he lost no time in offering Alda a Met contract, but before she could accept she was obliged to fulfil engagements at Warsaw, the Paris Opéra and in South America.

Her Metropolitan career began inauspiciously as Gilda, in the autumn of 1908.

> Miss Alda disclosed a voice of considerable power and some agility ... She was in general, though not invariably, respectful of the pitch, her lapses being mainly in singing sharp. It cannot be said that Miss Alda's voice was uniformly agreeable in quality. Her tones were marred by a vibrato, and they were often sharpened to a keen edge that cut shrilly upon the ear. She was effective in conventional fashion, and she may be looked to, no doubt, for useful work here.[1]

Ten days later came Anna in the first American performances of Puccini's *Le Villi*, then Marguerite and Manon; in none, however, does she seem to have worked any great improvement in her form.

The critics said little; her relationship with Gatti was soon common knowledge, and as Henderson observed it was 'useless' complaining, for she was going to sing 'no matter what is said'.[2] And so she did with only one season's absence until 1929. As time passed opinion was more complimentary, there was a 'decided improvement'[3] in her Mimi, she showed 'simplicity and gentleness'[4] as Desdemona, gave 'genuine art'[5] to Victor Herbert's Madeleine, was 'an attractive Roxanne'[6] in Damrosch's *Cyrano de Bergerac*; as Jaroslavna in *Prince Igor* 'she was

84 Frances Alda as Manon

always a delight to the eye, if not always to the ear',[7] the title-role of Henry Hadley's *Cleopatra's Night* gave her opportunities for the display of the 'unblushing contours of the body which are now practised on stage'[8] while 'her singing of the music' of the Princess in Rabaud's *Marouf* 'had more excellencies than some of her offerings'.[9]

She was most at home in lyrical roles with only a gesture or two of coloratura, while too dramatic music made demands of her singing and acting that she had neither the resources nor the temperament to cope with. As Micaëla, Manon, Manon Lescaut, Nannetta, Mimi, Desdemona, Lady Harriet in *Marta*, Susanna in Wolf-Ferrari's *Segreto di Susanna*, Rozenn in *Le Roi d'Ys*, and Anna in *Loreley*, her fine vocal qualities were heard at their best. Jaroslavna, the title-role in Zandonai's *Francesca da Rimini*, Margherita in *Mefistofele* and Ginevra in Giordano's *La Cena delle Beffe* were praiseworthy attempts to extend her range, but like Philine, Juliette, Ophélie and Violetta, they were not for her. Throughout her years at the Met she appeared only rarely in opera elsewhere, though she sang with the company on tour in the United States, and was heard frequently in recitals. Aldrich was present at one in 1911:

> Mme Alda's audience was a large one, ushers staggered under the weight of flowers that were sent up to the stage to do her honour, and there were all the accompaniments of a gala occasion. The singer was in good voice, and has probably never been heard to better advantage in a recital here. She did a good deal of fine singing of that type where vocal qualities are distinguished above the desire to portray the deeper moods or express strongly marked feelings. When her voice is at its best it has an evenness and flexibility in the upper portions that is capable of producing excellent results, and this was often in evidence. It was marred only by a tinge of acidity that often goes with the light voices, and a certain unsteadiness in the lower range.[10]

Her concert career continued for some years after her retirement from the Met, which incidentally coincided with her divorce from Gatti, and she liked to sing on the radio. However, she disliked changing the programme; when she sent the same one to her manager for the umpteenth time he cabled back: 'Hebrews xiii.8—Jesus Christ, the same yesterday, today and for ever'.

Alda's is a strong and bright lyric soprano with an especially lovely quality in the middle and upper ranges. She has many of the hallmarks of the

Marchesi method; the fine finish, clean attack and unambiguous trill. Her cantilena is generally smooth and well supported. Occasionally at the top, as on the high B at the climax of Wally's 'Ebben, ne andrò lontana' there is not sufficient breadth of tone, and the note acquires that sharp and vinegary quality to which critics allude. When she takes them within her means, however, they were conspicuously beautiful, like the B flat at the end of 'In quelle trine morbide'. Here her singing is colder in manner than the Italians', but one can think of few Latin performances that are so genuinely musical, relying solely for their effect on the expressive virtues of fine singing. When Puccini penned the difficult figures and trills in 'L'ora o Tirsi', we must believe he was in earnest and wanted them sung with the precision and delicacy that Alda offers; not as they so often come out, merely a squally approximation. Anna's 'Ah, dunque' from Catalani's *Loreley* is a justly famous interpretation of a rather meretricious piece. The tessitura is an assault course, awkwardly written and mined with trills which do not seem to fulfil any particular harmonic function. Alda despatches it with instrumental precision, stunning ease and brilliance. At the lower end of her range, in Margherita's 'L'altra notte' from *Mefistofele*, much of the music lies uncomfortably for her. The tone is slightly spread, and there are suggestions of the unsteadiness which Aldrich noted. She is sparing in her use of portamento—Toscanini's influence, no doubt—but here, where it might have helped to strengthen the foundations of her phrasing, it is wanting. Her Italian has some strange aberrations when she introduces diphthongs into the vowels, and their general lack of purity in the middle and lower range accounts for her poor diction, which is no better in English. Few of her records give such unadulterated pleasure as those she made of light music, pieces by Victor Herbert and Kalman, where her lovely voice and distinguished singing flatter the music.

   At the best of times there are comparatively few singers who never make an ugly sound; still fewer of whom it can be said that virtually every note—at least on gramophone records—is a thing of loveliness. In that select company may be numbered the Missouri-born lyric soprano EDITH MASON (1893–1973). She had her first singing lessons in Paris from Enrico Bertram, then returned to the United States and enrolled at the New England Conservatory of Music at Boston. There she took the opportunity to audition for Henry Russell who remembered her when he was suddenly short of a Nedda. So it was

85 Edith Mason

that at forty-eight hours notice she made her debut at the Boston Opera in 1912. She acquitted herself with honours and reappeared the following season repeating Nedda and adding Zerlina in *Don Giovanni* and, on tour, Micaëla. While in Boston she was so impressed with the skill of the tenor Edmond Clément that she determined to return to Paris to study the French repertory with him. In France she accepted an engagement with the Nice Opéra and then proceeded to Italy to coach with Cottone and Vanzo in Milan. A contract with the Marseilles Opéra was cancelled when war broke out. She made her way back to New York where she was recompensed with an engagement at the Metropolitan; she replaced Elisabeth Schumann. Her first appearance was as 'a very acceptable'[11] Sophie in *Rosenkavalier*; in the course of two seasons she sang Papagena, Gretel, the Woodbird in *Siegfried*, Oscar, Micaëla, a Flowermaiden in *Parsifal*, Marzelline, Samaritana in Zandonai's *Francesca da Rimini*, the Prioress in de Koven's *Canterbury Pilgrims* and Ah-Yoe in Leoni's *L'Oracolo*; the last three in their Met premieres. 1917 and 1918 were spent in Latin America touring with the Bracale Opera Company.

When the war ended she returned to France. Her debut took place at the Théâtre-Lyrique in what was incorrectly described as the first Paris production of Boito's *Mefistofele*, with Vanni Marcoux. 'Her very beautiful, very pure and very brilliant voice'[12] at once found favour. Almost immediately after some performances of *Faust* at Monte Carlo with Muratore, she was invited to the Opéra to sing Juliette, Gilda, Salomé in *Hérodiade* and Marguerite; then came

> a very successful debut at the Opéra-Comique in the role of Manon. Hers is a very pretty voice, pretty face and she is a charming actress. From the beginning it was clearly apparent that Edith Mason is among the finest interpreters of Massenet.[13]

In the United States again at Ravinia Park as Thaïs '[she] sang the score in a way that revived for the old-timers among the patrons memories of the days of Sybil Sanderson'.[14] With the appointment of her husband Giorgio Polacco as chief conductor of the Chicago Opera in 1921 it followed that Mason would become a leading member of the company. This was at the beginning of Mary Garden's season as 'Directa' but unlike a number of other sopranos on the roster Mason was busy throughout the season. It was probably unnecessary for Polacco to have had to use his influence for she created a sensation in her debut as Madama Butterfly. The beautiful quality of her singing at once established her as a favourite. She was heard subsequently as *Gilda, Marguerite, Manon, Juliette* and *Micaela*. She stayed with the company for twenty years returning regularly until 1930, expanding her repertory with the title-role of Rimsky-Korsakov's *Snegourotchka*, Margherita in *Mefistofele*, Eudoxia in *Ebrea*, Lady Harriet in *Marta*, Mimi, Sophie, Zerlina, Nanetta, Claris in Cadman's *Witches of Salem*, Susanna in *Le Nozze di Figaro* and the title-role in Mascagni's *Iris*, when *The Tribune* wrote: 'Miss Mason classifies among the company's golden throats, a gold that is close to being twenty-four karats fine'.[15] After a break of three years she came again and missed only one season thereafter until her retirement in 1941. In this second period, her voice and art having matured sufficiently, she undertook Violetta and Desdemona.

Abroad she was a guest at La Scala in 1923 as Mimi and four years later sang Marguerite in *Faust* under Toscanini. She appeared at Turin, Rome, at the Maggio Musicale in Florence and at the Salzburg Festival again under Toscanini as Nannetta in *Fal-*

staff. A season at Covent Garden in 1930 disappointed; she suffered throughout from a relaxed throat and was obliged to cancel a number of performances. In 1935 she returned to the Met as Butterfly and Violetta, but Chicago was always her artistic home and it was there that she made her farewell as Mimi in *La Bohème*. The audience 'tossed her enough flowers to start a shop'.[16]

Mason's was a voice of singular sweetness and was true from the lowest tones to the high D flat which she sustained with unparalleled ease at the end of Butterfly's Entrance. The registers were equalised through the entire range; there was no hoarseness at the bottom and it never became shrill at the top. Her record of the Jewel Song is a jewel indeed, the graces delicately yet brilliantly turned and there is something of Patti's genuine musical charm in her singing. She is a mistress of the correct interpretative style with the right proportion of expressive ritards yet without losing the rhythmic pulse. In Teresa del Riego's 'O dry those tears', which seems rather to have been calculated to set them flowing with renewed vigour, she offers the real portamento style, the line drawn through the intervals with differing degrees of completeness to give variety but always underlying it. The Entrance of Butterfly, where Puccini's lyrical and theatrical genius combine to make a most potent effect, has to withstand strong competition but it need bow to none, for its vocal ease and security are unsurpassed. Over the years, as a result of correct organisation, the voice matured nicely; alas, she made too few recordings. Some off-the-air transcriptions taken down after more than a quarter of a century's career show the voice only slightly less fresh, the mechanism largely untouched by time and still able to float the voice with easy grace—a lovely singer.

27. American Concert Sopranos

In her autobiography *You're Only Human Once* Grace Moore remembers ALMA GLUCK (1884–1938) with special affection: 'she was the first great star I ever heard'. She describes the warmth of her voice, the tenderness of her singing, her beauty and her kindness; after she had come to know her she recalls a conversation they had one day as they were driving out in Gluck's Rolls Royce. 'Then I asked her a peculiar question: "It's such a lovely car; does it cost much to get one?"' Gluck was not at all put out by such impertinence. '"I paid for it today with twenty thousand dollars which was part of a hundred thousand dollars check for royalties sent to me by the Victor company.''' Grace was dumbfounded. In fact the sum was only a fraction of Gluck's earnings from her records. One title, 'Carry me back to old Virginny' clocked up sales of more than a million copies. She ranked next after Caruso and with McCormack as one of the most popular gramophone singers of the day.

It was her records and her appearances in concert that made her famous; three seasons at the Metropolitan were only a short and not especially distinguished episode at the beginning of her career. Born in Roumania, she was brought to New York when only a child. There she studied singing with Arturo Buzzi-Peccia, a famous teacher and composer of several delightful trifles. Her operatic debut took place as Sophie in *Werther* with the Met company at the New Theatre. Subsequently at the main auditorium she sang Chloë in the interlude from Tchaikovsky's *Pique Dame*, Freia in *Rheingold*, Leonore in Flotow's *Alessandro Stradella*, the Priestess in *Aida*, Lucinde in Gluck's *Armide*, Nedda, Mimi, Esmeralda in *Verkaufte Braut*, and the Happy Shade in *Orfeo*, when 'she sang "E quest 'asilo" with exquisite taste'.[1]

She left the Met and opera in 1912 and went to Marcella Sembrich for a period of intensive study of the song repertory, and re-emerged in concert at Carnegie Hall two years later.

> One of the results of her study seems to have been the increasing volume of her middle and lower tones in a manner that might be called 'thickening'. There is a bigger and rounder tone than there was. In the upper ranges the voice is thin and frequently lacking in quality, and these tones are frequently also delivered as with effort.[2]

It took her a couple of seasons to get into her stride, but by 1916 the same critic could write:

> Mme Alma Gluck has gained a further and stronger place in the musical public's esteem in recent seasons, and with good reason: for her beautiful voice, for her serious purpose in mastering it wholly and putting it to the finest kind of service, for the artistic value and charm of her singing. Her voice had the aerial transparency and delicate lyric quality that have been so often veiled, and there were certain passages where more brilliancy of tone would have been effective. Mme Gluck's vocal mechanism has been continually bettered, and of the artistic side of her technique, as the

86 Alma Gluck

use of legato, the finish of phrasing, the clearness of diction, she has a firmer grasp. She still has something to acquire in fully embodying the finer spirit and significance of some of the songs she sings.[3]

Gluck's choice of recorded repertory has come in for a good deal of criticism over the years and certainly there are too many trashy pieces. Her recitals, on the other hand, included much that was

87 Hulda
Lashanska

attractive and which at the time must have seemed, in some cases, rather advanced. In 1910 her programme included Mahler's 'Rheinlegendchen', von Schillings's 'Wie wundersam', songs by Rimsky-Korsakov, Rachmaninoff, Moussorgsky and Smetana, and in later years works—and by no means the most familiar—by Strauss, Ravel, Reger, Loewe, Brahms and John Carpenter. She always began with a classical group, usually Bach, Handel, Gluck or Haydn. It was when she got into the recording studio that Victor were quick to point out the pecuniary advantages of 'Aloha Oe', 'Little grey home in the West', 'Perfect day', 'Such a li'l fellow' and so forth. Nevertheless the list does include some interesting titles, and nothing is more tiresome than adopting a superior attitude to the tastes of a bygone era; as if we were now, thanks to critical vigilance, living in the age of enlightenment when only the best was to be heard in the concert hall and at the opera house.

Even the trifles are graced by her remarkable vocal skills and fine musicianship. The voice is a pure lyric soprano, the middle and lower ranges warm and well-rounded and with just a trace of throatiness. At the top she seems to have taken to Sembrich's brilliant, sometimes walloping, attack but she could still sing a high note softly and with perfect security. As an interpreter she was not very imaginative. Her predilection for slow tempi and the narrow range of colour in the voice some-

times introduces a note of monotony, but at her best the extraordinary finish and the precision in detail provide a real musical pleasure. The unaccompanied air of Liuba from Rimsky-Korsakov's *Tsar's Bride* is extremely demanding. Her rhythmic instincts were not notably lively; the folk song 'When love is kind' she polishes with greater finesse than Bori, but there is no charm, no smile in the singing. Perhaps we should be grateful that her achievements are purely vocal and she never resorts to tricks, nor relies on personality to compensate for an indifferent technique. Her classical singing has many fine virtues, in particular the long phrasing and pure tone, yet, as we can hear in 'Come, beloved' from Handel's *Atalanta*, the interpretation is rather bland, and though the words are clear, she does not convince us that she means them. Her recording of Loewe's Canzonetta, a piece which starts out like Wallace and then offers a foretaste of Richard Strauss, is a famous tour de force; the fine shading of the line, the gracefully turned ornaments all beautifully shaped and proportioned, offer a genuine musical charm. If there is any criticism then we must agree with Aldrich 'it would have been improved by a less measured tempo'.[4]

Another of Marcella Sembrich's pupils was the New York-born soprano HULDA LASHANSKA (1893–1974). Her repertory was the same as Gluck's, for their voices were of similar character and range. Several recordings invite direct comparisons; in the case of Loewe's 'Canzonetta' it is a moot point who comes out on top. While still only in her teens Lashanska decided to become a singer. To begin with her family were discouraging, but they capitulated after she won a scholarship to the Institute of Musical Art. Her first teacher was Frieda Ashworth, but she went on for further study to Sembrich. The great lady was so delighted with her pupil's promise that she herself launched Lashanska in a concert at the Lyceum Theatre in 1909, describing her as the best pupil she had ever had—this was before Gluck came to her studio. Thereafter Lashanska went on a short tour in Europe and on her return, following an audition which Sembrich arranged, Walter Damrosch, then Director of the New York Symphony Orchestra, engaged her as a soloist for a concert in the autumn of 1910. She sang:

Liszt's 'Die Lorelei' with the orchestral accompaniment that he himself arranged for it. Miss Lashanska is young and still somewhat immature; but she has naturally a voice of unusually beautiful quality and she sings with real understanding and with a real artistic impulse. She is a singer of promise.[5]

To begin with her career was a series of stops and starts: she stopped for five years after her marriage in 1913, was busy again for a couple of seasons, then stopped to have a baby. It was not until 1921 that she actually took up her career with any real purposefulness, yet even then she never sang in opera or outside the United States; wherever possible she preferred family life, and singing took second place. She remained active in concerts until the mid-thirties, during which time she made many delightful records. For Columbia she recorded light music, for Victor songs by Brahms, Wolf, Strauss, Schubert and duets with the tenor Paul Reimers.

Compared with Gluck in the 'Canzonetta' her voice seems to have been naturally slightly less impressive, both in size and quality, but her singing is more alive, for she uses a faster tempo, which helps her organise the phrasing effectively so that the words come out more spontaneously. The resemblance in matters of technique, articulation of the high notes, command of dynamics, conception of tone are quite striking, and the influence of Sembrich is paramount in both. The detail of Lashanka's execution is not always quite as clear, but unlike Gluck, since the voice is more limpid, she does not permit the occasional trace of breath to escape through the more exacting intervals. As a singer of classical music she is correct and affecting. Gluck's 'Spiagge amate' from his *Paride ed Elena* and Secchi's arrangement of Sarti's 'Lungi dal caro bene' are sung with a graceful flowing legato and purity of style and at the same time with appropriate feeling. There is a warmth and sweetness in the colour of Lashanska's voice that is especially appealing; like Gluck she was a singer whose effects were achieved through the beauty of her art and without affectation or an ingratiating manner.

Though she had an attractive lyric soprano, light in weight but with 'a beautiful and pure tone', the career of ANNA CASE (born 1889) never amounted to much. Her training from Mme Ohrstrom-Renard was wholly American. She made her debut with the Metropolitan Opera in the 1909 season as the Dutch Boy in Massenet's *Werther*; the performance was given by the company during its brief tenure of the New Theatre. She remained a contract artist until the end of the 1916/17 season singing mostly small parts: a Bridesmaid in *Freischütz*, the Happy Shade in *Orfeo*, a Girl in the world premiere of Thuille's *Lobetanz*, the Priestess in *Aida*, the Second Youth in *Zauberflöte*, Feodor in *Boris Godounov* in which she cut a charming figure and sang as agreeably. The biggest thing she managed was Sophie in *Rosen-*

88 Anna Case

kavalier, but though she looked well 'those who had admired her exquisite voice last season were disquieted to hear it so seriously affected by hard usage so soon'.[6] Nothing, of course, wears away the quality of a voice more quickly than comprimario roles. A couple of performances of Micaëla in *Carmen* in the spring of 1917 wrote *finis* to her operatic career, henceforth for the next decade she busied herself as a concert singer and recitalist. As the critics noted, these circumstances were altogether more congenial to her.

Miss Case's voice is one of the most beautiful of its kind that has been heard for a long time. It is a light soprano of the most lyric quality, of delightful freshness and transparent purity when it is heard at its best; a voice that is not adapted for dramatic expression nor for the utterance of deep emotions but yet capable within its limits of a variety of colour and of manifold charming effects. Her programme was chosen with judicious regard to what she is best capable of doing, and also with a sense of musical contrast that spoke of a real musical feeling. She sang the eloquent Lament from Monteverdi's *Arianna* with fitting simplicity; perhaps a little more of such simplicity would have been better in the air 'Angels ever bright and fair'. There was grace in her delivery of Pergolesi's 'Se tu m'ami' and in Dr Arne's English air 'Lovely Celia' which she added to the group. Miss Case showed sympathy and understanding for German Lieder . . . yet there were two occasions when the quality of her sustained tones in Schumann's Röselein and Mondnacht was not maintained with purity and evenness . . . [and] she did not always succeed in preserving the beauty of her tone in imparting vigorous brilliancy.[7]

Case made a large number of recordings for the company of Thomas Edison, who much admired the pure quality of her voice; it suited his recording apparatus. She used to take part in his famous public 'Tone Test' demonstrations. The singer would stand next to the gramophone on the platform, the lights were dimmed and a record put on; at some point the singer would take over. The audience was challenged to state precisely when. In view of the generally poor quality of Edison's records, it is hard to believe that anyone could possibly have been taken in, yet apparently they often were. Which suggests that not only the equipment but the public's ears have also developed greater high fidelity over the years.

Case's is a high and bright lyric soprano. On the earliest recordings her singing is fresh and her manner attractive, although there are already evident traces of the hard use to which the voice was subjected during her years at the Metropolitan. By 1930, however, although she was only forty two, the tone is often hoarse and throaty. At her best in Handel's 'Rejoice greatly' there is much to admire in the spirited rhythm—firm but not mechanical—her smooth if not absolutely clear execution of the divisions and her excellent, if a little self-conscious, diction. A vocal arrangement of the Blue Danube Waltz does not suggest she had either the brilliance or charm necessary for this kind of thing. Massenet's 'Open your blue eyes' is more successful and her singing has a pure tone and smooth line.

EVA GAUTHIER (1885–1958), belongs to the small, but from this time ever-increasing, number of singers whom we find devoting themselves almost entirely to the art song. Her career began in Ottawa, Canada, where she was born, as a contralto soloist in a church choir. After a successful concert debut in 1901 she left for Europe to study, first in London with William Shakespeare, one of the elder Lamperti's most distinguished pupils, then in Paris with the Belgian baritone Jacques Bouhy, who also taught Lillian Blauvelt, Suzanne Adams, Louise Homer, Louise Kirkby Lunn, Clara Butt and Leon Rains, afterwards in Berlin with Anna Schoene-Renée, a pupil of Pauline Viardot, and finally in

Milan with Giuseppe Oxilia, who sang Otello with some success in the smaller Italian houses. With such a vocal pedigree, if lessons were all that it took, then we should have expected to find her numbered amongst the greatest opera singers of her day. In fact, her opera career was both brief and unimportant. It was not until after the First World War that her vocation really began and she was able to reveal the value of her wide and extensive studies.

Mme Gauthier is an artist who in two years has become the apostle of ultra-modern music from all countries. This musician, rich in sensibility, is in her absolute element in the modern French music from Chabrier to Satie, Delage, Roussel and Milhaud, with the melodies of Stravinsky and contemporary works from Italy, England and America.[8]

In her campaign on behalf of modern music she travelled throughout Europe and the United States, not only in regular concert and recital tours but also giving lectures in which she sought to introduce audiences to what must then have seemed advanced and strange sounding music. She settled in Greenwich Village, New York, at that time in its heyday as a centre of avant-garde artistic activity, and from whence she came forth regularly in the course of each season during the inter-war years to give recitals in one or other of the city's leading auditoriums. We may assume from the tenor of Aldrich's review of a concert in the winter of 1920 that it was not only with the public that she had to fight an uphill battle:

She presented a programme of music by some of the modern experimenters in the new effects, including three Americans—Winter Watts, Samuel Gardner and Bainbridge Crist. She began with Beethoven's arrangements of Irish, English and Scotch folk-songs, with accompaniment of piano, violin and 'cello . . . Of the modern songs, Ernest Chausson's 'Chanson Perpetuelle', with accompaniment of piano and string quartet, has the kind of glowing harmonic warmth that is remembered as his characteristic utterance. Thenceforward difficulties arose; as in Maurice Ravel's setting of verses by Mallarmé . . . in which the strings played in arpeggioed harmonics, gave the effect of suppressed squeaks, and the voice had little to say . . . Four very short Russian songs, 'Chansons Plaisantes', by Stravinsky, exemplified the fine flower of the composer's style . . . They were found pleasant or unpleasant in accordance with the listener's attitude toward that sort of thing. The scoring gives the

89 Eva Gauthier with Maurice Ravel

obvious intelligence and excellent diction it was not a real success.'[10] She had gone, literally, too far.

Eva Gauthier's voice was neither remarkable for size nor quality but her singing shows the effect of thorough schooling and she was an artist of distinction. In Duparc's 'Chanson Triste' the high notes are bright and true and although in the middle range the tone had become dry and slightly spread, probably from the exertion of stretching the voice through too many unvocal intervals in modern music, this is an affecting performance sung with unfailing taste. A souvenir of Java, a lullaby, sounds rather Europeanised but she contrives a suitably rapt intensity.

composer ample scope for instrumental pleasantries that sometimes escape the bounds of music. A setting of a poem by Shelley most unsuited to music, by Respighi, followed . . . Mme Gauthier sang all these productions with an equal devotion, with a serious attempt at their interpretation and with a sympathetic voice and style. How far she gained sympathy for some of her offerings was not sure.[9]

And her range went further than that. At an early age she had contracted a marriage with a Dutchman and gone to live with him in Java. It did not last, but she put the experience to good advantage. In the summer of 1925 she came to London and gave a recital entitled 'From Java to Jazz'. The programme ranged through Javanese folk songs, lieder, eighteenth century French airs and modern chansons to a group composed in the 'Chinese' style by Arthur Bliss. 'It was a bold experiment (she changed her dress for the Javanese group) but in spite of her

28. American Lyric Sopranos

The Virginia-born soprano ANNA FITZIU (1888–1967) had changed the spelling from Fitzhugh to suit Italian pronunciation; it was in Italy that she began her career. Her first stage appearances were in Chicago in musical comedy, thereafter she left for France to study with William Thorner, who was teaching in Paris prior to his arrival in New York. Her operatic debut took place at Rimini in 1912 as Elsa in *Lohengrin*; she was enthusiastically received. Engagements followed at Catania, as Elsa, Isabeau in Mascagni's opera, and she created the title-role in Savasta's *Vera* making rather more impression than the opera with 'her beautiful voice and its brilliant high notes'.[1] She was a guest at the Costanzi, Rome, in Florence, at Madrid and at the San Carlo, Naples, in 1914 as Fiora in *L'Amore dei tre Re*, again 'the beautiful voice and fine artistry earned great applause'.[2] In 1916 she returned to the United States and was engaged for the role of Rosario in the world premiere of Granados's *Goyescas* at the Metropolitan.

> She is in face, figure and personal presence not conspicuously fitted to portray the aristocratic Spanish lady. She showed sufficient familiarity with stage routine, however, and presented a figure at least plausible. Her voice is not notable for warmth or expressiveness; but there were some passages that she sang with success, especially in the last tableau, in her song to the nightingale and her duet with Fernando.[3]

From her point of view the experience was not a success for she was not invited to sing anything else, and she did not return to the Met. For Granados it was to prove fatal. With the war going on in Europe and in view of currency difficulties he asked to be paid in gold. For safety's sake he sewed it into the linings of his own and his wife's clothing. There was a grim sequel when the *Sussex* was torpedoed on the homeward voyage; they were among the few passengers who did not survive.

In the autumn of 1917 Fitziù made her bow with the Chicago Opera as Tosca, and for two seasons sang Marguerite in *Faust*, Mimi, Nedda and Azora in the opera of that name by Herbert Hadley. She

90 Anna Fitziu

sang it with the company on a visit to the Lexington Theatre, New York, but neither she nor the opera attracted much attention. In 1921 she appeared at Ravinia Park as Tosca and Manon and on more than one occasion joined the San Carlo touring company. At Havana in 1924 she was Tosca to Martinelli's Cavaradossi and was also heard as Desdemona. The next year she returned to the Chicago Opera adding Elsa and Desdemona to her previous repertory. In later years she sang as soloist with Kryl's band. In her retirement she moved to Chicago where she was a successful teacher of singing for a number of years.

It is a good voice, rather fluttery and with a touch of acid at certain moments in the upper range, but this is probably as much Pathé's fault as hers. 'Il bacio' is efficiently sung but not an endearing performance, there is little genuine charm and the high D is only managed after a fashion. The Bach-Gounod 'Ave Maria' requires greater smoothness and vocal poise in the long unfolding line and at the end the support is not certain enough for her to execute the awkward intervals clearly or accurately. She makes something very attractive out of Granados's 'Lover and the Nightingale' despite the diminished and faded accompaniment. This is interesting musically as well as historically—for we must suppose that Granados had gone over the interpretation—the phrasing tender, the voice sweeter than elsewhere, the singing more detailed and imaginative.

The career of the American soprano CAROLINA WHITE (1886–1961) was short and not especially resplendent, but the voice we hear on records seems to have had plenty of cut and thrust, the top notes brilliant and telling. She took lessons in Boston from Weldon Hunt and then sang in concert. In 1907 she journeyed to Italy where she continued her studies under Paolo Longone, later musical director at the Dal Verme, Milan, and afterwards at the Chicago Opera. They were married in 1910. Her operatic debut was at the San Carlo, Naples in 1908 as Gutrune in *Crepuscolo degli Dei*. She made guest appearances at Florence as Minnie in *Fanciulla del West* in 1912, at Parma as Aida in 1913 and at various other Italian theatres in the years before the First World War. In 1910 came a summons from the Chicago Opera. After singing Santuzza and Aida she created the role of Minnie in the first Chicago performances of Puccini's *Fanciulla del West*. These followed only fifteen days after the world premiere in New York and were preceded by a great deal of ballyhoo. In an interview White told the papers:

The whole thing is simply glorious. There are several passages that are unusually exquisite. One of these is where the Girl says goodbye to all the boys at the 'Polka'. There is so much feeling and pathos in the music here that I am afraid my throat will close up when I go to sing it.[4]

She need not have worried for in the event she was thought perfect; 'she looked the part and sang it well'.[5] But in spite of her vociferous advocacy both off and on stage, the reception was only polite. She sang the part subsequently in Boston with similar personal success.

In Chicago the following season, her roles included the Countess in *Le Nozze di Figaro*, Giulietta in *Les Contes d'Hoffmann*, Barbara in the world premiere of Victor Herbert's *Natoma*, in which Garden took the name part, Susanna in Wolf-Ferrari's *Segreto di Susanna*, Elsa in *Lohengrin* and Maliella in Wolf-Ferrari's *Gioielli della Madonna*; when the company appeared in New York Henderson was warm in his praise of her mastery of such 'appallingly exacting'[6] music. It was an arduous schedule and she protested to the Director, Andreas

91 Carolina White as Minnie in *Fanciulla del West*

Dippel; his reply that singers never over-work and only over-eat was particularly impertinent in her case, for she was a handsome woman with a slim figure. In her last two seasons her repertory was expanded further with Manon Lescaut, Salomé in Massenet's *Hérodiade*, Gioconda, Donna Elvira and Fedora. With the cancellation of the 1914 season her operatic career came to an end and she undertook a tour in vaudeville; thenceforth into the early twenties she was busy in concert and operetta. In 1918 she appeared in the silent film *My Cousin Caruso* opposite the great tenor; it was an unrewarding experience for both of them. After 1922 and her separation from Longone. She seems to have retired from the stage.

Hers is an interesting voice, the registers clearly established, but the middle and lower ranges are rather dull in timbre, vibratory and slightly throaty. She does not have a good line here and the execution of slurred intervals is clouded with aspirates. The upper range has striking presence; the ease, brilliance and certainty with which she puts out tones reminding us of a less dramatic version of that other, and great, American soprano Lillian Nordica. She does her best with 'I list the trill of golden throat' from *Natoma*, her diction is clear and she brings off the final difficult ascending phrases, but this is not the Herbert that we know and love; better by far 'A kiss in the dark'. 'Roberto tu che adoro' from Meyerbeer's *Roberto il diavolo* begins a little inexpressively and she cannot quite get the voice round the tricky middle section, but at the end when the expanding melody takes her up aloft the voice opens out to wonderful effect.

The career of the American-born soprano LUCILLE MARCEL (1887–1921) was cut short by her early death. Her recordings reveal a full and rounded lyrical voice of a particularly beautiful quality throughout its range, a singer of considerable skill and a refined artist. Born in New York, at first she studied the piano with Alexander Lambert, a pupil of Liszt, later taking vocal instruction from Mme Serrano. After a period spent in Berlin, she moved to Paris to the studio of Jean de Reszke; the obvious similarity in her tone production and style to other de Reszke pupils such as Marie Louise Edvina, Rachel Morton and to a lesser extent Carmen Melis has been noted before. In the spring of 1908 de Reszke recommended her to the conductor-composer Felix Weingartner who had just succeeded Mahler at the Vienna Imperial Opera. She made her debut there soon afterwards and was well received:

92 Lucille Marcel

stage with lightning rapidity. Her execution of the fearful dance . . . was demoniacal in the extreme.[8]

When Weingartner moved to Hamburg in 1910, Lucille went with him. Two years later they travelled to Boston together, where the obvious warmth of their attachment and its irregularity occasioned comment. There was, however, something so frank about Marcel's happiness that it disarmed criticism. When she was not singing herself she would sit in a prominently placed box and every time the maestro came on or went off wave to him ecstatically with her scarf, like Isolde, her face wreathed in smiles. Eventually in 1913 they were married. At Boston she sang Marguerite, Aida, Tosca, the title-role in Bizet's *Djamileh* in its first US performance, Desdemona and Eva, all under Weingartner's direction. Her singing was 'strong, full [and] rich in quality'.[9]

She was a soloist in a number of concerts in Boston, on one occasion with the violinist Jan Kubelik, on another in company with Melba. She sang works by Mozart, Beethoven and Weingartner. The couple made extensive concert tours together throughout Europe, at Antwerp programming songs by Berlioz, at Barcelona Gluck, Mozart and Weingartner. In Paris she was praised for her

> admirable voice, with its brilliant ring, well trained. She sang equally successfully in French and German with a mastery that roused the enthusiasm of the audience and she was obliged to repeat several pieces.[10]

Marcel was a guest with the Boston Opera at the Théâtre des Champs Elysées in 1914 as Desdemona and Eva. When Weingartner returned to Vienna she sang there too. She made her last appearance as Tosca in June 1921, only a week before her sudden death from atrophy of the kidneys.

The quality of Marcel's voice has been well caught on the short list of recordings she made in Vienna and later in the United States. Tosca's 'Vissi d'arte' is sung with a firm legato and warm tone; though others have managed the Jewel Song more brilliantly, her singing here is very lovely. It is also in Weingartner's song 'Thou art a child' which displays the limpid production in a long, smoothly-sustained piano line. It is an attractive if rather monotonous piece; a modulation or two would not have come amiss. The 'Ave Maria' of Desdemona she phrases affectionately with well-judged and graceful portamenti and the final, difficult ascent to the

Her low notes are wonderful but the voice is even throughout its register. Sobinov went into ecstasy [about her singing], an unusual voice, splendid training, intelligence and musical temperament.[7]

The biggest impression she made was on Weingartner, and there soon developed a romantic relationship. At his suggestion, the following year, she created the title-role in the local premiere of Strauss's *Elektra* and displayed

> unusual histrionic ability. Her movements were quick, graceful and cat-like, and she often darted across the

soft high A flat is brought off with perfect security and poise. Throughout the voice moves freely without any suggestion of being 'fixed' and there is a natural movement in it which gives the tone life and makes it affecting. On the other hand a curious deadness overtakes some of her interpretations, as if she had learned everything by rote; perhaps she was too much in awe of Weingartner—he provides the accompaniment on most, probably all, of her records—and one listens in vain for a little spontaneous temperament which would have put the final seal on her art. On none of her records does she seem very conscious of the words; this diminishes the impact of 'Vissi d'arte' considerably. In the American series they are often not very clear but since this was also a peculiarity of Columbia's recording system at the time, it is not possible to be certain whether the fault was hers alone. She was a conscientious rather than a great artist, but her finely schooled voice and its mellow tone provide a real musical pleasure.

The Alabama-born lyric soprano JULIA HEINRICH (1880–1919), daughter of a well-known German baritone, was not, so far as we can tell from her records, a great interpretative artist, but hers was a voice of singular purity and beauty. Her father was her only teacher and in her late teens her name already figured as a supporting artist on his concert bills. She made her operatic debut in Germany, and sang at Elberfield between 1910 and 1913; for the next two years she was at the Hamburg Opera and was heard there in *The Ring* cycle as Sieglinde. In 1915 she joined the Met making a 'quiet' debut as Gutrune, but failed to please and her only other roles were Waltraute in *Walküre* and the Second Lady in *Zauberflöte*. Probably her return to New York had been precipitated by the advent of war and her precarious position in Germany (in spite of her parentage). Thenceforth she sang extensively throughout the United States in concert and in 1919 went on tour as a demonstration artist for the Edison company. It was after a concert at a small Louisiana town, while she was waiting on the station platform for a train to Baton Rouge, that she was killed instantly by a derailed locomotive. Hers was the second of three such accidents involving singers. In 1914 the British light baritone Richard Green, who was the first London Silvio in *Pagliacci*, in a state of alcoholic depression had thrown himself in front of a train at Surbiton, Surrey. The year after the Heinrich accident Gervase Elwes was killed at Boston station, in circumstances described more fully elsewhere.

93 Julia Heinrich

A recording of Leonora's prayer 'Madre, pietosa vergine' from *Forza del Destino* though not perfectly idiomatic, is a piece of singing of rare beauty, the highest notes radiantly sweet and pure. The phrasing is chopped up a bit and hurried to fit as much as possible on to one side of a record, but she sings with feeling even if the emotion is rather generalised and she does not seem too secure in her use of the Italian language. Whatever its shortcomings, however, the lovely quality of her singing is a real joy.

MARGUERITE NAMARA (1888–1977) was an interesting and colourful personality. Her career never amounted to much for she could not decide which one to follow. As a child she studied the piano and singing with her mother. She made her debut as Marguerite in *Faust* at Genoa in 1908 when she was barely twenty. The experience seems to have convinced her of the need for further study and she journeyed to Paris to the studio of Jean de Reszke. After a season of operetta, she returned to the United States. She appeared at the Metropolitan in the 1912/13 season but only in a Sunday night concert. In the course of the next few years she was

94 Marguerite Namara

characteristic style at the keyboard, which in some songs of de Falla is a spinet made to order by Arnold Dolmetsch; in these later years she was especially interested in Spanish music.

Her voice was of modest size and range but an instrument of fine quality, the tone warm and rounded and in her fondness for portamento her style reminds us of another of Jean de Reszke's pupils, Maggie Teyte. The fragrant quality of Massenet's song 'Si les fleurs' suits her perfectly and the voice's neat but rapid tremolo is not unsuitable. Her account of Manon's Gavotte makes rather free but there is much pleasure to be derived from the sweetness and charm of her delivery; her trill flutters a little but the high notes are pure, even if the top D lay outside her range. A delightful morsel by Buzzi-Peccia 'Morenita' is similarly affecting. All her records are attractive even if she was never really more than an amateur.

29. *Gramophone Singers*

Over the years those who collect and comment on old records have shown a tendency to discount the very many beautiful recordings by British and American concert and ballad singers, often forgotten names now, who appeared only rarely, sometimes never, in the theatre. In this they are merely perpetuating the preoccupations of a society long gone when opera was the most glamorous entertainment in the world and few, if any, concert artists acquired the reputation, or enjoyed the fees of the greatest opera singers. The record companies were reflecting this, and not making an artistic judgment, when they dignified sometimes quite mediocre German and French opera singers with the red label and discriminated against so great a singer as, say, Peter Dawson, with the mournful colours of purple and black. Some concert artists lacked the resources to stand up to the rough and tumble of a career at the opera house, but just because they could not browbeat their audiences with sheer decibels of sound, distract attention with their dramatic skill (or the occasional glimpse of a curvaceous leg), they were obliged to rely on the quality of their singing. Many of the finest voices retained a freshness of quality and developed a technical finesse that we listen for in vain on records made by those whose careers were mostly taken up in the theatre.

busy as a soloist with various symphony orchestras and in recital as a supporting artist to a number of famous singers including John McCormack. At the same time she became interested in the dance and joined a class of Isadora Duncan who later declared Namara to be one of her best pupils. Namara sang with the Chicago Opera on odd occasions between 1919 and 1922, as Micaëla, Olga in *Fedora* and Thaïs. In Paris again, in 1923, she made her debut at the Opéra-Comique as Violetta and was subsequently heard as Manon and Mimi. We read of her next in Hollywood taking various parts in silent movies, including one opposite Rudolph Valentino. When the talkies arrived she was Carmen in the first sound film adaptation of Bizet's opera. On Broadway she starred with John Charles Thomas in Lehár's *Alone at last*. Her dramatic creations included Mme Darushka in *Claudia* and she played opposite John Lodge in *A Night of Love*, in both of these she sang a little. She remained active in concert and recital for many years in Europe and the United States, and was still making records as late as 1955. Although the voice was not what it had once been, these are delightfully impromptu. She accompanies herself in

95 Eleanor Jones-Hudson

ELEANOR JONES-HUDSON (1874–1946), whose career only just continued into the period of our discussion, was a popular British concert singer and her records of arias from opera and oratorio, ballads and songs sold prodigiously in her life-time and still appeal to lovers of fine singing today. Born in Wales, as a child she liked to raise her voice at local musical events; by the time she reached her late teens it was apparent that she had the talent to profit from professional training. A group of local music-lovers set up a fund to raise sufficient money to enable her to go to Cardiff and study with Madame Clara Novello Davies, a prominent figure in Welsh musical life; a soprano herself, later choral conductor, she taught many well-known singers including Clara Butt, and her son was the popular light opera composer Ivor Novello.

In 1896 Eleanor Jones, as she then was, secured a scholarship to the Royal College of Music, London, and became a pupil of Anna Williams, a famous concert soprano in Victorian days, whose own teacher, John Welch, like Santley, had been a pupil of Gaetano Nava in Milan. Jones proposed to travel to Italy herself but circumstances, namely Eli Hudson, a flautist of considerable distinction and later Chairman of Beecham's New Symphony Orchestra, intervened, and they were married in 1900. Thereafter she was busy in oratorio, concerts and recitals throughout Great Britain and especially in the recording studios of the Gramophone company, Zonophone and Odeon, under her own name, but sometimes as Alvena Yarrow and Madame Deering.

On the outbreak of war, at the instigation of the impresario Stoll, Eleanor with her husband and his sister Winnie, an accomplished executant on a variety of instruments, formed the Hudson Trio and toured the leading provincial theatrical circuits for the next three years; their programmes were a mixture of classical and light music. In 1917 at Knowsley Hall, Liverpool, they performed in front of King George V and Queen Mary. Later that year Hudson was drafted into the army; he was killed in the last weeks of the war. Immediately thereafter Jones-Hudson retired to Wales, though she did re-emerge from time to time for charity concerts and church functions, both as a singer and in melodramas and dramatic recitations.

Hers was not the kind of voice that rose over the Wagnerian flood and stirred vast multitudes, nor was she a high priestess buried in the interpretative depths. Her programmes did not demand such things; it was by the ineffable sweetness of the singing itself that she charmed. The voice is a high, pure, lyric soprano, the production easy and limpid throughout its range. The soft-grained warmth of the tone in Lurline's 'Sweet spirit hear my prayer' conjures up visions of evenings spent around the piano in the parlour, where the pleasure that beautiful singing can give was known and fully appreciated by thousands who never went to the opera. Hers was a cultivated art, the legato smooth and her diction an object lesson in clarity, but it

96 Ruth Vincent as Sophia in German's *Tom Jones*

never interferes with the flow of tone and there is no exaggerated ejaculation of consonants. She phrases gracefully and the voice is nicely responsive to shifting mood and tempo. Her account of the Israelite Woman's 'Let the bright Seraphim' from Handel's *Samson*, though accurately despatched in the divisions, lacks the boldness that would have come from theatrical experience; it rather peters out at the end without a cadenza or even a flourish. This absence of sensationalism, however, of all suggestion of artiness and contrivance, was in some measure a part of what makes her manner seem so truthful and spontaneous. Her record of Musetta's Waltz from *La Bohème* has the special interest of being one of the very few recordings of the original version of the song, only to be found in first editions of the score.

A British soprano whose career embraced operetta, opera and concert hall, RUTH VINCENT (1877–1955) made some delightful recordings. She was a pupil, perhaps the most successful, of Herman Klein, the critic and singing teacher whose books on singing and singers, especially Patti, still make interesting reading today. Her debut took place in 1896 at the Savoy Theatre as Gretchen in the first performance of Gilbert and Sullivan's *The Grand Duke*, and during the next two years she remained with the D'Oyly Carte company taking part in Gilbert and Sullivan pieces including *H.M.S. Pinafore* and *The Sorcerer*, and in an English version of Messager's *Véronique*. After 1898 she sang mostly in musical comedy; in 1907 she created Sophia in Edward German's *Tom Jones*. Three years later Beecham engaged her for his first season of opera at Covent Garden; in February 1910 she sang Micaëla in *Carmen*, Gretel and created Vrenchen in Delius's *A Village Romeo and Juliet*. In the summer that year she joined Beecham's English opéra-comique company at His Majesty's Theatre. Her roles included Gretel, Fiordiligi in *Così fan tutte*, Isidora in Missa's *Muguette* which 'she sang and acted with quiet charm'[1] and Antonia in *Les Contes d'Hoffmann*, when 'her rendering of the fine music . . . deserved great praise'.[2] At Covent Garden again that autumn she repeated Micaëla, Gretel and Antonia and was also Zerlina in *Don Giovanni*. She 'made a first appearance in oratorio' at the Albert Hall on Good Friday 1912, as soprano soloist in the *Messiah*, 'her operatic experience enabling her to give quite a fresh and characteristic interpretation to the familiar music'.[3]

Her records reveal an agreeable light soprano not remarkable in any way, but with an attractive

97 Lucy Isabelle Marsh

timbre which she uses expressively. Occasionally in the middle range the tone sounds a bit frayed, doubtless from nightly appearances in operetta. She puts across the Waltz Song from *Tom Jones* with a nice lilting rhythm and appropriate character, but the voice sounds fresher and the intonation rather more secure in Bemberg's 'Nymphes et Sylvains', and here too she manages to sustain the trills clearly.

If inclusion here depended solely on the magnitude of the singer's career in opera or concert, on his or her international repute, then there would hardly be a place for LUCY ISABELLE MARSH (1878–1956), for—so far as is known—she never appeared on stage or sang outside the United States. She studied first in New York with Walter Hall and then in Paris with Trabadello, the teacher of Mary Garden. Upon her return she established herself as a church singer and was in much demand as an oratorio soloist. The gramophone companies soon discovered that the soft and rounded quality of her voice made a suitable impression on records and she made many of them. She was a particularly fine duet singer; with McCormack in 'Parle-moi de ma mère' from *Carmen*, she contrives a ravishing effect with her sweet and steady tones. Like McCormack, she would have been unthinkable in the theatre in *Aida*, but their recording of the Tomb Scene is a performance of considerable musical distinction. Nowadays, in the name of dramatic verisimilitude all manner of wobbly, strenuous and inaccurate singing is tolerated in this duet. McCormack and Marsh remind us how much of its period the music is and closely related to popular ballad duets, how it depends for its effect on the simplest and most lyrical utterance, where the singers' tones are pure and limpid, perfectly matched and in tune. The clarity of her enunciation in Italian is rather embarrassing for she has a strong accent; in English, however, in Sir John Stevenson's setting of Shakespeare's 'Tell me where is fancy bred', another duet—where she is joined by the admirable Reinald Werrenrath—it is the beautiful marriage of word and tone which makes their singing so affecting.

Marsh was by no means the only American soprano whose name is known to us today only through her gramophone records. OLIVE KLINE (1885–1976) was another whose activities elsewhere seem to have been minimal, or at any rate gained little publicity. She was but one of many delightful and skilful singers whose voices may not have been as imposing as those found in the opera house or even in the recital room. Her vocal art and musicianship—though at the service of light music—were none the less genuine for that. The two idioms were then still roughly harmonious and there was some interchange of artists between them. In fact Kline began her career as an oratorio and church singer and never abandoned these activities, but the natural sweetness of her voice and her great facility found the biggest rewards in ballad and operetta singing. From 1912 she was a stalwart of the Victor company, popping back and forth to Camden recording anything and everything, what others would not or could not do, filling in the gaps, joining in ensembles, trios and duets. She turns up in the Love Duet from *Madama Butterfly* with the strenuous-voiced Paul Althouse; Kline is an affecting Butterfly. Then at the end of the Death Scene from *Don Quichotte*, when Chaliapin turns his gaze upwards to the stars and hears the angelic voice of his ideal beloved, it is the voice of Olive Kline, and her brief contribution is a good deal more true and no less idiomatic than that offered elsewhere by some French singers. Everything Kline touches she sings with the same fine competence, and with those virtues that were once commonplace among professional singers in England and the United States.

It is a moot point whether there is more music in, say, Mascagni, Rabaud or Humperdinck than in

98 Olive Kline

Liza Lehmann, Tosti or Kalman, but it is certain which trio had the more baneful influence on the singers' art. Richard Strauss once told his wife that he could not write like Lehár 'for in a few bars of mine there is more music than in a whole Lehár operetta'. Anyone who has ever been exposed to *The Love of Danae* or *The Egyptian Helen* may feel that he overstated the case. Certain it is that there is not a page in either of those pieces that any singer could make fall so gratefully upon the listener's ear and with such simple musical charm as Olive Kline does the Waltz from Lehár's *Alone at last*.

30. A Quartet of 'Coloraturas'

Melba heard the young coloratura soprano EVELYN SCOTNEY (1886–1967) while she was on tour in Australia in 1909, and was sufficiently impressed to arrange for her to take lessons with the great Mathilde Marchesi, her own teacher. After a year Henry Russell engaged Scotney for the Boston Opera, she made her debut as Frasquita in *Carmen*, singing La Charmeuse in *Thaïs* soon after, creating quite a stir. In the opinion of Hale hers was an unusual voice, 'extraordinarily pure and crystalline in its upper reaches, excellent in florid passages, and possessing a trill uncommonly good for her age'.[1] In the course of a three year engagement she reinforced the good impression she made as Gilda, Lucia, Violetta, Olympia in *Les Contes d'Hoffmann* and Lady Harriet in *Marta*. Later there were complaints that her tone was sometimes white and infantile-sounding in the middle range, but despite the competition from Tetrazzini in the first three roles, she seems to have acquitted herself with honours. After the war in 1919 she was engaged at the Metropolitan for two seasons. Her first appearance was as Eudoxie in *La Juive*, the last new production mounted for Caruso.

> Her voice is a high soprano, capable of great and piercing power, and with some dexterity in florid music, of which the part affords a few measures. Yet, as it was most often heard yesterday, it is not without an acid quality.[2]

Later she sang the Queen in Rimsky-Korsakov's *Le Coq d'or* and took part in some Sunday concerts and two galas, with excerpts from *Lucia*. Barrientos and Garrison were in the company at the time and Scotney got few opportunities for the kind of display in which she excelled. For the rest of her

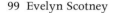

99 Evelyn Scotney

career she travelled widely in concert tours in the United States, Australia and Great Britain, where she made her final appearances in 1934 and where she lived during her retirement.

She made a sizeable quantity of records. Hers is a very light-weight soprano but there is a heady brilliance and point to the tone so that it would have told even in a big auditorium. In weight and range she reminds us of Maria Ivogün and both singers had problems sustaining the highest notes. Ivogün's voice is the sweeter, but Scotney's securer and in the Italian repertory she is a more stylish singer. Her performance of 'Una voce poco fà' lacks the vocal glamour of Galli-Curci, but it is delightfully done and the ornamentations, mostly traditional, are accurate and delicately turned all the way up to the high F, though at the end she contents herself with C. It is one of the best soprano versions on record. Her passage work is generally clean and the staccati particularly neat and clear, only the trill somewhat disappoints and is hardly up to a Marchesi pupil's usual standards. She makes something gay and dazzling out of Proch's famous set of variations Op. 164—what, one wonders, were the other one hundred and sixty-three like? In the electric period the voice is not as fresh and the singing not quite as easy, especially at the top, but she made several outstanding song recordings.

Frieda Hempel and Maria Barrientos were the ranking names in the coloratura soprano repertory at the Met in the years between 1915 and 1920, while the admirable MABEL GARRISON (1886–1963) was kept busy filling in the gaps and when it came to the top of the stave was, in fact, securer than either lady. From Baltimore, where she studied with Odenthal and then at the Peabody Institute, she moved to New York for further instruction with Oscar Saenger and Herbert Witherspoon. She made her debut in 1912 with a small provincial opera group as Philine in *Mignon*. Her skills were noted, and when in the following season she appeared at one of the Met's Sunday night concerts, *The Tribune* wrote that 'she possesses a light soprano voice of unusual purity and sweetness, a fluent and sure style'.[3] Her first stage appearance was in the small part of Frasquita in *Carmen*, after which she was heard as Berthe in Weber's *Euryanthe* and the Second Flowermaiden in *Parsifal*, then came her first important assignment as Urbain in *Les Huguenots*, in which direct comparisons were possible with Hempel as the Queen. Henderson thought Garrison 'sang very well'[4] but in view of the opera's illustrious performing tradition in New York, not

100 Mabel Garrison   101 Florence Macbeth   102 Luella Paikin

surprisingly he added 'without the voice, the experience or the style demanded by the role'.[5] In the course of the next six seasons other small roles included Biancofiore in the local premiere of Zandonai's *Francesca da Rimini*, Gretel, then, for her 'pluck and perseverence'[6] she was promoted to Rosina, Gilda and Lucia. She stepped in when Hempel had one of her frequent indispositions at the prospect of the Queen of the Night's high Fs. Later she sang the Queen of Shemakhan in Rimsky-Korsakov's *Le Coq d'or*, Lady Harriet in *Marta* and Adina in *L'Elisir d'Amore*. With the depletion of the older repertory after Caruso's death and Galli-Curci's engagement, Hempel, Barrientos and Garrison left. When Mozart's *Impresario* and *Bastien and Bastienne* were given at the Empire Theatre, New York, she was Mme Hofer in the former and Bastienne in the latter. She travelled to Europe and appeared at the Berlin State Opera and with the Hamburg and Cologne companies, returning in 1925 to accept an engagement as Rosina with the Chicago Opera. Thereafter she was principally active as a concert and recital singer. In her retirement she taught in Northampton, Massachusetts.

Her records include an accomplished rendering of the Doll's Song from *The Tales of Hoffmann*, not accurate in every detail—the intonation slips once or twice—but executed with neatness and considerable brilliance, the high notes especially true. Evidence of good schooling and security can be heard too

in the air 'Call me thine own' from Halévy's opéra-comique *L'Eclair*. She sustains the line smoothly and though there are no special nuances, the pretty quality of her voice is appealing.

Whilst Mabel Garrison was busy supporting Mmes Hempel and Barrientos at the Met, another young coloratura, FLORENCE MACBETH (1891–), was called in at Chicago after Tetrazzini had decided that her stage career was over. Three years later Galli-Curci arrived on the scene and it says something for Macbeth's voice and skill that although she was put very much in the shade, she withstood the competition and even survived Galli-Curci, for her Chicago career continued until 1928. She studied in New York and then Paris. Her first engagements were in concert; in 1912 she sang at the Dutch resort of Scheveningen. The following year she made a short tour in Germany appearing in concerts and as a guest artist at the Braunschweig Opera as Rosina and at Dresden and Darmstadt. The German critics were very complimentary. The same season she came to London and was the soloist in a concert at the Queen's Hall under the direction of Beecham.

She has a voice of much charm and wide compass, and the attraction in her singing of such show-pieces as the Bell Song from *Lakmé* and 'Una voce' was by no means solely due to neatness of vocalisation.[7]

This success led to a tour through the English provinces the following season; she appeared at Bournemouth, Liverpool, Birmingham and Manchester, as well as in London again. Had the war not intervened it seems likely that she would have returned.

In the autumn of 1913 came her Chicago debut as Rosina, but at first too much advance publicity seems to have taken the edge off the occasion. She was a member of the company in nine seasons between 1915 and 1928. Her repertory ranged through Lucia, Gilda, Philine, Olympia, Anna in *Loreley* (which she sang with the company on tour in New York), Ophelia to the Hamlet of Ruffo, Adina, Oscar, Mimi, Lakmé, Eudoxie in *La Juive*, Inez in *Africana*, Amina and Lady Harriet in *Marta*. She was heard as Gilda at the Ravinia Park summer season in 1921 and she returned in 1931 for the local premiere of Deems Taylor's *Peter Ibbetson*. Her career took her to the west coast and into the thirties she toured extensively in operetta, Gilbert and Sullivan, and in concert.

The voice, though small, is pure and of a most pleasing quality; finer than Garrison's. She is adept in all ornamentation but as with many voices of this type, sacrifices accuracy for smoothness in passage work. The staccati are especially true; in Benedict's Variations on the Carnival of Venice, she shows them off to fine if not perhaps dazzling effect. 'O luce di quest' anima' from *Linda*, though done neatly and with some grace, has not the spirit and dash that distinguish the greatest singers in this kind of music. The cadenza includes a couple of fine high Ds but she spoils the effect squeezing out the final C. Quite enchanting is Roberts's 'Pierrot', a typical period piece; her sweet, unaffected style and accurate intonation suit it perfectly.

The career of LUELLA PAIKIN (born 1900), one of the youngest singers included in this volume, began at La Scala, Milan, as the first boy in *Flauto Magico* under Toscanini's direction in 1923. The following season she was promoted to Amor in Gluck's *Orfeo* with Alfani-Tellini and Anitua, again conducted by Toscanini. Born in Manchester, she studied with Marie Brema, a distinguished British mezzo-soprano who could have made records, but did not. After La Scala Paikin appeared in 1920 as Lucia at the San Carlo, and at Cosenza before proceeding back to Great Britain. There she was successively a principal with the British National Opera and with the Carl Rosa Company. In 1927 she sang Lakmé at the Opéra-Comique. During the 1930s she appeared in musical comedy in London and

elsewhere. It was not until 1938 that she made her Covent Garden debut succeeding Pagliughi as Gilda in some performances of *Rigoletto* with Gigli and Tagliabue under Serafin. 'She made a charming Gilda, and sang with great skill and beauty',[8] In the autumn of the same year she was heard in the role again in Percy Heming's English Opera season, this time in company with Heddle Nash and Dennis Noble. Throughout her career she often sang in concerts and on the radio.

She was an artist of modest resources with a modest career. On records, though the voice is tiny, the purity of tone and the ease with which she sings are appealing. Nannetta's 'Sul fil d'un soffio etesio' has an appropriately fresh and girlish charm. The *Mignon* Polonaise is a game try but for this she has neither the voice nor the technique. She sings 'Ah yes 'tis so' from Bach's cantata *Phoebus and Pan*, with dainty grace and clear diction; a few variants, however, would not have been out of place.

31. English Lyric Sopranos

A graduate of the English *Ring* Cycle at Covent Garden in 1908, MAUD PERCEVAL ALLEN (1880–1955) was a pupil of William Shakespeare, the famous London teacher who had studied in Milan with the elder Lamperti. Allen's concert debut took place in 1905 and thereafter she was busy with engagements in the English provinces. Three years later she jumped in at the deep end as Brünnhilde in the *Twilight of the Gods*:

> She sang the music with great power, certainty of intonation, and fine musical effect . . . the occasion was her first appearance on stage; and her success was extraordinary, if we take this into account, for Brünnhilde in the last play of the trilogy is one of the hardest parts in music drama from the histrionic point of view; and if Miss Allen failed to convey the meaning of the character, she is praised for her courage in attempting it.[1]

She was also heard that season as the *Siegfried* Brünnhilde. Her operatic career continued at Covent Garden in 1910 when Beecham booked her for both of his seasons. In the first she was Brangäne in *Tristan*, a 'clear-sounding Rebecca'[2] in Sullivan's *Ivanhoe* and she also sang in Debussy's *L'Enfant prodigue*. In the second she repeated her Brangäne and sang Donna Elvira in a *Don Giovanni* with a cast that also included Giuseppe de Luca, Walter Hyde and Ruth Vincent. Beecham brought her forward again in his winter season of 1919/20; she sang Elisabeth in *Tannhäuser* and Isolde. Outside Great Britain she appeared in opera with the Quinlan Company on tour in the United States.

Throughout her career she was chiefly occupied in concerts and oratorio. We read of her attracting considerable attention as a soloist with the London Philharmonic Orchestra under Mancinelli by her 'very vivid singing of Isolde's Narration [in which she showed] how valuable her stage experience has been to her.'[3] In the autumn of 1910 she included Elsa's Dream and Elisabeth's Greeting in a programme conducted by Landon Ronald and 'sang with much brilliance and power'. The following season she was the Brünnhilde in an English *Ring* Cycle given in concert at Bristol, joined Clara Butt as one of the soloists in *Israel in Egypt* in the Handel Triennial Festival at the Crystal Palace, and sang in Coleridge-Taylor's *Endymion's Dream* and Elgar's

103 Maud Perceval Allen

Caractacus. She made extensive tours of the British Empire and also appeared in concert at Chicago, Philadelphia and Boston.

Allen's singing on records gives a good idea of the general standards prevailing among British singers in the second decade of this century. Her list includes a large number of ballads, too many doubtless for austere tastes nowadays, yet it was the exacting demands these made—the need to modulate the voice, to sing with a firm tone and ingratiating quality—that put a fine finish on the art of even the merely competent. Allen's was not a front-ranking instrument and it seems hard to credit that she had the reserves for Brünnhilde or Isolde, yet there is a compensating warmth of tone and smoothness of emission which are very agreeable and, used to nourish the lyrical episodes in Wagner's operas, would have spoken eloquently for them. Her singing affords a basic musical pleasure. As we can hear in Lucantoni's 'A night in Venice' with John Harrison (another good singer), she was a duettist of impeccable manners, and in Horn's lovely setting of 'I know a bank' the purity of her tone matches that of the mellow contralto of Edna Thornton to perfection. In both records the two voices are appropriately weighted, when responding to each other and in concert, and the intonation is clear and precise. It seems curious that only the finest singers today feel the need to do as much for great music, and that a shrill tone and agitating vibrato, which would never have been tolerated sixty years ago even in Behrend's 'Daddy' or Liza Lehmann's 'In my garden' is, alas, too often accepted in Wagner and Strauss by audiences who have come to expect nothing better.

A number of fine British singers established reputations, albeit local ones, with the Beecham Opera Company which was active at one London theatre or another almost continuously from the summer of 1915 until the autumn of 1920 when it finally went out of existence. One of its leading members, New Zealand born ROSINA BUCKMAN (1880–1948), had a good-sized lyric soprano with a warm and attractive quality. She studied singing in Australia where she made her first stage appearance in light opera. When Melba returned there in 1911 and organised her own opera company, Buckman was a supporting artist; she appeared not only in the opera but on the same concert bill as its leading tenor John McCormack. In 1913 she arrived in London and was engaged for the German season at Covent Garden the following February; she was a Flowermaiden in the first performance there of

104 Rosina Buckman as Madame Butterfly

Parsifal. By the summer she had graduated to Musetta in *Bohème* with Melba and Martinelli. After the outbreak of war she joined the Beecham company at the Shaftesbury Theatre where she created a leading part in Dame Ethel Smythe's *Boatswain's Mate.* Under Beecham she was heard in a variety of roles including Mimi, Butterfly, Aida and even Isolde. In 1919 at Covent Garden she sang the title-role in the first performances in London of Isador de Lara's *Naïl.* Over the previous quarter of a century this remarkable man had produced a whole stream of operas, of which the best known was *Messaline.* At one point he had almost succeeded in turning the Monte Carlo Opera into his own Bayreuth, but then the very rock upon which Monaco rests was shaken when his patroness, the American-born Princess

Alice, suddenly left the Principality—and the Prince—and de Lara went with her. Neither he nor his operas ever returned to Monaco.

From 1921 Buckman was a contract artist of the British National Opera Company and was heard regularly in concerts and recitals during the next six years. Her records show a well-schooled singer. In the middle range the quality is rather vibratory and sometimes pallid, the top, however, rises easily to the high C which we can hear in the 'Inflammatus' from Rossini's *Stabat Mater.* In duet from *Maritana* with Thornton the two voices make a pretty effect in the passage in thirds. Her singing of Leonora's Act One aria from *Trovatore* is accomplished and she introduces an arpeggio variant in the second verse which was traditional; it gives a good idea of the generally high standard of English provincial singing at this time. Elgar's song 'Pleading', which could have been written by almost any ballad composer of that period, is sung with much feeling and yet within the bounds of good taste; it is probably her best recording, showing off her voice and art at their most expressive. Her diction, however, is not ideally clear.

If the Beecham company had a prima donna then that was MIRIAM LICETTE (1892–1969). She studied in Paris with Mathilde Marchesi and took further instruction from Jean de Reszke. After a season spent in Italy in 1911, she returned to England. She joined the Beecham company at the Shaftesbury Theatre, appearing with it successively at the Aldwych, at Drury Lane and finally at Covent Garden in 1919 and 1920. She sang the gamut: after Juliette came Mimi, Constanze, Nanetta, Marguerite in *Faust,* Eva, the Countess in *Le Nozze di Figaro,* Desdemona, Jaroslavna in *Prince Igor,* Vrenchen in Delius's *A Village Romeo and Juliet,* Pamina and Eurydice. With the demise of Beecham's operations in the autumn of 1920, she moved to the British National Opera Company, adding to the list Louise, Zerlina, Thaïs, Manon, Butterfly and Santuzza. In 1928 she returned to Covent Garden, unexpectedly, as Desdemona:

Miss Sheridan had been originally cast for the part . . . but on this occasion Miss Miriam Licette was heard in her place. The latter has not a sufficiently big voice or a sufficiently broad style to combine well with Signor Zanelli, but she had a beauty and sympathy of quality in those passages where she was alone, and the orchestra allowed her to make her points without effort. The 'Salce' song and the prayer in the last act gave her the best opportunity for this.[4]

32. Miura and Bryhn-Langaard

105 Miriam Licette as Louise

The first important Japanese soprano outside her own country, the first to travel widely, TAMAKI MIURA (1884–1946), deserves a place in this anthology, though quite where, it has been difficult to decide; but since her biggest successes were in the United States, it seems fitting to include her here. She took her first lessons in Tokyo where she made her debut in 1914 as Santuzza. Soon after she came to Europe to study with various coaches, teachers and conductors, among them Henry Wood. He recalls 'a splendid voice, clear and penetrating though perhaps not colourful'.[1] She was a supporting artist at the charity concert in October 1914 at the Royal Albert Hall when Adelina Patti made her positively last public appearance. In the autumn of 1915 Max Rabinoff brought her to Boston where she made her first appearance in the title-role of *Madama Butterfly*, which understandably became her 'cheval de bataille'. She was enthusiastically received, but sage Philip Hale cautioned those budding western sopranos who were contemplating a trip to Japan to study Kabuki dancing that authenticity was not guaranteed by going to the lengths of Emma Abbot who spent a week in a mad-house before she undertook Lucia. The following year Miura returned to charm audiences in Mascagni's *Iris*, which was more than the opera did. According to Hale, Mascagni shot his bolt with the opening Hymn to the Sun, and he went on to suggest that both composer and librettist should join poor Iris in the sewer where they had made her fling herself.

Her Butterfly was heard in London with the Beecham company during the First World War. In 1918 she returned to the United States to sing for two seasons with the Chicago Opera; as well as Butterfly she was heard as Madame Chrysanthème in the local premiere of Messager's opera of that name. Apparently it had been adapted by the composer for the occasion, but not sufficiently for the taste of *The Tribune* critic who found the story warmed up Madame Butterfly. When she sang it in New York, Aldrich thought it a very suitable vehicle for her:

> She is captivating as the Japanese wife, with the grace and quickness, the sinuous movements, the picturesque attitudes that her Western companions in Japanese impersonations try in vain to imitate. She has a sufficient command of a voice not of the greatest beauty, and sings with intelligence and expression.[2]

She came again the following season as Donna Elvira in *Don Giovanni* with Stabile, Heddle Nash and Elisabeth Schumann.

Licette's sweet tone and simplicity of style contrast most agreeably with Frank Mullings in duet from *Othello*. She transposes Constanze's 'Ach ich liebte' a semi-tone and sings it in English. Perhaps her voice is a shade light for this music, but there is much pleasure to be derived from its purity, her correct intonation and neat—even brilliant—execution of the exacting fioritura, it is a pity that she did not include the appogiaturas.

In 1920 she was a guest at the Monte Carlo Opera, Barcelona, Florence and at the Costanzi, Rome, where the 'authenticity' of her stage business compensated for a want of Latin temperament and she enjoyed a success. In 1924, in the United States again, she toured with the San Carlo Opera Company and two years later returned to Chicago to create the title-role in Franchetti's *Namiko-San*; based on a particularly gory Japanese tragedy, the more graphic details had been toned down to allow for squeamish audiences. She sang in Italy again, but after 1930 spent most of her time in Japan.

In spite of her unfamiliarity with occidental manners, Wood recalls that she was not slow to cotton on: when she went to Manchester she asked an extortionate fee, plus an umbrella and carpeting on the station platform. He asked her to explain: the fee, she said, was the same that Melba and Patti earned and if they could get it why could not she, while the umbrella and carpet were to protect her from the Mancunian elements—wasn't it always raining there? There was a good answer to the first

107 Borghild Bryhn-Langaard as Tosca

106 Tamaki Miura as Madama Butterfly

which Wood gave her and she settled for something more reasonable; for the rest, he had to agree and she got both umbrella and carpet.

It would be nice to praise Miura's records, especially her 'Un bel dì', but the voice sounds rather small and white and she does not seem to have it under proper control.

Singers often change their names, sometimes for professional, sometimes for marital reasons. Both account for the several incarnations of the Norwegian soprano BORGHILD BRYHN-LANGAARD (1883–1939), alias Borghild Bryn, Borghild Langaard and Borghild Brunelli. She studied first in her own country before proceeding to London in 1907 where she kept herself by working as a governess. Whilst there she sang for Percy Pitt at Covent Garden and secured an engagement for the autumn season that year. Her debut took place on the same night as John McCormack's; she was Santuzza to his Turiddu, then came Laura in some performances of *Gioconda* with Litvinne in the title-role, Thornton, Vignas and de Luca. She was well enough liked to secure a return invitation the following January for the English *Ring* Cycle under Hans Richter. She took the part of Fricka in *Rhinegold* and her Brünnhilde in the *Valkyrie* was 'brilliantly sung'.[3] She reappeared that summer as Santuzza again and Venus in *Tannhäuser* when 'great interest centred round her striking costume, not least because she was a handsome and beautiful young woman'.[4]

In 1911 she was a guest at the Vienna Imperial Opera as Santuzza and Aida. Thereafter she was heard in Italy under the name of Brunelli and at Budapest. In 1914 with the Copenhagen Opera she sang Tosca and Elsa in *Lohengrin* and remained throughout the 1920s principally active in Scandinavia. In the United States her only operatic appearance was as Amelia in *Un Ballo in Maschera* with Bonci and Galeffi with the Chicago Opera in 1919.

Her list of recordings is a short one and though it does include operatic arias from *Tannhäuser*, *Fliegende Holländer*, *Gioconda* and *Cavalleria* many of the titles are Scandinavian songs, particularly the works of Grieg. Nothing could be more sweetly or lovingly sung than her rendering of 'Solveijgs vise' from Grieg's incidental music to *Peer Gynt*. The vocalise is delicately turned and ends on a perfect soft high A. It was said to have been the favourite record of the great Polar explorer Amundsen who took it to the Antarctic with him and played it every day to keep warm; however it was not her singing that did that but having to crank up the hand gramophone every time.

33. Ponselle and Easton

ROSA PONSELLE (1897–1981) was the first great American soprano to make her reputation entirely at home without previously having been to Europe, either to study or to gain experience. As a girl she sang in picture palaces and vaudeville, duetting with her elder sister Carmela Ponselle, a contralto. In the spring of 1918 she sang for William Thorner, who had worked for Jean de Reszke and was then an established coach and vocal scout in New York; it was he who introduced Galli-Curci to Campanini at Chicago. Thorner at once recognised Ponselle's possibilities and took her to Caruso and Romano Romani. An audition with Gatti-Casazza was arranged. The rest is history: she made her operatic debut at the Metropolitan in the first week of the 1918 season, as Leonora in the revival of *Forza del Destino* with Caruso, de Luca and Mardones.

> What a promising debut! Added to her personal attractiveness she possesses a voice of natural beauty

that may prove a gold mine. It is vocal gold, anyhow, with its luscious lower and middle tones, dark, rich and ductile. Brilliant and flexible in the upper register, she is given to forcing the column of breath with the result that the tone becomes hard to steeliness, yet a sweet appealing, sympathetic voice, well placed, well trained. The note of monotony in the tone colour that occasionally intruded may be avoided. Nuance, Nuance, Nuance. That must be mastered.[1]

Her next part was Rezia in Weber's *Oberon* when W. J. Henderson cautioned her against 'the inconsiderate praise of friends' and advised her to sing 'pure lyric roles . . . exercising the flexibility of her marvellous voice in the use of elastic florid music'.[2]

In the course of the next decade her roles included Rachel in *La Juive* with Caruso, Elisabetta in the Met's first production of *Don Carlo*, Santuzza, Elvira in *Ernani*, Margared in Lalo's *Le Roi d'Ys*, Mathilde in *Guglielmo Tell*, Selika in *Africana*, Maddalena in *Andrea Chénier*, Leonora in *Trovatore*, Aida and Gioconda. In these, as Henderson subsequently acknowledged, she demonstrated 'that the ripening of her talent has been the result of a sincerity of purpose and earnest study'.[3] The first major revival of which she was unquestionably the 'raison d'être' took place in 1925 when the Met mounted Spontini's *La Vestale*. It was a fine—perhaps her finest—achievement.

> The beauty, the range and the opulence of the voice have been common knowledge, but Miss Ponselle has not invariably been judicious and finished in its employment. Last night her native temperament and intuition for vocal effect found full play in a highly expressive and artistic interpretation—one that was thoughtfully and finely proportioned, that took account of text as well as song, and of histrionic representation.[4]

It was but a step to Norma. In this, as Oscar Thompson puts it 'it is not necessary to exaggerate Miss Ponselle's success in the role or to attribute it to a technical perfection that it did not altogether attain, to accord this Norma a respectable place in the royal line of Normas'.[5] 'Her Casta Diva was a genuinely beautiful piece of singing [and she] proved that she had given time and labour to the practice of vocalises, though there was much simplification and curtailing of the time-honoured cadenzas. She had also given study to the Bellini recitative. We are bound to confess, however, that in the recitatives, not only Miss Ponselle but every one else in the cast was heavy and monotonous'.[6]

Some of this had to do with the considerable amount of transposition that had been indulged in; by the end of the twenties Ponselle's high C was no longer a reliable note and wherever possible she took the opportunity to avoid it.

Norma represented the high-water mark of her career and she sang it on her first and hugely successful visit to London in 1929. It is an interesting comment on the extent of her reputation that apart from three summer seasons at Covent Garden and some performances of Giulia in *La Vestale* at the Florence Festival in 1933, her operatic career was wholly confined to the Metropolitan Opera Company in New York and on tour in the United States, though she did appear in concert in Havana in 1924. It would be hard to find a singer equally famous in the history of opera who sang comparatively so little and never set foot in a single Italian, French, German, Austrian or South American theatre. As with Galli-Curci, it was the records which established Ponselle's international renown, consolidated it and have sustained it even until today. London also heard her Leonora in *Forza del Destino*, Gioconda, Fiora in *L'Amore dei tre Re*, Fedra in Romani's opera of that name and Violetta, which she sang there for the first time. In pretty well all of them the reception was overwhelming. Newman brushed aside objections to her vocalism in *Traviata* 'in consideration of the fact that she can do practically anything she likes with her voice'.[7] She did, palpably, when she transposed 'Sempre libera' down a tone. In New York where during the last half century nearly all the greatest prima donnas had sung the part and critical memories were still fresh, it was the least successful of her assumptions hitherto:

> Though Miss Ponselle accomplished some beautiful and moving singing in the course of her first American *Traviata*, she will fortify her Violetta in the future, not through violent onslaughts on Verdi's melodic line but through the finished phrasing . . . the unblemished elegance his mid-nineteenth century style demands.[8]

For Henderson too 'she elected to disregard the fact that Verdi's music is essentially lyrical',[9] and he complained of her inappropriately 'declamatory' style.

At the Met her career continued with the title-role in Verdi's *Luisa Miller* and Donna Anna. In the former her singing found high favour and in the latter too she earned enthusiastic notices though the characterisation had a 'curious tentative

quality'[10]—which could hardly be said of the last addition she made to her repertory. In 1935 she undertook Carmen. The part has defeated many great singers from Patti onwards but for Ponselle it was Waterloo. There would be no point in dilating on its many infirmities here, the reader can find them all listed elsewhere.[11] He can also, if he has the stomach, sit through two live recordings, which are relatively easily obtainable; both leave the matter beyond reasonable dispute. Apparently the best that could be said in her favour was that she looked well; photographs suggest more like Carmen Miranda, only without the fruit.

The official version of what came next goes something like this: the Met wanted her back, but up in the realm where she had been undisputed Queen—as Norma particularly and in the operas of Verdi—but she insisted on *Adriana Lecouvreur* as a vocal stepping stone. Johnson declined to oblige. Both parties having established their positions, there was an impasse with neither prepared to make any concessions; meanwhile her last season having come and gone, she had, as it were, departed by default. So far as it goes it is no doubt true, only it does not go far enough. By the mid-thirties, as radio transcriptions of *Traviata*, *Carmen* and various operatic arias testify, the voice was not what it had once been. It had become slightly unsteady, lost much of its brilliance at the top and the high notes were giving her trouble. A role with only a modest range, Adriana Lecouvreur, was just what the doctor ordered. Norma was out of the question; she had been a secret transposer for years but to have brought anything further down would have made it impossible for the other singers. She left, leaving the impression of having done so when still at the top. She continued to sing in concert and on the radio for a few more years and has never ceased to do so at home. Private recordings made during the forties and a couple of LPs of songs in the early fifties show the rested voice had regained much of its old bloom and steadiness, but not the high notes. Privileged guests who heard her at that time came back raving; she must have been delighted when they begged her to make a come-back, but she knew better.

Of one thing there can be no two opinions: Rosa Ponselle's voice is one of the most remarkable on records; a full, lyric-dramatic soprano of characteristic quality, the registers correctly equalised and blended from the low A to, in her early days, an easy if rather steely high C. The production is smooth and secure and she is able to modulate it from a well

108 Rosa Ponselle as Violetta

poised mezza voce through to an imposing forte. Despite its size the tone is always warm and well-rounded, and made an exceptionally good impression on wax. Her virtues are shown off to their best advantage in slow and stately music, as in the two arias of Giulia from *La Vestale* where the noble delivery almost makes us forget how dull and pompous the music is. The steady emission and repose commended her in the operas of Verdi, above all in *Forza del Destino*. Set next to the edgy and tremulous tones of, say, Burzio or Callas in 'Pace, pace mio Dio' how pleasant it is to hear the soft high notes so beautifully taken, the listener can rest assured; yet these notes are somehow meaningless and dislocated, for she does not contrive to frame them, as both those ladies do, within the overall shape of the phrase and give them relevant intensity. Her Leonora falls agreeably on the ear, but without a knowledge of the text the nature of the drama is obscure; there are no subtleties in the rhythm or in the inflection of the words, she sings quickly rather than urgently, and without anguish. A want of expression, apparent to some degree in almost all her recordings, is not simply a deficiency of temperament, but arises from a peculiarity in her voice production. Although not throaty in the usual way, the voice is not completely free; she seems to be holding the tone in the mouth, especially in the middle and lower ranges, so compromising the purity of the vowels and obscuring them with that characteristic diphthonged 'ow' which is present in all her singing. It restricts the range and variety of vocal colour and leads to a certain monotony in her delivery, an inability to differentiate effectively between, say, Violetta, Norma or Giulia. It also accounts for Ponselle's often unclear diction and for the heaviness of her recitative singing which the critics noted. In 'Sediziose voci', before 'Casta diva', the only memorable thing is the soft, high A flat, a traditional interpolation; Ponselle makes a feature of it, and it does not appear, as it should, to be the logical conclusion of all Norma has 'said' before. (The Italians would say 'detto'. Callas and Burzio elsewhere in *Norma* actually 'speak' the recitatives in pure singing tone; Ponselle merely vocalises.)

Her recording—there are three of them in fact—of Elvira's cavatina from *Ernani* has been much praised for the way she manages to negotiate such difficult music for so dark a voice. Certainly it is admirably secure, smoothly sung, neat and with a good trill. But if we apply the strictest standards, the voice does not really flow, slurred notes are not cleanly articulated, the ritards are only the regulation ones and the phrasing is unmemorable. In the cabaletta too, there is a want of grace, accuracy and brilliance.

She is at her best in simple things, where her vocal skills were sufficient and appropriate. 'Scenes that are brightest' from Wallace's *Maritana* delights; the warm manner, poised high notes and attractive variants in the second verse are most affecting. It is unfortunate that her diction is not clearer; it would appear to have been least good in

English. We have a golden opportunity to admire the wonderful support of the piano singing in Rimsky-Korsakov's 'Eastern Romance', a ravishing record. Very lovely too, is Tosti's 'A vucchella'; though she has not the spontaneity that makes Caruso irresistible here, there is a quality in the expansive delivery which helps explain why he himself dubbed her 'the Caruso in petticoats'. She reached the apogee of her fame following her retirement, in the period of the Second World War and immediately thereafter when, understandably, standards were low and there was a dearth of good young singers. Nowadays, when Rossini and Bellini are once again oiling voices, we can agree with contemporary opinion that her achievements in florid music were no more than decently accomplished. As an artist she suffered from provincialism and from a want of international experience. Throughout her career her musicianship remained unformed, like a lesson well-learned, lacking refinement and an identity of its own. Her records are impressive, but as with Nordica, Destinn and Flagstad they cannot reproduce the thrill of being in the presence of such a great voice; it had, as it were, to be seen as well as heard.

Despite the fact that FLORENCE EASTON (1882–1955) was singing the role of Rezia for the first time and despite the tremendous vocal difficulties with which Weber invested his heroine's music, she sang with truly remarkable poise and assurance. In the comparison with her predecessor which is inevitable, Miss Easton chalked to her credit every quality that belongs in the realm of the artistic. In point of diction, style, phrasing and in revealing histrionism she was Ponselle's superior. Only in the matter of natural vocal endowment did she yield precedence.[12]

It was but one of more than forty of Easton's achievements in the course of eleven seasons' sterling service at the Metropolitan. Several of them she undertook at short notice—on occasion in less than forty eight hours—and often when she had never appeared in the part before. In the fortnight between 3 and 17 November 1927 she sang Maddalena in *Andrea Chénier*, Gioconda, Rachel in *La Juive*, Butterfly and the Marschallin; if it was surprising that she could manage them all and in such a relatively short space of time, it was astonishing that the critical response to nearly every one was laudatory. Though unlike her in so many ways Easton had this much in common with Lilli Lehmann; by dint of application, intelligence, musical facility and sheer hard work, she was able to transform a lightweight lyric soprano into a dramatic instrument capable not merely of scaling the Wagnerian heights but with the stamina to stay up there season in and season out.

Born in England, she spent her childhood in Canada but in 1899 returned to study at the Royal College of Music, London, with Agnes Larkom. Afterwards she went to Elliott Haslam, an English singing teacher then living in Paris; in later years it was Haslam whom she acknowledged as her only teacher. In 1903 she joined the Moody-Manners opera company, a reputable touring group active in the English provinces. Her debut was in Newcastle as the Shepherd Boy in *Tannhäuser*. That autumn with the company in a short season at Covent Garden, she sang Stephano in *Romeo and Juliet*. In the spring of 1904 she married one of its principals, the American tenor Francis MacLennan. The next year husband and wife embarked for the United States and an engagement with the Savage Opera company. Easton's American debut took place at Boston as Gilda in *Rigoletto*; the critic Parker, usually hard to please, was much taken with her 'voice of girlish musing and girlish romance'.[13] Subsequently she sang Marguerite and, the next season, Butterfly. At a performance, among the first given in New York city, she shared the role with two other singers, each of them having an act apiece. In 1907 husband and wife were back in Europe to join the Berlin Imperial Opera. Easton made her bow as Marguerite and then, at very short notice, undertook Aida. Her other roles included the First Boy in *Zauberflöte*, a Dryad in Richard Strauss's *Ariadne*, Marie in *Regimentstochter*, Perdita in Goldmark's *Wintermärchen*, Änchen in *Lustigen Weiber von Windsor*, Sophie in *Rosenkavalier* and Madama Butterfly.

The contracts permitted them to make guest appearances elsewhere, and in the winter of 1909 they were at Covent Garden once more. Easton created the role of Beatrice in Edwin Naylor's *The Angelus* and sang Butterfly; she was, incidentally, the first in London to take the high D flat at the end of the entrance.

> Miss Easton has a voice of very agreeable quality, and her acting in the lighter scenes of Act One was quite convincing . . . In the more earnest scenes there was a charming sympathetic quality in the voice, and so much taste in the singing that the pathos was fully brought out.[14]

About this time she began her forays into Wagnerian territory; Elsa and Elisabeth in Berlin, and on tour in Great Britain with various companies 'she distinguished herself'[15] as Sieglinde and Gutrune. When the five years in Berlin were up, they moved on to Hamburg. There her repertory matured: she sang Valentine in *Hugenotten*, Senta, Martha in Kienzl's *Evangelimann*, Grete in Schreker's *Der ferne Klang*, the title-role in Goldmark's *Königin von Saba*, Desdemona, Salome, Venus and Minnie, which she sang opposite Caruso when he came on a visit. In 1915, notwithstanding the hazards of travelling on the high seas in wartime, they ventured across the Atlantic to accept an invitation with the Chicago Opera. In the first season Easton sang only the *Siegfried* Brünnhilde but she came back for Nedda, Gutrune and Butterfly. In 1917, when it became apparent that the United States was being drawn into the war willy-nilly, they decided not to return to Germany. She sang Serpina in New York in the American premiere of Pergolesi's *La Serva Padrona*. With MacLennan she auditioned for the Met, and although Easton came a cropper on the difficult high C in the Nile aria from *Aida*, it was she who was engaged. For the first time their careers were separated; it was the beginning of the end of their marriage.

She made her bow as Santuzza,

> [and] gave a performance of intelligent, refined and musicianly skill, never forcing, but always colouring her tones to suit the emotion of the moment.[16]

She progressed through Ah-Yoe in Leoni's *L'Oracolo*, a vehicle for Scotti, St Elisabeth in the Met's staging of Liszt's oratorio, 'when she stepped into the first rank of Metropolitan stars',[17] Lodoletta, in lieu of Farrar, Lauretta in the world premiere of *Gianni Schicchi*, singing with 'such grace, such sweetness, such modesty, with such beauty of tone as to bring down the house',[18] the title-role in John Hugo's *The Temple Dancer*, Berthe in *Le Prophète*, when Muzio was indisposed, Mother Tyl and Maternal Love in Wolff's setting of Maeterlinck's *L'Oiseau bleu*, Nedda, Rezia, Butterfly, Margherita and Elena in *Mefistofele*, Rachel with Caruso and later Martinelli, Kundry, Fiora, again as a replacement for Muzio, Aida, Isolde, and the Marschallin, of which Krehbiel wrote:

109 Florence Easton

Florence Easton's diction and enunciation was impeccable. She is an artist who always satisfies the demands of critics, but ever and anon brings us a shock of pleasurable surprise. Her predecessors, Mesdames Hempel and Kurt, seemed inimitable as the Princess. Miss Easton invested the character with greater dignity than either, and by voice, action and sincerity won for it a large measure of sympathy.[19]

As Fiordiligi in the first performances at the Met of *Così fan tutte* she drew even more enthusiastic notices, she 'sang with authority, with a true perception of Mozart's style, and many qualific ations to present it brilliantly, artistically, with a power and expression'.[20] Then came Eva, Maddalena, Elisabeth in *Tannhäuser*, Pilar in Laparra's *La Habañera*, Elsa, Gioconda, Leonora in *Trovatore*, Tosca, Dulcinée in *Don Quichotte* mounted for

Chaliapin, Brünnhilde in *Walküre* and *Siegfried*, Maliella in Wolf-Ferrari's *Gioielli della Madonna*, Aelfrida in Deems Taylor's *The King's Henchman*, Anita in Krenek's *Jonny spielt auf*, Turandot and even Carmen, which she sang quite often. In pretty well all of these, critical opinion found little to complain of and much to enthuse about.

And this was not the sum of her virtuosity. In the course of the Met years, with the company at Brooklyn, she stepped in for Ponselle as Selika in *Africana*, a part that she had never sung before and never did again. At the Ravinia Park summer seasons she took several roles she was not heard in elsewhere including Zazà, Manon Lescaut and Violetta. In 1929 she left the Met and with her second husband went back to live in England. Two years previously after an interval of eighteen years, she had made an unheralded but triumphant reappearance at Covent Garden. It happened that Raisa was unable to come to London to recreate Turandot there and the management was obliged to recourse to Bianca Scacciati; she did not please. When someone spotted Easton in the audience taking a busman's holiday, she was quickly pressed into service and 'hey presto—she did it again'. In the Wagner season in 1932 she sang the *Siegfried* Brünnhilde with Melchior, and was praised for her 'beautiful voice [used] with great subtlety'[21] as Isolde; she was now in her fiftieth year. She travelled to Birmingham and was heard as Carmen and Tosca; it was with her protegé, the tenor Arthur Carron, that she made her last operatic appearances in Great Britain at Sadler's Wells in 1934, again as Tosca. She returned to the United States in 1935 and sang a solitary Brünnhilde in *Walküre* the following season at the Met by way of farewell.

There was a great burst of applause when Miss Easton was first glimpsed . . . and another storm of plaudits arose at the conclusion of her brilliant negotiations of the 'Ho-yo-to-ho!' which was voiced with ringing tones alive with exultation. The high Bs and Cs flowed forth without effort and were admirably true to pitch.[22]

And this in spite of Flagstad's enormous vogue at the time and though Easton was in the thirty-fourth year of a career, during at least twenty-five of which she had sung unstintingly, in some of the most demanding roles in the repertory and in the world's most important theatres.

Nor was this the end of it. She had been busy for years as a concert singer with bleeding chunks of

Wagner, and as a recitalist. During her retirement . . .

> Since she left the fleshpots of opera, the soprano has been refreshing her spirit in the land of the Lied, and she came back to her Manhattan admirers with much Brahms and Strauss bespeaking the labors of her year of rest. Wisely enough, she placed her numbers in English first, and contrived to establish at once the qualities of an art in which words are never sacrificed for notes or vocal expediency.[23]

She continued to appear regularly, sometimes on the radio, until her last recital in 1943. Thereafter she taught in Montreal and finally in New York.

Whereas the fine commercial recordings made by Ponselle have done much to sustain, even to enhance, the reputation of a singer whose operatic career was hardly extensive (off-the-air transcriptions suggest things did not always go smoothly in 'real life'), with Easton it was the other way about. Broadcasts of her in excerpts from Wagner and in recital show that even towards the end of her exceptionally busy career, her voice remained unimpaired and she was still extending the range and depth of her musical sympathies. Unfortunately the Vocalion and Brunswick companies chose to record her in an unrepresentative motley of pieces, though these cannot disguise the splendid quality of her brilliant soprano. It was not perhaps a great voice but she used it with such great skill she almost persuades us that it was. The tone is forward and steady on the breath from the low A to high C. The ringing top is its principal glory but the registers are properly equalised and blended throughout the entire range. She sings safely, perhaps too much so, for in her concern to keep the voice against the hard palate occasionally the tone gets a little fixed sounding, when a trace of breath escapes through difficult and slurred intervals; but this is a slight, one may say, healthy blemish. The purity of tone is particularly remarkable and as a result her diction in every language is abundantly plain but never exaggeratedly so, for the words sit perfectly in the tone and there is no dislocation.

Her versatility, unlike Lilli Lehmann's did not embrace Lucia, but she frequently sang Gilda and Marguerite. If her coloratura had not the dazzle and finish that would have been expected a generation of so previously, in the Jewel Song she surprises us by the neatness of her execution of the ornaments and she shows a stylish command of this music, singing with grace and sweetness of tone. There is in all of Easton's records an honesty about the singing, a boldness and spontaneity that is affecting. No wonder her Butterfly was such a success in New York; after years of having to endure Farrar fighting a losing battle with an increasingly recalcitrant voice what a relief, a refreshing pleasure, it must have been to hear a soprano shape and phrase 'Un bel dì' with such unfailingly secure and lovely tone (at the end she takes the high B flat on the second syllable of the word 'aspetto' and then finishes an octave lower, an option indicated in early editions of the score). In Solveig's Song and the Song of the Indian Guest from *Sadko* there is no cheating, no reliance on charm and personality to trick a way through the exacting tessitura. 'O mio babbino caro', a souvenir of a role she created at the world premiere, is sung with a perfectly controlled column of sound supported on the breath and she does not overdo a good thing by labouring Lauretta's not very serious threat to commit suicide. This aria is an isolated lyrical episode and needs precisely Easton's unfussy, simple and classical delivery to set off the music to its best advantage. A Scotch dialect song 'My Laddie' by Thayer she finds alien corn, but her account of the Bach-Gounod 'Ave Maria' is done with radiant tone and masterly assurance, especially the awkwardly written wide intervals in the concluding measures. Again it is the lovely tone and the poise and sweep of her phrasing that is admirable in Victor Herbert's 'Kiss me again', and she eschews sentimentality and the flirtatious manners of the soubrettes who have not the tone to fill out the melody. It is the expansive treatment of the big tune that puts her recording of 'O divine Redeemer' among the very best. Altogether she was an important artist who made the most out of her voice in an all embracing career and her records, despite the inadequacy of the selections, reveal a singer of classical virtues.

34. Contraltos

We need look no further than any one of her many records to find an eloquent advocate for the inclusion of CARMEN HILL (1883–   ) in these pages. Born in Aberdeen, Scotland, she came to London to study with Frederick King at the Royal Academy of Music. Her first important engagement was as a supporting artist to Emma Albani on one of the diva's, as it seemed, endless tours in search of solvency after the ravages her fortune sustained as a result of the financial adventures of her husband. Hill ventured on stage only once; in Beecham's season of opéra-comique at His Majesty's Theatre in 1910, as the Dewman in *Hansel and Gretel* with

Maggie Teyte and Ruth Vincent. Thereafter she was busy with various activities: as a soloist in oratorio and choral works, with Lieder recitals and ballad concerts—she was a regular artist at the Chappell series over many years—and she was often heard in arias and songs at the Promenade concerts. She 'sang the part of the Angel [in the *Dream of Gerontius*] with great charm'[1] in cities throughout Great Britain. In Dublin she appeared in a programme of Irish music with Agnes Nicholls, Ben Davies and Robert Radford. She joined Percy Grainger in an evening of folk music, to which he added a few numbers of his own composition to help strengthen the diet. As a ballad singer she was in great demand, introducing some particularly treasured numbers, including several by Dorothy Forster; like Eleanor Jones-Hudson she often programmed that great favourite

110 Carmen Hill as the Dew Fairy in *Hansel and Gretel*

CARMEN HILL.

'Rose in the bud', but in this they were both trumped by Clara Butt.

In journeys round the country she 'further established her claims as a Lieder singer of high rank'.[2] Ezra Pound heard her sing Mignon's 'Connais-tu le pays?' 'in French, quite good French for an English singer. She sang with clear enunciation and delicacy'.[3] At the Grosvenor Room of the Great Eastern Hotel in 1923, in an after-dinner recital she included songs by Hugo Wolf, Brahms, Harty and Peel; could British Rail provide such classy fare today? When Hubert Bath's 'Look at the Clock' was introduced at a Queen's Hall Choral Society concert, she was one of the 'excellent' soloists; it was conducted by Franco Leoni, the composer of *L'Oracolo*. For a special charity affair at the Albert Hall in 1919 she matched her tones with Edna Thornton, Ethel Hook and Clara Butt in an all-contralto programme; the four came together for Liza Lehmann's 'Birth of the Flowers'.

Though she appeared at the Albert Hall, Carmen Hill's voice was of the sort better suited to smaller, more modest auditoriums, for she had off to perfection the fine art of modulating her tones so as to give an appropriate intimacy to the light music which she so often sang. The limpid production, correctly blended and equalised registers, the range and especially the soft and mellow tone remind us of Julia Culp. For all that Eric Coates's 'Green hills o' Somerset' and 'Fairy tales of Ireland' are much the same song, in either the utter simplicity of Hill's singing is telling. The works of Mme Guy d'Hardelot are an acquired, or possibly not-to-be-acquired taste, and there will be some for whom 'Roses of Forgiveness' is too strong to stomach. Those, however, who enjoy a little nostalgia will appreciate the perfect manners, unsentimental delivery and eloquence with which Hill puts the piece in its best light.

The Welsh mezzo soprano LEILA MEGANE (1891–1960), was a pupil of Jean de Reszke. She sang in concert before making her operatic debut at Covent Garden in the summer season of 1919, in the title-role of Massenet's *Thérèse*.

The only possible excuse for the infliction of *Thérèse* was that it served to introduce Miss Leila Megane, a young singer of ability, in a part in which she would not have to face comparison with the famous contraltos of the past. No doubt it was meant kindly. We could not help feeling, however, that Miss Megane might have been far more interesting, even if she could not instantly be pronounced superb, in a part which gave the chance of more positive characterisation. She has a beautiful voice, one of those voices which rings true in all circumstances, except when on low notes she is anxious to prove she really is a contralto. Then one begins to wonder whether she is or not. Through most of the opera one could only feel that she was making the best of a trying situation.[4]

Her success led straight away to an engagement at the Opéra-Comique. She sang Charlotte in *Werther* with Léon Beyle and Charles Panzéra who was also making his debut as Albert. Subsequently she took the role of Jeanette in the world premiere of Lévadé's *La Rôtisserie de la Reine Pédauque*. In 1923 in Wales she won the coveted first prize at the National Eisteddfod. That season she appeared in concert at the Queen's Hall, London, and then went on tour throughout the United States.

It is an interesting and most attractive voice with now and then a glint of drama in it. A typical mezzo extending to an easy high B flat and with a properly dark hue in the chest register which she uses to tint phrases tellingly. Dalila's 'Amour, viens aider ma faiblesse' is a little immature, lacking weight of tone and breadth in the phrasing that would surely have come from stage experience, but there is already a sense of character. An air from *La Reine Pédauque* she does her best with but it avails little. She sings the 'Jour de juin' from *Thérèse* affectingly, with a smooth line and complete mastery of the French style—doubtless as a result of her study with de Reszke, for there is much in the production of tone that also reminds us of his soprano pupils. Massenet here is rather obviously re-treading old ground, when that is so fertile we shall not complain.

Not a great deal is known about CAROLINA LAZZARI (1891–1946), whose career seems to have been very short. She studied in New York and then went to Milan. Her first appearances in the United States in opera were with the Chicago company in the 1917/18 season. She took the part of Giglietta in the United States premiere of Mascagni's *Isabeau* with Raisa, Crimi and Rimini. Thereafter she sang the Goatherd in *Dinorah* with Galli-Curci, and Trine in a solitary presentation of *Le Sauteriot* by Silvio Lazzari, no relation. The next season she added La Cieca in *Gioconda* and Dalila opposite the Samson of John O'Sullivan. In 1920 an engagement at the Metropolitan amounted to a solitary and 'very agreeable'[5] Amneris. She journeyed to Buenos Aires the following year and sang in a couple of *Aida*s there too. And that would appear to be the sum total of her important operatic engagements. For several

111 Leila Megane

years in the 1920s she was a member of the Metropolitan Opera Quartet, which included Frances Alda, Charles Hackett and Giuseppe de Luca, touring widely throughout the United States.

Her voice was a wide ranging mezzo-soprano of a particularly fine and lovely quality. The exacting intervals of Rossini's 'Fac ut portem' present no difficulty; the tone has solidity at the top and sonority in the bass. Her execution of fioritura is neat and tidy and she sings the long recitative and canzonetta of the Goatherd from *Dinorah* with charm and sweetness. She was specially affecting in ballads; though she does not savour to the full Nevin's 'The Rosary'—Schumann-Heink and Butt are more sanctimonious—she knows how to launch the melody in Shelley's 'Love's sorrow' and make

112 Carolina Lazzari

113 Edna Thornton as Dalila in *Samson and Dalila*

colourful use of registration for effect. Her diction is always clear and without mannerisms. Why her career never amounted to much we can only guess but the comparative rarity of her records is easily explained by the generally indifferent quality of Edison's products.

The Beecham opera company had its contralto stars too, of whom the most formidable was EDNA THORNTON (1875–1958). She was a student at the Royal Manchester College of Music with Mme Lemmens-Sherrington, a well-known English soprano who had sung at Covent Garden on several occasions in the eighteen-sixties. In London Thornton took lessons from Santley and it was there that she began her career, albeit in a modest way, in a musical comedy *Ib and Little Christina* at Daly's

Theatre in 1899. She was soon busy in concert work, eventually as soloist in *The Messiah*, Bach's *Mass in B Minor* and the *St Matthew Passion*. In 1904 she was brought to Covent Garden but only to sing small roles; her largest assignment was Maddalena in *Rigoletto*. She reappeared regularly until 1910 progressing through Madelon in the Covent Garden premiere of *Andrea Chénier* with Caruso and Destinn, Ulrica, La Cieca in *Gioconda*, Lola in *Cavalleria Rusticana*, Mary in *Fliegende Holländer*, Emilia in *Otello*, Magdalene in *Meistersinger*, Giulietta in *Les Contes d'Hoffmann*, Geneviève in *Pelléas et Mélisande*, Erda in *Rhinegold* and *Siegfried*, Fricka in the *Valkyrie* and Waltraute in *Twilight of the Gods*, and she took leading roles in Leroux's *Le Chemineau*, Naylor's *The Angelus* and Franchetti's *Germania*.

114 Sophie Braslau

She toured widely both in England and abroad as a member of the Quinlan Opera, and then in 1915 joined up with Beecham. She was heard in leading roles from *The Ring* mentioned above as well as Ortrud, Marina in *Boris Godounov*, Marfa in *Khovanshchina*, Kontchakovna in *Prince Igor*, Dalila, Brangäne, Amneris, Azucena and in Holst's *The Perfect Fool*. She was a member of the British National Opera Company and appeared in their seasons at Covent Garden between 1922 and 1924. Thereafter she retired and devoted herself to teaching.

It is hard on Thornton that her best-remembered performance on record is her contribution to the *Rigoletto* quartet with Melba, McCormack and Sammarco. It was made on the day of King Edward VII's funeral. Melba, probably with some reluctance, had had to subtract herself from a celebratory lunch and arrived at the studio punctually as was her wont, but not in a very good humour. When McCormack showed up half an hour late, she admonished him in a not very lady-like fashion. Thereupon there was an exchange of language never to be forgotten by at least one bystander, Fred Gaisberg. Eventually, when the protagonists had simmered down sufficiently, the record was made, and as is often the way on such occasions their contributions are the best. Sammarco, who must have wondered what on earth was going on, for it is doubtful if he spoke that kind of English, is not at all his usual ebullient self. Thornton, trying to jolly things up a bit, did not measure her effects too well; she sounds as if Sparafucile's Inn were the 'Rose and Crown' and she the principal adornment behind the saloon bar. Hers is a good quality contralto, strong at the top and bottom but often a little hoarse in between. She sings smoothly, though not without some flickering in the tone. Her contributions to the duets with Rosina Buckman and Maud Perceval Allen referred to before are more typical of her art. Sometimes she is a bit solid and dull—in company with Austral in *Aida*, for example. But she surprises with 'Gentle Troubadour' from Wallace's *Lurline*, singing with finesse and grace, every word beautifully delivered on the breath. Very attractive too is, 'My heart is weary' from *Nadeshda* of Arthur Goring-Thomas; an under-rated composer whose lyric charm at its best is fresh and engaging.

Born in New York of Russian parents, SOPHIE BRASLAU (1892–1935) took piano lessons as a girl, and when she was old enough started to study singing. Hers was a wide ranging pedagogic experience for she went the rounds: to Buzzi-Peccia, Sibella, Witherspoon, Marafioti and finally Sembrich. Her operatic debut took place at the Metropolitan in 1913 as the Voice in *Parsifal*. She was a contract artist for the next seven years, singing Feodor and the Innkeeper in *Boris Godounov*, an Orphan in *Rosenkavalier*, the Sandman in *Hansel und Gretel*, Hua-Quee in Leoni's *L'Oracolo*, Javotte in *Manon*, Lola in *Cavalleria Rusticana*, the Third Boy in *Zauberflöte*, the First Knight in *Parsifal*, Altichiara in Zandonai's *Francesca da Rimini*, Maddalena in *Rigoletto*, Amelfa in *Le Coq d'or*, the title-role in Cadman's *Shanewis*, Albine in *Thaïs*, La Comare in the Ricci brothers' *Crispino e la Comare*, Preziosilla in *La Forza del Destino* and Marina in *Boris Godounov*. Throughout that time she was a regular contributor to the Sunday-night concerts, taking on the weightier stuff denied her during the week: she sang 'Che farò' from *Orfeo*, 'Stride la vampa', 'Voce di donna' from *Gioconda*, 'Adieu forêts' from Tchaikovsky's *Jeanne d'Arc* (in Russian), 'Mon coeur' from *Samson*, 'O mio Fernando' from *La Favorita*, 'My heart is weary' from Goring-Thomas's *Nadeshda*, 'Il segreto' from *Lucrezia Borgia*, 'Gerechter Gott' from *Rienzi*, 'O bien aimée' from Massenet's *Marie-Magdaleine* and 'Re dell'abisso'.

From 1916 she was a regular recitalist in New York and on tour round the United States; in 1931 she ventured to Europe. After her departure from the Met she sang only on occasion in opera, at Ravinia Park in 1918 and with the Philadelphia Company at the end of her career as Carmen and Marina. Her recital programmes were wide-ranging, including works by Bach, Handel, Gluck, Schubert, Schumann, Brahms, Strauss, Tchaikovsky, Arensky, Moussorgsky, Rubinstein, Rachmaninov, Rimsky-Korsakov and Korganov as well as pieces in a lighter vein.

[In all of these] she exhibited a thoroughly musicianly attitude toward her work, displayed a sense of the correct values in Lieder singing, and, in general, demonstrated that she is a recital artist of personality and one with serious aims.[6]

Recordings introduce us to a dark-hued contralto descending in Schubert's 'Der Tod und das Mädchen' to a bottom D. The voice is of lyric dimensions, rather guttural in quality. This affects the clarity of her enunciation, clouding over the vowels and restricting the range of colour. At her best the top has a bright focus on the tone—as we should expect from a pupil of Sembrich—and the emission, in Moussorgsky's 'Chant Juif', is smooth, the line expressively inflected and with a melancholy intensity that is very affecting. She makes something beautiful out of Halsey's 'Swedish Love Song' with its gracefully nuanced legato and downward portamento in the falling intervals at the end of each phrase. It was not a voice that wore well, for as time passed the tone became increasingly throaty and unsteady and the top dulled, and she overindulges in the chest register. She was not a cheerful soul, a lugubrious tempo and the minor mode suited her best. Rubinstein's 'Night' is an attractive performance; Maffio Orsini's Brindisi, Carmen's Habañera and Schubert's 'Die Forelle' make demands of her that she is not equal to; in the last the poor fish seems half-dead at the beginning.

Many of the most important American singers in the early years of this century travelled to Europe to finish their studies and to gain some experience before making an assault on the leading opera houses in their own country. ELEONORA DE CISNEROS (1878–1934), née Broadfoot, though she eventually took this route to success, at first tried to short-circuit it. After some lessons in New York she made her debut at the Metropolitan as Rossweisse in *Walküre* and subsequently sang the Second Boy in *Zauberflöte*. She was quick to get the measure of her inexperience and left after a season. In 1901 she went to Paris to work with Trabadello, (a teacher of Mary Garden), Victor Maurel and Jean de Reszke. During the next two years she was busy in the Italian provinces. In 1904 came an engagement for the autumn season at Covent Garden; her first appearance was as Amneris, when her 'vocal methods were thought to be well suited to the large spaces of Covent Garden',[7] then came Ulrica, 'a

115 Eleonora de Cisneros as Laura in *Gioconda*

stately and dramatic'[8] Princess in *Adriana Lecouvreur*—these were the first performances of the opera in London, and Ortrud in an Italian *Lohengrin*. The next year she added Azucena in *Trovatore*. A few months later came her Scala debut as the Countess in Tchaikovsky's *Dama di Picche*; the same season she created Candia in the world premiere of Franchetti's *Figlia di Jorio*.

In the autumn of 1906 she stopped briefly at Covent Garden on her way back to the United States to join Hammerstein in his classic attempt to challenge the Met's monopoly in New York. During the first year she sang Amneris, 'an imposing stage presence with a voluptuous voice',[9] Urbain in *Ugonotti*, Lola, Ulrica and Nancy in *Marta*. In the next season she added Laura, Nicklausse in *Les Contes d'Hoffmann*, Maddalena in *Rigoletto* and Madelon in *Andrea Chénier*. In Milan again in 1909 she was Clytemnestra in the first Scala production of Strauss's *Electra*. The following season she spent in Naples, at the San Carlo, as Fides in *Profeta*, Ortrud and Eboli. In the autumn of 1910 she joined the new Chicago Opera and sang Amneris on the opening night; thereafter her roles included Azucena and Herodias in *Salome*. Melba engaged her to join the Melba-Williamson opera company touring Australia in the summer of 1911; that autumn she was again in Chicago, adding to her previous accomplishments Gertrude in *Amleto* with Ruffo, which she also sang with the company on tour in New York, and Santuzza in *Cavalleria Rusticana*. After spending some months in Latin America in 1915, she reappeared in Chicago the following year. She was a guest at Parma as Eboli in the special production of *Don Carlo* to commemorate Verdi's centenary in 1913. In Paris the following year she was Brangäne at the Théâtre des Champs Elysées, then appeared at St Petersburg, Vienna and Lisbon. She was still busy at La Scala in the 1924/5 season as Herodias. For a few years at the end of her life she taught in Paris and finally in New York.

It is hard to reconcile what we hear on her often admirable records with descriptions of the voice as 'voluptuous'. It seems a warm and attractive mezzo-soprano with notably clear diction, but on the evidence one would have thought Amneris and Azucena rather heavy for it. 'I dreamt that I dwelt in marble halls' disappoints; it is a plodding performance lacking charm, with the regulation upward portamento but unimaginatively phrased. It needs Caruso to do anything for Bartlett's 'A dream'. The Page's Song from *Ugonotti* is quite nimble and the passagework mostly clean but her intonation, especially in the upper passaggio, is unreliable; the first F comes out very flat.

35. *A Quartet of American Tenors*

It is appropriate to bracket the next four tenors together. They were all Americans, all enjoyed sturdy careers, were generally appreciated at home and had some measure of success in Europe; and perhaps most important, all were deeply and to some extent adversely affected by the supreme tenor example, Enrico Caruso. RICCARDO MARTIN (1874–1952) (he changed his name from Hugh Whitfield) first studied the violin and then at Columbia University joined the composition class of Edward Macdowell. He did, in fact, compose a few songs and choral pieces before deciding to become a singer in Europe he took instruction from Giovanni Sbriglia, Jean de Reszke, Léon Escalaïs and Vincenzo Lombardi; if a pedigree were all that was needed, then he should have been the greatest. A debut at Nantes in the title-role of Gounod's *Faust* in 1904 was a modest affair. Two years later Henry Russell invited him to New Orleans for a season of French opera. In 1907 he came to the Met as Faust in *Mefistofele* revealing 'a true tenor voice of pretty quality'[1] and obvious lack of background. He stayed with the company for eight successive seasons working through Canio, Pinkerton, Des Grieux in *Manon Lescaut*, Iolan in Converse's *Pipe of Desire*—the first American opera to make it to the Met—Cavaradossi, Don José, Hagenbach in *La Wally*, Manrico, Gounod's Faust, Turiddu, Radamès, Rodolfo, Enzo, Christian in Damrosch's *Cyrano de Bergerac* and Quintus in Parker's *Mona*. There was a postscript when he returned for a solitary Rodolfo in 1917. As a result of the Gatti-Russell pact he also sang in Boston in 1910.

A Covent Garden engagement the same year included Radamès, Angel Clare in d'Erlanger's *Tess*, Des Grieux, Pinkerton, in which 'his voice was robust, round and pleasing, and his powers as an actor showed uncommon intelligence',[2] Faust which disappointed—'wanting the lyrical grace the part demands'—and Cavaradossi; in this, though he occasionally forced the voice, he revealed considerable histrionic skill. The following season he added Dick Johnson in *Fanciulla del West* and in 1920 sang again Pinkerton and Cavaradossi. In the United States between 1915 and 1917 he appeared with Rabinoff's company in Boston in *Madama Butterfly*, *Faust*, *Cavalleria Rusticana* and *Aida*, and in New

York at the Lexington Theatre, as Avito in *L'Amore dei tre Re*. From 1920 to 1923 he was a member of the Chicago Opera and there widened his repertory with Nicias in *Thaïs* and Siegmund in *Walküre*.

A recording of the 'Winterstürme' is one of his best; the agreeable quality, point on the tone and general accuracy of execution compensate for some weakness in the lower range. The obvious model of Caruso for 'O souverain' from *Le Cid* has not provided him with the necessary expansive breath span, and despite a generally artistic approach, the phrasing does not seem to hold together. His singing is not notable for polish and Manrico's 'Ah si ben mio' lacks finish in detail—a trill, for example—and he makes no very suave impression in what is, after all, a love song. A sound artist and a good second rate singer.

The early career of ORVILLE HARROLD (1878–1933) was spent in light music. As a young man he was one of the 'Pumphouse Gang', a vocal quartet which 'found saloons the most convenient auditoriums in which to dispense their particular variety of close harmony'.[3] He was five years touring vaudeville circuits and then appeared on the programme at the old Victoria Theatre, where Oscar Hammerstein heard him and characteristically took charge of his affairs. Harrold was sent to Oscar Saenger for lessons and in 1910 made his debut at the Manhattan Opera as Canio, subsequently singing the Duke opposite Tetrazzini's Gilda. When Hammerstein shut up shop the following year and moved across the Atlantic to his new London Opera House, Harrold went with him. He sang a 'robust-voiced'[4] Alfredo, was not much liked as Roméo, and 'made altogether a splendid' Edgardo:

> Not for many a day has a tenor been heard in London so lavish, so unsparing of his high Cs and C sharps . . . and his acting was not perhaps more conventional than such a conventional part compelled. But as a rule he would do well to leave a little more strength in reserve for the broad melody and soaring phrases of the final 'Tu che a Dio' which is in more senses than one the true climax of an Edgardo's career.[5]

In 1912 back in the United States he was a guest with the Chicago Opera, at Ravinia Park and with the Century company. He came to the Met in 1919 and sang there for five seasons; at first, as Leopoldo in *La Juive*, he used the voice cautiously, but after Dimitri in *Boris Godounov* and Pinkerton, his Rodolfo revealed 'big and powerful'[6] tones. He sang Turiddu, Don José, Meiamoun in Hadley's

Cleopatra's Night, Julien in *Louise* 'with sufficient ardour and vocal power',[7] Tsar Berendy in *Snegourotchka*, Almaviva, Faust, Lohengrin, Parsifal, the Italian singer in *Rosenkavalier*, Win-San-Luy in *l'Oracolo* and Paul in Korngold's *Die Tote Stadt*.

> It requires much uninterrupted singing, much outpouring of high tones in full voice, which Mr Harrold is not averse to doing, and is difficult and ungrateful in its dramatic outline.[8]

The consensus of opinion is that it ruined his voice. After his departure from the Met he returned again to light music and vaudeville.

Of this quartet Harrold's is undoubtedly the finest voice with a brilliant and vibrant tone. He makes the most out of the passage 'Depuis longtemps j'habitais cette chambre' from *Louise*; the interjections are from Eva Gauthier. As with Martin the diction is notably clear but unaffected, if not always perfectly idiomatic. The phrasing has sensitivity, and the singing is both musical and pleasant on the ear; at the climax he seems to have reserves to spare. There is some genuine charm in a spirited number after the Spanish fashion—complete with castanets—from Ganne's *Les Saltimbanques* and here the phrasing is shaped with gracefully-launched portamento.

After some lessons from Arthur Hubbard in Boston, at the age of twenty three, CHARLES HACKETT (1887–1941) took the title-role in a concert version of *Faust*. During the next couple of seasons he was busy as a church and concert singer, but in 1912 decided to travel to Europe to study the Italian opera repertory with Vincenzo Lombardi in Florence. He made his stage debut in Italy at Pavia in 1915 as Faust in Boito's *Mefistofele*, then sang at Reggio Emilia and Genoa in *Mefistofele*, *Mignon*, *Traviata* and *Bohème*. In the autumn of 1916 came a summons to La Scala for some performances of *Mignon* and it was as Wilhelm Meister that he was heard the same season at the Costanzi, Rome with de Hidalgo, Besanzoni and Enrico Molinari. In the summer of 1917, braving the submarine warfare in the Atlantic, he visited South America. At the Colon he created Ruggero in the local premiere of *La Rondine* and was also Cavaradossi and Almaviva. In the winter he was again at the Costanzi as Ruggero, Fenton, Wilhelm Meister and Rodolfo. On this occasion he does not seem to have pleased so well:

> The tenor Hackett, of whom, since his successes last year on this stage, we expected a perfect performance

116 Riccardo Martin as Enzo in *Gioconda*

117 Orville Harrold as the Duke of Mantua

of Rodolfo, failed us. The colour of his voice has become fixed, uniform; throaty in the middle, nasal and without brilliance at the top; nor did we hear again those delicate effects of mezza voce. Hackett has become too pre-occupied with trying to enhance the sonority of his voice, looking for ways of developing the resonance of the high notes, and instead has finished up by spoiling it.[9]

He returned to the Colon the following summer for Faust, the Duke, Fenton, Don Ottavio and Des Grieux and got some good advice from Caruso who told him not to sing so much.

A Met contract began in 1918 with Almaviva in company with Hempel and de Luca, after which came Alfredo, when Henderson commended 'his mastery of mezza voce', Vincent in *Mireille*, the Duke and Cavaradossi. During the next two seasons he added Rodolfo, Pinkerton, Des Grieux and Lindoro, in an unfortunate revival of Rossini's *Italiana* with Besanzoni. Hackett sang 'with spirit, not always with beauty of voice or vocal style'.[10] In spite of the pressure brought to bear on the management to engage native talent, he was unable to survive in the same company as Gigli, Pertile, Lauri-Volpi and Martinelli, and after three years Gatti let him go. From this time he was increasingly occupied with lucrative concert tours, joining the Metropolitan Quartet with Frances Alda, Carolina Lazzari and either de Luca or Zanelli. He appeared in opera at Ravinia Park, with the Scotti Grand Opera Company and in 1922 went back to Europe.

118 Charles Hackett

119 Mario Chamlee in the title-role of Rabaud's *Marouf*

At La Scala he reappeared as Almaviva; in Paris he sang the Duke in *Rigoletto* with Battistini and Gabrielle Ritter-Ciampi. He was a guest at the Opéra-Comique, the Liceo, Barcelona, and for three seasons at Monte Carlo. In London he joined the British National Opera Company for some performances of *Bohème* and *Tosca*, when he used the original text and the company preferred the vernacular. In the 1926 summer season he took part in *Barbiere di Siviglia* and *Falstaff* and also sang in Act Two of *Roméo et Juliette* on the occasion of Melba's farewell. Between 1924 and 1932 and in 1935, 1937 and 1938, he was a principal tenor at the Chicago Opera. There he extended his repertory with Nadir in *Les Pêcheurs de perles*, Arnold Talbot in Cadman's *Witches of Salem*, Tsar Berendy in *Snegourotchka*,

Eisenstein in *Fledermaus*, Alessandro in Moret's *Lorenzaccio*, Armand in Forest's *Camille*, Don Ottavio and Rinuccio in *Gianni Schicchi*. From 1934 until 1939 he was again on the Met roster of artists, but it is debatable whether the engagement reflected a real improvement in his performance, or merely the comparative shortage of good tenors at that time. In the later part of his career he was chiefly a concert and song singer.

Hackett joins Ponselle in the final duet from *Aida* in a Columbia recording and makes a bold pass at music obviously outside his range in the theatre. The top notes have an easy resonance but in the lower range, as we hear in 'Che gelida manina', the tone becomes dry and colourless. His singing in everything he undertakes is accomplished but characterless. His Italian diction, though clear, suffers from some curious notions of stress and inflection. Another capable but largely uninspired singer.

The youngest of the quartet, MARIO CHAMLEE (1892–1966), né Archer Cholmondeley, first raised his voice in public when he was a student at the University of Southern California and sang in the College Glee Club. He took his first singing lessons from Achille Alberti in Los Angeles. It was there that he made his debut with the Lombardi Opera Company as Edgardo in *Lucia* in 1916. Soon afterwards he journeyed east to continue his studies with Sibella and Dellera in New York. These were interrupted when the war came and he joined the American Expeditionary Forces. Following the armistice in 1919 he took part in a celebration concert in Paris, then returned to the United States. His first few months back home were spent singing in cinemas before Scotti heard him and booked him for a season with his Grand Opera Company. This led directly to an engagement at the Metropolitan. With Farrar and Scotti, Chamlee made his debut as Cavaradossi. Aldrich praised his

> . . . tenor voice of excellent quality, of unspoiled freshness, not without warmth and colour, vibrancy and power, and he made intelligent use of it.[11]

He remained with the company for eight seasons and was heard as Edgardo, Christian Brehm in Weis's *The Polish Jew*, the Duke, Pinkerton, Faust, Faust in *Mefistofele*, Win-Say-Luy in *L'Oracolo*, Des Grieux in *Manon*, Wilhelm Meister, Alfredo, Enzo, Vasco in *l'Africana*, Hoffmann, Pedro in Vittadini's *Anima Allegra* and Turiddu.

After leaving the Met he made guest appearances at the Deutsches Oper in Prague, the Volksoper in Vienna, the Paris Opéra and Opéra-Comique, at Lille, Bordeaux and the Monnaie, Brussels, where he was greatly admired in the title-role of Rabaud's *Marouf* in 1928. He sang it the year after with equal success at Ravinia Park and when he returned to the Met in 1935. At San Francisco he was heard as Lohengrin and Walther in *Meistersinger* and between 1935 and 1939, at the Met again he sang Jenik, and leading parts in the New York premieres of Hagemann's *Caponsacchi* and Menotti's *Amelia al Ballo*. In the latter his entrance, in the manner of Tarzan, sliding down a rope, greatly astounded the audience and he proved too that he was still 'the possessor of a voice'.[12]

In many of Chamlee's recordings the influence of Caruso is very striking; Barthélemy's 'Triste

ritorno', Geehl's 'For you alone' and the Serenade from *Don Pasquale*, for example. It is not simply a matter of copying the externals of the interpretation—tempo, phrasing, rubato and so forth—but the production of the voice itself, the attack, the way of launching ascending phrases and general conception of tone is all almost a carbon print of Caruso. The trouble is that since these effects have been artfully acquired they do not come forth spontaneously and, as with Martin's 'O souverain', there is something dead about Chamlee's performances. In Ernesto's Serenade, instead of refining the focus of the tone so as to manage the vocal line with proper grace and accuracy, he blows up the middle range; the voice does not move easily and aspirates impede its progress. For style there is only sentimentality. His singing is generally attractive and though he vociferates a little too much in Enzo's 'Cielo e mar', the line is smooth and secure and he embraces the high B flat with ease. The quality of the voice is well caught in 'Adieu Mignon', where he seems content to sing more lyrically.

36. A British-born Trio

Today EDWARD JOHNSON (1878–1959) is probably best remembered as the General Manager of the Metropolitan, a position he held from 1935 until 1950. Yet for nearly a quarter of a century before he was a successful tenor in many of the world's leading opera houses, so we must take with a pinch of salt the story he liked to tell in later years, of how one day a young soprano of the company burst into his office, waving aloft one of his records: 'But you never told me you were a singer!' Johnson was born in Canada and, like many other tenors of that period, began his career in oratorio, concert and musical comedy. In 1902 he was Robin Hood in Reginald de Koven's musical play and the following year sang in a concert version of Gounod's *Faust*. He came to New York to take lessons from von Fielitsch and had his first big success as Niki in the 1908 Broadway production of Oscar Straus's *Waltz Dream*. With the proceeds he went off to Italy and the studio of Vincenzo Lombardi for further study. Eventually in 1912 he made his operatic debut as Andrea Chénier at Pavia; for the next six years he was busy in the country's most important theatres. He sang at Ancona, Brescia, Florence and Bologna before arriving at the Costanzi, Rome, where he returned regularly until the end of the First World War, taking principal roles in *Isabeau*, *Fanciulla del West*, Zandonai's *Melenis*, Tommasini's *Uguale Fortuna*, Micchetti's *Maria di Magdala*, *Pelléas et Mélisande*, Marinuzzi's *Jacquerie*, *Fedora*, *Manon Lescaut*, *Andrea Chénier*, *Tabarro* and *Gianni Schicchi*. In 1913 he was introduced at La Scala in the name part of the first Italian production of *Parsifal*, then sang in the world premiere of Alfano's *l'Ombra di Don Giovanni*. Throughout his Italian career he adopted the nome di teatro of 'Edouardo di Giovanni'. He seems to have been much appreciated for his good looks, intelligent stage-craft and the general accomplishment of his singing. At La Scala he was heard as Loge in *Oro del Reno*, Walter in Catalani's *Loreley*, Ippolito in Pizzetti's *Fedra*, Andrea Chénier and Marco in Montemezzi's *La Nave*. In 1916 he journeyed to the Colon, where among other parts he sang Walther in *Maestri Cantori*. In Madrid the year after he added Tannhäuser.

Johnson's American operatic debut was with the Chicago Opera in 1919 as Loris in *Fedora* when 'his "Amor ti vieta" literally stopped the show'.[1] He remained with the company for three seasons as

120 Edward Johnson as Avito in Montemezzi's *L'Amore dei tre Re*

Luigi and Rinuccio, Avito in *l'Amore dei tre Re*—which he sang at the Lexington Theatre in his New York opera debut and was commended as 'a man of excellent figure, of virile and picturesque action, of moderately good voice'[2]—Mazurec in Marinuzzi's *Jacquerie*, Canio and Lohengrin. His Met debut in 1922 was also as Avito:

> He has a voice of warm tenor quality which he uses with skill and with telling dramatic effect; a voice of power but capable of reserves and subject to the discipline of musical understanding . . . Here is a tenor who is something more than a voice, who is an artistic personality.[3]

His Met career lasted for thirteen years as Avito, Dimitri in *Boris Godounov*, Des Grieux in *Manon Lescaut*, Cavaradossi, Don José, Canio, Pinkerton, Faust, Roméo, Pelléas, Radamès, Loris, Rodolfo, Licinio in *La Vestale*, Aethelwold in Deems Taylor's *The King's Henchman*, Fra Gherardo in Pizzetti's opera of that name, the title roles in Rimsky-Korsakov's *Sadko* and Deems Taylor's *Peter Ibbetson*, and Sir Gower Lackland in Howard Hanson's *Merry Mount*. In the 1920s he was busy elsewhere in the United States, at San Francisco as Ruggero in *La Rondine*, at Ravinia Park as Julien in *Louise*, and he travelled to England to appear with the British National Opera Company at Covent Garden as Faust opposite Melba's Marguerite.

Throughout his career Johnson was busy as a concert and recital singer, not only in North America and Europe but on tour in the Orient.

> His robust voice he delights in using in a robust manner, and it is effective and resonant when so used. His mezza voce was heard at its best after he had been singing for some time, and at its best is not one of his strong points. If his singing does not at all times show all the refinements of vocal art, his straightforward and energetic style, his discernment of the emotional and dramatic significance of the music he deals with and his skill in presenting it impressively make his performances interesting and often engrossing. His diction is commendably clear.[4]

The records of Johnson are something of a mystery and it is hard to reconcile what we hear on them with the reputation he enjoyed, at least at the beginning of his career. Possibly the strenuous roles he undertook in Italy permanently damaged the voice. Even the best 'Amor ti vieta' from *Fedora*, sounds strained, the tone thick and constricted. It is a strong voice but he appears to have little control over it, the phrasing is lumpy and the climaxes forced. Wrighton's 'Her bright smile haunts me still' at least enables us to hear the good natural quality.

Born in England, brought up in the United States, ALFRED PICCAVER (1883–1958) sang almost all of his career as principal 'Italian' tenor at the Vienna State Opera. His inclusion here is to some extent arbitrary but since his singing is neither German nor Italian in style, it seems appropriate to list him with two other Anglo-Saxon tenors, Edward Johnson and Joseph Hislop, whose careers were also largely made outside their own countries, and in the Italian repertory. After a period spent as a pupil at Heinrich Conried's Metropolitan Opera School in New York, in 1907 he departed for Europe. Angelo Neumann, then Director of the German Opera Company, Prague, offered him a contract but sent him first for a period of further instruction with Mme Prochazka-Neumann. He sang in Prague until 1911 and was heard in many of the roles with which he would later delight Vienna audiences, including Fenton, Roméo, Lionel in *Martha*, Faust, Canio— which at that stage seems to have been too strenuous for him—Alfredo, Tamino, the Duke (perhaps his most popular assumption), the title-role in Flotow's *Alessandro Stradella*, Riccardo in *Maskenball*, Rodolfo, Don José, Turiddu and Cavaradossi. In 1910 and 1911 he was a guest with Battistini's touring opera in Prague and Vienna, his first appearances in that city; he sang the Duke, Alfredo, Riccardo and Don Ottavio, in casts that included Elvira de Hidalgo and Vittorio Arimondi, as well as Battistini. These exposures led to his engagement with the Imperial Opera. His debut took place in 1912, as the Duke; he stayed there, despite some interruptions in the thirties, until his retirement in 1937.

In the course of a quarter of a century he sang more than twenty-seven different roles, and in the early years appeared often up to fifty times a season. To the roles mentioned before he added: Belmonte in *Seraglio*, Dick Johnson, Edgardo, Nemorino, Des Grieux in *Manon*, the same part in Puccini's opera, Werther, Radamès, Enzo, Vasco in *Afrikanerin*, Barinkay in *Zigeunerbaron*, Andrea Chénier, Hoffmann, Florestan in *Fidelio*, Luigi in *Tabarro* and Babinsky in Weinberger's *Schwanda*. The contract enabled him to make guest appearances abroad. He sang often in Berlin and at various other German houses, in Chicago in 1923 and 1924, but there, like Tino Pattiera, he made no impression, and in the latter year at Covent Garden, when he was heard as Cavaradossi and the Duke:

121 Alfred Piccaver as Dick Johnson in *Fanciulla del West*

His voice is full and round in quality, and of great power, even at the biggest moments one felt he had in reserve quite as much as he gave out. It has not the brilliance of some of the big Italian tenors we have heard but . . . Mr Piccaver's singing is entirely free from tiresome mannerisms. The music was taken simply and without over-emphasis of its emotional quality. This restraint made 'E lucevan le stelle' the more effective given such turn of phrasing, nothing in the way of vocal sobs need be added.[5]

In Paris in 1928 he was at the Opéra with a visiting troupe from Vienna as Florestan, Ottavio and Cavaradossi. In the later part of his career he appeared in various operettas; it was in one of these— *Dreimäderlhaus*, a confection made out of various pieces of Schubert, which Tauber subsequently made famous in the English version, *Blossom-Time*—that Piccaver made his last stage appearances at Salzburg in 1937.

His is an exceptionally attractive, full lyric tenor, with a characteristic quality and his singing is unfailingly agreeable; we can imagine what a refreshing treat that must have been in Vienna. The tone has just the right note of voluptuousness for Hoffmann's 'O Dieu de quelle ivresse' (in German). In 'Deserto in terra' from Donizetti's *Don Sebastiano*, the suave emission and persuasive phrasing to an extent compensate for a lack of limpidity and brilliance, for the voice is throaty and insufficiently responsive. Although 'Questa o quella' goes with an elegant lilt, we can hear in a crudely cut passage from another Donizetti opera, *Belisario*, that he is unable to give to the opening strongly marked dotted rhythm either spontaneity or urgency; neither does he make any real distinction between the aria and cabaletta. His backward production divorces the words from the tone, but whereas most singers of this period, particularly the French, prefer to articulate at the expense of song, he puts tone first; it is no less decadent. It leads to a different kind of monotony; in Rodolfo's 'Che gelida manina', without the words to give dramatic variety to the shifting phrases, these simply follow one another with hardly any range of colour, and the music loses coherence. He manages a passage from Weber's early work *Silvana* with some skill, taking the uncomfortable tessitura in his stride, and in this the words are of less importance.

As a young man JOSEPH HISLOP (1884–1977) sang in the choir of St Mary's Cathedral, Edinburgh, the city where he was born. It was not until after he moved to Sweden to work for a printer that he decided to switch professions and study singing seriously. He went to Gillis Bratt in Stockholm, the teacher of Ivar Andresen, Göta Ljungberg and Gertrude Wettergren. His operatic debut took place at the Stockholm Opera in 1914 in the title-role of *Faust*. He remained a contract artist with the company through five seasons, singing nineteen different parts in the Italian and French repertory. After the war he went to Milan for further study with Tullio Voghera, one of Caruso's accompanists, and auditioned for Paolo Longone who booked him for the 1919/20 season at the San Carlo, Naples. Hislop sang Edgardo, Cavaradossi and the Duke, and seems to have enjoyed a generally enthusiastic reception. The following summer he made his Covent Garden debut as Rodolfo.

122 Joseph Hislop as Sir Walter Raleigh In German's *Merrie England*

The principal tenor part was sung by Mr Joseph Hislop who, after some continental experience, was making his first appearance here. His is a voice of good quality, thought not of exceptional power, and it has the advantage, which not all bigger tenors have, of keeping its quality on the middle notes. His singing, too, was musical, showing a feeling for melodic outline which suggested that he will be a valuable addition to the company.[6]

Subsequently he sang Pinkerton in lieu of Riccardo Martin. In 1923 and the winter of 1924 he was a guest artist with the British National Opera Company in their seasons at Covent Garden as Rodolfo to Melba's Mimi, Cavaradossi and the Duke with de Hidalgo and Umberto Urbano. He was again at

Covent Garden in the summer season of 1924 singing Rodolfo, Pinkerton, Canio, Cavaradossi and Alfredo, in 1927 as Cavaradossi, and in 1928 as Faust.

Hislop's North American debut took place in the autumn of 1920 with the Chicago Opera. He appeared in *Tosca*, *Bohème*, *Aida*, *Butterfly*, *Rigoletto* and *Roméo et Juliette*. The next year with the Scotti Grand Opera he joined a roster of tenors that included Mario Chamlee, Charles Hackett, José Palet and Morgan Kingston. In 1922 he was in Stockholm again, returning often thereafter until his farewell as Faust, his last stage performance in 1937. In 1923 he was in Italy, at the Fenice, Venice, and at Turin, as Edgardo, Julien in Charpentier's *Luisa* and Rodolfo. That autumn he succeeded Pertile at La Scala as Edgardo with dal Monte, Stracciari and Pinza. The next spring he was

engaged at the Monnaie, Brussels, and afterwards as a guest in Ghent, Liège and Antwerp singing in his usual repertory as well as Des Grieux in Massenet's *Manon* and *Werther*. In the summer he went to the Colon, Buenos Aires, but his voice did not seem big enough; he sang Fenton, Rinuccio in *Gianni Schicchi*, Roméo and Rodolfo. In 1926 he was engaged at the Liceo, Barcelona and at the Opéra-Comique as Werther, Rodolfo and Cavaradossi. He was a great success in opera in Australia and returned to Stockholm again, adding Gérald in *Lakmé*, Des Grieux in *Manon Lescaut* and Don José to his previous achievements. In 1930 he starred in the film *The Loves of Robert Burns*, the music of which was arranged from Scottish folk songs by Leslie Heward, and the following year he played Goethe in Lehàr's *Frederike*, first in London and then Australia and New Zealand. Throughout his career he was busy in extensive concert tours. After the Second World War he returned to England and taught in London at the Guildhall School of Music.

His is a sound lyric tenor, not large and with nothing especially individual about it; for glamour of quality it does not compare to Piccaver, but his singing is cleaner, more vigorous and everything is done with a generally high degree of competence. Although he is not notably imaginative in all songs, he produces just the right effect with old ballads such as Pinsuti's 'Queen of the Earth' or Tosti's 'Good-bye'.

123 John O'Sullivan as Raoul in Meyerbeer's *Ugonotti*

37. High Cs and Heroic Voices

The Irish tenor JOHN O'SULLIVAN (1878–1948) was the possessor of a powerful and brilliant tenor voice and his clarion high notes were greatly appreciated by his countryman, James Joyce.

> It is incomparably the greatest human voice I have ever heard, beside which Chaliapin is braggadocio and McCormack insignificant . . . . I have been through the score of *Guillaume Tell* and I discover that O'Sullivan sings 456 Gs, 93 A flats, 54 B flats, 15 Bs, 19 Cs, and 2 C sharps . . . . Nobody else can do it!

O'Sullivan was a student at the Paris Conservatory, but came to London in 1909 and joined a touring company in the title-role of *Tannhäuser*. Between 1910 and 1914 he sang in the French provinces, at Toulouse, Geneva and Lyons as Max in *Freischütz* before arriving at the Paris Opéra. His first appearance there was as Arnold in *Guillaume Tell*, afterwards came Raoul in *Les Huguenots*, the title-role in Reyer's *Sigurd* with Laute-Brun and Noté, Fernand in *La Favorite*, Nicias in *Thaïs* and Dick Johnson in *La Fille du Far-West*. In 1917 he was principal tenor in a season at the Gaîté-Lyrique, singing in *Lucia di Lammermoor*, *L'Africaine*, Auber's *La Muette de Portici* and Halévy's *La Reine de Chypre*. The following year he was invited to Chicago for a couple of seasons where he sang Arnold, Samson, Prinzivalle in Février's *Monna Vanna*, Canio, Faust, Jean in *Hérodiade*, Don José, Roméo and Werther. The last two he repeated at the Lexington Theatre on the company's visit to New York; in these he was pronounced 'mediocre' and 'inferior' respectively. At Bordeaux in 1921 he took the leading parts in Massenet's *Roma* and *Tannhäuser*, the next season he travelled to Italy for performances of *Ugonotti* at the Lirico, Milan, and Parma. Farther afield in 1923 at the Colon, Buenos

Aires, his roles included Arnold, Radamès, Manrico, Faust in Berlioz's *La Damnation de Faust* and Julien in *Louise*. In 1924 at Monte Carlo he took leading roles in Galeotti's *Anton*, and he sang Faust in Lili Boulanger's *Faust et Hélène* as well as Berlioz's *La Damnation de Faust*. At the Verona Arena in 1926 he was Manrico in *Trovatore*. He sang Raoul at Covent Garden in 1927 in the last and most unfortunate revival of *Ugonotti*:

> [He] was obviously not at his ease in the difficult scene and romance in Act One, but his high notes made their effect when they came and he is a tenor who should prove a considerable acquisition.[1]

He should have, but did not; projected performances of *Otello* were cancelled and he never appeared in London again. In Paris he sang Arnold in the centenary production of *Guillaume Tell* at the Opéra in 1929 and returned in the years between 1932 and 1934, when he was also heard as Eléazar in *La Juive* and Otello.

It is a remarkable instrument; the high notes, in a big theatre, must have made a tremendous impression but his singing is very provincial, too vehement, the line not securely based. A pronounced vibrato present throughout the voice makes it impossible for him to produce the sustained legato necessary for Vasco's 'O Paradiso' or Raoul's 'Bianca al par'. A couple of excerpts from *Otello* sandwiched together, 'Esultate' and 'Ora e per sempre addio', though crudely done are not without effect. 'Di quella pira' too, has its points: a couple of stentorian high Cs. His splendidly clear and vivid diction, in spite of a slight accent in Italian, gives intensity in declamatory music.

It was probably just because FRANK MULLINGS (1881–1953) never sang outside Great Britain, and hardly ever in any language but English, that he was so greatly admired there. Beecham, Cardus, Wood and Newman, who were by no means always a consensus, though they acknowledged profound limitations in his vocal technique, were fulsome in their praise of him. Mullings was a student at the Birmingham School of Music and in 1907 sang Faust in a concert performance of the opera at Coventry, for which he was paid £2.12.6d. In the next few years he began to develop a reputation as an oratorio and concert singer and was already programming works by Lane Wilson, Quilter, Bantock, Stanford and Holbrooke. His earnest advocacy of the 'serious' British composers was undoubtedly an important

124 Frank Mullings as Canio

factor in commending him to the critics. In 1913 he joined the Denhof Opera, a touring group which did sterling work introducing many of Wagner's operas to the English provinces; Mullings sang Tristan. His association with Beecham began in the summer of 1914 at Drury Lane when he sang Gwyddno in Holbrooke's *Dylan*. In 1915 Mullings became the leading dramatic tenor of Beecham's own opera company; during its five years of activity he was heard as Don Whiskerandos in Stanford's *The Critic*, Hoffmann, Otello, Radamès, Tristan, Tannhäuser, Canio, Siegfried, Samson and Midas in Beecham's dramatisation of Bach's secular cantata *Phoebus and Pan*. The company set remarkably high standards and outside London nothing like it had been heard before; many of its leading principals left an enduring impression in the memory of younger opera-goers who were probably hearing the works for the first time.

> In the days of the Beecham opera, we in Manchester knew that one of the greatest living actors in opera was Frank Mullings; I call him actor because his voice, a tenor, was often strangled by unnatural production, yet was the most histrionic voice I have heard amongst all the tenors known or suffered by me.[2]

With Beecham he sang at Covent Garden in the summer and autumn season of 1919, joining Rosina Buckman and Percy Hemming as Hadjar in de Lara's *Naïl*. When the company was finally disbanded, along with many of his colleagues he became a member of the British National Opera Company. This gave seasons at Covent Garden between 1922 and 1924, and travelled widely throughout Great Britain until its demise in 1929. During that time Mullings sang most of the heroic roles and added to his repertory Apollo in Rutland Boughton's *Alkestis*. With one company or another he continued to appear during the 1930s but only on occasion in London. His concert career lasted until after the Second World War.

Mullings was a big man and he made a big impression on the stage, as Newman tells us, ranging 'with extraordinary ease and veracity from the most elemental fury to the most pitiful pathos'.[3] Beecham describes how 'when he stormed certain high passages . . . I used to hold my breath in apprehension of some dire physical disaster averted only by the possession of an iron frame . . .'[4] but adds that 'his singing of quiet passages had a poetry, spirituality and intelligence which I have never heard in any

other native artist and in very few elsewhere.' It would be nice to have some confirmation of all this fine enthusiasm; unfortunately, the gramophone has preserved only the throaty—often strangled—voice production, vague intonation and imprecise execution. Was there, one wonders, something chauvinistic, fashionable, about the praises he drew? The fact that he virtually never sang in any other language but English and as we are so often told made it sound 'clear and beautiful'[5] would have suited Beecham, Cardus and Newman at a time when opera in English was fashionable in 'intellectual' circles. Then, too, it must have helped reconcile British audiences with Wagner when the country was at war with Germany; possibly Mullings's powerful personality and projection of the words persuaded them that the operas were really English. There is a hint of something of this sort from Cardus who after recalling his 'noble towering presence as Othello', goes on '[he] constantly reminded [us] that Othello, after all, is Shakespeare's and not Verdi's creation'.[6]

Records do not confirm the clarity of his enunciation; certainly his declamation is full of vigour and interest but the throaty production in some degree obscures all the vowels and especially in dramatic passages makes it difficult to catch more than a word or two. Clutsam's 'I know of two bright eyes' does not tax him unduly and the voice here is largely without the unfortunate juddering that can be heard, for example, in Othello's music. In the Love Duet with Miriam Licette his singing is tender and eloquent by intention but not smooth enough, there is no line and the climax becomes strident and disagreeable. Licette's appealing Desdemona, after the fashion of Melba—the tones pure without being white—puts his singing in a poor light. Whatever was remarkable in his art the gramophone has not succeeded in preserving.

38. The Ballad and Oratorio Tradition

It is surprising that the name of Gervase Elwes is better known than that of JOHN COATES (1865–1941); though Elwes had a prettier voice, in almost all other respects he was nothing like so finished a singer and Coates's career which continued until he was over seventy was wider in its range of accomplishments. Gerald Moore refers to him as 'the finest and most imaginative of tenors'.[1] Almost any of the large number of records he made confirms this. As a boy singing in a church choir, he came under the

125 John Coates

he underwent an operation on the vocal cords; to his surprise when the voice returned it was fresher and unequivocally a tenor. He made his operatic debut at Covent Garden in 1901 as Claudio in Stanford's *Much Ado About Nothing*, and followed it with Faust. Until the First World War he was busy in a wide variety of musical activities. At Covent Garden in seasons given by Moody-Manners, the Carl Rosa, Beecham and Raymond Roze, he sang Don José, Faust, Lohengrin, Pedro in *Tiefland*, Hoffmann, Tannhäuser and Tristan. In the provinces he appeared with the Denhof and Quinlan companies and at His Majesty's with Beecham, and the Lyric with Moody Manners, as Mark in Dame Ethel Smythe's *Wreckers*, Siegfried, Lionel in Missa's *Muguette*, Dick Johnson and Radamès. Abroad he was a guest at Cologne as Roméo, Faust and Lohengrin and also at Dresden, Hamburg, Dusseldorf, Frankfurt and Amsterdam.

From 1901 he was a popular figure at most of the big English music festivals, at Leeds, Worcester, Brighton and Norwich as well as at the Crystal Palace. His oratorio repertory was all-embracing and included the *Messiah* and *Belshazzar* by Handel, Mendelssohn's *St Paul* and *Elijah*, Bach's *St Matthew Passion*, Elgar's *Dream of Gerontius* and *King Olaf* and Saint-Saëns's *Promised Land*. In 1906 he was at the Cincinatti Festival and during the next twenty years often returned to the United States. Occasionally he reappeared in musical comedy but it was as a singer of songs that he was most greatly renowned. A typical programme embraced works from Morley and Bach to Cyril Scott and Reger. He was a regular soloist in Wagner concerts and often sang the title-role in concert performances of *Parsifal*;

As a singer he is a master of many styles, from the grave to the gay. He can bill and coo the most tender phases of the great passion, or he can electrify you with his dramatic intensity. His diction makes his singing as plain as speech, and his phrasing and accentuation, both musical and verbal, show a rare sensitiveness to fine subtleties. But after all it is the obvious sincerity of the expression and the intellectuality of his singing that magnetise his hearers. The best of the finest music is revealed. He is best with the best music and can only move when he is moved.[4]

After the war he made comparatively few appearances on stage, though in 1921 at Covent Garden he sang Don José and Lohengrin with the Carl Rosa company. During the twenties he was

influence of Gregorian chant 'and grasped the idea that truth of accent was the life of singing'.[2] At first his progress was slow and his studies without system. In 1893 after an engagement as Valentin with the Carl Rosa company he took some lessons from William Shakespeare, who advised him that he had 'the typical tenor E'.[3] However, it was as a baritone that he appeared with the D'Oyly Carte company the following year at the Savoy and subsequently on tour in the United States. After a couple of seasons spent in musical comedy, in 1896 principally occupied in concert work, giving four or five recitals each season in London, ranging over German, French and English song. He undertook tours throughout the provinces and abroad, especially in Australia and South Africa.

Coates's voice is a sound instrument of good quality: it is his way of using it that is exceptional. His singing represents the English ballad and oratorio tradition at its most admirable. Though sorely taxed at moments in 'Cielo e mar' he makes no compromises, there is no blustering; the execution is of exceptional accuracy, every note cleanly attacked and the whole piece given life and vitality through the clarity of the diction. This is one of the most beautiful features in Balfe's lovely setting of Tennyson's 'Come into the garden Maud', where tone and text are blended with a classical perfection, the two inextricably interwoven. It is a fascinating performance, rich in detail, full of affection without sentimentality—how vividly he conveys expectation in the coda by his lithe, responsive command of rhythm. A couple of Weckerlin arrangements of old French songs 'Entendez vous?' and 'Le beau séjour' are done with delightful spirit, the enunciation idiomatic yet without the affectation heard in recordings of many French singers. 'John's Wife' by Roeckel shows off his considerable skill in mezza voce and clever management of the head voice. This he uses to particular effect on the difficult high B flat at the end of 'Heavenly Aida'; those who must have Radamès with a brilliant Italian voice miss a great deal, for here is a splendid piece of declamation in the English tradition reminding us of Edward Lloyd. His singing had genuine charm, as we can hear in Brewer's 'Ninetta' and his perfect taste is an object lesson. Remarkable for imagination is Wright's 'La vie est vaine' and Mallison's 'Eldorado' (Kipling), where the graces have a chiselled perfection. He went on making records into the twenties, his interpretative skill unimpaired, but the voice shows the strain of his various operatic activities, not to mention the long runs in musical comedy. One of the finest English singers on record.

It was only after a number of years' study with various teachers, including Demest in Brussels and Bouhy in Paris, and after he had finally abandoned a career in the diplomatic service that GERVASE ELWES (1866–1921) decided to seek his fortune on the concert platform. He was born into a landed Northamptonshire family and in those days there was a great deal of prejudice against a man in his social position becoming a professional singer. In

126 Gervase Elwes

1903 he sang at the Westmoreland Festival in a cantata of Somervell and Elgar's *Coronation Ode*, under the direction of Coleridge-Taylor. An engagement at the Bechstein Hall, London, followed but the critical response was qualified: 'he has a beautiful quality voice and intelligence, but the production is not clear and the voice requires more training in the upper range'.[5] It was a testament to his character and determination that in spite of his age—he was already thirty eight—he took the advice and went to Victor Beigel for a further course of study. Beigel not only assisted him with technical problems but awakened his interest in Lieder, especially the songs of Brahms. In 1904 he sang Gerontius in Elgar's *Dream of Gerontius* for the first time and enjoyed a considerable success; in the course of the next sixteen years he took the part more than a hundred times. For many his was *the* interpretation; Elgar, however, preferred Coates's. With Beigel and Fanny Davies, a pupil of Clara Schumann, in 1907, he went on an extensive tour of Germany. Two years later in New York under Damrosch he sang Gerontius and the Evangelist in the *St Matthew Passion*. On his return Vaughan Williams invited him to give the first performance of his song-cycle 'On Wenlock Edge'; in the opinion of at least one critic the music owed much of its initial popularity to Elwes's earnest advocacy.

In the period before the war Elwes established himself as one of the country's leading concert artists and this in spite of his refusal to sing anything that did not suit his voice or please his taste. He never appeared in opera and declined to take part in ballad concerts. This gave him the image of a serious artist which was much appreciated by the critics and helped to reconcile him to those in society who felt that it was undignified for a squire of the manor to sing for his supper. And, in spite of his rigorous taste, and his fee of one hundred guineas, he was much in demand for after dinner engagements. In the war he was occupied with concerts for the Red Cross and other charities and sang in hospitals, and entertainments at camps and barracks. When the war ended he took up his career again and in the autumn of 1920, after eleven years' absence, travelled again to the United States for a series of concerts on the east coast. The day before he was to sing in Boston he took the train from New York. Upon arrival, was walking along the platform when he realised he had taken someone else's coat. Rushing back to the train, which was now pulling out he threw the coat for a guard to catch. In so doing he lost his balance and fell between the carriages. He died a few hours later from the injuries.

Elwes's recordings include the complete 'On Wenlock Edge' and a variety of English songs as well as pieces by Bach, Handel, Dvorak and Grieg. Save for the last all are in English. The voice is of pleasant quality and, as we might have expected, there is a certain gentlemanliness in his manner which is ingratiating without being precious. In all the songs the diction is clear but it has not the classical excellence of Coates, nor has his singing the same finish. He puts across Maude Valérie White's 'Absent yet present' with genuine feeling and intensity and without exaggeration. In Sir George Henschel's 'Morning Hymn' he shows himself a master of mood; this is an interesting piece.

Like John Coates, WALTER HYDE (1875–1951) sang with equal success in opera, oratorio, musical comedy and songs. At the Royal College of Music he was a pupil of Gustave Garcia, the son of Manuel Garcia the younger, and also took instruction from Sir Charles Stanford and Walter Parratt. He made his debut at Covent Garden in 1901 in the same performance of Stanford's *Much Ado About Nothing* that also introduced Coates. Thereafter he was busy in musical comedy: at Terry's Theatre in 1905 with Sydney Jones's *My Lady Molly*, in Rubens's *Miss Hook of Holland* and in 1907 he created Squire Thornhill in David Bispham's production of Liza Lehmann's *Vicar of Wakefield*. The following winter in Richter's English *Ring* cycle at Covent Garden he sang Siegmund' in capital style'.[6] In the summer season 'he sang [Pinkerton] with such excellent tone and expression that the result was not in any doubt'.[7] He repeated Siegmund in Richter's second cycle and added Loge, as well as Walther in *The Mastersingers*. He was Siegmund again, this time in German, in the summer of 1909. In 1910 he was engaged for Beecham's winter and autumn seasons at Covent Garden as an 'entirely admirable' Ivanhoe in the title-role of Sullivan's opera, Sali in Delius's *A Village Romeo and Juliet*, Hoffmann, Ottavio, Faust, Laërte in *Hamlet*, and Erik. In the summer he joined Beecham in a season of opéra-comique at His Majesty's Theatre, as Ferrando in *Così fan tutte* and Lionel in Missa's *Muguette*. Somehow he also found time to make a concert tour in the United States and Canada and sang a solitary performance of Siegmund in *Walküre* at the Metropolitan with Gadski, Fremstad and Whitehill. Outside Great Britain he was a guest in opera in Budapest. In 1913, once again with Beecham, he appeared in opera in Birmingham.

At Covent Garden in 1919 his roles included Dimitri in *Boris Godounov*, Belmonte in *Seraglio*, Haroun in Bizet's *Djamileh*, Parsifal, Sali in *A Village Romeo and Juliet* and Tamino. From 1922 he was a member of the British National Opera Company, later being appointed a Director, and sang at Covent Garden between 1922 and 1924, Julien in *Louise*, Loge, Siegmund, Don Miguel in Offenbach's *Goldsmith of Toledo*, Belmonte, the Troubadour in Holst's *Perfect Fool*, Samson, Tannhäuser, Tamino, Parsifal, Midas in Bach's *Phoebus and Pan*, and Admetus in Rutland Boughton's *Alkestis*, which he created; his 'beautiful voice made the part ring true, especially

127 Walter Hyde in Rimsky-Korsakov's *Ivan the
Terrible*

128 Paul Reimers

in Act Two'.[8] After his retirement he was
appointed Professor of Singing at the Royal College
of Music, London.

Hyde's is not a voice of remarkable power or
sonority. Typically English, it is a respectable
lyrical instrument with a pleasant quality, a little
throaty, but only rarely does a rapid tremolo verge
on a bleat. His singing has many virtues, in parti-

cular the clean attack; a perfect example of what
Garcia meant by the coup de glotte and there is only
the slightest suggestion of ictus. He is a fine Handel
singer in 'Where'er you walk' from *Semele* and
'Waft her angels' from *Jephtha*. In these the line is
smoothly composed, the divisions cleanly managed
even though the tone gets a bit constricted in the
upper range. In these too his splendidly clean

diction, especially in the recitative 'Deeper and deeper still thy goodness, child', is very telling; very accomplished is the way he draws the portamento from D to F sharp on the word 'thy' and there is a wide range of expression. His skilful management of the registers in the upper range greatly enhances the quality of the voice, though occasionally he over-does the mezza voce, as we can hear in Bishop's delightful old song 'The Pilgrim of Love'. In other respects this is a stylish piece of singing and he gives a lesson, by command of nuance and variety of rubato, on how to make an effect in this music. The Flower Song from *Carmen*, in English, is a distinguished performance and without any of the extravagant manners popularised in the post-Caruso period.

An attractive singer with a light but pleasing voice, PAUL REIMERS (1877–1942) was born in Germany and took his first lessons in Berlin from Spengel. In due course he came to London to study with Sir George Henschel. He tried a season on stage at Hamburg in 1903, making his debut as Max in *Freischütz*, but quickly realised he had not sufficient resources for opera and thenceforth devoted himself entirely to concert work and recitals. In Germany he was one of the founders of the Brahms quartet and travelled abroad with it to France and England. He sang solo recitals with great success throughout Europe and the United States, his programmes ranging widely from the works of Schubert, Schumann, Wolf and Brahms to popular ballads, and he was fluent in English, French and Italian, as well as German. In London in 1913 and 1914 he appeared in duet with Elena Gerhardt and 'well sustained the inevitable comparison'.[9] He was one of the few German born artists whose American career was not interrupted by the war. In the twenties he often appeared with Alma Gluck and Hulda Lashanska in joint recitals. Every summer at Baden-Baden he organised a series of master classes for advanced students and after 1924 joined the faculty at the Julliard School of Music, New York.

The catholic taste in his concert programmes is displayed in his choice of recorded repertory. The voice is small, well-schooled though a little tight in the upper range. His singing is always pleasant and has genuine charm. In White's 'To Mary', the English diction is impeccable and there is a fine polish on his art. In Dalcrôze's 'Le coeur de ma mie' it is possible to feel that his imitation of a French tenorino is too good, the tone as dry as a whisper, though he turns the graces more deftly than most French singers of the period.

39. McCormack

JOHN McCORMACK (1884–1945), like so many tenors of his day, fell under the spell of Caruso. In 1904, after having spent somewhile studying in Dublin with Vincent O'Brien, McCormack came to London. One evening he went to Covent Garden, to a performance of *La Bohème*, and heard Caruso for the first time; thirty years later he could write: 'that voice still rings in my ears, the memory of it will never die'. McCormack was by no means the first important Irish tenor: apart from the legendary Michael Kelly, the creator of Don Basilio in *Le Nozze di Figaro*, in the early years of this century Joseph O'Mara and Barton McGuckin—both tenors of repute—made records, but we should have to go back to Kelly to find one who travelled to Italy for instruction. It was Caruso who fired McCormack with the ambition to succeed in Italian opera. To judge from recordings made before his departure and those made upon his return the Italian experience—three month's study with Vincenzo Sabatini—gave him a mastery of the language, a knowledge of the repertory and a skill in the correct style and performing tradition. What Sabatini did not manage was to secure McCormack's high notes. His voice was a naturally high lyric tenor of a sweet and characteristic quality extending to top D. Had he elected on a career in ballads and ballad opera, like so many of the English-speaking tenors of the period, he would have produced the upper tones, in the fashion we hear in recordings of O'Mara, Coates, Beddoe and others; without increasing the breath tension so as to make more out of them than nature had put in. But the example of Caruso and the need to contrive a forceful effect in climaxes in, say, the music of Cavaradossi and Turiddu, which he often sang, encouraged him to open the top notes and shout. As a result the voice ascended with ease only to A; he could produce a B flat and B natural but the quality of these was not consistent with the rest of the voice while top C and above was distinctly a gamble. This failure with the high notes was one of the factors—and an important one—in bringing his operatic career to an untimely conclusion in 1923 when he was not yet forty.

McCormack made his operatic debut at Savona in 1906, as Beppe in *L'Amico Fritz*. Thereafter he sang elsewhere in the Italian provinces but after failing to secure an engagement at La Scala, where at the audition he cracked on the high C in 'Salve! dimora', he returned to London. In the autumn of 1907 he made his first appearance at Covent Garden, as

Turiddu, then came the Duke—with Tetrazzini—and Don Ottavio. He came again the following summer and every season until 1914, adding Edgardo, Alfredo, Elvino, Gérald, Rodolfo, Almaviva, Cassio, Pinkerton, Faust in both Gounod and Boito's operas, Roméo and Cavaradossi, in all of them enjoying an enthusiastic press. He made an equally good impression on the public and his colleagues; Melba engaged him as principal tenor for her company in Australia in 1911. L. A. G. Strong, in his biography of McCormack, has written a diverting account of their turbulent friendship, yet with it all went a high degree of mutual respect. His attachment to Tetrazzini was warmer; he called her his 'fairy godmother' and it was through her good offices, so she tells us, that Hammerstein booked McCormack for the Manhattan Opera, New York, in 1909. His debut took place in *Traviata* with her and despite a bad cold he was an instantaneous success:

> The voice was beautiful in quality, and it was controlled with a skill one does not hope for nowadays from a tenor not born in Italy, and a good taste that is rare. Such command of mezza voce, such smoothness in legato, such fluent execution, such grace of phrase bear witness to fine schooling of fine natural gifts. An Italian might well take pleasure in the clear enunciation of his beautiful language.[1]

It is a fact not without some interest that at this stage of his career McCormack was regarded as an 'Italian' tenor and we find few comments on his Irish brogue; Sir Henry Wood recalls his contribution to a performance of the Verdi *Requiem*, in 1911 as being in the 'truest Italian tradition'[2] and records made at the time confirm that he sang Italian opera in fine style and with hardly a trace of an accent. It was after his arrival in America that the Irish in him began to reassert itself in his singing. Shaw observed that no man is so patriotic as when he is abroad; it was in America that McCormack rediscovered his Irishness. At his Met debut in 1910, again as Alfredo, this time opposite Melba, a clamorous delegation of his countrymen secured for him the success that was denied Clément, Constantino, Jadlowker and Smirnov, none of whom made much headway with audiences infatuated with Caruso's magnificent outpourings. Inevitably, and no doubt gratefully, McCormack responded to their enthusiasm in concert and recital by turning his attention to the popular music of his homeland and even, in revolutionary ballads like 'The wearing of the green', coming forth as a champion of

Irish nationalism. Apart from anything else it was profitable. In the United States, where there were more Irishmen than in Ireland, his drawing power was enormous. At a recital at the New York Hippodrome in 1918, 7,000 people heard him sing; 5,000 sitting in front, 1,000 behind and another 1,000 standing, and such large audiences were the rule. After 1912 McCormack stepped up his concert activity, and his appearances in opera became fewer and further between. He was a guest with the Boston and Philadelphia-Chicago companies; it was with the latter that he made his only appearance in a new work, creating Lt. Paul Merrill in the world premiere of Victor Herbert's *Natoma*. But after his debut season at the Metropolitan, he did not return until 1917/18 and then only for two Rodolfos and one Cavaradossi; the following year there was a solitary Pinkerton which, with a Rodolfo opposite Galli-Curci for the Chicago Opera, wrote *finis* to his operatic career in the United States. His very last stage appearances took place at Monte Carlo: in 1921 he sang Almaviva and Tamino in *Zauberflöte*; in 1923 he appeared with Mercedes Capsir in *Marta*, *Barbiere* and *Bohème*, with Gilda dalla Rizza in *Tosca* and *Butterfly* and he created Gritzko in Raoul Gunsbourg's edition of Moussorgsky's unfinished *La Foire de Sorotchintzi*. Thereafter and until the end of his career McCormack sang only in concert and recitals. In his later years he broadcast frequently and appeared in several films, in one of which *Song O' My Heart* there is a whole uncut concert sequence which may not be good cinema but is certainly good McCormack.

The best of McCormack's operatic titles, made in the period before 1920, represent his singing at its freshest; largely without the obtrusive Irish accent and nasal tone that later on became tiresome. The influence of Caruso is apparent in 'Una furtiva lagrima' but in its own right this is an elegant and expressively shaded performance and there are few finer on record. The Tomb Scene from *Lucia*—without the mourners' interjections and shorn of the final phrases—has always been highly regarded. The voice moves easily in the difficult high tessitura, leaving no doubt as to its natural disposition. His careful avoidance of jerkiness when executing the dotted notes, and eloquent use of rubato in the repeated phrase 'o bell'alma innamorata', is a model of style. The aria from *Figlia del Reggimento* appears only in the original French edition of the score; Gilibert introduced McCormack to it when he sang Tonio at the Manhattan and he himself translated it into Italian. It is

129 John McCormack

slightly abbreviated but sung with unfailing sweetness of tone and suave line and it is easy to overlook the hair crack that opens up on the high B flat when he attempts so ambitious a diminuendo. Wilhelm Meister's 'In her simplicity' from *Mignon* is equally fine. The songs from the *Bohemian Girl* and *Maritana*, with their delicious enunciation—the words framed in a stream of lovely tone—are both classic renderings; even 'Celeste Aida', so obviously copied from Caruso, with the same conception of tone and big scale portamento, comes off better than the singer had any right to expect. From the beginning in those early years he transposed a number of arias: 'Spirto gentil', 'Che gelida manina' and 'Salve! dimora' are all down a semi-tone so as to avoid the high Cs. In fact it is hard to find a high C in all his many recordings. He surprises us, however, with a D flat, in the song 'The vacant chair', but here he is supported by a 'backing group', and it sounds like an accident; we can hardly imagine him venturing it without cover. Elsewhere there may be other notes above B but these must be few; it seems likely that after his mishap with top C in a performance of *Faust* in Florence as a young man, he rarely if ever ventured the note in public or on records again.

McCormack made a sizeable quantity of records in company with various colleagues. A series of duets from *Bohème*, *Gioconda*, *Barbiere* and *Pescatori di Perle* is spoiled by the gruff sounding baritone of the Sicilian Sammarco. His singing is crude, vehement and inaccurate; it is difficult to imagine a less suitable partner for so polished an artist as McCormack. He finds an altogether worthier companion in the delightful soprano Lucrezia Bori; their singing of 'Parigi, o cara'—lays good claim to be the best on record. But perhaps the perfect duet was that of McCormack and the violinist Fritz Kreisler. They made a large number of recordings together. Every title is a gem. When the singer enquires, in the Braga, 'from whence come those lovely strains?, there can be only one answer; Kreisler's playing is indeed an angel's serenade, such sweetness and fullness of tone—those low notes—and such graceful portamento. Singer and violinist echo each other in perfection of phrasing and weight of tone so that each seems to blend into the other. The Berceuse from *Jocelyn* was for more than a generation a favourite record; it would be hard to imagine it better sung, for McCormack finds—as French tenors so rarely have—a perfect balance between text and music, word and tone, consonant and vowel. The most important group is the songs of Rachmaninov; McCormack sings these in English, apparently in his own excellent and most musical translations. His light tenor with its slightly plaintive timbre suits Russian music and despite strong competition, notably from Ivan Kozlovsky, few versions in the original are as idiomatic. The legato is full of delicate and expressive nuances while his exquisite enunciation of the text makes the English words seem inevitable. And in them all Kreisler's fiddling is so telling that at any minute we expect him to burst into words.

Much, perhaps too much, has been made of McCormack as a classical singer, partly by record collectors but also—a quarter of a century or so ago—by critics when, as it seemed, no tenor any more could manage a trill or negotiate divisions. These days, with the revival of interest in classical

and pre-classical music, such accomplishments have once again become relatively commonplace. McCormack, like most tenors of his time, sang little music of the seventeenth and eighteenth centuries. His operatic repertory included only two classical roles, he rarely took part in oratorio and his recitals included at most a handful of pieces written before 1800. The small number of recordings he left of Bach, Handel and Mozart are very fine, and better sung than most, but it cannot be said that his singing here has genuine spontaneity—save possibly in the late record of 'Where'er you walk', which he turns into a ballad—or that he shows any real understanding of the classical style. His 'Il mio tesoro' is certainly the smoothest and, with Tauber's, the most accurate performance on record, but it is deficient in character and suffers—as do all of his records of works of this period—from the typically Anglo-Saxon notion then, and still, extant that classical music does not require any passionate or characterful expression, even when, as here, the dramatic situation and the text explicitly call for it. 'O sleep' is famous for his execution of the long division on the word 'wandering' in one breath and this is certainly a feat, even if it is contrived by putting on a spurt towards the end; altogether this is a smoothly composed piece of singing but as in Lotti's 'Pur dicesti', there is not sufficient tension in the line and he is not able to establish stylishly the subordinate function of the graces. If we compare him in the latter piece with Patti, we hear the difference between a singer whose coloratura was merely an acquired skill and now that his voice is in decline is already marred with aspirates, from one for whom it was an inextricable part of her technique so that even at the end of her career it remained, like the Cheshire cat's smile, when pretty well everything else had vanished.

His Lieder singing has always divided opinion and although there are many beauties contained in it yet it is not entirely satisfying. Mostly this has to do with his incomplete command of the German language; he often seems to be overcompensating for it and there is a fussiness, a lack of the directness and simplicity that make his delivery of English and Italian so immediately affecting, while the heavy Irish accent is disconcerting, at times risible. An embarrassing comment on the tenor's ignorance of German is provided by Gerald Moore who tells of an incident at the press conference given prior to McCormack's Farewell recital at the Albert Hall in 1938. After the singer declared that his favourite song on the programme was Hugo Wolf's 'Herr was trägt der Boden hier?' ('Lord, what will grow in this ground?'), a reporter demanded to know what that meant. There was a deafening silence which was eventually broken when Moore came to McCormack's rescue. It is possible to believe that much of his Lieder singing was the result of exterior promptings; from the critics, from his accompanist and coach Edwin Schneider and, even, from feelings of guilt over his colossal earnings indulging popular taste—a few Lieder and he felt shriven. His approach in all the songs is very much of the old school and his performances do not plumb the interpretative depths in the modern fashion, where the singer seeks out every hidden colour and nuance suggested by the text, whether the musical setting allows for them or not, and frequently at the expense of tone and line. For McCormack these always came first and he looked to the cadence for guidance as how best to inflect the words. In this respect at least his Lieder singing is stylish.

McCormack's concert programmes often featured songs by Vaughan Williams, Parry, Quilter and Bantock, and he recorded a number of them. With their rather arty taste in verses and often dry music, they now seem quite as dated as the sentimental songs of the day, and rarely as attractive. McCormack's earnest advocacy puts the best complexion on them but these excursions were into the byways, like Caruso, Gigli, Schipa and Tauber, it was as a great singer of the popular music of his day that his reputation was made and still survives. In his youth he was deeply affected by Italian opera and a measure of its influence remained with him until the end of his career, in his concern for a pleasing tone and suave line. But the ballad and song tradition was in his blood, it was a part of the Irishman and would not be put down. There was nothing at all intellectual about it; his art, though supremely accomplished, spoke with the eloquence of a minstrel. In some of the triter songs this could be too much for sensitive spirits. A friend once took Yeats to a McCormack recital, at some point in the course of the evening he became aware that the poet had left his seat, going outside he came upon him pacing up and down. 'Don't you like it, W.B.?' he enquired anxiously. 'Oh! he's wonderful,' came the reply, 'but the damnable clarity of the words!' Over the years familiarity and changing taste have staled the songs he sang, but the singer's expression remains so potent that they move us still. What could be more magical, a more direct statement to the heart, without the prissy mannerisms he affected in art songs, than 'Take, oh take those lips

away'? And in a ballad that almost became his signature tune, 'I hear you calling me', the singing is ineffably beautiful with its soft high notes and delicately poised glissandi. And there was variety in his art; the swaggering rhythm of 'It's a long way to Tipperary'—a piece of nostalgia that still speaks to us vividly—recalls the high spirits of the young men who rushed into an early and futile death in the trenches. Even when the voice was on the wane, the diseur's skill remained but of that there will be opportunity to speak later.

130 McCormack as Don Ottavio

40. Baritones and Basses

One of America's most distinguished concert baritones, REINALD WERRENRATH (1883–1953) took his first lessons from his father. Later he went to several other teachers including Victor Maurel. He made his debut in 1907 and thereafter was active in numerous recital tours throughout the United States and in Europe; he sang in London regularly until the late twenties. He appeared at most of the leading festivals as a soloist in oratorio and concerts. In New York after 1909 his annual recital was a feature of the season. Of the second of these Aldrich wrote:

Mr Werrenrath has a voice of unusual beauty and is clearly one possessed of artistic instincts that lead him to the diligent cultivation of the talent with which he is endowed. He has studied and worked to excellent purpose. The voice, the style, the interpretation are such as belongs to an artist. His first three numbers were old Italian airs that require a command of legato style, and fine phrasing and enunciation. These he sang with much finish, with mastery of the difficult technique that they require, as well as with taste. He sang songs by Beethoven, Brahms, Wolf and Grieg that evinced a nice understanding of the widely differing characterisation that they needed.[1]

In 1919 came his operatic debut in *Pagliacci* at the Met. Henderson thought him the finest Silvio he had ever heard 'in respect of style, diction, phrasing and beauty of expression'.[2] These same qualities were displayed as Valentin and Escamillo, but though he remained with the company for three seasons they were his only roles. Thereafter he returned to the concert hall. In London he sang in a number of early radio concerts. Throughout his career he was heard frequently as soloist with various choral societies and himself composed several pieces for male chorus.

The fine quality of his attractive light baritone voice is well caught in Scarlatti's 'O cessate di piagarmi'. He sings with grace, a nice mezza voce and with some variety of expression. The aria 'Ecco pur ch'a voi ritorno' from *Orfeo* is probably the earliest recording of a Monteverdi piece, when the revival under the aegis of Respighi and others was just beginning. This too he sings with a simple and classical dignity.

Few other singers in this anthology made, and sold, as many records as PETER DAWSON (1882–1961); at one time there could hardly have been a home throughout the entire British Empire which boasted a gramophone that did not have at least one

131 Reinald Werrenrath

132 Peter Dawson

title of Dawson's. His list of recordings was prodigious and though overwhelmingly composed of ballads and popular songs, excerpts from Handel, Rossini and Wagner leave no doubt as to the accomplishment of his art. Blanche Marchesi told John Freestone that his vocal technique was as near perfection as any she had ever heard. Dawson's decision to sing only in concert, his preference for translating everything into English, and his appearance on the cheaper plum label records encourage the idea that he was somehow second class. It is true that he was not an intellectual interpreter, there was nothing cerebral in his approach, but his musical instincts were of the finest and his singing has that kind of perfect composure and simplicity that conceals the greatest skill. The control, detail and finish of his art put him in the very highest league and it is no exaggeration to compare him to Santley and Battistini. Perhaps this should not surprise us, for he was a pupil of Santley, and Battistini was the example he acknowledged throughout his career.

Dawson was from Adelaide, Australia. He studied there with J. C. Stevens before coming to England in 1900 to work successively with E. L. Bamford and Santley. It was through Santley's good offices that he made his debut; as a supporting artist with Emma Albani in a tour through the West Country in 1902. In 1904 he made his first recordings for the Edison company and began another career that was to last almost half a century. By 1925 his record sales amounted to over eight million. In 1909 he sang the Nightwatchman in the *Mastersingers* under Richter at Covent Garden. The experience was not congenial to him and he never appeared in opera again. The voice was not powerful enough for the big heroic baritone roles, nor did he have the temperament for a stage career. Instead he embarked on extensive concert tours, throughout Great Britain, Australia, New Zealand, South Africa and the Far East. Between these he sang in oratorio, at the Promenade Concerts and was one of the pioneers on the radio.

Dawson's range extends from the bass E flat to the baritone A. The topmost notes he claims to have acquired from a certain Professor Kantorez, some years after he was already launched on his career. Yet even in the earliest recordings the high notes up to G are brilliant, easy and secure. Kantorez may have assisted him to secure his control over them but, as with Santley, they were made possible by resisting the temptation to try and produce a big sound, especially in the passage notes. The registers are

133 Robert Radford

correctly equalised and blended, the tone finely focussed and there is not an infirm note throughout his compass. Although the voice is not remarkable for resonance or sonority, his singing is of classical excellence, clean and accurate in the divisions of Handel's 'Honour and Arms', 'O ruddier than the cherry' and 'The Lord is a man of war', (with Robert Radford), Shield's 'The Wolf' and Reeve's 'I am a friar of orders grey'. In all of these there is a splendidly vigorous and buoyant rhythm. In suaver, more lyrical music, the line is carried in a portamento of the breath much as that was understood in the days of Tosi and Mancini and all the graces—mordents, gruppetti even trills—are beautifully polished; the aspirate is unknown to Dawson.

The song titles include a lot of dross but the best period pieces—Crampton's 'Lackaday', Coates's 'Green Hills of Somerset' and Amy Woodforde-Finden's 'Indian love lyrics'—are distinguished by his good taste and eloquent delivery. In everything he does he gives a lesson in interpretation and shows how a clear diction is not contrived by artful over-enunciation but by a perfect reconciliation between the vowel which colours the tone and the consonant which articulates it. Thus everything from the simplest to the most difficult piece is done with complete spontaneity; speech is simply heightened into song, the words coloured by singing tone. The very ease of it is the art that disguises art. We hardly notice the attack which is at the basis of his skill; it is a perfect example of what Garcia really meant by the 'coup de glotte'. Its precision accounts not only for the notable accuracy of his intonation but it helps launch and project every word. In spite of his repertory Dawson's singing retains much of the art of bel canto.

HORACE STEVENS (1876–1954) was for many years a church singer and was well past forty when he made his only operatic appearances. Born in Melbourne, Australia, he came to London and was a lay clerk at St Paul's Cathedral. He appeared at the Queen's Hall in concert in 1919 under Sir Henry Wood. The conductor was so impressed he urged Stevens to abandon his successful dental practice in Melbourne for the concert platform. Soon afterwards, again under Wood's direction, Stevens sang Elijah for the first time. The *Morning Post* critic hailed him 'the greatest Elijah since Santley', Elgar demurred—'he is the greatest Elijah the world has ever known, not excepting Santley'. He quickly gained an enviable reputation at leading choral festivals throughout Great Britain, the United States—he sang in Chicago and at Cincinnati—and in the British Empire, singing the bass parts in Handel's *Messiah* and *Samson*, Bach's *St Matthew Passion*, Brahms's *Requiem*, Elgar's *Dream of Gerontius* and Bantock's *Omar Khayyam*. In 1924 he created the role of Hiawatha when Coleridge-Taylor's trilogy was presented in a dramatised version at the Albert Hall. Throughout the 1920s he was a member of the British National Opera Company. On tour he sang Falstaff, Hans Sachs, Méphistophélès in *Faust*, the Dutchman, the Landgrave in *Tannhauser* and at Covent Garden, in 1923, Wotan in the *Valkyrie*. He sang the role there again in a season of opera in English in 1931.

134 Horace Stevens

Mr Horace Stevens's Wotan is the equal of any Wotan we have seen. Dignified in bearing and magnificently sonorous, he yet gave full value to the details of the part, and his outbursts of thwarted fury had an almost terrifying power. His only failure—and it was comparative—was in the quieter parts of his colloquy with Brünnhilde. Here his vocal tone lacked the colour and smoothness which marked his more tense passages in the last act.[3]

In 1934 he returned to Australia where he taught singing at Melbourne University and was still active as a choral conductor at the time of his death.

His is indeed a 'magnificently sonorous' bass-baritone voice as we hear it echoing in the sepulchral acoustics of Hereford Cathedral during a live performance of the *Dream of Gerontius* at the Three Choirs' Festival in 1927 under the composer's direction. He surprises us in the Barcarole from Federico Ricci's *Prigione d'Edimburgo*, a rumbustious florid piece, singing with much character and despatching the coloratura easily, even if his Italian is not very idiomatic. The voice is wide ranging, easily produced and he is a singer of considerable technical skill.

The Australian bass MALCOLM McEACHERN (1883–1945), a singer of remarkable gifts, preferred concert and oratorio work to the opera, though he did appear with the Melba-Williamson Company, on one of the diva's tours of her native country. In his early years in Australia he sang in *Elijah*, *The Messiah*, *The Creation*, *Samson*, *Judas Maccabeus* and Sullivan's *The Golden Legend*. In 1916 with his wife as accompanist, he embarked on a world tour. Of his performance as the bass soloist in *The Messiah*, an American critic wrote:

Stalwart Malcolm McEachern made the florid and exacting bass solo part stand out with more than usual prominence. His opening recitative was taken at a faster tempo than commonly heard; and his singing of the really tempestuous music of the part, in which 'The Nations Rage so Furiously Together' was faster than it has ever been sung here, perhaps faster than any other human being could sing it, was a veritable study in breath-conservation and control. He possesses a voice of unusual resonance, and one sufficiently powerful to fill the largest of halls.[4]

In due course husband and wife settled in England where he was very much in demand as a concert soloist with symphony orchestras appearing with Henry Wood and John Barbirolli. But at heart McEachern was a ballad and popular singer. He met the composer of light music, B. C. Hilliam and in 1925 they formed a partnership, 'Flotsam and Jetsam'; for almost twenty years they were active touring the halls and on the radio, and 'Jetsam's' splendidly rotund, dark and finely focussed tones were admired throughout the country. His death in 1945, as Peter Dawson put it, 'robbed the world of a master of song and one of Australia's greatest ambassadors to Great Britain.'

McEachern's was a noble basso profundo, extending from the high F down to low C, even B flat in Jude's 'The Mighty Deep'. His voice production like that of Dawson was a model, the registers perfectly blended and the weight of tone even throughout its entire range. As a singer of oratorio he left some outstanding records. Polyphemus's 'O ruddier than the cherry' is notable for its bouncy rhythm, nimble and clear execution of the divisions, also for its 'mummerset' accent. If he does not quite wrest the palm from Dawson with 'Honour and Arms', a greater weight of tone in the lower range gives him the edge in Mendelssohn's 'I am a roamer'. Procida's apostrophe to his native city, from *Vespri Siciliani* (transposed a semi-tone into F) he sings with a beautifully firm and suavely drawn line, suggesting

the operatic career that he might have had. Emmanuel's 'The Desert' is a collector's piece; the song as much as the singing. 'Oh! God! I am lost in this desolate place', calls the singer, as vultures wheel over-head—and in the orchestra too—then in the nick of time the caravan train arrives—mostly the percussion section—and 'I am saved! I am saved!' The beauty of his tone and clear but unaffected diction are most affecting in 'Hear me gentle Maritana . . . The Mariner in his barque' from Wallace's *Maritana*, an outstanding example of the correct style in ballad opera.

135 Malcolm McEachern

PART V

The German Style in Evolution

41. Lyric Sopranos

The operatic tradition at Dresden was long and notable and produced many fine singers. Few of them were more gifted than EVA VON DER OSTEN (1881–1936). She studied with August Iffert, one of the many teachers then active in Dresden, and whose pupils included Erik Schmedes and Katharina Fleischer-Edel. Her debut took place at the Dresden Opera as the Page in *Hugenotten* in 1902; she remained a member of the company for twenty seven seasons. From the beginning she was greatly admired and in 1907 made a considerable impression as Lisa in the local premiere of Tchaikovsky's *Pique Dame*. Less than four years later Richard Strauss selected her to create the title-role in the world premiere of *Der Rosenkavalier*. When the opera was brought to Covent Garden in Beecham's spring season in 1913, von der Osten and Siems, the original Marschallin, again headed the cast. *The Times* wrote:

> For richness of quality the mezzo-soprano [sic] of Fräulein von der Osten comes first; [she] not only thrilled one by her singing but looked and played the high-spirited, irresponsible boy.[1]

She reappeared at His Majesty's Theatre that summer, also in company with Beecham, when she undertook the leading role in the London premiere of another Richard Strauss opera, *Ariadne auf Naxos*. In the spring of 1914 she was Kundry in the first production of *Parsifal* at Covent Garden:

> Madame von der Osten is the possessor of one of the most beautiful voices of modern times. In the second act, [her] singing was extraordinarily fine from the first terrible wails with which she answered the call of Klingsor, through the scene of temptation her voice had the thrill of a wonderful musical instrument, the one fault was she was too commanding, entirely too big a creature to suggest seductive art, but her singing was a joy to hear.[2]

The performances were packed out and the sensation of the season. She was also heard as Isolde 'the best since Ternina'[3] and Sieglinde in *Walküre*; had not the war intervened she would surely have returned.

At Dresden where she continued to sing every season, she took part in the first performances of Bittner's *Hollisch Gold* and Schreker's *Der ferne Klang*. There she was as much celebrated in the Italian repertory; as Zazà when Leoncavallo's opera was heard for the first time and an outstanding Tosca opposite the Scarpia of George Baklanov. In

136 Eva von der Osten as Elsa in *Lohengrin*

1912 for a season she was seconded to the Berlin Komische Oper and there created the role of Blanchefleur in Kienzl's *Der Kuhreigen*. After the war in the 1922/3 season she joined Leo Blech's company touring the United States before German language performances had been restored at the Met. When the company appeared at the Lexington Theatre, von der Osten sang Isolde and a 'splendid' Sieglinde. She remained busy throughout the 1920s and gave her farewell at Dresden in 1930 as Brünnhilde in a performance of *Walküre* in which her husband Friedrich Plaschke was the Wotan. In her retirement she became a director; in 1933 she assisted in staging the world premier of another Strauss at Dresden, *Arabella*.

Von der Osten's voice on records is a full lyric soprano and, as her contemporaries noted, of an exceptionally fine quality. Her method is less inhibited and contrived than the Dresden sopranos of the previous generation, partly at least because she did not attempt, as so many of them did, everything in the repertory from Gilda to Brünnhilde. The registers are not however fully equalised nor correctly blended, though the joins are well enough smoothed over. The chest voice is separate and immature with the result that in the middle and upper range the tone is shallow, white rather than pure in quality and not firmly based and her intonation sometimes strays. The singing is nevertheless generally attractive and she was an interesting artist. Two excerpts from *Zazà* are affectingly done and without the strident exaggerations of her Italian contemporaries. Indeed her restrained manner and affectionate phrasing with a particularly eloquent use of portamento put the best value on the music. A spirited rendering of Mignon's 'Styrienne' shows off a little coloratura and a neatly turned trill. She is very fine, the tone fresh and radiant in Elsa's Dream and though her legato style is not perfect, with some pinched tone in the head register, she avoids monotony and gives proper expression and feeling to the details of Elsa's narration. None of her records suggests the voice of a Brünnhilde or Kundry, however.

LUISE PERARD-PETZL (1884–1936), or Perard-Thiessen as she is sometimes known, sang with success in a number of German theatres and on visits to London, Brussels, Budapest and elsewhere. She made her debut in the 1908 season at Hamburg and soon established herself as a principal soprano in the lyric and lyric-dramatic repertory. Beecham engaged her for his season at Covent Garden in the spring of 1910. She succeeded the American sop-

137 Luise Perard-Petzl as Eva in *Meistersinger*

rano Frances Rose as Chrysothemis in the first London performance of *Elektra* and was considered vocally superior. She returned the following autumn repeating Chrysothemis and was heard in *Tannhäuser* as Elisabeth and Venus, on one occasion singing both roles in the same performance. In Beecham's 1913 season she sang the Marschallin in succession to Siems in two performances of *Der Rosenkavalier*. In the same year in the summer she was an 'admirable'[4] Gutrune in *Götterdämmerung*, Elsa and Rosine in von Walterhausen's *Oberst Chabert*. In the last, however, like the opera itself, she failed to make any impression.

In 1912 she was a guest at the Monnaie, Brussels, in *The Ring* cycle in company with Edyth Walker, Jacques Urlus and Ernst van Dyck; she sang Freia in *Rheingold* and Sieglinde.

Mme Petzl has a very pretty voice, brilliant and without hardness in the upper range and she truly

138 Zinaida Jurjevskaya as the Countess in
Figaros Hochzeit

captivated her audience. She was by turn dramatic and
passionate to a degree that was entirely appropriate to
the role of Sieglinde. And as Freia she was full of charm
and youthfulness.[5]

From Hamburg she moved to Munich and was a
popular favourite as Tosca, Aida, Donna Anna,
Pamina, Salome, Sieglinde and Freia which she sang
at the Munich Festival of 1913. She continued to
sing at Hamburg until her retirement, after which
she taught singing in Munich.

Perard-Petzl made only four records; arias from
Zauberflöte, *Ernani*, *Troubadour* and *Aida*. The voice
is a warm and rounded full lyric soprano, the tone
firm and secure and it is easy to believe how
effective vocally she would have been as Chrysothemis or Sieglinde. Her singing is accomplished
after the German fashion; in Pamina's lament from
Zauberflöte she negotiates the difficult high-lying
tessitura with instrumental precision and notable
accuracy. The performance is full of light and shade,

though the voice itself seems rather inexpressive
and hardly reflects the prevailing minor mode.
'Ernani, involami' (in German, as are all her records)
has some interesting details; she nicely graces the
opening measures with trills and in the descent from
the top A flat alters marcato to staccato. As with
many of the German singers of the day, there is some
squeezing or contrivance in her manipulation of the
voice; this and the hard attack take the smoothness
out of the line. A want of a floating legato keeps
'D'amor sull' ali rosee' earth bound and the attempt
to get it all on to a single 78 side robs the phrasing of
breadth. The Nile aria from *Aida* is also hurried
over, so preventing a competent and assured performance with an excellent high C from being
numbered among the best.

The career of the Russian-born ZINAIDA
JURJEVSKAYA (1896–1925) lasted only three
years, but during that time she established herself as
a front-ranking artist. We know little of her early
life, even the date of her birth is not certain, and it
was not until after the Revolution when she and her
family fled Russia and came to Berlin that she began
her vocal studies. From the beginning she showed
remarkable talent, the attractive and characteristic
quality of her voice quickly securing her an engagement at the top: in 1922 at the Staatsoper in Rimsky-
Korsakov's *Der Goldene Hahn*. She was a principal of
the company until her death. Her roles included
Sophie in *Rosenkavalier* and Jenufa, which she
created in the local premiere of Janacek's opera in
1924 under Erich Kleiber with Margarethe Ober and
Fritz Soot. In Paris that year she had a great success
in a couple of recitals notwithstanding stiff competition from Vallin, McCormack and Barrientos
and Smirnov:

What a pleasure to discover among the innumerable
foreigners who make their debuts in Paris, an artist as
wonderful as this young Russian singer. What a
marvellous voice; it reminds us of Ninon Vallin, and
she has the technique of the greatest Italian singers,
taste, musicality and exceptional interpretative skill.
Mme Jurjevskaya uses all these qualities to blandish
us. She sang airs by Pergolesi, Scarlatti, Mozart and
Lully, as well as operatic arias and Russian songs. In all
of them she made a notable impression with the
beauty, charm and spontaneity of her art. Bravo
Madam![6]

At the second she was joined by Sergei Prokofiev
and introduced a number of his songs: 'Cinq
mélodies sans paroles', Op. 35 and 'Suis-moi', Op. 23.
André Mangeot wanted to know how it was that the

Germans had had such good fortune to find so fine an artist; was she, he asked, part of the war reparations? It would appear that she was on the verge of making a great career when in the summer of 1925, after she had sung with an ensemble from the Berlin Opera at Amsterdam, on a visit to Andermatt in Switzerland she threw herself into a mountain river and drowned. It was said that she was overcome by an unrequited passion for another soprano.

In the middle and upper part of her voice the quality is pure and lovely, by comparison the lower range is somewhat pallid and inexpressive. Iolanthe's aria from Tchaikovsky's opera, which she sings in the original, lies uncomfortably low for her; it was, after all, written for Medea Mei who was almost a mezzo-soprano. In general her technique is sure, but without a fine finish and there are occasional aspirates in the middle range. The exacting tessitura of Iphigénie's 'O toi qui prolonges mes jours' (sung in German) holds no terrors for her but she has not the real classical style and solidity of legato. The best of a short list of records is an excerpt from Janacek's *Jenufa*. The awkwardly written, sometimes downright ugly, vocal line she sings with feeling and notable precision. It is a very musical performance in marked contrast to the kind of approximate and inaccurate screaming we usually hear; for that, however, the composer's own ignorance of or lack of sympathy for the singing voice must bear a large measure of the responsibility.

It was hardly a coincidence that the Dresden soprano who enjoyed the widest international reputation should have been the youngest, ELISABETH RETHBERG (1894–1976). Her singing is altogether freer sounding, more natural and spontaneous than anything to be heard in the recordings of her predecessors. Hers was a first class voice and, in the upper octave particularly, in her best days, of a remarkable purity and brilliance. She joined the Dresden Conservatory in 1912, first to study the piano and later voice under Otto Watrin. She made her first stage appearance at the Hofoper in 1915 in the soubrette role of Arsena in Johann Strauss's *Zigeunerbaron*. As a contract artist for seven years she sang Agathe in *Freischütz*, Christkindchen in Pfitzner's *Christelflein*, Hansel, Marie in *Verkaufte Braut*, Micaela, both Sophie and Octavian in *Rosenkavalier*, Constanze, Susanna, Mimi, Tosca, Butterfly and the Kaiserin in the first Dresden performance of Richard Strauss's *Frau ohne Schatten*.

Glowing reports travelled the Atlantic, reaching Gatti-Casazza who invited her to the Met in the autumn of 1922.

139 Elisabeth Rethberg as Agathe in *Freischütz*

> Mme Elisabeth Rethberg made her most favourable impression at the start in Aida's lamenting air 'Numi, pietà', her high clear, liquid tones of a singular brightness floating above Verdi's orchestration with unforced ease. The Dresden soprano dominated sufficiently the noisier ensemble of the Theban trumpet scene, and she was dramatically acceptable in spite of crude costuming . . . In the Nile Scene, there was again opportunity for singing to win its way, which, after all, is the main point; a success, in essentials, distinctly was Mme Rethberg.[7]

As indeed she remained, a favourite principal of the company for nearly a generation. Her roles included Pamina, both Donna Anna and Donna Elvira in *Don Giovanni*, Nedda, Sieglinde, Sophie in *Rosenkavalier*, Butterfly, Amelia in *Un Ballo in Maschera*, Maria in *Simon Boccanegra*, Elsa, Desdemona, Elisabeth, Agathe and Maddalena in *Andrea Chénier*.

Although she spent the major part of her career thereafter in New York, she returned to Europe every summer. In 1925 she made her Covent Garden debut as Aida, and according to Ernest Newman,

> raised the season to a height it had not yet attained; all in all, the best artist we have had here since Lehmann left us; her voice is pure, warm and steady, and always in tune; she phrases beautifully and altogether has a fine sense of style.[8]

Though her success in performances of *Butterfly* that followed was if anything even greater, she did not return to Covent Garden until 1934, and then only by accident. When Borgioli, who was engaged as Ramiro in *Cenerentola*, became indisposed, the management was obliged to substitute *Bohème*; the Mimi of the season, Noréna, being unavailable, Rethberg—who was in London at the time—was hastily pressed into service. She was re-engaged in her own right the following season as Elsa 'singing with that purity of tone for which she has long since been famous',[9] Dorota in Weinberger's *Schwanda* and Yaroslavna in *Prinz Igor*. In 1936 she sang the Marschallin, Aida, Mimi and Sieglinde, though in this Newman thought her voice not quite equal to the climaxes. Nor was she much appreciated in her final season three years later when Donna Anna seems to have greatly taxed her.

Elsewhere in Europe, at La Scala in 1929 she succeeded Arangi-Lombardi, as Aida under Toscanini, and thereafter appeared with Martinelli in Respighi's *Campana sommersa* at the Rome Opera. Her Aida earned golden opinions in Paris the following year and at Florence in 1934 she was Leonora in *Forza del Destino*. She took part in the Salzburg Festivals, in 1922 as Constanze and in 1933 as Leonore in *Fidelio* and Donna Anna. She continued to appear regularly in Germany and in 1928 created the name part in Richard Strauss's *Aegyptische Helena*. She was a great success not only with the public and critics but with other musicians. Lauri-Volpi compared her voice to a Stradivarius; Toscanini and Mengelberg, who were agreed over little else, praised the purity and beauty of her singing. By the middle thirties however, the voice was no longer as fresh and steady as it had once been and repetition seems to have staled her artistry. Of the Met's 1937 revival of *Otello* with Martinelli and Tibbett, Oscar Thompson wrote:

> Mme Rethberg's performance was one of seasoned routine and security in the music, with the 'Salce! Salce!' and the 'Ave Maria' smoothly and sympathetically sung but otherwise rather nondescript.[10]

It is unfortunate that various off-the-air transcriptions, chiefly of Met broadcasts made in the later thirties, have achieved such wide currency for these do her reputation a disservice. Though she was only in her early forties, the voice is already passé and sounds taxed by the more dramatic pages of *Otello*, *Trovatore* and *Simon Boccanegra*. They confirm what her earliest and best records for Odeon and Brunswick indicate: that hers was never more than a full lyric soprano and in much of the music she sang, in the middle and lower range, the voice lacked breadth of tone and colour. Even as Aida, probably her most successful role in the Italian repertory, it is the high notes which are so telling. The first of three recordings of the Nile aria is the best; here she manages with supreme ease and brilliance what is often faltered over, screamed through or at best contrived. The high C is one of the finest on records. There is the same radiant quality and limpid execution in Elsa's 'Euch Lüften' and Elisabeth's 'Allmächt'ge Jungfrau'. She claimed to have more than a thousand songs in her repertory; it would be hard to imagine any more ravishingly sung than Strauss's 'Freundliche Vision'. This is a study in genuine piano singing, utterly unaffected and without any of the Teutonic slitherings and artful manipulations of at least one of her contemporaries. She surprises us too in the 'Londonderry Air' and one of McCormack's stand-bys, 'The Snowy-Breasted Pearl'; others have sung them with more charm but few as well. The role of Mimi lay perfectly in her voice and though Tosca's 'Vissi d'arte' is rather lacking in temperament, it is largely free of ugly German mannerisms.

In the face of so much excellence it may seem unkind to complain that her voice is often characterless, and that the tone, though pure, is bland and anaemic, especially in the middle and lower range. She has a good line but her legato style is not affecting, the emission is not ideally smooth and there is a want of poise, of tension in the phrasing. In Mozart this slackness makes her interpretations

140 Grete Stückgold

soprano in Berlin until 1927. At the end of that time she secured an engagement at Covent Garden as Aida.

> Miss Stückgold is a fine singer, her voice is warm and sympathetic, but lacks the keen edge necessary to get the notes through the big ensembles of Act Two. She was somewhat overweighted in her scenes with Amneris by Madame Onegin's powerful voice. She made an ideal Aida in Act Three and final duet.[11]

Although an attempt was made to engage her for Gutrune in 1934 when she was not available, she never sang at Covent Garden again. In the autumn of 1927 she journeyed to New York to make her debut as Eva. Henderson thought hers a 'fresh and most agreeable voice'[12]; for Aldrich she had:

> the valuable asset of a young and fresh voice, and she is a plausible if a little over-kittenish Eva on the stage. In this much she gave pleasure. She must be heard in other roles to be fairly estimated. Her Eva of the first two acts had no very distinctive or eloquent characteristics.[13]

She stayed at the Met until 1934 missing only one season and returned again in 1939. Her roles included Eva, Aida, Elsa, Sieglinde, Agathe, Octavian and later the Marschallin. She travelled on the spring tours with the company and was heard in San Francisco, Chicago and Philadelphia. Her position was difficult for she was overshadowed by Rethberg and Müller but in later years she earned quite a reputation singing on the radio. In her retirement she taught singing at Bennington College, Vermont.

At its best her voice is an attractive lyric soprano but the registers are not properly equalised and blended. The head voice is pure and brilliant but the middle and lower range, though pleasant in quality, sound dull and without any focus on the tone. There is something curiously tentative, almost amateurish in her delivery of 'Ruhe sanft' from *Zaide*; it lacks a solid line in the middle range and at the top she seems almost to be crooning. Her execution of the elaborate vocal writing is neat enough but the attack is not always clean and the intonation variable. Less demanding arias, Elisabeth's 'Allmächt'ge Jungfrau' and Elsa's Dream, are sung with lovely tone but there is a want of finish in the singing and she has no assumption or authority. In the Nile Duet from *Aida* her contribution is obscured by the ugly and forcible delivery

dull and dispiriting. There is in her singing much of the best of the modern approach, which is perhaps why Toscanini so much admired her. She is thorough and after the fashion of her day, a correct musician and she sings all, or almost all, of what is written, but we listen in vain for any individual or imaginative touches that distinguish the great artist from even the best singer.

The general standard of accomplishment among the German sopranos of this period was remarkably high, as is apparent in recordings made by those whose careers, though significant, were not momentous: GRETE STÜCKGOLD (1895–1977), for example. Born Grete Schneidt in the suburbs of London, her father was German, the director of a cable company, and her mother English. Her musical training began after the family moved to Munich in 1913 and she became a pupil of Jacques Stückgold. Subsequently she married him, but the relationship did not last and later she switched her affections to the character baritone Gustav Schützendorf. Her debut took place at Nuremberg in 1917. She stayed with the company five years making guest appearances elsewhere in Germany: in concert with the Leipzig Gewandhaus Orchestra under Artur Nikisch and at the Berlin Staatsoper. The latter led to a long term contract and she was a leading of Fritz Krauss and neither here nor as Desdemona is the voice quite secure, occasionally there is some tremulousness. Bizet's 'Pastorale' she manages attractively.

42. Lyric-Dramatic Sopranos

ELSA BLAND (1880–1935), a favourite singer of Gustav Mahler, was one of the big stars of the Vienna Opera from 1906 until her retirement in 1924. She was born in the city and studied there with Marianne Brandt. Her debut took place at Olmütz in 1903 as Leonore in *Fidelio*. Thereafter came seasons in Magdeburg and Altenberg. A guest appearance at the Imperial Opera in 1905 led to her engagement as a principal of the company the following season. The Imperial—and as it later became, the State—Opera remained the centre of her activities throughout her career. She sang abroad on a number of occasions. She visited Italy in 1909 and appeared at a number of leading theatres there during the next couple of seasons. Her Isolde in particular was acclaimed at Parma, Turin, Verona and the Dal Verme, Milan, on each occasion in company with Ferrari-Fontana. At Bologna she was Elisabeth in *Tannhäuser* and took the name part in Respighi's *Semirama* with Giuseppe Borgatti and Maria Llacer. In 1911 she sang Amelia at Covent Garden, but seems to have made no effect. In Vienna her repertory embraced a wide range of mostly dramatic roles drawn from French and Italian as well as German opera. She was Amelia in *Maskenball* under Walter with Kurz, Walker, Slezak and Demuth, Martha in *Tiefland* in performances directed by the composer himself, Valentine in *Hugenotten*, Berthe in *Prophet*, Aida, Desdemona and Sulamith in *Königin von Saba*, all opposite Leo Slezak, Marguerite, Rachel in *Jüdin*, both Elsa and Ortrud in *Lohengrin*, Elisabeth and Venus in *Tannhäuser*, Leonore in *Fidelio*, Kundry and Isolde. In 1913 she was a guest artist at the German opera house in Berlin, and in 1921 at Bucarest she was 'much appreciated'[1] as Tosca and Aida. Two years later she travelled to South America where she sang Brünnhilde in *Walküre*, Isolde and Elektra in performances conducted by Strauss. After her retirement she taught singing in Vienna.

Her records, made early in her career, show a full and powerful soprano. The top is its chief glory, the high notes are brilliant yet soft-grained. The quality, if not as characteristic, is reminiscent of Destinn, and like hers it is also a top-heavy voice; by

141 Elsa Bland

comparison the middle sounds dry and slightly spread. The chest register is immature and not properly equalised and there is a very obvious catch in the tone when she has to pass back and forth across the break. Both of Aida's solos impress, in spite of the German language and an explosive attack which disturbs an otherwise smooth line. A souvenir of her Amelia, 'Morrò ma prima in grazia', phrased eloquently and smoothly, rises to an impressive climax. Elsewhere, in Elsa's 'Euch Lüften' and Leonore's 'Komm', Hoffnung', there are signs of a wobble and the intonation is not always accurate. Something of the fine quality of the voice can be discerned in part of Desdemona's Willow Song but the voice is not under perfect control and the pitch is never quite precise. She was an accomplished but rather provincial singer and there was lacking in her technique the finesse we associate with the leading artists of her day.

The Swedish soprano LILY HAFGREN (1884–1965) was from a musical family; her mother was a concert singer and her brother a pianist and composer. she studied in Berlin and later at the Raff Conservatory, Frankfurt-am-Main. In 1907, whilst in Italy for some coaching in the Italian repertory, she chanced to sing for Siegfried Wagner. He was greatly impressed and invited her to Bayreuth the following summer. She made her debut as Freia in a performance of *Rheingold* conducted by Hans Richter with Walter Soomer, Luise Reuss-Belce, Carl Braun and Hermine Kittel. Present on the occasion was the Intendant of the Mannheim Opera who

142 Lily Hafgren as Freia in *Rheingold*

immediately offered her a contract; she was a principal lyric soprano there for the next four years. She reappeared at Bayreuth in the summer of 1909 as Elsa under Siegfried Wagner's direction and Eva in *Meistersinger* in 1911 and 1912. In the latter year came two proposals from the Director of the Berlin Hofoper, Dr Waag; she accepted them both—a contract from the theatre that was to last eight years and his hand in marriage.

During her years at Berlin she expanded her repertory and began to sing increasingly dramatic roles: Brünnhilde as well as Sieglinde in *Walküre*, Venus and Elisabeth in *Tannhaüser*, Iphigénie in Gluck's *Iphigenia auf Tauris*, Elsa, Kundry, Gutrune, Freia, Isolde, Brünnhilde in *Siegfried* and *Götterdämmerung*, Pamina and the First Lady in *Zauberflöte*, the Countess in *Figaros Hochzeit*, Agathe, Ariadne, Octavian, Chrysothemis, Herodias in *Salome*, Selika in *Afrikanerin*, Rachel in *Jüdin*, Charlotte in *Werther*, Carmen, Tosca and the Kaiserin in the local premiere of Strauss's *Die Frau ohne Schatten*. Throughout the 1920s she was active as a concert and recital singer in Germany, Austria, Scandinavia and Italy and often included in her programmes modern works by Strauss, von Schillings and Hafgren. She sang in opera, chiefly the big Wagnerian roles, at Stockholm, Madrid, Warsaw and at La Scala where she was Brünnhilde in two *Ring* cycles, one in 1926 under Panizza and the other under Siegfried Wagner in 1930. In 1924 she returned to Bayreuth as Eva and in 1933/4 was a principal at the Dresden Opera.

Hafgren's was a pure and attractive voice which developed considerably in the ten years that separate the Odeons she made in 1911 from the later Grammophon series. Records suggest, however, that she never became a dramatic soprano: the voice lacks the expansion for Isolde's Liebestod or Kundry's Narration and the high notes are thin. She produces them lightly in the head voice and is careful not to weight the tone, but by so doing, as we can hear with the high B at the end of Elisabeth's Greeting, she robs the climax of its proper effect. Her carefully measured enunciation of the opening of Agathe's 'Wie nahte mir der Schlummer' nicely establishes the mood, but in this music the voice production is not smooth enough, she has not a real legato and the concluding allegro she only sketches. A passage from d'Albert's *Tiefland*, music not without some melodic character, suits her intense manner better and here she sings more smoothly. She was an intelligent, sensitive artist but not an outstanding singer.

BARBARA KEMP (1881–1959) was first a pupil

at the Strasbourg Conservatory and after 1903 an apprentice at the Opera there (at that time Strasbourg was in Germany). Between 1906 and 1908 she sang at Rostock then moved to Breslau where she remained for five years. Her long association with the Berlin Imperial, later State, Opera began in 1913. The following year she made her Bayreuth debut as Senta, returning in 1924 and 1927 as Kundry in *Parsifal*. In Berlin her repertory embraced roles from Italian and French opera as well as Wagner. She sang Aida, Leonora in *Troubadour*, the Marschallin, Salome, Elektra, Elsa, Donna Anna, the Dyer's wife in *Frau ohne Schatten*, Santuzza, Carmen, Berthe in *Prophet* and Valentine in *Hugenotten*. In 1919 when artists' self-government was proclaimed at the leading theatres, she contrived to get Max von Schillings, later her husband, 'elected' Director. Out of gratitude or from a genuine regard for her talent, or perhaps a bit of both, he composed an opera especially for her: *Mona Lisa*. The story takes a bit of beating; it is set in Renaissance Florence in the home of an elderly and wealthy goldsmith. When the curtain rises the famous portrait with its enigmatic smile is seen hanging on the wall. The husband, however, is not happy, his wife never smiles at him. His suspicions that she has a lover are confirmed when he surprises a young man hiding in the house, in an airless treasure vault; quickly turning the key he leaves him to suffocate. The wife realises where he is and frees him. Some time later when the husband goes into the vault expecting to find a corpse, the wife waits for him to get inside then quickly slams the door and turns the key on him. The tables are turned; only then does she face the portrait and return its smile.

It was as Mona Lisa in 1923 that she made her Met debut.

> Mme Kemp disclosed fine histrionic talent in the climactic moments but compelled no great admiration for the quality of her voice or her vocal skill.[2]

She also sang Isolde, but in this 'the limitations of range and power in her voice were quite evident'.[3] The following season after a solitary performance of *Mona Lisa* she bowed out pleading ill-health and Gatti made the usual polite noises. Schillings, however, in a press interview blamed the Met's heavy scheduling and the lack of proper rehearsal arrangements. The air was soon thick with recriminations: Gatti declared that Schillings had 'lost a splendid

chance to keep silent';[4] Kemp had simply not measured up to Met standards. Thereafter she was busy in Vienna until 1927 and also made guest appearances at Budapest, Prague, Munich, Dresden, Hamburg and Amsterdam. When her career was over she taught singing in Berlin.

The voice we hear on records is a mature lyric soprano, the tone for the most part bright and rounded. The registers are well blended though the quality is thinner and drier in the chest voice. Her singing is generally accomplished but wanting in finesse and here and there the emission is flawed, as if the support were not always reliable. She moves easily enough through the sweeping line of Leonora's 'D'amor sull'ali rosee' and though not always able to sustain the trills clearly, this is one of her best records. The attack is in the main clean but occasionally, as at the beginning of the Valentine-

143 Barbara Kemp in the title-role of von Schillings'
Mona Lisa

Marcel duet from *Hugenotten*, she reaches up to the high notes rather than taking them cleanly. Her technique is simply not equal to Donna Anna's 'Non mi dir'; there is not the poise or classical smoothness necessary for the opening measures and the end is altogether without brilliance; her extreme caution does not disguise the difficulties. Senta's Ballad she takes in her stride, but from this it seems hard to believe that she ever had the sonority or weight of tone to cope with Isolde in a big theatre. In the final scene from *Afrikanerin*, where Selika inhales the deadly perfume of the mancanilla tree, she makes a bold climax but her singing is not suave enough or sufficiently controlled. Ideally the music needs an electric recording to reveal the felicities in the orchestration. Under the benign influence of her husband she flourished; in a less conducive atmosphere one can imagine why she might have disappointed.

The Hungarian soprano CHARLOTTE VON SEEBÖCK (1886–1952) spent the major part of her career as a principal at the Budapest Opera. She was a pupil of Rosa Papier-Paumgartner, a well known Viennese teacher with whom Lucie Weidt and Anna Bahr-Mildenburg studied. Her debut was at the Vienna Opera in 1905, where she stayed for two years and then moved to Frankfurt before returning to Budapest. To begin with she sang only light coloratura roles, but during fifteen years she gradually began to undertake more dramatic roles. A short list of recordings includes Norma's 'Casta Diva', Aida's 'O Vaterland', one of Leonora's arias from *Troubadour*, both of the Queen of the Night's and 'M'odi, ah m'odi' from *Lucrezia Borgia*, also in German. Hers is a typically German method and the attack often far from accurate. The florid passages are a bit lumpy, but she manages them to some effect and has a good trill. The interpretation is very free and she likes showing off the high notes up to the top C sharp but the lower range is rather weak in comparison. It is an important sounding voice and if her manners are somewhat provincial we can imagine that they had an effect in Budapest.

43. Dramatic Sopranos

The Viennese soprano MELANIE KURT (1880–1941) studied the piano with the legendary Theodore Leschetizky, teacher of Paderewski and Schnabel, before taking singing lessons from Fanny Muller, Marie Lehmann, and later her famous sister Lilli Lehmann. Her career began in 1902 at Lubeck

144 Charlotte von Seeböck

as Elisabeth in *Tannhäuser*. After a few seasons at Leipzig and Brunswick, in 1908, she moved to Berlin. There she was both at the Imperial Opera and at the German Opera. In 1910 she was invited to Covent Garden and sang Brünnhilde and Sieglinde in performances of *Walküre*. Later that summer she was one of the Ladies in *Die Zauberflöte* with Lilli Lehmann and Hermine Kittel at the Salzburg Festival. She appeared at Covent Garden again in February 1914 as Kundry in *Parsifal*.

The following year she joined the company at the Met, making her debut as Brünnhilde in *Walküre*, adding Sieglinde and Brünnhilde in *Götterdämmerung*:

> The music of Brünnhilde has rarely been sung with a finer art, a more thrilling dramatic quality and poignancy of vocal utterance, a more eloquent declamatory potency and truth. It was equally as fine upon the histrionic side. Mme Kurt's conception lays the right emphasis upon the essentially womanly feeling of Brünnhilde deprived of the attributes of the goddess; the tenderness, the bewilderment and despair at the web of deception that envelops her, the outraged dignity, the majesty of her final proclamation over Siegfried's bier.[1]

She was also heard as Pamina, Kundry, Leonore, Elisabeth, Isolde, Amelia, Fricka in *Rheingold*, the Marschallin and Santuzza. Though she was not uniformly successful in them all, at her best, as Isolde—the voice 'fresh, unworn, youthful'[2]—hers was 'the work of a finished artist'.[3] Henderson particularly praised the Battle Cry from *Walküre* sung 'precisely as it is written without any of the familiar evasions'.[4] Her career in New York came to an abrupt halt when the United States joined in the war in 1917.

She was still busy in Germany and Austria into the 1920s: at Dresden, Berlin, Zoppot and Vienna. After her retirement she taught singing in Berlin and then in Vienna until 1938. In that year the Anschluss forced her into exile. It was a twist of fate that the First World War should have driven her from the United States and brought her international career to a premature conclusion, while the advent of the Second World War obliged her to return there to seek refuge. It was in New York that she died in 1941.

Kurt's voice in recordings is a splendid dark coloured and full dramatic soprano with more than a slight—and hardly coincidental—resemblance to Lilli Lehmann. There is the same authority in her every utterance, the grand manner, and also, it must be regretted, the same imprecise attack on the high notes rather than a cleanly poised portamento. Like Lehmann, and unlike the majority of German sopranos of the day, the chest voice is of imposing dimensions and fully equalised, giving colour to the entire voice. Senta's Ballad is a formidable performance, the vocalise and opening phrases hurled out with great force and yet there is a soft and tender line, at the end she quite tears through the difficult allegro. As Sieglinde others have produced a more radiant tone, sung more tenderly too, but she brings a great variety of shade and feeling to the Narration 'Der Männer Sippe'. It is a pity that she has no time to give the phrasing sufficient breadth in Isolde's Liebestod, which is chased through to get it onto one side of a 78 record. Notwithstanding the rather squeezed out Lehmann-style legato in Amelia's two arias from *Maskenball* and some consequent sharp intonation, she gives us a good idea of the Verdi manner in Germany at the beginning of the century. She is at her finest in the music of Kundry, in 'Ich sah das Kind' and 'Seit Ewigkeiten harre ich deiner', the declamation full of character and fascination, the voice responsive across the wide ranging tessitura; for all her faults she was a noble singer.

BERTA MORENA (1878–1952) was a leading soprano at the Munich Opera throughout her entire career. After completing her studies with Frau Röhr-Brajnin and Aglaia von Orgeni she made her debut there as Agathe in *Freischütz* and left a very pleasing impression. During the next decade she sang a wide variety of roles, gradually gaining a reputation, especially in the operas of Wagner. In

145 Melanie Kurt as Berthe in *Prophet*

1908 she was engaged at the Metropolitan, where she appeared during four seasons. To begin with opinion was not particularly enthusiastic. Of her Leonore in *Fidelio* the best that could be said was that she 'was in accord with Mr Mahler's ideas and was consistent' but she could not erase still vivid recollections of Lilli Lehmann and Materna in the role. After 1910, however, she seems to have worked some improvement on her form. As Elisabeth in *Tannhäuser* she sang the 'music so beautifully that critical opinion can only be a description of excellencies and she was a 'fine' Sieglinde. Many years later, in 1925, she reappeared for a solitary Brünnhilde in *Götterdämmerung*. She sang widely as a guest artist at Berlin, Vienna, Hamburg and in 1914 came to London. There her Isolde did not please, for the voice already sounded worn, but her Sieglinde was thought 'wonderful from the dramatic point of view'. As Kundry, however, she could not compare to Matzenauer, while her dressing-gown-like-garb' made it easy to appreciate why

146 Berta Morena as Rachel in Halévy's *Judin*

took guest appearances elsewhere. Gradually she began to make excursions into the soprano repertory but even in 1913 we find her still singing Brangäne, Fricka, Erda and Waltraute. It was not until she accepted an engagement at Stuttgart the following year that she completed the soprano conversion and was heard chiefly in the dramatic repertory of Wagner. From 1918 she was at Berlin, first with the State Opera and after 1925 at the City Opera. In 1919 she made her debut at the Vienna State Opera and returned there often as a guest artist until 1932. In 1924 at the Stockholm Opera she sang Valentine, the following year she was invited to La Scala as Kundry in *Parsifal*, and though the rest of the cast were Italians and sang in the vernacular, Wildbrunn used the original text. Weingartner engaged her for the 1922 season at the Colon. Thus it was that she came to take part in the first German language performances given at that theatre. She was Kundry in *Parsifal*, all three Brünnhildes in a *Ring* cycle in which the casts also included Lotte Lehmann, Walter Kirchhoff, Emil Schipper and Carl Braun, and subsequently she was heard as the Marschallin in *Rosenkavalier*. In the twenties she visited Zurich, Amsterdam, Budapest and Paris.

In 1927 she was engaged at Covent Garden as *Fidelio* in company with Lotte Schöne, Fritz Krauss and Paul Bender under the direction of Bruno Walter. She did not make a good impression, the voice was showing signs of wear, and it seems that the high notes did not come easily to her. After 1932 she sang only occasionally and in concert. She was a Professor at the Vienna Musical Academy from 1932 until 1950. She died in Vienna three days after her ninetieth birthday.

Wildbrunn's is an outstanding dramatic soprano on the grand scale and there is much in her manner and method to remind us of other Papier-Paumgartner pupils, especially Anna Bahr-Mildenburg. Her chest register too is fully developed and this helps to give solidity to the tone and colour throughout the entire range of the voice. Lotte Lehmann has written admiringly of Wildbrunn's 'noble art' and we can hear that, perhaps nowhere better, in the great scene of *Fidelio*. Though she sings this more after the fashion of Lilli Lehmann—including all the appoggiaturas—in a grander and more expansive style than Lotte, she adds to it something of the latter's warmer delivery. The opening recitative is incisively declaimed with great authority and purity of tone, even if she has to squeeze the high notes to get them out. The central aria 'Komm,

Parsifal did not find it difficult to resist her blandishments. She remained active in Munich until 1927 after which she taught singing.

Morena's is a bright and secure soprano rather more lyric than dramatic but the telling edge on the tone is some compensation for a lack of weight especially in the lower range. She sings with a tremulous intensity and some passion, as we can hear in Rachel's 'Il va venir' (in German), though there is no great variety of colour and her legato is mostly a matter of good intentions. Her voice is not so imposing as Kurt's in Sieglinde's 'Der Männer Sippe' but it is brighter sounding and her attack generally more accurate.

HELENE WILDBRUNN (1882–1972) was a pupil of Rosa Papier-Paumgartner who had previously taught Anna Bahr-Mildenberg and Lucie Weidt. In the early part of her career she sang contralto and it was as such that she made her debut at Dortmund in 1907; she remained there seven years but under-

147 Helene Wildbrunn as Isolde

148 Gertrude Bindernagel as Fidelio with ear-rings!

Hoffnung' is sung with a correct use of portamento and she spans the wide phrases and difficult tessitura with assurance, though above A the tone hardens under pressure. Throughout she shows a grasp of the overall structure of the scene and she accomplishes the awkwardly written and exacting concluding measures with the same fine intensity. This is a great interpretation.

GERTRUDE BINDERNAGEL (1894–1932), the possessor of a full dramatic soprano voice with a dark almost mezzo quality, died a violent death at the height of her career. She was born in Magdeburg where she studied at the local conservatory and then at the age of seventeen became an unpaid apprentice at the Municipal Theatre. Between 1913 and 1917 she was a pupil at the Berlin Musikhochschule. After graduating, for the next four years, she appeared successively with the Breslau and Regensburg Operas. The fine quality of her voice brought her to the attention of the management at the Berlin Staatsoper where she made her debut in 1921. During six seasons she was a leading member of the company, at first in lyric roles, as Nedda and

later Aida, and eventually as Isolde. In the spring of 1927 she sang Leonora in the first Berlin performances of Verdi's *Die Macht des Schicksals*; the opera was directed by Leo Blech and the cast also included Genia Guszalewicz, Tino Pattiera, Heinrich Schlusnus, Leo Schützendorf and Emanuel List. After 1927 she also appeared at the Städtischen Oper and sang elsewhere in Germany, at Hamburg, Munich, Mannheim and the Zoppot Festivals on the Baltic coast. Abroad she was a guest at Barcelona and in 1930 at the Vienna Staatsoper. There she was the Marschallin in *Rosenkavalier* with Adele Kern, Margit Angerer and Richard Mayr conducted by Clemens Krauss. It was in Berlin after a performance of *Siegfried* in the autumn of 1932, as she was walking through the opera arcade, that her second husband, a banker, Wilhelm Hintze, shot her at point blank range; she died a few days later as a result of her injuries. At the trial it transpired that Hintze's finances having suffered greatly from the economic uncertainty immediately before the Nazis took office, he imagined that there was a conspiracy afoot organised by his wife and her lover to ruin him. The tragic irony was that there was not only no conspiracy, there was no lover either.

Bindernagel made only a short list of recordings. Hers is a secure, powerful instrument, the tone not perfectly free but the voice moves easily up to the high C, the registers are well blended and the emission is generally smooth. As Gretchen in Gounod's *Margarethe*, the Jewel Song and part of the Love Duet with Alexander Kirchner sound rather too staid and mature. She makes an imposing impression as Anna in Marschner's *Hans Heiling* but the music is hardly distinguished. She is at her best in Aida's two arias. 'O Vaterland' in particular, in spite of the German method where the tone is squeezed out rather than floated, is attractively phrased and sung with feeling.

Few Wagnerian sopranos of this time were more greatly admired than GERTRUDE KAPPEL (1884–1971), who sang principal roles with great success in London, Vienna, New York, Hamburg and Munich over more than twenty years. She was a student at the Leipzig Conservatory, and she too began in the mezzo, even alto range, for we find her in concert programming arias of Dalila and Azucena. Eventually when the voice settled she made her debut as Leonore in *Fidelio* at Hanover. There she was a principal until 1920. She sang Donna Anna, the Countess, Pamina, Aida with Slezak, Amelia in *Maskenball* with Piccaver, Santuzza in performances of *Cavalleria Rusticana* conducted by Mascagni, Elektra, Octavian, Saffi in *Zigeunerbaron* and Rosalinde. In 1912 she made her Covent Garden debut as Brünnhilde in *Walküre*; 'with a voice of great beauty she unites a simplicity of style'.[5]

> Simplicity too, was the salient feature of Fraulein Kappel's performance as Brünnhilde in *Götterdämmerung*. It was clear at once that she had power in reserve, from the first there was a richness of quality and expression in her singing which she had not shown us in *Walküre*.[6]

She reappeared at Covent Garden the following summer adding Elisabeth and Venus in different performances of *Tannhäuser* and in 1914 was the Brünnhilde in a complete *Ring* cycle under Nikisch. Ten years later with the resumption of the International seasons Kappel returned for another *Ring* cycle under Walter and was heard in London for the first time as Isolde. She came again in 1925 and 1926 singing Isolde, Senta, Elektra, various Brünnhildes, and the Marschallin but she was less well-liked in Strauss.

After the war she appeared regularly at the Vienna State Opera, as the Marschallin with Gutheil-Schoder, Brünnhilde in a *Walküre* with Lehmann, Olczewska and Melchior, Ortrud in *Lohengrin*, the Dyer's Wife in Strauss's *Frau ohne Schatten*, the title-role in Korngold's *Violanta* directed by the composer, the Queen in Goldmark's *Königin von Saba* with Maria Nemeth as Sulamith and Aida opposite Slezak. She made her Met debut as Isolde in January 1928.

Her performance was uneven in some particulars but it was sufficient to give unmistakeable evidence of a

149 Gertrude Kappel as Brünnhilde in *Walküre*

highly gifted artist. It has been many years since we heard an Isolde who did not bawl in indiscriminate fortes and fortissimos her rage and resentment against Tristan. In Kappel's tones were to be felt every fluctuating shade of passion and feeling, [and] in accomplishing this, [she] matched the text with the tone and the tone with the text, and every act and word had significance to the audience. The voice is uncommonly warm and lyrical, of the necessary range, and fitted for dramatic expression. Sometimes it was forced, with resultant brilliancy but loss of quality and ease of emission.[7]

In New York she was heard as all three Brünnhildes, Kundry, offered 'generally beautiful and sometimes ravishing singing'[8] as Fidelio, Ortrud, 'a rather dowdy Marschallin',[9] Fricka in *Rheingold*, Rachel in *La Juive* and Elektra in which . . .

[She] was deplorably miscast . . . she was not within a thousand miles of being Elektra. Maniacal intensity is not within the power of Mme Kappel to suggest. This cherishable artist, a moving and noble Brünnhilde, an admirable Isolde, is hopelessly unfitted for such a role.[10]

Throughout her career she was a soloist in the concert hall; we read of her in Bologna in 1913 in Bach's *St Matthew Passion*. Between 1927 and 1932 she was a prominent member of the company at Munich and made guest appearances elsewhere in Germany where her repertory also included: Ariadne, Marietta in Korngold's *Tote Stadt*, Myrtocle in d'Albert's *Toten Augen*, Rezia in *Oberon*, Agathe and the title-role in von Schillings's *Mona Lisa*.

Kappel was a fine artist and her voice, if not especially big, was a lyric soprano of pure and attractive quality. Her singing has a certain charm and though, as in Brünnhilde's Immolation, she does not have the breadth in her phrasing or the power we are accustomed to in this music, yet she is able to affect us. Unfortunately this is almost entirely vitiated by her poor attack. She squeezes the tone out on the high notes and when she feels it is in the right place, sets it free to vibrate; it is not a pleasant or a musical way of proceeding, nor is it successful. An unpublished recording of the Battle Cry from *Walküre* makes it easier to understand the affection in which she was held. There is less sliding around, a breadth of tone and an assumption—also a well articulated trill—that impresses.

For the late Roberto Bauer, author of *Historical Records* and for many years vocal talent-scout in Europe for the Metropolitan Opera, there were prima donnas and there was FRIDA LEIDER (1888–1975) in a class by herself. Those who enjoyed Bauer's acquaintance are never likely to forget that inimitable voice, at the same time hoarse and raucous, launched on a seemingly endless flow of anecdotage. With his impossibly retentive memory he would detail the entire programme of a Leider recital in 1932, including the encores, and then give a quick run through of those present in the audience: musicians, politicians, society figures and critics. For him as for so many it was Leider's deep intensity that was so affecting and then, too, hers was a wonderful voice, warm and full of colour. Her technique—no one dared tell Roberto—was by no means perfect and, though she had rid herself of many of the bad habits of her colleagues, yet the upper part of her voice did not ring forth freely and in later years the effort involved in producing it was obvious. She did not compromise, however, and declined to take the easy way up; she never felt her way on to the pitch but always tried to attack tones cleanly. A snippet of film of her in action in the final measures of *Siegfried* with the tenor Max Lorenz has an overwhelmingly exultant quality about it; once seen it is not easily forgotten.

Leider went to several teachers, of whom the most important was Otto Schwarz in Berlin. She made her debut as Venus in *Tannhäuser* at Halle in 1915 and soon afterwards, at Nuremberg, sang her first Brünnhilde in *Walküre*. From 1916 to 1919 she was a contract artist at the Rostock Opera, moving briefly to Königsberg and in 1920 to Hamburg, where her career really began. There she was busy not only in the Wagnerian repertory but also as Donna Anna, the Countess, Leonora in *Troubadour*, Fidelio, Aida, Tosca, Ariadne and Amelia in *Maskenball*. In 1923 she made her first appearance at the Berlin State Opera as Fidelio under the direction of Erich Kleiber; she remained with the company until her retirement. In 1924 she began a love affair with the London public which continued despite failing powers until 1938. She was Brünnhilde in the Covent Garden *Ring* cycles of 1928, 1930 and every season from 1932 until 1938. She sang Isolde eight times, and her other roles included the Marschallin, Senta, Donna Anna, Leonora in *Trovatore*, the title-role in Gluck's *Armide* and Kundry. Her success in pretty well all of them—even as the Marschallin, where she had on several occasions to contend with Lehmann's classic example—was complete and overwhelming. Failings were remarked but they did not affect the quality or sincerity of her perfor-

150 Frida Leider as Isolde

mances. In her last years she shared the honours with Flagstad, then at the height of her prodigious powers, but in spite of the latter's vocal freshness, the easy brilliance of her upper range and fecundity of her powers, the public and critics remained with Leider to the end.

She was honoured by La Scala in 1927 and 1928 when she appeared in *The Ring* cycle under Panizza; in the first year she sang Brünnhilde in *Walküre* and *Götterdämmerung*, in the second she was Brünnhilde throughout. In the summer of 1928 she sang at Bayreuth as Brünnhilde and Kundry and returned again in 1933 and 1938, in the latter year adding Isolde. In the winter of 1928 she accepted an invitation to Chicago and appeared there during the next four seasons as Brünnhilde in *Walküre*, Kundry, Isolde, Donna Anna, the Marschallin, Venus, Fidelio, the First Lady in *Zauberflöte* and in the title-role of von Schillings's *Mona Lisa*. She took part in the Zoppot Festivals in Germany and in 1931 visited the Colon, Buenos Aires. Her Metropolitan debut the following season was as Isolde and although by then past her best she made a great impression.

> Mme Leider's Isolde has long been famous abroad. Her embodiment has been called, indeed, the greatest Isolde now on stage. I am not sure that any living Isolde could seem 'great' or 'greatest' to those whose memories are not wholly within our time. Yet it would be scarcely extravagant to say that Mme Leider's Isolde is one of singular beauty and expressiveness. Her voice is a true Isolde voice. It is not so powerful nor so resonant, not so full and secure in its upper ranges, as it was some years ago. But in its middle register the voice is of rare loveliness and purity; and in the mezza voce or piano passages it is often enamouring . . . This Isolde is not cyclonic; but she has a sovereign dignity, an elect intensity, a passion that remains patrician, that does not bawl and shriek. Above all it has a deep and enlarging tenderness, a richness of feeling, and a poetry of the imagination that set it apart from the Isoldes of our time.[11]

She found neither the New York weather nor her fee sufficiently attractive and stayed only two seasons. It was her defection that obliged Gatti to call in an unknown Norwegian soprano to take over her roles. In the later part of her career Leider's position in Germany became increasingly difficult; her husband, the violinist Rudolf Deman, was a Jew and she refused to have the marriage annulled to oblige Nazi dogma. Eventually Deman withdrew to Switzerland but they were re-united after the war. She sang in concert for some years after her retirement from the stage and was later busy as a teacher, first at the voice studio of the Berlin State Opera and subsequently as Professor at the Berlin Music School.

Leider's great interpretative gifts remained unimpaired to the end of her career, but it must be admitted that in the later recordings there are some uncomfortable moments vocally. Even in 1929, in the *Tristan* Love Duet with Melchior, a tremendous account of the music, she squeezes out the high notes and then has to let them go with a sharp ejaculatory yelp. A comparison between two recordings of Kundry's Narrative, a piece that falls perfectly within her range and to which she devotes her full

expressive powers, reveals as we might have expected greater maturity in the second made in 1931, but although she displays a finely drawn line in both, in the earlier version the voice is more responsive and she even manages to give an impression of floating the tone. Throughout her phrasing is remarkably sensitive to the intricate and constantly shifting pattern of the music. In Weber's mighty 'Ozean' there is the same sure and telling overall command. Others have dealt more emphatically with the opening recitative, and she does not offer the optional high B flat, but her voice has a variety of colour and expression throughout the entire range that is not equalled elsewhere. As in Wagner the declamation has a majestic repose, yet is suffused in a warm and womanly glow. Her Verdi singing is interesting too, although she has not quite sufficient polish for it; an occasional lightly aspirated slurred quaver or mordent is more obtrusive here and the voice is without alacrity for a piece like Leonora's 'Di tale amor' from *Trovatore*. It was as a Wagner singer that she was supreme; she had not the security or brilliance of Nordica, nor the surpassing ease of Flagstad; instead she brought to Brünnhilde and Isolde an intense and passionate quality of her own which deeply moved a whole generation of lovers of his music.

44. Schumann

The name of ELISABETH SCHUMANN (1888–1952) is inseparably linked with Richard Strauss's *Der Rosenkavalier*. Her repertory embraced a variety of light lyric soprano roles, in many of which she greatly charmed, but it was as Sophie—though she did not create the part—that she enjoyed the widest acclaim. Schumann came from a musical family, her father was a church organist and on her mother's side she claimed descent from the great nineteenth-century soprano Henriette Sontag. Her only teacher was Alma Schadow, who subsequently gave lessons to Lotte Lehmann. Her voice and the technique she acquired have always been matters of contention. At the top it had a silvery quality, but in range and size was never more than a soubrette. Florence Easton, who sang with Schumann in her early days in Hamburg, recalls: 'the biggest thing she ever did was Sophie. She was very limited. She never had much of a voice and she used to have to fake'.[1] Records suggest the limitations arose chiefly from technical inadequacy and the voice sounds frail and insubstantial because it was not fully developed and lacked support.

She made her debut at Hamburg as the Shepherd Boy in *Tannhäuser* in 1909, remaining there until 1919. She took a number of small roles as well as Eva in *Meistersinger*, Bastienne in Mozart's *Bastien und Bastienne*, Mimi, Cherubino, Dot in Goldmark's *Heimchen am Herd*, the Woodbird in *Siegfried* and Sophie in the first Hamburg performance of *Rosenkavalier* with Fleischer-Edel and Edyth Walker. It was as Sophie that she appeared at the Metropolitan for the first time in the 1914/15 season; Hempel was the Marschallin and Ober Octavian.

Mme Schumann's voice, as it was disclosed in the difficult tessitura of the music she sings in the second

151 Elisabeth Schumann

act, is a clear and high soprano of pure quality and agreeable timbre, a voice possessing the bloom of youth, that will be listened for with high expectation in other music as the season advances.[2]

Her Musetta, Papagena, Woodbird and Gretel passed without further comment, but when she sang Marzelline Aldrich noted that 'she was acceptable though she did not quite have all the beauty of vocal quality in her songs that might have been expected.'[3] She did not return to the Met.

Her career continued in Hamburg and with guest engagements elsewhere, then in 1919, largely through Strauss's initiative, she moved to Vienna. Under his direction she sang Despina in *Così fan tutte*, Ilia in *Idomeneo* and Pamina, as well as Sophie. Other roles included Micaëla, Nedda, Norina, Marguerite and Mimi. She sang at the Munich and Salzberg Festivals and in 1921 was supporting artist to Richard Strauss on a coast to coast recital tour of the United States. Her London debut took place in 1924 as Sophie with Lehmann, Reinhardt and Mayr under Bruno Walter, a classic cast. She was much admired though 'a certain hardness of voice and maturity in acting was [sic] noticed'.[4] She returned regularly until 1931 adding the Composer in *Ariadne*, a 'delightful' Eva, Susanna, Zerlina, a 'sprightly and melodious' Blonde in *Seraglio* and her Adele in *Fledermaus* was pronounced 'inimitable'. After 1930 she appeared less often in opera, usually in the same handful of parts, and was increasingly busy in the concert hall and recital room. She continued to give Lieder recitals almost to the end of her life and in her later years was appointed Head of the Vocal department at the Curtis Institute, Philadelphia.

Schumann's daughter-in-law in a little manual entitled *The Teaching of Elisabeth Schumann*, the usual mixture of the unexceptionable and the obscure, does let drop one revelatory sentence:

> Although she allowed [the] deeper and bigger voices to mix chest with head resonance in their lower notes, from approximately B flat downwards, she made an iron rule that the higher type of soprano, lyrical, soubrette and coloratura, should on no occasion make use of chest notes, even in a mixed form.[5]

What every important teacher from Tosi to Garcia would have thought of such extraordinary wisdom one can only speculate but it is certain that Schumann acted upon it herself all her career. There is no sign of a chest register in her singing on any of her many gramophone records, with results that are obvious not only at the bottom where the tone is pallid and lacking resonance, but its absence is felt across the entire range. The chest register provides the source of colour throughout the soprano voice, the basic palette which the singer uses when painting the tones so as to give them variety of expression, which is one of the principal reasons why all the greatest singing teachers have put such a premium on the full equalisation of the registers. There is another more compelling reason; the vocal muscles like any others will not develop or retain their health and vigour when not fully exercised.

The top was the best part of Schumann's voice in her youth, as Aldrich noted, with a fresh bloom on it. It was partly out of concern to preserve this that she came to confuse lightness for brilliance and partly the consequence of another technical failing: records show that her breathing was shallow and not sufficiently expansive to have supported a fully developed voice. Pictorial confirmation is provided in a couple of action photographs of her reproduced in *The Teaching of Elisabeth Schumann*, where she stands erect but with her shoulders set and drawn up slightly; when the breathing is deep and correct the shoulders do not move. Since Lehmann—very audibly—had the same problem, it does not say much for Alma Schadow's teaching that she was unable to correct either of them. Schumann did contrive to keep something of the freshness and facility in the upper range throughout most of her career, but the rest of the voice came to sound rather dropped with a throaty attack and as her daughter-in-law tells us she suffered increasingly over the years from hoarseness. In contrast to her contemporary Lucrezia Bori, a soprano of similar natural resources, whose voice as she grew older acquired a warmer and fuller quality in the middle range, which gave to her singing an appropriate maturity, Schumann's did not develop. Obliged by diminishing vocal powers to abandon most of her operatic career some years before Bori, she switched to Lieder, but her perspectives were the same and she did not acquire in compensation a wider range of expression. The charm and girlishness of her manner were engaging in her youth, but a middle-aged soubrette seems pert and coy, even tiresome. The charm of an older woman is something different and, as we hear in Patti's records, frailer. A note of experience is sounded in the warm, well-honed quality of the voice, achieved in spite of, or perhaps just because of, diminished powers.

Records leave no doubt that it was not only Schumann's personality that made Sophie so out-

standing; the part perfectly suited her voice and technique. Nobody has excelled her interpretation nor, to date, equalled it; it is not desirable anyone should try. Strauss wrote for the voice in a debased portamento style—debased, because he did not use the device in the classical fashion, so as to relate words and melody with maximum eloquence. Strauss's melodies were not conceived vocally in breath spans, but in paragraphs ranging across wide intervals and the sweeping portamento in the vocal line merely echoed—as we have already noted— that of the violin writing. Nothing could have accommodated Schumann better for, as is plain even in her earliest recordings, she always had difficulty in attacking a note cleanly; generally she would scoop up to it and then slither down again. The extra harmonies this introduced were lost in, or perhaps even enriched, the elaborate web of Strauss's orchestration while the delightful silvery quality of her upper register matched that of the swooping strings, precisely the effect Strauss was aiming for. In the operas of Mozart, however, in which she was much admired in her day, her recordings are less attractive. The incessant slithering and sliding, pecking and twittering, the lack of a solid legato assume a greater prominence than they would have in the opera house or concert hall with the artist's physical presence to distract us. Records do not deal kindly with her failings. Even on the early Edisons, for example, Ännchen's two airs from *Freischütz*, though she characterises piquantly, the execution is tentative and after an uncomfortable high B flat in the concluding measures of 'Trube Augen' the voice collapses. It was by charm that she held audiences captive for a complete recital, for by the time she was forty her voice was no more than a wisp of tone. Hers was an achievement of personality, like that of a diseuse. She was not capable in her Lieder singing, as Sembrich was, of charming us through the singing alone without affectation, by purity of tone, smoothness of line and the simplicity of her delivery. We are all too conscious of the winsome ways of the soubrette.

Though not perhaps a star, BERTA KIURINA (1881–1933) was a great favourite in Vienna through more than a generation. She studied at the Vienna Conservatory, first piano under Fischoff and later voice with Geiringer. Less than a year after her debut at Linz in 1904, Mahler heard her and she was offered a contract at the Vienna Opera where she sang every season until 1927. She began modestly as the Duchess's Page in *Rigoletto*, then came Zerlina in *Don Giovanni*, Marzelline in *Fidelio*, Oscar in

152 Berta Kiurina as Gretchen in Gounod's
Margarethe

Maskenball, Urbain in *Hugenotten*, Margiana in
Cornelius's *Barbier von Bagdad*, the Wood Bird in
Siegfried and assorted Rhine and Flower maidens in
other Wagnerian works, Cherubino, Martha in
Kienzl's *Der Evangelimann* and Musetta. In due
course she sang Marie in *Verkaufte Braut*, Jutta in
Dalibor, Micaëla, Eva, Nedda, Diemut in *Feuersnot*,
the three heroines in *Les Contes d'Hoffman*, Madama
Butterfly, Desdemona, Adina, Gilda, the Queen in
Hugenotten, Leonora in *Troubadour*, Leonore in

Alessandro Stradella, Marguerite, Sulamith in *Königin von Saba*, Constanze and even the Queen of the
Night. She took various parts in several of Strauss's
operas: Chrysothemis in *Elektra*, Octavian, Naiade
in *Ariadne auf Naxos* and on different occasions
both the Empress and the Dyer's Wife in *Frau ohne
Schatten*. She was Esmeralda in Franz Schmidt's
Notre Dame and Ighino in Pfitzner's *Palestrina*; it
was an extraordinary range of accomplishments.

Nor was that all, for she was a successful concert
artist, in Verdi's *Requiem*, Brahms's *Deutsches
Requiem*, Mahler's Eighth Symphony and
Beethoven's Ninth, and, perhaps most remarkably,
Schoenberg's *Gurrelieder*. She travelled throughout

153 Lola Artôt de Padilla

Austria and Germany and appeared in opera in Berlin, Budapest and in 1928 at the Colon, Buenos Aires.

Kiurina made a long list of recordings over a period of more than twenty years. It was a well trained lyric soprano with some good high notes, the technique quite enough to cope with most of the demands she made of it over many years. Fiordiligi's 'Per pietà' (in German, as are all the titles) rather catches her out in the awkward fioritura at the end, but she surprises us in 'Casta Diva', managing it with some skill; but even maids-of-all-work draw the line somewhere, and wisely she never sang Norma in the theatre. Over the years the voice dried out and her intonation was not always accurate. In the earliest recordings, for example the Page's Song from *Hugenotten*, there is still some sheen left; this is a neat, attractive performance, not brilliant, but the coloratura is clearer than it became later on. The vocal arrangements of Strauss Waltzes 'Freut euch des Lebens' and the more famous 'Wo die Zitronen blühn' will appeal to those who like this kind of thing; she is not a virtuosa but then she spares us the yards of trill that Mme Kurz liked to indulge in on such occasions and offers instead a little spirit and grace. Not a great, and certainly not a perfect singer, but one who gave much satisfaction in her lifetime and whose records still have the capacity to please.

For an aspiring artist to have one famous singer as a parent may be an advantage; two, it might be thought, would be more likely to prove an embarrassment, yet the career of LOLA ARTOT DE PADILLA (1880–1933), although she was never an international star, did credit to the memory of both her father the Spanish baritone Mariano Padilla y Ramos and especially her mother the mezzo-soprano Desirée Artôt, one of the most important of Pauline Viardot's pupils, who was her daughter's only teacher. Upon the completion of her studies in 1902, Artôt de Padilla sang in concert in Paris and then on tour in Poland and Scandinavia. The following season she made her stage debut at Wiesbaden as Mignon, after which she appeared at the Opéra-Comique as a Fairy in Halphen's *Cor fleuri*. From 1907 she sang in Berlin, first with the Komische Oper, then the Gura-Sommer-Oper, and after 1909 for seventeen years at the Imperial Opera. She was Berlin's first Octavian in company with Hempel, Dux and Knüpfer and first Composer in the revised version of *Ariadne auf Naxos* with Hafgren, Kirchner and Bronsgeest. She was a famous Zerlina; in 1909 with Lilli Lehmann and d'Andrade, and

thirteen years later with Frida Leider and Gertrude Bindernagel. Her other roles included Marie in *Verkaufte Braut*, Micaëla to the Carmen of Labia, Charlotte, Lola in *Cavalleria Rusticana*, Mimi, Orlovsky in *Fledermaus*, Cherubino with Denera, Hempel, Knüpfer and Hoffmann, Papagena also with Hempel and Knüpfer, Frau Gertrude in Leo Blech's *Versiegelt*, Oscar in *Maskenball* with Kurt, Ober, Kirchoff and Bronsgeest, Marguerite, and she sang in the local premieres of Delius's *Village Romeo and Juliet*, Gounod's *Le Médecin malgré lui* and Humperdinck's *Königskinder* in which 'she was a charming and delicate country girl with her voice so pretty yet properly disciplined'.[6]

Her voice is a light lyric soprano of no great range or remarkable quality, but her singing shows the results of fine schooling. The tone is pure and firm and she has a sound legato style. Most of the titles she recorded are in German and the consonants often have an awkward way of digging into the line but her attack is always clean. She was a fine Mozart singer, in Cherubino's 'Non so più' rather overdoing the ritards but 'Voi che sapete' has just the right amount of spirit in the delivery, full of delicate inflexions, shading in the line and at one point an appropriate touch of peevishness. The same fine skill and character distinguish her interpretations of both Zerlina's arias. The first shows off a lovely line, the intervals cleanly and clearly articulated and the singing full of imaginative detail. The 6/8 section is taken faster than the plodding tempi preferred today, introducing not only variety of pace but giving a touch of brilliance to the roulades, which Artôt de Padilla executes with delicate finesse. In 'Vedrai carino' it is her singing itself that charms, the graceful portamento style and use of tremolando as a legitimate musical effect.

Of all the German sopranos whom Beecham introduced to London in his various seasons immediately prior to the First World War the most successful was CLAIRE DUX (1885–1967). She was fêted by press, public and even her own colleagues; Melba actually went so far as to claim Dux as her successor. Though she was born in Poland, her family were Germans. At a very early age she showed signs of musical talent and when only twelve sang the part of Gretel in a school production of Humperdinck's *Hansel und Gretel*. Her vocal studies began in Berlin under Maria Schwadtke and Adolf Deppe, later she went to Milan to work with the famous Austrian born soprano Teresa Arkel. In 1906 she made her debut at the Cologne Opera as Pamina in *Die Zauberflöte*; it was to remain through-

154 Claire Dux as the Goosegirl in Humperdinck's
Königskinder

out her career her most popular role. During five years at Cologne she sang Marzelline in *Fidelio*, Aennchen in *Lustigen Weiber von Windsor*, the Countess in *Figaros Hochzeit*, Marguerite Agathe, Desdemona, Gilda, Eva and Benjamin in Méhul's *Josef*. She made various guest appearances at other leading German theatres, notably at the Berlin Imperial Opera in 1909 as Mimi opposite Caruso. In 1911 she became a member of the Berlin company where she stayed until the end of the war.

Her international career began in London in January 1913 at Covent Garden as Sophie in the local premiere of Strauss's *Rosenkavalier*. In the course of eight performances, although there were four different Octavians and Marschallins, Dux was the only Sophie. The purity of her tone and the beauty of her singing made a great impression. She was hardly less striking in her only other role that season, Eva in *Meistersinger* opposite Walter Kirchhoff's Walther. She repeated the part at Covent Garden the following year and was heard again in London that summer at Drury Lane both as Sophie and Pamina.

The excellence of the German singing was a surprise.

The greatest personal success was made by Miss Claire Dux in her singing of 'Ah! lo so.'[7]

After the war she was more active in the concert hall than on the stage, though in 1920 she starred in an operetta specially composed for her, Kalman's *Das Hollandweibchen*, at the Metropol Theatre, Berlin. The next year she left for the United States and save for some guest appearances in Berlin in 1925 did not sing in opera in Germany again. Her North American debut took place in the autumn of 1921 as Mimi with the Chicago Opera, followed by Nedda, in which part she was also heard in the company's annual visit to New York. In both cities she was warmly received but sang only a handful of performances; this was in Mary Garden's season when the 'Directa' showered contracts like confetti and hardly any of the artists engaged actually sang all the performances that they were bound to do and had been paid for. In the following year she joined Leo Blech's touring company, and was Lady Harriet in *Martha*, and Eva. In Chicago again on Christmas Day 1923 she introduced Humperdinck's Goosegirl in *Königskinder*, as she had done in Berlin, and though the performance was 'flagrantly under-rehearsed',[8] hers was a personal triumph:

The Hellabrunn clock struck the hour of noon, the gates of the city were opened, and there stood a goose girl, golden crown on golden hair, her geese waddling and cackling about her feet, a scene that by its complete simplicity and sincerity was one to touch the heart and live in the memory.[9]

The geese at any rate seemed to know their role.

Dux was married three times, to a writer, an actor, and the great Chicago meat magnate Charles H. Swift. Possibly it was on his account, directly or indirectly, that she sang only infrequently after the mid-twenties.

The voice we hear on almost all her recordings was a beautiful lyric soprano. One can imagine the pure and bright upper notes sounding out brilliantly in the theatre. On records however, the very German technique contrives to make her singing often bland and uninteresting. The middle of the voice, by comparison with the top, is rather dull and colourless and the chest register not properly equalised. Mozart's 'Dove sono', despite the pure tone, suffers for want of a really smooth and solid legato, her attack is imperfect and the intonation by no means impeccable. Leonora's 'D'amor sull'ali rosee' finds her rather out of her depth; the trills are not clearly defined and though the high notes are prettily done, she is unable to make them a fitting part of the sweeping phrases. She makes something pretty out of Leila's 'Comme autrefois', though here the pure tone verges on whiteness. The music of Mimi and Mignon suits her voice. Raff's instrumentally inspired Cavatine shows off her technique to good advantage, the voice sounding extraordinarily like a violin, though one could imagine a violinist doing it more effortlessly. Two numbers from Kalman's *Hollandweibchen*, with more than a sprinkling of paprika in the Edam, she sings beautifully though without any of those touches that make an artist like Fritzi Massary so inimitable. Altogether it is not difficult to hear why in spite of a lovely voice she failed to capitalise on her early successes; her manner is inexpressive and musically she is not interesting.

The career of VERA SCHWARZ (1884–1964) embraced both opera and operetta with equal success. She was a pupil of Philipp Forstén in Vienna. As a young woman the voice was rather small and he advised her to become an operetta singer. So it was that she made her first stage appearance at the Theater an der Wien in 1908 opposite a favourite operetta tenor, Alexander Girardi. During the next four years she was a member

155 Vera Schwarz in the title-role of *Rosenkavalier*

of various operetta companies, at first singing only small roles but in due course she was well received Rosalinde in *Fledermaus*. Her success encouraged her to undertake a period of further study, at the end of which she secured an engagement at the Hamburg Opera. She remained there for several years. After 1916 Lehmann had gone to Vienna, and Schwarz sang a variety of leading roles from Carmen to Aida. In 1919 she was a guest at the Berlin State Opera and two years later made her debut at the Vienna State Opera as Tosca with Alfred Piccaver. In the heyday of Jeritza this was bold, not to say hazardous, but she succeeded triumphantly. Since Jeritza was now spending a large part of each season in New York, Schwarz went on to inherit a number of her other roles. For five years from 1924 she was a leading principal of the company with a repertory that included Pamina, the Countess, various lyrical roles of Wagner from Eva to Sieglinde, Verdi's Amelia, Aida, Elvira in *Ernani* and Leonora in *Troubadour*, Strauss's Oktavian, Ariadne and Helena, Korngold's Marietta, Heliane and Violanta and she was Anita in the Vienna premiere of Krenek's *Jonny spielt auf*.

She made guest appearances in Germany and sang Octavian at the 1929 Salzburg Festival. When her Vienna contract ran out later that season she turned again to operetta and for the next five years was busy with Lehàr's *Paganini* and *Land des Lächelns*, starring in all of these opposite Richard Tauber. In 1934 she was re-engaged at the State Opera adding to her previous accomplishments Minnie in *Das Mädchen aus dem goldenen Westen*, Saffi in *Zigeunerbaron* and Leonora in *Macht des Schicksals*. In 1935 she created Renate in Franz Salmhofer's *Die Dame in Traum* and three years later, again with Tauber, sang in the *Land des Lächelns*. With the Anschluss she left Austria, travelling first to England, where she was Lady Macbeth in Verdi's *Macbeth* at Glyndebourne in the summer of 1939 and then on to the United States. After some guest engagements there she retired. With the cessation of hostilities she returned to Austria and organised master classes at the Salzburg Festival, later settling in Vienna.

In her early days Schwarz's lovely but light lyric soprano with its soft and rounded tone was perfectly suited for carrying the sweet melodies of operetta. The voice is ravishing in 'Liebe du Himmel auf Erden' from *Paganini*. But in opera too, she could be effective, making Kate's air from Goetze's adaptation of the *Shrew* sound as if it might be worth giving the piece an airing. With 'Psyche wandelt durch Säulenhallen' from d'Albert's *Die Toten Augen* she challenges comparison with Lotte Lehmann and survives the test admirably, for if she has not the latter's intensity, she offers instead more expansive phrasing and a voice no less attractive. Even at the beginning, however, it was not perfectly secure and an occasional German tendency to slide about is apparent. By the time she came to make electric records, the whole voice seems as it were to have come unstitched. The support is uncertain, top notes are not properly based and miss their mark, and her coloratura amounts to little more than gestures in the direction of specific notes. Her teacher Forstén was probably right in his

original diagnosis: the voice was not really suited to opera, certainly not for the big Verdi roles, Sieglinde or Salome. And she never developed any individuality of manner or particular skill in characterisation by way of compensation; in duet with Tauber she sounds merely dull.

The Hungarian soprano MARIA IVOGUN (1891–1986), though not an impeccable singer, was a wholly delightful and captivating artist. Her voice was small and could not compare in size to that of Kurz or Siems but we can hear, in her records, how she had shed so many of the artful contrivances of the older German style and her art was more spontaneous, fresh sounding, to the manner born. She studied at the Vienna Conservatory from 1909 to 1913. In the latter year she gave an audition at the Imperial Opera. Bruno Walter who had just retired from the staff so as to take up the post of Director at Munich, was present on the occasion:

> One of the many differences of opinion between Gregor (Director of the Vienna Opera) and myself gave me great and lasting pleasure. A pupil of the well-known singing teacher Irene Schlemmer-Ambros appeared on the stage. When she had sung a coloratura aria and, unless I am mistaken, Mimi's racconto from *La Bohème*, I knew that I had been listening to a future star. At the same time I realised that within the hour she would be leaving Gregor's office with a contract for the Vienna Opera. My premature sorrow was turned into joy when, after the young woman had finished singing, Gregor turned to me and expressed his judgment with the words: 'Not a chance!' I hurried back stage and had quite a long conversation with the shy girl. A few days later . . . Maria Ivogün was a member of the Munich Opera.[10]

There she was a principal for twelve years. Her debut was as Mimi; soon afterwards, in the Mozart Festival of 1913, she sang the Queen of the Night for the first time. As well as Nannetta in *Falstaff*, Oscar, Marie in *Zar und Zimmermann*, Undine in Lortzing's opera of that name, Norina, Despina, Marzelline, Zerlina, Rosina, the Queen in *Hugenotten*, Violetta, Susanna and Zerbinetta, she appeared in a number of modern pieces that failed to establish themselves: Pfitzner's *Palestrina*, *Der arme Heinrich* and *Christelflein*, Braunfels's *The Birds* based on Aristophanes, and Korngold's *Ring des Polykrates*.

During that time she made guest appearances in Berlin as Gilda and Rosina, at Vienna as Zerbinetta and Norina, which she shared with Elisabeth Schumann, and she was Zerlina in *Don Giovanni* at the 1925 Salzburg Festival. In the 1921/2 season she was engaged at the Chicago Opera but as with Claire Dux

156 Maria Ivogün as Frau Fluth in Nicolai's *Lustigen Weiber von Windsor*

First must be mentioned Miss Maria Ivogün, in her recent wonderful performances of Zerbinetta in Strauss's *Ariadne auf Naxos* she has shown herself to be a great coloratura singer in a part in which very few singers have excelled. Here as Gilda we were given an opportunity of hearing her in a part which all the great sopranos of the last seventy years or so have in turn made their own. She was excellent in the Courtyard Scene, the way in which she phrased both the duet with Rigoletto and the famous 'Caro nome' was not only in the great tradition, and not only had the purity which is the first requisite of such singing, but also had a fine distinction of its own, it was coloratura plus musical personality. In the more emotional duet of the next act, her voice sounded a little too light . . . but again in the quartet, her musicianship compelled admiration.[12]

She came again in 1927 but on that occasion, as Constanze in *Seraglio*, she seemed over-parted, 'she sang with some difficulty and one missed the ringing quality and the certainty of intonation which made so great an impression when she was last here'.[13]

From 1925 for the rest of her career Ivogün was a leading singer at the Berlin Staatsoper. She sang most of her Munich roles and also the Doll in *Hoffmanns Erzählungen*, Mignon, Rose in Maillart's *Das Glöckchen des Eremiten*, Manon, Lady Harriet in *Martha*, the title-role in Braunfels's *Galathea* and Tatiana in *Eugen Onegin*. It may be doubted whether all of these suited her voice; recordings made at the time of her premature retirement from the stage in 1932, when she was only forty, suggest that she had imposed too heavy a burden on an essentially light and fragile instrument. Her singing has become tentative and uncertain and there is no longer the same brilliance and alacrity in the upper range; frequently she is obliged to cut down the highest notes and her intonation is often false. She continued to sing in concert for a couple of years more, giving her last recitals in 1934. Thereafter she taught, first in Vienna and after 1950 at the Berlin Academy. Her pupils included several post-war German sopranos of whom the most outstanding was Elisabeth Schwarzkopf.

The grace and charm of Maria Ivogün's singing have always commended it to record collectors and music lovers. She was not, as is sometimes stated, a bel canto singer, for save for Rosina and Norina she was heard in scarcely any of that repertory and her singing has only the narrowest range of colour and expression; the coloratura is simply embroidery, delightful but not in itself affecting. At its best the

she was another victim of Directa Garden's largesse, and sang only one performance, as Rosina, which she repeated with the company in New York at the Manhattan Theatre. She revealed a voice of 'beautiful quality and remarkable high range' as well as a mastery of 'every feat of the colorature soprano'.[11] She returned to the United States again the following season with the touring German Opera company of Leo Blech, and took the role of Frau Fluth in Nicolai's *Lustigen Weiber von Windsor*. In 1924 she was invited to Covent Garden as Zerbinetta and Gilda:

range extended to the high F; later she was not always able to sustain this note. Her technique included a fine trill and feather light staccato but she was less adept in passage work and in general not so proficient as Hempel or Kurz. Her singing, however, had more spontaneity than either of theirs, a natural grace and sweetness which was also more attractive. Put next to Galli-Curci or Tetrazzini her limitations are obvious—she sounds amateurish—and though she does not sing as consistently flat as the former, not all of the florid detail is quite on the centre of the pitch. Her recordings of the Queen of the Night's two airs are among the best, for if she lacks the driving thrust for the second, how agreeable to hear it sung without sacrificing a pure tone. In vocal arrangements of the Blue Danube Waltz and Kreisler's Liebesfreud it is the delightful variety of ornamental effects, the instinctive command of rhythm that appeals, and her charm is not pasted on from outside with little sly winks and knowing nudges. Rosina's 'Una voce' (sung in German) is hardly idiomatic and like Hempel she gets lost in a maze of elaborate and unstylish embellishments; at the end instead of the climactic high F she attempts, out comes a little squeak. 'Teurer Name' from *Rigoletto* is more pleasing, though rather studied and she has not the breadth of phrasing to knit the piece into a convincing whole. Her most famous recording, made when she was past her best, of Zerbinetta's Rondo from *Ariadne auf Naxos* is undoubtedly the finest recorded performance of this music; she does not exactly disguise its difficulties but she manages to make out of them something musical. As with Galli-Curci she is not to be numbered among the greatest of singers, but the sheer beauty of her tone and the fine quality of her singing—even when some of the detail is suspect—give a very real satisfaction. Had the voice been properly trained, and the chest register—which seems to be virtually non-existent—fully developed, she might well, when the voice matured, have been able to cope with Mimi or Tatiana. As it was, the attempts cut short her career.

45. Jeritza and Lehmann

No diva was more celebrated in her day than the glamorous MARIA JERITZA (1887–1982). She enjoyed sensational successes in Vienna, London,

157 Maria Jeritza as Blanchefleur in Keinzl's *Kuhreigen*

Munich, Paris and New York. Everywhere she went, the public's appetite was whetted with tales of her temperament and tantrums, and her performances were mostly sold out before she arrived in town. She was the favourite not only of audiences, but directors, conductors, composers, her colleagues and even crowned heads vied with each other to enjoy a little of the diva's condescension; it is said that it was through the direct intervention of the Emperor Francis Joseph, who was delighted with her performance of Rosalinde in *Die Fleder-*

maus in a summer season at Bad Gastein, that she was offered a contract at the Imperial Opera in 1912. At the Artists' Theatre, Munich, the great stage director Max Reinhardt, captivated by her youthful beauty, built his entire production of Offenbach's *Schöne Helena* around her. Strauss and von Hofmannsthal in their correspondence mention her more often than any other singer; the composer refers to his efforts to secure her services to create leading roles in a number of his operas, sometimes successfully, as in *Ariadne auf Naxos* and *Frau ohne Schatten*, and sometimes unsuccessfully, as in *Aegyptische Helena*, notwithstanding every blandishment he offered—'it would be madness, would it not, if we did not try our utmost to get her?'[1] Her great beauty and histrionic skill especially appealed to composers like Strauss and Korngold whose subject matter demanded singers more decorative than the traditional fat Hausfraus of the Wagnerian music dramas, all of which tended to obscure the fact that she was a singer of very considerable accomplishments. When she came to London in 1925 Ernest Newman wrote 'her voice is beautiful, powerful, delicate by turns and admirably under control'.[2] In New York too, her singing was praised and despite the presence of Ponselle, Easton, Bori and Muzio, she quickly established herself the company's leading, as well as highest paid, soprano.

Her career began modestly in the chorus of the Municipal Theatre at Brunn in Austria where she was born. But when she produced a brilliant high C in the Triumphal scene from *Aida*, her debut was arranged at Olmütz as Elsa in *Lohengrin*. After Olmütz came Munich where she was heard by the Director of the Vienna Volksoper, who lost no time in signing her up. There she sang Marguerite, Elsa, Agathe, Manon Lescaut in Puccini's opera and Blanchefleur in Kienzl's *Kuhreigen*. Thence it was but a short step to the Imperial Opera. She was soon the reigning diva, singing in both the Italian and German repertory. In German opera she sang works by Goldmark, Kienzl, von Schillings and Schreker. She took the name parts in Strauss's *Salome* and *Rosenkavalier* and in 1912, at Stuttgart, created Ariadne in the first version of *Ariadne auf Naxos*, and repeated the role in the premiere of the revised edition in Vienna in 1916. Three years later she created the Empress in *Frau ohne Schatten*. She was Vienna's first Minnie in Puccini's *Das Mädchen aus dem Goldenen Westen* and first Jenufa in Janacek's opera. She sang Elsa, Elisabeth, Violanta in Korngold's opera of that name and Marietta in his *Tote Stadt*, and she was the most famous of all

Vienna's Toscas. She remained a member of the State Opera until 1935. After the Second World War she was active in the campaign for the restoration of the opera house and sang there again in 1950 Salome and Tosca, and four years later Tosca and Minnie; she was then sixty-seven.

Gatti-Casazza heard Jeritza in 1913 and planned to bring her to New York the following season, but the war intervened and it was not for another seven years that she finally arrived at the Met. Her debut was as Marietta, and she made a great impression but this was entirely surpassed a fortnight later in her first appearance as Tosca.

> No one who saw [her] Tosca is likely soon to forget her. She gave a performance of thrilling beauty and intensity, every tone and gesture of which was instinct with authority and imagination. She sobbed at the end of 'Vissi d'arte' and more than one of her hearers wept with her. She is a great artist, there is no doubt of that. One would have to forsake the opera stage and go back to Sarah Bernhardt to find a Tosca that could hold an audience so spellbound. Just before the 'Vissi d'arte' she crouched on the sofa, from which Scarpia roughly pushed her so that she half slid, half fell, to the floor. It was from this prone position that she sang the whole aria—a vocal feat as difficult as it was effective. Her voice was as beautiful as her acting. Only once or twice did she fall into her fault of 'scooping' her notes. But even then she scooped to conquer.[3]

158 Jeritza as Tosca

She remained with the company until the 1931/2 season singing many parts including: Elsa, Sieglinde, Santuzza, Thaïs, Fedora, Maliella in *Gioielli della Madonna*, Elisabeth, Turandot, Jenufa, Violanta, Carmen, Helena in Strauss's *Aegyptische Helena*, Octavian, Minnie, Senta, Boccaccio in Suppé's operetta and Rene in the same composer's *Donna Juanita*. Towards the end her increasing disposition to exaggerated stage business and careless vocalism hardened critical arteries though her box office appeal remained unaffected. There was a postscript to her Met career too: in 1952 she returned for a benefit performance of *Die Fledermaus* when, as Kolodin puts it, her acting if not her singing could be condoned.

Jeritza's recordings, save for the early Odeons, have never been rare for they sold in large quantities. Though record collectors have found little to favour in them, anyone hearing them for the first time cannot fail to be struck by the brilliant and fine quality of the voice, its generally easy production over a wide range and her attractive singing, though less characterful than we might have expected. The habit of attacking high notes from below which the New York critics complained of grew with her over the years; it is the most disagreeable feature of what is otherwise not a very German-sounding technique. In one of the best of the Odeons, Ariadne's Monologue, there is scarcely any of the vocal contrivance which can be heard in much of the singing of Strauss's music in this period. A couple of arias from Goldmark's *Heimchen am Herd*, based on Charles Dickens's story *The Cricket on the Hearth*, show off a little coloratura, also some charm and personality. Both are absent from Musetta's Waltz Song and though she sings 'Vissi d'arte' well enough, it is obvious that she depended more for her effect on the stage business than musical imagination. She is impressive in Minnie's 'Laggiù nel Soledad', the tone attractive, the high C cleanly attacked; it makes an interesting contrast to Poli-Randaccio's more exuberant Italian manner.

Of all the German sopranos of her day LOTTE LEHMANN (1888–1976) was the greatest artist. There are few singers on records whose musical personality is so potent and in everything she sings there is an extraordinary communicative energy. Her achievements were all the more remarkable in view of the tight German technique that she had acquired in her youth and which throughout her career she had to overcome so as to give full expression to her interpretative gifts. Her success was not, however, complete and she never did realise the full extent of her artistic ambitions; her repertory remained narrow, increasingly so with the passage of time. As a girl at the Berlin High School she had taken some lessons from an older student and then won a scholarship to study at the studio of Etelka Gerster, an erstwhile rival of Patti and pupil of Marchesi, whose career though short had been exceptionally brilliant. Lehmann was put in the charge of an assistant, Eva Rheingold. Theirs was not a happy relationship; the kind of pure, emasculated tone and instrumental clarity of execution that the Gerster school put before everything and which we can hear in so many recordings made by German singers in the early years of the century, completely inhibited Lehmann. After a time this became apparent to her teachers and she was expelled. Unfortunately, as is so often the way, though she left without having acquired much skill, she was there long enough to develop certain bad habits: the hard, glottal attack, tight emission in the upper range and shallow breathing, which she was never able to correct. Thereafter her experience with teachers seems to have been chiefly a matter of experiment. She went to Mathilde Mallinger, the first Eva in *Meistersinger* of whom probably the best that can be said is that she left Lehmann to follow her own instincts, Alma Schadow the teacher of Elisabeth Schumann—not much of a reference, Hedwig Francillo-Kauffmann, Katharina Fleischer-Edel, Elise Elizza and Felice Kaschowska, all of whom no doubt contributed something to her artistic development but whose own methods, records suggest, were too various to have provided any really solid example.

Lehmann's career began at the Hamburg Opera in 1909 as the Third Boy in *Zauberflöte*. At first her progress was slow and she was mostly kept to tiny roles, though she was heard as Aenchen in *Lustigen Weiber von Windsor*. During the next couple of seasons she sang Freia in *Rheingold* under Nikisch, in which she found little favour with the critics, May in Goldmark's *Heimchen am Herd* with Schumann, Agathe in *Freischütz*, Martha in *Evangelimann* and Elsa under Klemperer, when she had her first real success, and Micaëla in *Carmen*. On the last occasion the Director of the Vienna Imperial Opera was present, he had come to hear the Don José but instead went away with Micaëla; he gave her a contract to appear in Vienna as Eva in *Meistersinger*. Before taking up that she came to London to sing in the summer of 1914 to sing Sophie in Beecham's last season before the war at the Drury Lane Theatre but she quite failed to make any impression on a public enchanted with Claire Dux. Her debut at the Vienna Opera was as Agathe but her first great triumph was in the premiere of the revised edition of *Ariadne*, when she replaced Gutheil-Schoder as the Composer. Other roles in Vienna included Charlotte in *Werther*, Lisa in *Pique Dame*, Tatiana in *Eugen Onegin*, Manon, Desdemona, the Dyer's Wife—another Strauss creation, Mimi, Maddalena in *Andrea Chénier*, Heliane in *Das Wunder der Heliane*, Butterfly, Manon Lescaut, Octavian and she was Vienna's first Suor Angelica.

Her international career began in South America in 1922; under Weingartner's direction she appeared at the Teatro Colon, Buenos Aires, as Freia, Sieglinde and Gutrune. Two years later came her Covent Garden debut when she switched for the first time to the role of the Marschallin in *Rosenkavalier*. This time she was the toast of the town, and Newman was ecstatic: 'an exquisite singer with a voice capable of the most delicate inflexions, and an actress whose quiet ease is the perfection of the art that conceals art'.[4] She reappeared at Covent Garden every season until 1935 and again in 1938, singing: Ariadne, Elsa 'sung and acted as it had not been perhaps for twenty years',[5] Eva, Desdemona, Donna Elvira, 'a most moving and beautiful'[6] Elisabeth, a 'delicious'[7] Rosalinde, the Countess in *Figaros Hochzeit*, Sieglinde, Gutrune and Fidelio. Like Leider and Olczewska, her colleagues on many occasions, she made her American debut at the Chicago Opera, in 1930, as Sieglinde. 'It is one of the loveliest voices ever heard on the Civic Opera stage. It is of a freedom and purity seldom discovered in German singers and employed with an eloquence and artistry that moved the audience to a great demonstration.'[8]

Lehmann's first appearance in New York was delayed for almost another four years when she again chose Sieglinde:

> Mme Lehmann's voice is not immense in volume as operatic voices go, yet she used it so beautifully it seemed far larger than it is. Her pianissimo of exquisite quality, carried to the furthest corner of the house; her fortissimi pierced without difficulty the climaxes of the orchestra. At the beginning of the scene with Siegmund, and indeed well into the middle of Act One, it was not a warm voice and there were moments of slight departure from pitch, and apparently slight forcing at the top, as in the final apostrophe to Siegmund. But in Act Two her performance had an electrifying quality that swept the critical faculty away and made even the guarded listener a participant in the emotions of the anguished Sieglinde.[9]

als „Eva"

159 Lotte Lehmann as Eva in *Meistersinger*

Her New York repertory included only one role which she had not sung in London: Tosca, and in that criticism was not unanimous. Of her Marschallin, however, there were not two opinions and to this day it remains a classic performance:

> Mme Lehmann has long been famous for this characterisation, which has everything—the lightness of touch, the manner and accent of the nobly born; the flaming embers of a last passion, the pathos and ache of renunciation.[10]

During the thirties Lehmann was active as a concert singer, her programmes including works by Schubert, Schumann, Franz, Brahms, Wolf, Strauss, Pfitzner, Mahler, Reger and Marx and she even ventured into the French repertory with a few songs by Fauré, Duparc, Hahn and Paladilhe. With these as Philip Miller has put it 'it was not so much what she sang that mattered but the way she sang it; it was the personality of the singer that opened up the songs for her hearers'.[11] She appeared for the last time in opera at the Met as the Marschallin in 1945 and made her recital farewell in 1951. Thereafter she remained active as a teacher at Santa Barbara, where she lived in the later years of her life and ventured abroad on occasion, giving master classes at the Wigmore Hall in London in 1957.

Lehmann's records are among the most satisfying ever made. In the first place her voice, especially in the earlier recordings, is of a rare loveliness and then by the truth of her accents she contrives to give it a greater beauty still; it is the perfect marriage of verbal and musical accent that makes her art so compelling. Although hers was not a classical method, she has the two fundamental virtues that would have been recognised in the eighteenth century: spontaneity and intensity. Small wonder that she swept Viennese audiences off their feet, for after all they had been raised on a diet of artifice and contrivance, on singing that managed to be ugly and inhibited at the same time, and Lehmann must have seemed like champagne in the desert. Alone among the German sopranos of this period she convinces us equally in the Italian repertory; her 'Vissi d'arte' (the earlier version) is sung with tremendous passion. Perhaps at the very end she does go a little too far, but it is one of the greatest performances on record—perhaps *the* greatest—or so she persuades us as we listen to it. And unlike many of her Italian contemporaries she contains her temperament within the bounds of good taste. In the music of Wagner she transforms Elsa's Dream, letting the voice free and giving full measure to the words; suddenly, instead of a pallid monologue, Elsa comes to life and her narration is full of interest and fascination. That fine artist Michael Bohnen joins Lehmann in the Eva/Sachs duet from *Meistersinger*. This is a richly characterful and stylish performance. The light conversational, almost casual, ease of their delivery disguises considerable vocal skill. The wide range of nuance and variety of expression are contrived entirely musically. The notes are accurately sung and the words clearly enunciated and set in a limpid tone. There is none of the usual consonantal coughing, stage whisperings and hence only approximate execution. Of her greatness as a song singer we can speak later and of that there is much to tell, for hardly a record in her entire repertory has not some delight, even in music that did not fall easily within her compass. And her faults, what of them? Like those of Maria Callas they are so glaringly obvious that even the most insensitive ear can identify them. To mention them again would be gratuitous; one may as well complain that the Venus de Milo has no arms.

46. Five Contraltos

The international career of one of Germany's outstanding singers the mezzo soprano MARGARETHE ARNDT-OBER (1885–1971) was frustrated by circumstances surrounding the First World War. She was from Berlin where she studied with Benno Stolzenberg and Arthur Arndt, whom she subsequently married. Her stage debut took place at Frankfurt in 1906 as Azucena in *Troubadour*; within a year she had joined the Berlin Imperial Opera and began a career there that was to last with certain interruptions until her retirement in 1945. Throughout that time she sustained all the leading as well as a variety of supporting roles in the mezzo and contralto repertory.

In 1913 she was engaged by the Metropolitan, New York, and made an impressive debut as Ortrud 'the creation of a true tragic actress'.[1] She confirmed this initial impression and showed something of the range of her skills when she created Octavian in the local premiere of *Der Rosenkavalier*.

> A more brilliant piece of work has not been enjoyed here for a long time. The fire, vivacity and youthful ardour, the mischievous comic spirit of her acting, the adroitness with which she carries off the somewhat difficult task of a young man are wholly delightful. She engages all the sympathies of her listeners at once . . . Her voice has been admired in the few times she has sung here this winter, and she sings this music with warmth and beauty of tone and with excellent diction.[2]

Her New York repertory included Marina in an Italian *Boris Godounov*, Erda in *Siegfried*, and following Schumann-Heink's precedent, Erda and Flosshilde in *Rheingold* and Flosshilde and Waltraute in *Götterdämmerung*; in the latter she was 'so beautiful in voice and so potent in utterance that she became one of the grand figures of the drama',[3] Brangäne, Laura in *Gioconda*, Amneris, the Witch in Humperdinck's *Königskinder*, Nancy in *Marta*, Katharina in Goetze's *Widerspenstigen Zähmung*, Azucena, Eglantine in which though 'her representation was very fine . . . her technique did not prove equal to singing properly the difficult florid passages',[4] and the Wife of Bath in Reginald de Koven's *Canterbury Pilgrims* when her English seems to have been largely incomprehensible.

What looked like a future full of promise came to nothing in 1917 when the United States entered the war. Along with Otto Goritz, Johanna Gadski, Johannes Sembach, Melanie Kurt and Carl Braun, Ober was summarily dismissed, as indeed were the works of Wagner and Strauss which she and her colleagues had sustained, for the most part, so well. Ober sued the Met for 50,000 dollars, twice as much as her contract was worth, to compensate, as she put it, for 'the inconvenience' of having to travel to the United States. The gesture served to provide exactly the opportunity the Met's advocate was looking for; he cited her 'intense hatred of America' as an excuse for breaking her contract. The war had only been over a year when she returned to New York, in company with Goritz and Braun, to attempt a comeback in a season of German opera at the Lexington Theatre. Memories were too fresh and the venture had hardly managed more than a concert when it collapsed. In Germany her career continued in Berlin and at the Zoppot Festivals where she sang every season from 1922 to 1942, in which last year she can be heard in parts of a live recording of *Meistersinger*.

Ober's was a fine mezzo soprano in the tradition of Marianne Brandt. The technique is very German with a hard attack and some pinched and typically hooted tone in the upper range, but the voice is smoothly produced and sits easily on the breath. Unlike Brandt and Matzenauer she never attempted soprano music. Although the quality is not as dark or resonant as Schumann-Heink's she makes a very grand Fidès and includes among the excerpts a less familiar passage from the Cathedral Scene. Eboli's 'O

160 Margarethe Arndt-Ober as Fides in *Prophet*

161 Ottilie Metzger

don fatale' (in German) is one of the few versions from this period apparently in the original key though she leaves out the high C flat; it is nobly sung, even if the high line takes her to the upper limits. The Veil Song is notably accurate, particularly the slow trills. The slow speed of the central section and the sudden accelerando before the second verse are interesting stylistically. In Brangäne's Warning her absolutely steady tone makes the kind of effect one rarely hears. Although she was not the most fascinating or imaginative of singers, her singing has a polish and smoothness that always makes it a pleasure to listen to, notwithstanding an occasional disfiguring German mannerism.

OTTILIE METZGER (1878–1943), a pupil of Selma Nicklass-Kempner the teacher of Frieda Hempel, had a splendidly resonant, dark contralto voice. She made her first appearance on stage at Hamburg in 1898. From 1900 to 1903 she gained valuable experience at Cologne in the basic contralto repertory. She left in the latter year but returned frequently thereafter, usually for performances of *The Ring* cycle. She was principal contralto at Hamburg from 1903 until 1915 and was heard in Italian as well as German roles; in 1912 when Caruso made some guest appearances as Radamès, she was the Amneris in a cast that also included Lucille Marcel under the direction of Felix Weingartner. In the years before the war Metzger travelled widely, singing in opera in Berlin, St Petersburg, Brussels, Munich, Frankfurt and Covent Garden, where she was a member of the company in both of Beecham's 1910 seasons. In the first she followed Anna Bahr-Mildenburg as Clytemnestra in the first London performances of Strauss's *Elektra*; in the second she was an 'appropriately furious and vindictive Herodias'[5] in Strauss's *Salome*—another Covent Garden premiere—and had a 'triumph' as Carmen.[6] Between 1901 and 1904 and again in 1912 she took various parts in *The Ring* cycle at the Bayreuth Festivals: Flosshilde, Erda, Waltraute and a Norn. Throughout her career she appeared regularly in the concert hall and recital room; in 1910 in Prague, Pfitzner accompanied her in a programme of his songs and the same year at the Munich Festival she was a soloist in Mahler's Eighth Symphony. In 1915 she moved to the Dresden Opera where she stayed until 1923. Her United States debut took place in the season of 1922/3 with the touring German Opera company organised by Edouard Mörike and Leo Blech; she was heard as Brangäne in *Tristan* with von der Osten, Jacques Urlus and Alexander Kipnis.

After her retirement she taught in Berlin until the Nazis took power, when she moved to Brussels, where, however, in 1940 she was overtaken by the German occupation and sent to Auschwitz from which she never emerged.

The characteristic German method is apparent in all her recordings; the voice is dark and weighty, yet the tone has point and brilliance. A narrow and fast vibrato is a matter of intensity and does not introduce warring harmonics. She is very fine in slow and stately music; in Wagner's 'Schmerzen' from the Wesendonck Lieder and an aria from Bruch's cantata *Odysseus*, once beloved of German contraltos. Unlike Schumann-Heink the voice can not easily negotiate the rapid coloratura of Maffio Orsini's Brindisi from *Lucrezia Borgia* and she has no trill. She makes a grand Fidès, phrasing with breadth and feeling and we can overlook some skidding up to thin and rather shallow high notes. In this opera, in duet, she is joined by the Berthe of Melanie Kurt. Beethoven's 'In questa tomba oscura' was once a great favourite and there are memorable recordings of it by Chaliapin and Clara Butt. Metzger's is not perhaps in that class, without interpretative genius, but she sings with a firm line, dark tone and in suitably lugubrious style, also in bad Italian. With Josefine von Artner and Maria Knüpfer she recorded the Rhinemaidens' trios from both *Rheingold* and *Götterdämmerung*, outstanding examples of ensemble singing. The singers' clean and focussed tones match perfectly revealing the polyphony with instrumental clarity and make these brief but affecting episodes more musically satisfying than we are accustomed to hear them in spite of the thin accompaniment.

Little is known of ANKA HORVAT (1888—   ) another fine contralto of this period. She was almost certainly Hungarian, though she does not appear to have sung at the Budapest Opera. She was a member of the Dresden Opera between 1914 and 1917 where she introduced Kundry in the local premiere of *Parsifal*. Her other roles there included: Carmen, Azucena, Ulrica, Amneris and Brangäne. In 1918 she was a guest in Vienna and two years later at Munich, after which we can find no trace of her.

She made only a few gramophone records and these are very rare. In Azucena's 'Stride la vampa' (sung in German) she shows off an outstanding voice with a wide range and easy delivery throughout. The quality is warm and rounded and somewhat reminiscent of Matzenauer. It is a well sung though not especially dramatic rendering and her rhythmic sense is not always quite precise.

162 Anka Horvat

crude attack, but she makes a great effect contrasting the registers. In the difficult and rather grotesque cabaletta she manages to squeeze out most of the high notes but takes advantage of the simplified optional passages when it comes to the bravura.

Many leading German singers at this time appeared regularly in the concert hall and recital room as well at the opera; few managed to do so as successfully as EMMI LEISNER (1885–1958). Upon the completion of her studies with Helene Breest, she made an impressive recital debut in Berlin. At Hellerau in 1912 she took the name part in a famous revival of Gluck's *Orpheus* conducted by Jacques Dalcrôze. The following year making one of her rare visits outside Germany she sang in the *St Matthew Passion* at Bologna. The same season the Berlin Imperial Opera offered her a contract; she remained a member of the company until 1921. Her repertory ranged through supporting as well as leading roles. In the concert hall she was a noted interpreter of Bach and Handel and her recital programmes included songs by Schubert, Schumann, Brahms, Wolf, Mahler and Pfitzner. We read of her providing the vocal illustrations for Max Friedlander's lecture on 'Schiller and Music'. Before 'Seine Majestät' at Potsdam she sang Brahms's 'Zigeunerlieder'.

163 Sabine Kalter

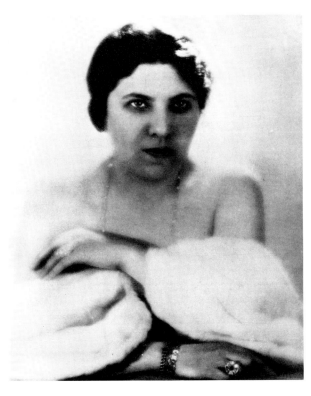

SABINE KALTER (1889–1957) was from Galicia and studied at the Vienna Musical Academy before making her debut in 1913 at the Volksoper. Two years later she was engaged to replace Ottilie Metzger at Hamburg as principal contralto, where she remained until the Nazis seized power in 1933 and was obliged to leave Germany. She settled in England and appeared at Covent Garden in four seasons between 1935 and 1939. Her roles included Ortrud, Fricka in *Rheingold* and *Walküre*, Waltraute in *Götterdämmerung*, Herodias in *Salome* and Brangäne. She was liked well enough, though her voice was by that time passé and she could 'hardly eclipse memories of Olczewska and Onegin'.[7]

In its best days hers was a big, solid, wide ranging contralto. The quality was neither especially individual nor attractive but, as we can hear in the Prison scene from Meyerbeer's *Prophet*, she was a dramatic singer. It is a bold and thrusting interpretation marred by the hard and sometimes

164 Emmi Leisner as Brangäne in *Tristan und Isolde*

In 1925 she was a guest at Bayreuth as Erda and the First Norn. Her career continued into the 1930s.

Leisner's is a big, voluptuous contralto. Her singing is without the fixed placement that we can hear in the recordings of Ober, Metzger and Kalter. Strangely, for a Lieder singer, the voice lacks much variety of colour and expression and she has a predilection for slow and stately tempi which often render her interpretations dull and monotonous. The early recordings are the best when the upper range still has some point on the tone and the voice is steadier; later it becomes slightly spread and loses its focus. The air 'Ich wob das Gewand' from Bruch's *Odysseus* with its curious pre-echo of Mahler in the opening phrase, she sings with a dark and solemn majesty and with some dramatic feeling. This is relatively free of a besetting infirmity which eventually took charge of everything she sang and makes it difficult to understand how cultivated ears could have found her musicianship tolerable: she became incapable of attacking any note in the upper

middle range cleanly. Her Bach and Handel is impossibly slovenly, the incessant scooping and slithering introduces all manner of incongruous harmonies. She is hardly more agreeable in Wagner; in *Tristan*, when Brangäne's voice is heard descanting over the orchestral reiteration of the love music, precision of attack and absolute purity of intonation are essential.

47. Two Great Lieder Singers

For close on forty years the name of ELENA GERHARDT (1883–1961) was synonymous with Lieder. She was by no means the first great Lieder singer—at the beginning of this century Gustav Walter, Felix Senius and Ludwig Wüllner were still active—but Gerhardt was certainly the first female singer to devote virtually her entire career to singing Lieder. She studied with Marie Hedmont in Leipzig, where she gave her first recital in 1903. The same year she joined the Leipzig Opera. There she sang Mignon and Charlotte in *Werther*, but soon discovered she had no theatrical talent and left after one season. While there, however, she had the good fortune to make the acquaintance of one of the great musical personalities of the age, Arthur Nikisch, who was then the Director of the Gewandhaus Orchestra. When Gerhardt told Nikisch of her intention to give Lieder recitals, to her great delight he offered to accompany her. Their first collaboration in Leipzig was a huge success and it led to a tour throughout Germany and in 1906 to the Queen's Hall, London. The critics praised both singer and accompanist and predicted a great future for Gerhardt. The two returned for several seasons thereafter, when 'the perfect sympathy between singer and pianist increased one's admiration for their art. It must now be considered one of the chief events of the musical season'.[1] In 1912 Gerhardt made her New York debut, though without Nikisch.

She soon made it clear that she is an artist of no common fibre, and that by her intelligence and understanding, her musical feeling, she has penetrated deeply into the essence of the German song. Her program ... comprised songs by Franz, Schubert, Strauss, Brahms and Wolf—songs of widely diverse expression, for which she was almost uniformly successful in finding beautiful, varied and characteristic expression. Her voice is not in itself of the highest type of beauty, yet at its best sympathetic, amply endowed with power and controlled on the whole, with a keen appreciation of varieties of color and expressive nuance. It is most satisfying when she uses it in mezza voce, but it sometimes happens then that there is a throaty quality brought into thcm that is injurious. Miss Gerhardt's phrasing and care for the melodic line are exercised with finished skill, and are those of an artist, and her technique of breath control is such as to second her artistic intentions in this respect almost unerringly.[2]

Throughout her long career her admirers consistently praised Gerhardt for the range and intensity of her powers of expression; it was even said that she could 'project laughter and gaiety'[3] but it was not for them that she became famous, nor indeed do the lyrics of Schubert's songs—and especially those of Schumann and Wolf—call very often for the display of unrestrained mirth. It was for the deep and abiding seriousness of her approach to her art that she was held in such regard. Her programmes were, and they must have seemed doubly so in those days, ruthlessly high-brow and there were no concessions to the uncultivated taste. This particularly appealed to the English critics at that time, led by Ernest Newman. Newman regarded it almost as a holy duty to improve the public taste, to expunge so far as his pen was able to effect it, anything at all of a diverting or purely entertaining character from the music or its performance in the concert hall and the opera house. The worship of the Lied was part of his religion and Gerhardt the perfect high priestess. In the United States much the same temper was abroad among the critics save that though her high ideals were praised there too, the quality of her singing, which as time passed the London critics were content to dilate on less and less, was subjected to closer and hence less flattering scrutiny. Even at the beginning Aldrich's detailed description of it was not unequivocal.

165 Elena Gerhardt

> In the first song, 'Das Meer hat seine Perlen', by Franz, her voice was rather unsteady, and the broad phrases of the music were not always so equably delivered as they need to be. But she soon gained a better control of her resources, and in Schubert's 'Die Forelle' and 'Wohin?' she sang with great charm and vivacity. There might have been some question as to the disposition of her phrasing in Schubert's 'An die Musik', but there was much breadth and warmth of sincere expression in it . . . In her singing of 'Der Erlkönig' she did something creditable, but it has been sung with greater power and intensity. It seemed a little outside her range. Miss Gerhardt's singing of Brahms, Strauss and Wolf was in many respects fine; as in 'An die Nachtigall', in its breadth of phrase and its suggestion of ecstasy; the 'Sapphische Ode', a test of phrasing and command of legato; and, to a degree, in 'Immer leise wird mein Schlummer', though by forcing she produced a bad tone to the injury of the last line. She did little that was more delightful than Strauss's 'Morgen' . . . Of the songs of Hugo Wolf she was most successful in 'Auf einer Wanderung', wherein she expressed with great skill and subtlety its changing moods. Miss Gerhardt is in fact a mistress of variety and characteristic interpretation of a wide gamut of moods and emotions as they are embodied in the German Lied . . . It is a pity that her diction is not a little better than it is, which it might be.[4]

Though Gerhardt was not the first great Lieder singer, she was perhaps the first of the modern school to make fashionable a generally different style of delivery and hence vocal production from that heard in the opera house. Throughout the nineteenth century there was no such discrimination; in his day, all the available evidence suggests, the music of Schubert was sung much as was that of Weber or Marschner, or even Rossini. We cannot know how Michael Vogl sang† but the records of Gustav Walter, who studied with a pupil of Vogl's, reveal him using essentially the same method and technique in Thomas's *Mignon* as he does in Schubert's 'Am Meer', and one could cite many other such examples. It is true that the leading singers of Schubert's day often sang his and other composers' songs in public—Wilhelmine Schroeder-Devrient, for example—but the pieces they chose, rightly, were the most theatrical and dramatic, those best suited to large halls and they were almost invariably accompanied by an orchestra. The Liederabend as we understand it, where the singer on his own, save for his accompanist, performs a whole evening of songs including one or more cycles, in an auditorium as big as Carnegie Hall or the Royal Festival Hall, was quite unknown. Many of Schubert's songs, even some of the most difficult, were composed for amateurs and meant for performance in intimate circumstances.

From the beginning of this century when the song recital became increasingly popular in the big metropolitan centres—London, Paris and New York—the ambitious singer had various options. Like the prima donna or primo tenore on leave from the opera house, in mufti as it were, he could engage a group of supporting artists, ostensibly to relieve himself of the weight of a whole evening's singing, but which also served to cover up the fact that he had not the art to carry it off alone anyway. Then there was the example of one of the most venturesome singers of that era, the soprano Marcella Sembrich; her reputation became quite as great in the recital room as it was at the opera house and she was not afraid to sustain the whole programme herself, creating a great effect with her consummate vocal skill in generally lyrical music. The way favoured by the American baritone David Bispham was to translate most of the songs into English, so that even though his voice was not a thing of loveliness, he could always command the audience's attention with his clear and compelling utterance of the text. What Gerhardt attempted was

†We do know, however, that his ornaments for Schubert's songs, many of which survive, are in a similar style to that of his Italian contemporaries.

more pretentious than any of them, and increasingly so as time passed and the programmes became more stringent, for neither her voice in itself nor the finish of her vocal art could compare to that of Sembrich, and unlike Bispham she declined to accommodate her audiences' linguistic ignorance. To make her effect she relied on an extraordinary musical intensity, on the boldness of her conceptions and on as great a range of dynamics and variety of colour as her voice was capable. With this artillery she held audiences, even those who understood little or no German, in her sway. It is a testament to her integrity that she succeeded so completely almost from the beginning—no matter what criticism was made of her—and that throughout her career she never failed to do so even when, as her accompanist and admirer Gerald Moore admits, she had gone on for too long.

Unfortunately the style that Gerhardt evolved, and which has been so much aped since, like anything pretentious involved risks, both to her art and to her voice. The basic claim which it made, and for which she was so much applauded by critics at the time, was that it had shed operatic mannerisms. The fact, however that she had eliminated stage gestures, the old fashioned plastique of Delsarte, which so many opera singers delighted to bring on to the concert platform—often as diversionary tactics—should not disguise the fact that her style remained extremely dramatic, only in a different way, as we can hear easily enough on almost any of her recordings. How could it have been otherwise? To project for a whole evening drawing room music (it is a pity that this perfectly legitimate description should have acquired so many perjorative overtones) across the spaces of a large hall, inevitably involves some dramatisation; without it no artist could succeed in keeping the attention of persons in the audience farther back than the first half dozen rows for more than five minutes. Gerhardt's dramatic artillery was concentrated on vocal colouring and slow tempi. The latter we can hear particularly in the early recordings, no doubt because she had greater breath control to play with. In the concert hall it made an imposing effect but on records, in Schubert's 'An die Musik' for example, which she delivers as if it were a funeral ode, it sounds pompous. Her concern for vocal colour is more apparent in her electric recordings when she was especially associated with the songs of Hugo Wolf, in which their intimate character and very subtle relationship between words and music, demanded the kind of varied response that she endeavoured to give full expression to. But she went too far. Her attempt to colour every word, mark every shifting rhythm and underline the structure was too ambitious and imposed too great a burden on a technique that had never been properly based. In the course of time her singing became a prey to all manner of bad habits. They had always been present in some degree, as the French critic Paul de Stoecklin who did not fall under her spell, was not slow to remark:

> Her voice is admirable, her craftsmanship fine. Mlle Gerhardt does what she wants to do and as she wants. Her voice has real quality but she has the disagreeable fault of German singers, almost without exception, of always attacking notes from below. She sings Schubert with a sentiment that is not mine. I do not understand all the ritards, which the singer likes to display so lovingly. She abuses the voix-blanche and the pianissimi are without quality. Sometimes the result is charming but as with all good things one can have too much of it. I much prefer her in the Lieder of Strauss than in those of Schubert, which call for more style, more affection and less extravagance.[5]

In Wolf's 'Und willst du deinen Liebsten' from the Italienisches Liederbuch, we hear how fond she was of the white voice, and of unsupported portamento, as on the descending sixth on the word 'Fäden'. Her very studied approach in Wolf seems appropriate; in Schubert it is unstylish. It led inexorably to the artifice of Schwarzkopf and Fischer-Dieskau; in large halls alternately ranting and whispering to pompous accompaniments provided by 'grandpianists' like Moore. Though all very well in their own way, and not as inflated as Beecham's Handel or Stokowski's Bach, they nevertheless impose on Schubert. Mostly his songs suit small auditoriums and intimate music making, the singers need to be less intellectual and more spontaneous, less concerned with weighing the meaning of each word and more with quality of tone and suiting this to the light and characterful timbre of the forte-piano.

The singing of the Dutch mezzo-soprano JULIA CULP (1880–1970), one of the finest recital artists during the first quarter of this century, exemplified simpler, basically more musical virtues. Hers was 'a widely comprehensive art and her high intelligence captured the most characteristic and varied notes of expression',[6] which she achieved with an instrument of great natural beauty, musical in itself, like a fine Guarnerius cello, and she played upon it with a noble poise and breadth of phrasing. Perhaps that came easily to her, for as a girl she had studied the

violin before becoming a pupil of Cornélie van Zanten at the Amsterdam Conservatory. Later she travelled to Berlin to work with Etelka Gerster. Her debut took place at Magdeburg as a supporting artist to the great composer-pianist Ferruccio Busoni. Soon afterwards she appeared in Berlin and then undertook a concert tour throughout Germany and Holland. Her international career began in 1906. In London in 1912 she replaced Elena Gerhardt as the Angel in Elgar's *Dream of Gerontius*. Henry Wood, who conducted, recalls her 'devout delivery, her repose, the lovely even quality of her voice, her diction (her English was perfect) seemed to bring the Catholic Church into the Queen's Hall'.[7] In a concert programme the same year she included Monteverdi's Lament of Arianna and some Schubert, in which 'she gave free wing to her temperament without danger to the music, and her singing throughout was that of an exceptionally fine artist'.[8] Her American career began at the Carnegie Hall in 1913.

> [Her] voice has an altogether remarkable richness and silken smoothness; it is admirably equalised throughout its whole range; it has great power and fullness, which she can modulate to the extreme of pianissimo. There are many technical excellencies in her employment of it, and one of the most noteworthy is her breath control, which, with her artistic intelligence, enables her to do unusual things in the way of phrasing.[9]

She reappeared very often thereafter and in her programmes showed the variety and extent of her musical sympathies. Though her art was not like Gerhardt's, yet her choice of repertory began to reflect in some degree the taste for songs of a more intricate and complicated musical expression. It did not, however, corrupt the classical perfection of her style or undermine her vocal technique:

> Of the four songs by Hugo Wolf, not well known, 'Heimweh' seemed the best from the musical point of view—not the point of view always adopted by the thick and thin admirers of Wolf. Some of these would celebrate the ironical suggestion of innocence so skillfully conveyed in 'Ihr jungen Leute', or the fine wit and brilliancy of 'Mausfallen-Sprüchlein'; but the success of these is attained at the expense of specifically musical values, heightened as it may be by the exceedingly felicitous interpretations of Mme Culp, who obviously rejoiced in the opportunities afforded her for subtle declamation and vocal delineation in them.[10]

from a perfect legato and adversely affects her intonation. It is rare to find on any of her records an expressive device either of colour or dynamics which she is not able to manage with the utmost smoothness. We may agree with Aldrich that she could be accused of a 'certain monotony in her delivery'[11], and she was not at her best in fast-moving and joyous music. Within those limitations much that she did still gives real pleasure. How beautifully, and accurately too, she draws the long line of Brahms's 'Muss es eine Trennung geben'; the delicate nuances, occasional ritards and accelerandi are all in proportion and done with perfect taste. Coenraad von Bos, her much admired accompanist over many years felt that she often abused her remarkable breath span—'she is like a violinist whose bow is a mile long'—hanging on to notes without any good reason. It is difficult to complain about these too strenuously, for her breath span enabled her to accomplish musical effects beyond the capabilities of less well-endowed singers. Her Dalila never appeared on the stage and perhaps she would not have had the cut and thrust for dramatic exchanges, but a recording of 'Mon coeur s'ouvre à ta voix' is done with the classical suavity of a piece by Gluck, and not inappropriately, for Saint-Saëns admitted his indebtedness to and admiration for the great eighteenth-century master. And she could also be charming and utterly without affectation. When one thinks of what some of her famous contemporaries would have done to Horn's old song 'I've been roaming' what a genuine pleasure to hear it sung so sweetly and simply and without being larded with personality. In this we hear her admirable English and the way tone and word are held in the correct classical balance.

166 Julia Culp

Culp's career continued into the 1920s but after her second marriage she moved to Czechoslovakia and appeared less often. In 1938 she returned to Holland and lived in Amsterdam where she died at the age of ninety. She made a large number of recordings many of which are very lovely and do justice to the fine quality of her voice. It is not a wide ranging instrument and she attempts no music that lies high in the voice and though she was sometimes advertised as a contralto, the character of the voice is that of a lyric mezzo-soprano. The registers are correctly blended, and the only real weakness in her technique arises from the not always accurate attack which occasionally detracts

48. Baritones

The career of JULIUS VON RAATZ-BROCKMANN (1870–1944) was not especially eventful, though he was a well-known concert and Lieder singer in Germany throughout the first quarter of the century. As a young man he had abandoned the study of the law so as to take up singing; first in Berlin and later in Milan. Although encouraged to seek a career in Wagnerian opera by no less a person than the composer's widow, almost from the beginning he decided to devote himself to oratorio—he was greatly admired in the works of Bach and Handel—and the art of the Lied, and he became an authority

167 Julius von Raatz-Brockmann

in his field. In 1907 still at the height of his career he began teaching in Berlin and in 1923 was appointed Professor of Singing at the Berlin Music School. He remained active throughout the 1920s.

He made recordings for several companies over a number of years; these show a good quality baritone voice, the tone slightly throaty and with a marked but not disagreeable vibrato. A recording of Loewe's ballad 'Fredericus Rex' gives us some idea of the interpretative style in this music when it was still popular. Although his voice is not in itself anything remarkable, he makes a striking effect. In order to create the impression of telling a story he delivers the words cleanly and clearly but at the same time satisfies the musical requirements; speech is heightened into song and an underlying tension in the line sustained throughout in properly supported singing tone. This he accomplishes so successfully that at the most intense moments in the declamation he is able to alter the line upwards for effect and yet still contain it within the musical phrase. It is an extension of the same mechanism that a great actor uses when raising the pitch of his voice in speech and without shouting; he does it from the diaphragm, not from the throat. When the intensity relaxes in the more lyrical passages, as we can hear, his voice melts into something approaching a legato style and without there being any obvious mechanical adjustment in the voice production.

We shall get a useful idea of prevailing standards in the leading German theatres in the first quarter of this century from the recordings made by the baritone FRIEDRICH BRODERSEN (1873–1926), a principal at Munich between 1903 and 1926. He began studying as an architect but on the encouragement of some friends decided to take some singing lessons. These were so successful that in 1900 he made his debut at the Nuremberg Opera, where he stayed for the next three years. At the end

of that time he moved to Munich and began there a career which was to last until the time of his death twenty three years later. Throughout that period he was one of the Munich public's great favourites. He created many roles and took part in several world premieres: in 1903 Wolf-Ferrari's *Le Donne Curiose*, six years later the same composer's *Segreto di Susanna*, in 1912 von Waltershausen's *Oberst Chabert*, in 1917 Pfitzner's *Palestrina* and the following year in *Das Chriselflein*. In 1913 he journeyed out of Germany for the only time and was a member of Beecham's season at Covent Garden. His roles included Orest in *Elektra*, Kurwenal in *Tristan* and he was London's first Faninal in *Rosenkavalier* with Siems, von der Osten, Dux and Knüpfer, when 'he kept his particular form of pomposity distinct from and subservient to the Baron'.[1] In the later years of his life he was active as a recitalist, usually accompanied by his daughter, Linde Brodersen, but on one occasion with Richard Strauss.

His voice on records is hardly of the first quality but he is an intelligent artist and he sings with feeling. His Malatesta in 'Bella siccome un angelo', as that comes out in German, hardly rivals de Luca

168 Friedrich Brodersen as Kurwenal in *Tristan und Isolde*

or Scotti; he has a way of shutting off the support and coasting through the cadenzas. The upper range of the voice sounds as if it were made from dead wood; possibly this is exaggerated by the recording, but the voice is not resonant. Nevertheless it is a spirited rendering sung with fine feeling, elegantly phrased, and he even suggests a floating line. He has not the sonority of voice for Wolfram's 'Als du in kühnem Sange', but as a song singer he makes something lovely out of Schubert's 'Sei mir gegrüsst', full of intensity and feeling, drawing the voice with the finest line, skilfully swelling and diminishing the tone in the head register and with all manner of lively rubato. The style here is much as he uses in Donizetti and seems entirely appropriate in showing off the song's lyrical qualities in music of much the same period. Only questionable is the occasional exaggerated rolled *r* as he repeats 'sei mir gegrüsst'.

HEINRICH REHKEMPER (1894–1949) was a popular singer of Lieder as well as opera in Germany between the wars. Upon completing his studies in Düsseldorf, he made his stage debut at Coburg in 1919 in Kalman's *Die Faschingsfee*, subsequently he

169 Heinrich Rehkemper

sang there in *Lustigen Weiber von Windsor, Lohengrin, Carmen* and *Cavalleria Rusticana*. Two years later he moved to Stuttgart where he remained for three seasons, during which time he sang more than forty principal roles. It is not difficult to understand why he decided to break his contract. For the year that he was forbidden the opera stage he began to develop his art as a concert singer. He sang recitals of Schubert, Schumann, Wolf and Mahler and was a soloist in Beethoven's Ninth Symphony and, in Vienna, in Bach's *St John Passion*. In 1925 he resumed his operatic career at Munich, where he soon established himself as the successor to Friedrich Brodersen and spent the remainder of his career, until the theatre was demolished in an air-raid in 1943. His repertory included: Papageno, in which following the Schikaneder's own tradition he extemporised freely in the spoken dialogue, the Count and Figaro in Mozart's *Figaros Hochzeit*, Guglielmo in *Così fan tutte*, Don Giovanni, Amfortas in *Parsifal*, Michele in *Tabarro*, Giovanni Morone in Pfitzner's *Palestrina*, Jokanaan in *Salome*, Macbeth, Donner in *Rheingold*, Beckmesser, Posa in *Don Carlos*, Malatesta in *Don Pasquale*, Don Carlo in *Macht das Schicksals* and Marcello in *Bohème*. He also took leading roles in Pfitzner's *Das Herz*, Egk's *Zaubergeige*, Schultze's *Schwarzer Peter*, Goetze's *Widerspenstigen Zähmung*, d'Albert's *Tiefland*, Humperdinck's *Königskinder* and Lortzing's *Wildschütz*. He seems to have sung abroad only once as Papageno at Amsterdam, but he made frequent guest appearances elsewhere in Germany, at Cologne, Darmstadt, Bremen and Berlin, where he sang Rigoletto with Lotte Schoene and Don Carlo with Giannini, Roswaenge and List.

His recital repertory was considerable and included a number of cycles, among them Schubert's 'Winterreise', Mahler's 'Lieder eines fahrenden Gesellen' and von Hausseger's 'Hymnen an die Nacht', as well as individual songs by the same composers and also Schumann, Wolf, Grieg and Richard Strauss, who accompanied Rehkemper in a recital of his songs at Munich in 1931.

The voice on records is a high baritone, the tone rather gravelly and throaty and it does not sit too firmly on the breath; his singing conspicuously lacks a good legato style. The instrument is not an ingratiating one, a pleasure to listen to in itself, which ought to be a pre-requisite for any recital singer—it even improves genius. What should we think of a string or wind player who ventured a solo recital with a poor quality instrument, imperfectly tuned and which he could not play with real accuracy? Yet Rehkemper's singing of the Count's aria from *Figaros Hochzeit* has no legato, the intonation is not precise and the difficult concluding passage roughed out instead of cleanly sung. In his Lieder singing what would be applauded as praiseworthy artistic ambitions from a singer with a proper control over his instrument, sounds merely pretentious. It is no use trying to colour the words so as to give weight and meaning to each phrase when this cannot be accomplished within a securely poised and flowing line. The constant nudgings and smudgings—he seems not to be able to turn the simplest ornament cleanly—the way the top notes are either shoved out or crooned undermines the music and soon wearies the listener. He is best when he is least affected, in Schumann's 'Meine Rose', though the tone is not really supported. His records are rare, which is hardly surprising for there was too much competition when they were made. One can understand that his contemporaries would have had no difficulty choosing between his records and those of, say, Schlusnus.

The Viennese baritone HANS DUHAN (1890–1971) was not a great singer but he was a leading member of the Vienna State Opera for many years and as Hugo von Hofmannstal describes him 'a courtly singer' who sang a large number of parts; he created the Music Master and Harlequin in the revised version of *Ariadne auf Naxos*. He was a student at the Vienna Music Academy and made his debut at Troppau in 1910. He stayed there for three years, then moved for a season to Teopliz-Schönau before arriving at Vienna. He was a member of the company until 1940, during which time he was heard at the Salzburg Festivals but rarely travelled abroad. After 1932 he taught singing at the Vienna Music Academy. In the latter part of his career he was also a stage director and on occasion even conducted.

Duhan was a very successful concert artist and made among the first complete recordings of Schubert's 'Die Schöne Müllerin' and 'Winterreise'. His was a light baritone, somewhat dry in quality and with no special character but as we hear him in Liszt's 'O quand je dors', he sings with some affection and sensitivity and though the phrasing is not especially distinguished, he avoids those exaggerated devices that encourage the singer to take the voice off the support. Fritz's 'Pierrot-lied' from Korngold's *Die Tote Stadt*, as we might have expected, provokes an appropriate response stylistically, and he reveals a sure sense of character.

The vocal range of HERMANN WEIL (1876–

170 Hans Duhan as Arlecchino in Strauss's *Ariadne auf Naxos*

1949) was that of a classical baritone; though he was capable of taking the high G, even A flat, the voice was not pitched comfortably in this altitude and he preferred the tessitura to lie in the centre of his range. As a young man he had originally planned to become a chorus-master and with this goal in view took some instruction from the great conductor Felix Mottl, but the fine quality of his voice eventually persuaded him to become a singer himself and he went to Frankfurt to study with Adolf Deppe. His first stage appearance was at Freiburg in 1901 as Wolfram in *Tannhäuser*. Three years later he moved to Stuttgart where he was a prominent member of the company for more than thirty years. In the course of that time he sang in many leading theatres in Germany and abroad. At Bayreuth in the 1911 and 1912 seasons he was Günther and Amfortas and in 1924 and 1925 Hans Sachs. Beecham brought him to London for his winter season at

171 Herman Weil

The black and beetle-browed Lysiart of Mr Weil was intelligent in a melodramatic conception, and there were numerous well-executed touches in his action. He sang some of the music well, especially the declamatory parts, but found difficulties in some of the florid music.[4]

When the United States entered the war in 1917, along with many of his compatriots, he was summarily dismissed. In the autumn of 1919 he attempted a come-back at the Lexington Theatre in the company of a number of other German artists. At the inaugural concert when Weil launched into Hans Sachs's Apostrophe to German art it seemed as if hostilities would break out anew. As a result of the powerful pressure exerted by anti-German groups led by the war veterans, the season was shut down almost before it had begun. He did, however, return to sing Sachs in the season of German opera at the Manhattan in 1923. For Weil all this had its special irony, for he was a Jew. In 1933 when the Nazis came to power he was obliged to flee Germany; he sought refuge in the United States.

In the Monologue from Act Two of *Meistersinger* 'Was duftet doch der Flieder' we can agree with contemporary opinion; it is not a sympathetic reading, yet the voice is imposing, the declamation intelligent and delivered firmly.

He makes a fine effect with 'Eri tu' in spite of the German translation. The voice is dark and resonant, not perhaps perfectly smooth but he sings with some line, phrases well and takes the high tessitura in his stride.

A leading baritone at the Berlin State Opera over many years, CORNELIS BRONSGEEST (1878–1957) studied first in Berlin and later at Frankfurt with Julius Stockhausen, a pupil of Manuel Garcia. His stage debut took place at Magdeburg in 1900, where he remained a principal throughout three seasons. The following three years he spent at Hamburg. A casual appearance as Amonasro in some performances of *Aida* in Berlin led to a regular engagement and thereafter the Imperial (later State) Opera was the centre of his activities. In the early years of his career he made tours of Northern Europe and in 1914 Beecham brought him to Drury Lane to sing Papageno in some performances of *Die Zauberflöte* with Frieda Hempel, Claire Dux and Johann Sembach. He appeared elsewhere in Germany too and was especially praised for the fine quality of his singing as Wolfram in some performances of *Tannhäuser* at Cologne. A review of a concert in Berlin in 1913 shows another facet of his art with which he

Covent Garden in 1913; he sang Jokanaan in *Salome* and 'a sound rather than sympathetic' Sachs.[2]

He made his United States debut at the Metropolitan in 1911 and was a member of the company for the next six seasons. Opinion was not enthusiastic, the voice was thought rather dry in quality though it was well-schooled and he provided strong support in most of his roles. His first part was Kurvenal, subsequently he was heard as Gunther, Braun in Blech's *Versiegelt*, Telramund, Wotan in *Rheingold* and *Walküre*, 'a wooden and unsympathetic'[3] Sachs, the title-role in Monteverdi's *Orfeo*, this was given in concert form and was one of the first modern revivals of the work, Amfortas, Faninal in the local premiere of *Rosenkavalier*, Pizarro and Don Fernando in *Fidelio*, and the Speaker in *Zauberflöte*. He was generally commended in an unstylish revival of Gluck's *Iphigenia auf Tauris*, and was perhaps most successful in Weber's *Euryanthe* under Toscanini's direction.

became increasingly preoccupied after the First World War.

> He has a brilliant ringing voice and a good if not entirely pleasant mezza voce with which he produces some lovely effects. But if he wishes to be a successful concert singer he must not juxtapose these so obviously nor be so free with the tempo.[5]

After 1923 he became interested in the presentation of opera on the radio and was appointed Director of Radio Opera in Berlin and assisted in the foundation of the radio orchestra and chorus. Until the early

172   Cornelis Bronsgeest as Amfortas in *Parsifal*

1930s he continued to appear at the Berlin Opera and to make tours with various opera companies. In 1933, however, when the Nazis came to power he was obliged to resign from the radio and subsequently returned to Holland. After the war he organised some of the first performances of opera given in Berlin and thereafter lived in the city until his death.

His first recordings date from 1906, the last from 1928, when he sings Amfortas in a complete recording of Act Three of *Parsifal* under Karl Muck. Over the years the voice changed little. In Wolfram's 'Als du in kühnem Sange', we hear an agreeable, well-schooled though not quite smoothly produced baritone. He knows how the piece should go and bends into the melody effectively but his legato is not ideally firm or suave enough. He was an excellent routine artist.

Another Dutch baritone JOSEF GROENEN (1885–1959) though not a front ranking artist left some attractive recordings. He studied first in Amsterdam then travelled abroad to Stuttgart and Milan. He made his debut at Mainz in 1913. In the course of the next decade he established himself as a leading baritone in the heroic repertory. In 1914 he was at Hamburg, thereafter moving successively to Vienna and Berlin. Three years later he returned to Hamburg where he remained a contract artist for the rest of his career; however he continued to make guest appearances elsewhere and sang in Vienna on many occasions during the 1920s.

Groenen's voice on records is of agreeable quality rather vibratory but with a good focus on the tone and easy production. He sings Nelusko's 'L'avoir tant adorée' (in German) with some skill and appreciation of the style. He differentiates effectively between the various sections and manages the strongly marked rhythmic passage cleanly and incisively. In Wolfram's 'O du mein holder Abendstern' the vibrato rather spoils a spaciously conceived legato style and the singing has little variety of colour or expression though it has the virtues of honesty and solidity.

Although born in Riga, Latvia, then a province of Tsarist Russia, JOSEPH SCHWARZ (1880–1926) was of German Jewish extraction, and the great triumphs of his career came in the German speaking countries. He trained first in Berlin with Alexander Heinemann and then travelled to Vienna to study at the Conservatory there. His debut took place at Linz in 1900 as Amonasro in *Aida*. In the succeeding years he sang at Graz, Riga and other provincial theatres, eventually arriving at the Marinsky, St

173 Josef Groenen

side of the drama a little too early. One did not get the impression ... that this Rigoletto had ever been a merry jester, a creature of light wit and abandoned morals. He took everything seriously and in the famous entrance when he came seeking his daughter he gave us more of the snarl than the grin.[6]

By this time his voice was on the wane; his addiction to alcohol and consequent failing health undermined his vocal technique. He died the following year.

Schwarz was the most naturally talented of all the German baritones of this period, before Friedrich Schorr established himself, and his was the finer voice. On records we hear a glorious high baritone, the quality outstanding, the registers fully equalised and blended and the production limpid in a way rarely heard among German singers at that time. Like Maurice Renaud he knows how to use the vibrato as an affecting device; later on, unfortunately, it gets the better of him and the tone spreads. At his best, however, the command of nuance, skill in dynamics, especially when he shades a note away, remind us of Battistini. He has not the Italian's charm or ultimate finesse but he informs the fioritura with feeling and his mastery of the portamento style, especially in mezza voce, recalls his great predecessor. There is a fine example of this in the first lyrical episode in the *Pagliacci* Prologue; the vocal poise and melting line can only be compared to that of Battistini, and like him he avoids sentimentality. Notwithstanding the German translation, it is one of the finest renderings on record, singing full of imagination and colour with a great variety of nuance, and the declamatory and legato passages beautifully contrasted. At the most intense moment, just before the big tune, he breaks out into ironic laughter; generally this sort of thing becomes tedious rehearing, but he contrives it in a classical parlando fashion, entirely musically, marking each laugh on a note in a descending phrase completed by the orchestra. It is but one vivid effect in a remarkable record.

In some excerpts from various operas of Verdi, the German language may sound odd, but it is not unmusical and in fact his singing is generally more stylish than that of all but a very few of his Italian contemporaries. There is still something of the traditions of bel canto; the words and tone are held in perfect balance, and instead of the words being used to push out the voice, the voice informs the words with musical tone. The vowels are pure and the consonants, though they articulate the flow of tone, do not disrupt it. In his utterance of the text

Petersburg. In 1909 he returned to Vienna and was a member of the company at the Volksoper and later at the Imperial Opera, where he remained until 1915. In that year he moved to Berlin. During the war he appeared in Scandinavia and in 1921 visited the United States for a recital and a concert with the New York Philharmonic. Between 1922 and 1925 he sang with the Chicago Opera. His roles included Tonio, Athanael, Amfortas, Rigoletto, Iago, the four villains in *Les Contes d'Hoffmann* and Germont; the last two he repeated on tour at the Manhattan Opera House in New York, and the critics were impressed. In these years he was also a guest artist at Berlin, Vienna, Prague and Budapest, and sang Rigoletto to the Gilda of Eidé Noréna at Covent Garden in the summer of 1925.

In the early scenes the emotional tremolo in Mr Schwarz's voice made some of his high notes uncertain in quality or pitch, but he has a clear conception of the part and the power which grips, and in the third act he got all the human feeling possible out of Verdi's theatrical melodies, perhaps he fastens on the tragic

49. Basses

MICHAEL BOHNEN (1887–1965), a fine singer and outstanding actor who appeared for many years with success in Germany and the United States, lacked the self-discipline to fulfil his great potential. He could never resist the temptation to overdo a good thing; thus, what often started out fresh and imaginative too often ended up odd, even grotesque. For Méphistophélès in Gounod's *Faust* to wear a grey-tinged costume was an original departure, and effective too; as Kezal in *Verkaufte Braut*, his 'astonishing variety of sounds, gestures and grimaces'[1] added up to a superb piece of clowning. But when Tonio came cart-wheeling on and Hagen turned up in three different sets of costumes and make-up in that many performances, critical enthusiasm waned. It was all manna at the box-office, however, and the public was eager to see what he would do next, but it undoubtedly debased a very considerable talent.

He studied singing in Cologne under Schulz-Dornburg and made an effective debut as Caspar in *Der Freischütz* at Dusseldorf in 1910; This lead to a four year contract at Wiesbaden. In 1914, at short notice, he deputised for an indisposed Knüpfer as Gurnemanz in *Parsifal* at Berlin and created a sensation. That summer he made his first visit outside Germany to London, where he sang König Heinrich in *Lohengrin* at Covent Garden, and with Beecham's company at Drury Lane succeeded Knüpfer as Ochs in some performances of *Der Rosenkavalier*. Afterwards he travelled to Bayreuth where he took the parts of Hunding in *Walküre* and Titurel in *Parsifal*. A contract with the Berlin Imperial Opera was postponed when he was drafted into military service on the outbreak of war, but he was able to join the company in 1916 and remained with it until the end of the war.

At about this time he became interested in the cinema and formed his own production company. A film he made then *Herrin der Welt*, has earned a footnote in the history of the cinema. Throughout the inter-war period, in one capacity or another—producer, director or actor—he was associated with a number of films: *Lady of the World*, *Book of Esther*, *Der Rosenkavalier* and *Tiefland*, and after the introduction of the talkies: *Weiner Blut*, *The Emperor Waltz* with Leo Slezak, *Private Life of Louis XIV*, *Victoria and her Hussar*, *Johann Strauss* and *Mutterlied* with Gigli. His operatic career continued at the Metropolitan in 1922 when he made his debut as

174 Joseph Schwarz as di Luna in *Troubadour*

there is something of the dramatic intensity that we can hear in the great German actors of this period, Alexander Moissi for example. He is able to declaim, even make some slight changes in the pitches of certain notes, as in Rigoletto's 'Cortigiani', so as to give full expression to the German text, yet contain it within the musical phrase. The many fine recordings that he made leave us in no doubt that he was one of the greatest German singers of his, or any other, day.

the jealous husband Francesco in Max von Schillings's *Mona Lisa*; 'he sang in an effective bass, with much dramatic virility and command of emotional colour'.[2] In the course of eleven seasons in New York he was heard as Grunemanz, which although it was splendidly sung and admirably acted included 'an inordinate amount of walking around in the Grail scene',[3] Wotan in *Rheingold* and *Walküre*, the Wanderer in *Siegfried*, Amonasro, Hagen, a Caspar 'whose magnetic force and dramatic power vitalised the whole performance',[4] a Kezal of 'superb vocal accomplishment', Ochs, König Marke, Daland, Hunding, Tonio, König Heinrich, Hans Sachs, the Landgrave and Méphistophélès. In 1933 at the Colon he sang several of his usual parts and Pizarro in *Fidelio*. Two years later he joined the Berlin City Opera where he continued to sing for nearly a decade. After the war, briefly, he was director of the company. In 1951 he made his farewell in Berlin as Sachs.

Bohnen made many records, and especially on the early ones he is a singer of considerable accomplishments. The voice was wide ranging, enabling him to sing a number of baritone roles with ease and, as we can hear in Sarastro's prayer, he could plumb the depths, though there the line gets a little thin. His voice production was free, the registers well blended and he was capable of a wide variety of expression. He has more musical personality than Mayr and is a better singer. A recording of Pizarro's 'Ha, welch ein Augenblick' is a remarkably accurate account of unspeakably difficult music and the malevolence is wonderfully suggested by vocal colour alone. He could be richly humorous too, as in the duet 'Weiss'ich doch eine' from *Verkaufte Braut* and 'Salemaleikum' from *Der Barbier von Bagdad*. Both show his beautifully pure enunciation, the words simply roll out on the tone, and nowhere is there any trace of ranting. His rhythmic sense here too is remarkably acute; this is only possible when the voice is responsive. In both of these pieces he communicates a genuine sense of enjoyment. The music of Amonasro or Iago, though it lies comfortably in his range and is full of character, he manages less successfully and occasionally gets a bit carried away. In the 'Transformation' duet from *Faust* his attempt to inject into the declamation something of the style of the German actors of that period in Goethe's *Faust*, only succeeds in undermining Gounod. He was not a subtle or refined artist, but at his best, where broad characterisation is appropriate and important, there are few finer German singers on record.

175 Michael Bohnen as König Marke in *Tristan und Isolde*

Not many singers have remained with one company for as long as did the bass PAUL BENDER (1875–1947); he was a principal at the Munich Opera for more than forty-four years. In that time he notched up over two thousand performances. Upon the completion of his studies with Luise Ress and Baptist Hoffmann, in 1900 he made his stage debut as the Hermit in *Freischütz* at Breslau. He stayed there for two years, during which time he was invited to Bayreuth to sing Fasolt in the 1902

Festival. The following season he was engaged at Munich. His repertory was vast and included Polyphemus in Handel's *Acis*, both Bartolo and Basilio in *Barbier von Sevilla*, Boris Godounov, Rocco in *Fidelio*, Sulpice in Donizetti's *Regimentstochter*, Sentlinger in Strauss's *Feuersnot*, Lysiart in Weber's *Euryanthe*, the King and Ramfis in *Aida*, the Landgrave in *Tannhäuser*, Sarastro, Falstaff in *Lustigen Weiber von Windsor*, Ochs, Morales in *Carmen*, Orest in *Elektra*, Marcel in *Hugenotten*, and a variety of roles in contemporary works.

Throughout his years in Munich he made frequent guest appearances elsewhere. In 1910 at Nuremberg he was Germany's first Don Quichotte in Massenet's opera. In Vienna he was heard on several occasions, in *Faust*, *Hoffmanns Erzählungen*, *Fliegende Holländer* and *Parsifal*. At the Théâtre des Champs Elysées, Paris, with Russell's company in 1914 he sang Sachs in a performance of *Meistersinger* with Lucille Marcel and Johannes Sembach under the direction of Weingartner but the voice, though robust was 'ill at ease in the upper range';[5] with Bruno Walter in the same theatre fourteen years later, he was Sarastro and the Commendatore. His London debut took place in Beecham's 1910 season at Covent Garden as Orest in the local premiere of Strauss's *Elektra*. He returned twice in 1914 to sing a 'superb'[6] Amfortas in *Parsifal* (the only time he sang it); Wotan, Sachs, and Jacob in Méhul's *Joseph*. He was at Covent Garden again in 1924 as 'a resonant'[7] Hunding, Ochs, Hagen 'his voice as black as his beard'[8] and in 1927 as a 'very droll'[9] Osmin in *Seraglio*. In the United States he was a member of the company at the Met between 1922 and 1927, where he seems to have provided dutiful service but was generally rated a dull singer with a 'ponderous',[10] 'doleful',[11] 'sepulchral'[12] voice. He was blamed for the failure of a revival of Cornelius's *Barbier von Bagdad*.

At the age of sixty-three in 1938 he sang Fafner in *Rheingold* at La Scala under the direction of Clemens Krauss and returned the following year to take the same part in some performances of *Siegfried*. At Salzburg in 1926 he was Osmin in *Seraglio* with Marie Gerhart, Richard Tauber and Hans Duhan and at the 1939 Festival gave a recital at the Felsenreitschule of Brahms and Loewe. In the later part of his career especially, he was busy in the concert hall and his programmes included works by most of the leading German song composers, but with a particular partiality for the ballads of Loewe. One of these, 'Der Mummelsee', has inspired a critic of his recordings to compare him with Plançon. It is

certainly a very artful piece of singing—too much so at times; coyness from a soubrette is tolerable, from a bass absurd. All the changes of colour and dynamics he attempts cannot disguise the fact that he has not the technique to accomplish so demanding a piece; the difficult florid figures he either whispers or blusters, and they are only an approximation of specific note values. In opera, when he is not being ambitious, we can hear what a fine, dark and well-focussed voice it was, extending easily to the high F and down to a firm if not exactly sonorous low E flat. At the beginning of his career he often sang in the bass-baritone range but later confined himself entirely to the lower range. He is imposing in Sarastro's music but has not a really smooth legato and as Osmin, though he manages a serviceable trill, there is no particular character or personality. As Wagner's various Kings, and in other lay roles, his ponderous dignity is suitable and he makes the right noises. He represents the best

174 Paul Bender

Paul Bender   30

kind of house singer and one can well imagine how useful his versatility must have been in a repertory company like Munich.

Although he did not create the role of Baron Ochs in Strauss's *Der Rosenkavalier*, the Austrian bass RICHARD MAYR (1877–1935) came to be more closely associated with it than any other singer of his day; it remains, through the medium of recording, a classic interpretation. As a young man he contrived to study medicine and singing at the same time; one at Vienna University, the other at the Vienna Conservatory. But after he had sung successfully in concerts in the winter of 1898, he determined on a career in opera. He renewed his vocal studies under Johannes Ress and in 1901 secured an engagement to sing Hagen at the Bayreuth Festival the following summer. At this time Gustav Mahler heard Mayr and engaged him for the Vienna Imperial Opera. He made his debut as Silva in *Ernani* with Selma Kurz, Leo Slezak and Leopold Demuth

177 Richard Mayr as Pogner in *Meistersinger*

and soon afterwards sang König Heinrich, St Bris and Marcel in *Hugenotten*, Fasolt, the Landgrave, König Marke, Colline, Hunding, Hagen and was a soloist in Liszt's oratorio *Heilige Elisabeth*. He remained a principal with the company until his death in 1935 and was heard in a great variety of roles. After 1906 he was a frequent visitor to Salzburg, the last time in 1926 in Pergolesi's *Serva Padrona*. He was a favourite singer of Strauss and created the role of Barak in the world premiere of *Die Frau ohne Schatten* in Vienna in 1919, and also sang in the first Viennese performances of *Intermezzo* and *Arabella*.

Mayr's Covent Garden debut took place in the 1924 season as Ochs; Newman thought it 'a constant joy . . . and his smile and whistle during Annina's reading of the letter said more than a few pages of words could do'.[13] He returned to London on several occasions until 1931 to sing König Marke, Figaro in *Figaro's Hochzeit*, a 'genial'[14] Daland, 'a dignified and genial'[15] Pogner and a 'dignified'[16] Gurnemanz. He was a greater success in London than New York; by the time of his first appearance at the Met in 1927, though he was only fifty, not a great age for a bass, his vocal powers were already diminished.

There was an artist on the stage last night who, if his vocal results had been equal to his fine intuitions, his sense of dramatic values and his knowledge of style, would have been the distinguishing feature of the performance. This was Richard Mayr [whose] resonance did not always fill the spaces. His tone colour, in the upper register was inclined to pale. He showed himself, nevertheless, the artist of high and deserved reputation in Europe, as those who have seen his performances in operas of Mozart and Beethoven, for example, will testify.[17]

In his best days Mayr's voice was a supple and smooth bass; in the Barcarolle from Auber's *Stumme von Portici*, he even gets a little florid. It was not, however, in itself a very colourful or expressive instrument, and the tone at the top often sounds rather dry and the production constricted. His masterful sense of comedy, skill in characterisation and natural good taste which so much distinguished for his contemporaries his interpretation of Baron Ochs is clearly apparent on recordings, but this was not by any means—as we should expect in a Strauss-Hofmannsthal collaboration—achieved solely through the music. Newman gives us the hint there; his stage presence was an important ingredient in it. No doubt this sense of characterisation made something rather special out of Wagner's König Marke, Pogner and the Landgrave, yet the voice does not seem, on records at any rate, to have the right kind of weight or solidity of tone for this music; basically he was a buffo singer. A splendidly rumbustious account of Rocco's Gold-arie from *Fidelio* is a souvenir of his performance in this role in Mahler's production in Vienna.

The voice of WALTER SOOMER (1878–1955) was a black and baleful bass, notably telling in roles like Hagen and Hunding which, however, he sang only in the later years of his career, when he had relinquished his baritone ambitions. He studied in Berlin with Hermann Stoeckert and Anna Uhlig. Following a successful debut at Colmar in 1902 he was engaged by the Halle Opera for four seasons. From the beginning he was associated with the music of Wagner and in 1906 made his first appearance at the Bayreuth Festival singing Kurvenal and Donner. He came again in 1908 as Wotan, the Dutchman and Sachs and in 1924 and 1925 when he shifted down for Hagen, Hunding and Gurnemanz. His first appearances outside Germany were at Covent Garden in 1905 in *Meistersinger* and *Lohengrin*. In 1908 he was invited to the Metropolitan where he sang for three seasons and only Wagnerian roles: Wolfram, Sachs, Wotan in *Rheingold* and *Walküre*, the Wanderer, Kurvenal, Telramund and Gunther. In Germany after 1906 he was a contract artist at Leipzig remaining there for the rest of his career until 1927, save for a period at Dresden between 1911 and 1915. After his retirement he opened a singing school in Leipzig.

It was a fine and resonant bass extending to the high G but in the upper range, as we can hear in Wotan's 'Nicht straf'ich dich erst' from *Walküre*, the voice was not at its best. Wolfram's 'Blick ich umher' is done with some intensity and character and if the singing is not exactly suave, there is little here of the ejaculatory style of Bayreuth. The voice is of excellent quality and he quite lacks the tremolo which is omnipresent in the later recordings of van Rooy though he has little of that great artist's majesty repose, legato style or breadth of phrasing.

When he was only eighteen CARL BRAUN (1886–1960) became an apprentice at the Berlin Imperial Opera. He was a student of Hermann Gausche in Kreuznach and later of Eugen Weiss. His career began at Wiesbaden in 1906; five years later he moved to Vienna for a season, and then spent two years with the Berlin City Opera. In 1906 an invitation came to sing at Bayreuth, and during the next twenty-five years he was heard often as

178 Walter Soomer as Wotan in *Walküre*

Gurnemanz, Hagen, Pogner, Fasolt, Fafner and Wotan. The same year he ventured abroad for the first time to London where he appeared in *Rheingold*, *Walküre*, *Tristan* and *Meistersinger* in the summer season at Covent Garden; but these were early days , he came and went without making much of an impression on audiences who had just heard Clarence Whitehill and Anton van Rooy. He never sang in London again. His Met debut took place in 1912 as König Marke; in the course of five seasons in New York his repertory included Wotan in *Rheingold* and *Walküre*, Pogner, Sarastro, Hagen, which gave him 'a chance to sing, not shout',[18] Fafner, Fasolt, König Heinrich, the Landgrave, Thoas in *Iphigenia auf Tauris*, an 'excellent'[19] Rocco in *Fidelio*, a 'wholly German'[20] Marcel in *Ugonotti*, the Wanderer in *Siegfried* and Gurnemanz. When war came he was banished but he returned in 1929

179 Carl Braun as Hans Sachs

Of all the bass singers of the German school under consideration here the most famous was ALEXANDER KIPNIS (1891–1978). Though he was born in the Ukraine, he never sang in Russia, and his career was principally associated with the great Wagnerian bass roles. He studied at the Warsaw Conservatory and then in Berlin. He was there when the First World War broke out, and was promptly interned as an enemy alien. Eventually, however, he was allowed free to make his debut at Hamburg in 1916. For the next two seasons he was a contract artist at Wiesbaden. In 1919 he returned to Berlin and sang there for the rest of his German career until 1933, both at the City Opera and later with the Berlin State Opera.

His United States debut took place in the 1922/3 season when he joined the German Opera Company which appeared first at the Lexington and subsequently at the Manhattan Theatre in New York. Another newcomer was the baritone Friedrich Schorr and for the critics these two singers' contributions were among the highlights of the season. Kipnis sang Pogner, König Marke, the Landgrave, Rocco and Hagen. In the last Henderson compared his 'subtle, sinister and commanding' interpretation to that of Edouard de Reszke but, in the aftermath of the war, the Met's attention was focussed on other matters than Wagner and Kipnis's potential was ignored; it was not for another seventeen years that he sang in New York on a regular basis. He joined the Chicago Opera in the autumn of 1923 and stayed with them every season until 1931, returning in 1938 and 1942. There he sang a wide variety of parts including several which he later relinquished, among them: the Wanderer in *Siegfried*, Don Pedro and the High Priest of Brahma in *L'Africana*, the King and Ramfis in *Aida*, the Prior in *Le Jongleur de Notre Dame*, Cardinal Brogny in *La Juive*, Palémon in *Thaïs*, Alvise, Albert in *Werther*, Arkel in *Pelléas et Mélisande*, Escamillo, Tommaso in d'Albert's *Tiefland*, Mefistofele, Wotan in *Walküre*, Méphistophélès, Leporello and the Marquis in *Forza del Destino*.

In 1926 he accepted an invitation from the Colon, Buenos Aires, and appeared there six times in the course of the next fifteen years. His repertory included Hunding, the Hermit in *Freischütz*, the Landgrave, König Marke, Pogner, Figaro in Mozart's *Le Nozze di Figaro*, Fafner, Ochs, Tiresias in Stravinsky's *Oedipus Rex*, Fasolt, Hagen, Kezal in *Verkaufte Braut*, Waldner in *Arabella*, Daland, König Heinrich, Gurnemanz and Sarastro. He sang Sarastro at Salzburg, and Gurnemanz,

and 1932 with Gadski's company at the Manhattan and his voice sounded as good as before. In Europe he was a prominent member of the Berlin State Opera Company between 1920 and 1927. He sang in South America at the Colon, Buenos Aires, in some of the first performances of Wagner's operas in German under Weingartner in 1922 and again in 1923. After 1933 he was busy in Berlin as a stage director, and finally as a concert agent.

His was a typical German bass voice of the best kind, secure, firm and dark coloured through a wide range and though he was not an elegant or refined singer, he had the voice and stature to make the proper effect in the big Wagnerian roles.

His rendering of Wotan's Act Two monologue from *Die Walküre* is not notable for musical or dramatic imagination, there is little variety of nuance, but he makes an imposing if rather stolid godhead.

180 Alexander Kipnis as Gurnemanz in *Parsifal*

1933 to 1938, following the arrival of the Nazis, he moved to Vienna, but after the Anchluss settled in the United States.

His belated Met debut took place in 1940 as Gurnemanz.

> Mr Kipnis immediately won the favour of his audience. He invested the role with the utmost significance. The richness of the voice made one of several fine attributes of the singer and the dramatic interpreter. The text was admirably delivered; the treatment of the melodic line was that of a true musician. The character developed with a noble consistency. The tenderness and wisdom exemplified by the later scenes were the continuation of one of the most authoritative and sympathetic representations of the character that the Metropolitan stage has seen in recent years.[21]

He remained at the Met until his retirement in 1946, making his familiar contributions to *Rosenkavalier*, *Tannhäuser*, *Pelléas et Mélisande*, *Tristan*, *Fidelio*, *Zauberflöte*, *The Ring* and *Parsifal* and was also heard, rather surprisingly, as Nilakantha in *Lakmé* and as Boris Godounov, which he was the first to sing in the original since the days of Chaliapin.

There are few more noble bass voices on record, the quality rich and mellow, moving with ease and security over a wide range. It is this flow of the voice, without any of that suggestion of fixed placement that we can hear in the recordings of so many of his contemporaries, which is so agreeable to the ear and also accounts for the remarkable purity of his intonation. As Sarastro his singing has not so pure and suave a legato as Plançon, but the voice has more naturally the requisite gravity for this music. The simple repose, in an early recording of Prince Gremin's aria from Tchaikovsky's *Eugen Onegin*, the dignified and spacious phrasing and expressive inflections in his enunciation of the text, notwithstanding the German translation, put it among the best renderings of this piece. There are the same fine qualities in a lengthy excerpt 'So ward es uns verheissen' from *Parsifal*, in which the orchestra is directed by Siegfried Wagner. His account of Fiesco's 'Il lacerato spirito' is deservedly famous and again shows the evenness of the voice. A number of excerpts from *Boris Godounov* made much later in his career are disappointing; the voice has lost some of its quality and there are traces of wear. As an interpretation it suffers from exaggerations, particularly in the declamatory passages, and is not convincing. In later years Kipnis enjoyed a considerable reputation as a Lieder singer. This aspect of his career will be considered in due course.

König Marke, the Landgrave and Pogner at Bayreuth between 1927 and 1933. His London debut took place in the unfortunate revival of *Ugonotti* in 1927; his contribution as Marcel was one of its few saving graces. In the course of the next eight years to his familiar roles he added Sparafucile, the Commendatore, the Magician in Weinberger's *Schwanda* and Khan Kontchak in *Prinz Igor*. From

50. *Tauber and the Lyric Tenors*

There were German tenors of this period with larger, more beautiful, more brilliant voices, there were some who were greater actors and some who were better—far better—looking, but none was a greater musician or a finer artist than RICHARD TAUBER (1891–1948). Neither was any as popular with the general public, as respected by his colleagues, by composers, even—grudgingly—by the critics, at a time when it was fashionable to deplore a 'serious' musician who busied himself with light music so ostentatiously and with such evident satisfaction as Tauber did. He was accused of preferring money; was there ever born an opera singer, performing musician or composer, who was unconcerned with such things? To the critics it was inconceivable that he actually enjoyed singing popular songs and ballads and loved giving pleasure to thousands who probably would never set foot in an opera house or attend a Liederabend. This was the age when any voiceless wonder who offered a programme of obscure and pretentious songs could be assured of rapt attention, and in the notices expect, at the least, polite comments on his musicianship and artistry. As if artistry were merely a matter of serious intentions, of carefully dotting the right crotchets and being properly respectful of the printed page: as if it were possible to make music without a musical instrument.

Tauber's disarming honesty, his democratic attitude—'Bless this house' and Mozart's 'Dies Bildnis' are sung with the same fine vocal art, instinctive musicianship and good taste—were not calculated to endear him to those who had a vested interest in demonstrating the superiority of their taste and knowledge. Yet criticism of him was difficult; his exceptional musicianship was transparently obvious and had been widely praised by composers such as Strauss, and conductors like Beecham. So it was claimed that his familiarity with operetta and ballads had contaminated his interpretations of the classics, undermined his taste and ruined his voice. Records, however, paint a very different picture. It seems rather that his art elevated everything; it would be hard to imagine a more scrupulous, utterly unsentimental and still effective rendering of Böhm's glutinous 'Still wie die Nacht'. And though Max's 'Durch die Wälder' from *Freischütz* was recorded in 1946, his voice has faded much less than we might have expected after a strenuous career that had already lasted more than thirty

years. It is an impeccable performance; the difficult low-lying tessitura cleanly sung and with characteristic rhythmic energy. There is none finer on record.

Though his voice was not in the same class, in a very real sense Tauber was the successor of Caruso. Like him, and unlike Gigli or Martinelli, he succeeded equally as a singer of opera, art songs and popular light music. That his success was not as complete, and decreasingly so with the passage of time, was the result of various musical developments which became obvious during the 1920s. In

181 Richard Tauber as Antonio in Graener's *Don Juans letztes Abenteuer*

Caruso's time the same, essentially vocal, style was common to all, or almost all, music. By the time Tauber entered his maturity this was no longer true. Opera composers had largely abandoned traditional lyricism (some would say it had abandoned them), and were embarked upon all manner of difficult and vocally exacting experiments; Tauber ignored most of them. At the same time, the invention of the radio, consequent growth in mass audiences and America's new ascendancy in the field of light music had helped to popularise an alien idiom, Afro-American jazz. In the course of time its syncopated rhythms impregnated a great deal of music composed on both sides of the Atlantic. For a time Tauber kept clear of this but in later years he attempted songs by Irving Berlin, Cole Porter and others. Of all his recordings these are undoubtedly the least successful, though often delightful. Although he brings to bear all of his accustomed skill, he is unstylish and out of his element; the attempt to impose the Viennese manner produces incongruous, sometimes grotesque results.

Tauber was born in Linz, Austria. His parents were married, but not to each other. Both were in the theatre; his mother was a soubrette, his father an actor. With the latter's encouragement he determined to become a singer. At first he met only with rebuffs and his admiration for the Heldentenor Heinrich Hensel encouraged in him Wagnerian ambitions which were quickly squelched: 'he has not even the ghost of a chance'.[7] At length, however, he was accepted in the class of Carl Beines, whose pupils also included Gotthelf Pistor and Herbert Ernst Groh. He made rapid progress; in less than a year he was ready to sing in concert. The following year his father was appointed Director of the Municipal Theatre, Chemnitz, and it was there in 1913 that Tauber made his debut as Tamino in *Die Zauberflöte* and only a few days later sang Max in *Der Freischütz*. Count Seebach, the Director of the Dresden Opera, was at the latter performance and offered the young man a five-year contract. He remained a principal at Dresden until 1922, at first in small roles but soon graduating to Don José, Tonio in *Regimentstochter*, Pylades in *Iphigenia auf Tauris*, Leopold in *Jüdin*, Pedro in *Tiefland*, Mathias in *Der Evangelimann*, Turiddu, Belmonte, Ottavio, Tamino, Fenton in *Lustigen Weiber von Windsor*, Hoffmann, the Vagabond in *Der Vagabund und die Prinzessin* by Poldini, Rodolfo, Pinkerton, Cavaradossi, Almaviva, Jenik in *Verkaufte Braut*, Sandor Barinkay in *Zigeunerbaron,* Eisenstein in *Fledermaus*, Bacchus in *Ariadne auf Naxos*, the Italian singer in *Rosenkavalier*, Lenski in *Eugen Onegin*, Wilhelm in *Mignon*, Fenton in *Falstaff*, Max, Froh in *Rheingold*—this last was the only important Wagnerian role he ever undertook—Alfredo in *Traviata* and Faust.

> What always completely captivates, besides the dazzling gifts and fully developed technique for which he has to thank Nature, is his musicianship. Together with this he has respect for the smallest note, not only in the bravura parts, but all the time.[2]

Much of the refinement in his musicianship was the result of his early and thorough studies in piano and composition; these were to be of assistance to him again in later years when he started to conduct and compose operettas and from the beginning they gave him a remarkable facility. In his many guest appearances during the Dresden years, his capacity to learn a role, on several occasions in less than forty-eight hours, earned him the soubriquet 'the S-O-S tenor'.

After 1919 he was busy all over the place; chiefly in Berlin, the Vienna Volksoper and Vienna State Opera. When the latter offered him a regular engagement in 1922, he accepted and broke his Dresden contract, but he returned there frequently as a guest artist and in 1926, when he stepped into the breach for an ailing Curt Taucher and sang Calaf in the local premiere of *Turandot*, creating a sensation—'he sang with just the right mixture of poetical ardour and masterly Italian cantilena'[3]— amid all the critical euphoria, the management graciously waived the fine it had previously imposed. Hardly had he made his first appearance with the Vienna company at the Salzburg Festival than, to fill in the gap before the regular season began, he undertook his first stint in operetta, playing the role of Armand in *Frasquita* at the Theater an der Wien; everyone, except the Director of the State Opera, was vastly entertained, but of that more later. His career at the Staatsoper, which was henceforth to occupy him, with some interruptions, for twenty years, added to his repertory Paul in *Die Tote Stadt*, Riccardo in *Maskenball* with Vera Schwarz, Selma Kurz and Mattia Battistini, Canio, Primus Thaller in Kienzl's *Der Kuhreigen*, and even Prince Sou-Chong in *Land des Lächelns*, to which there were objections that the tone of the house was being lowered.

His first Berlin engagements as Alfredo and Almaviva, again in 1919, were not particularly successful but he returned the following season as

Don José with Artôt de Padilla as *Carmen*, Cavara-dossi with Leider and Amato, when the critics commented on his bel canto and Amato's 'Sprech-gesang' (it was virtually at the end of the Italian baritone's career) and Ottavio.

> There is no necessity to write more of the culture of his singing. He is the polished, fine musician who not only knows his part, but the whole score and creates from the complete work, which is extremely important in Mozart. He makes a fine character study of it, gives the nobleman a manly, refined mien and sings the two arias incomparably. At the end of the G major aria by the power of his cantilena he gives the octave leaping melody a soaring poised line and the way he fills the coloratura of the B flat major aria is without pre-cedent.[4]

He reappeared regularly in Berlin with the State Opera company and in various seasons of operetta until 1932. He was a guest elsewhere in Germany, especially often at Hamburg and Munich; he travel-led with the Berlin company to Sweden; with the Vienna State Opera to the Paris Opéra in 1928. His first visit to the United States was for a concert tour in 1931. The previous year he had made his London debut; after he left Germany he returned with increasing regularity. It was not, however, until 1938 that he appeared at Covent Garden, as Tamino, subsequently he was Belmonte and the following season Jenik and Ottavio; it was in the role of Ottavio at Covent Garden, as a guest of the visiting Vienna State Opera in 1947, when he was already stricken with a fatal disease, that he made his last appearance on stage. Between 1913 and 1922 Tauber had sung principally in opera; from 1923 until 1932 he divided his time about equally bet-ween opera and operetta; after that he was chiefly occupied with operetta, concert tours, films and the radio. It seems fitting therefore to consider him here principally as an opera singer and to keep for later a full discussion of his unique career in light music.

His was a light, lyric tenor but not a tenorino and with an attractive mellifluous quality. It was in no way a remarkable instrument and from the begin-ning the limitations it imposed on his artistic ambitions were a challenge to his technical re-sourcefulness; it is a tribute to his skill that he overcame these with supreme assurance. Having been obliged to abandon the notion of becoming a Heldentenor, as he tells us himself. Caruso's de-velopment into a dramatic singer with only a lyric voice furnished him with an example. He set out to

suggest the same kind of ardent and manly quality, to deploy the breath tension in a similar way so as to give the maximum resonance to the tone and yet still keep it forward and bright. His solution was not, however, like Caruso's, though it may have sounded so to him; it was a German translation. In order to avoid weighting the voice and to keep it off the throat, he used a greater proportion of nasal resonance than was consistent with a pure tone. The attack was placed high and kept free with a dash of vibrato which he would intensify for emotional effect; of all the characteristic devices of his singing it was this that gave it its peculiarly affecting quality. It also enabled him to sing cleanly, without any of the scooping and sliding that we hear in recordings of so many other German tenors, and it accounts for the remarkable purity of his intonation.

To accomplish this he was obliged to make certain compromises, in particular he sacrificed the highest notes. The voice was not, as is sometimes alleged, a naturally short one; in a recording of the duet 'Schön wie die blaue Sommernacht' from *Giuditta* he takes a soft high D flat; a head note. But by darkening the A and B flat so as to make them sound more imposing, it was not possible to rise to the high C in full voice, and he let it go. The danger of inflating the tone is that the voice will stiffen, as indeed in some measure Caruso's did, and lose its responsiveness, but Tauber, throughout his career, returned regularly to Mozart and even in operetta interpolated many of the antique graces of bel canto—mordents, gruppetti and so forth—which helped to oil the voice and keep it limpid. He was also careful not to dispense too much of it in a performance and concentrated ceaselessly on refin-ing the dynamic range. When playing in a long run of a musical show he was not too proud to avail himself of the support of the microphone, though he never became hooked on it, or really needed it. As we can hear even at the end during that last *Don Giovanni* at Covent Garden, the tones are still projected forth with point and ease.

He was always able, whenever he so wished, to shed those favourite emotional effects of his and sing simply and unaffectedly. A broadcast of Lohengrin's 'In fernem Land' made about 1937 (he never took the role in the theatre) is a remarkable piece of pure singing. Few other performances so clearly establish that this is a narration, the de-clamation spontaneous-sounding, yet contained within the musical tone and disciplined by the line and the shape of the phrase. As with Lehmann's

'Liebestod' we can only regret that he lacked the resources to sing the part in full. On the occasion of Tauber's Covent Garden debut, Newman, in the pious vein then affected by critics, wrote that by the end 'he allowed us in the audience to forget that he was Richard Tauber, and became more and more Mozart's Tamino'.[5] Well, Newman may have forgotten it, but it is doubtful if anyone else did, and indeed why should they have? The operas of Mozart, Verdi and Wagner require interpreters and would cease to exist without them. The idea that it is desirable or even possible that the interpreter should efface himself, as if he were a crystal vessel, as Toscanini put it, and in some unexplained way transmit the music like a well-programmed computer untouched by human agency—and music of such deep human feeling—is absurd. Mozart's Tamino remains a collection of notes and words on paper until the interpreter puts it into three dimensions and once again brings it to life. It is precisely the strength of the personality of a great interpretative artist that illuminates; his vitality and energy that enables us to be touched by the spirit of the work. In that last *Don Giovanni*, so infinitely moving, even in the face of death Tauber's art is still full of life, as fresh and spontaneous as it ever was.

The baritone Adolf Robinson, a noted teacher, himself a pupil of the elder Lamperti, gave lessons to a number of outstanding singers including Leo Slezak, Joseph Schwarz, Rudolph Berger and ALEXANDER KIRCHNER (1876–1948). Of these Kirchner was probably the least well known for he seems to have sung outside the German-speaking countries on only a few occasions, yet he was a lyric tenor with a fine voice and a singer of evident breeding. From Robinson in Brunn he went to Vienna for further instruction from Amelia Materna, a famous Wagnerian soprano who created the role of Kundry at Bayreuth and who, like Robinson, had been a prominent member of the Damrosch seasons at the Met in the 1880s. In 1909 Kirchner made his debut at the Imperial Opera in Vienna as Des Grieux in Massenet's *Manon*. Subsequently he was Don José, Manrico and Tamino before accepting an engagement at Stockholm for a couple of seasons; this sojourn accounts for a number of recordings of excerpts from French, Italian and German opera rendered in Swedish. In 1912 he sang Florestan in *Fidelio* at the German Opera in Berlin. In 1914 he became a member of the Berlin Imperial Opera, and remained there through various changes of management until he was nearly sixty in 1935. His repertory included Florestan, Huon in Weber's

182 Alexander Kirchner as Manrico in *Troubadour*

Oberon, Lenski in *Eugen Onegin*, Max in *Freischütz*, Walther, Bacchus in *Ariadne auf Naxos*, Don José, Parsifal and in later years Otello. 1914 was a busy year for Kirchner; after taking the title-role in some performances of *Lohengrin* at the Budapest Opera, he travelled to London to sing Tamino in Beecham's Drury Lane season with Hempel, Dux, Bronsgeest and Knüpfer. In such company it was perhaps not surprising that he was rather passed over, and since the war was only days away there were no further British engagements. From London he went to Bayreuth where he was engaged as Erik in *Fliegende Holländer*. Throughout his lengthy career he was active as a concert and oratorio singer, as soloist in Verdi's *Requiem*, Handel's *Judas Maccabeus*, Haydn's *Seasons* and Beethoven's Ninth Symphony.

Kirchner's admirably produced lyric tenor of pure quality comes in marked contrast to the strangulated cries of so many German tenors. It is not a voice notable for its size or strength and the

183 Johannes Sembach as Parsifal

disappoints; the attack is pinched and he does not seem to have decided whether it shall indeed be taken 'piano'. His performances here give us some inkling of how it was possible for Jean de Reszke to make so great an effect in such disparate roles. The fine lyric qualities of his singing are perhaps most revelatory in the role of Parsifal; though he lacked vocal stature and personal fascination, in the passage 'Nur eine Waffe taugt' the marriage of legato and declamation is a lesson in the correct performing style.

The only one of the important German singers active at the Metropolitan in the immediate pre-war period who returned afterwards was JOHANNES SEMBACH (1881–1944); he had kept his nose clean and played no part in the abortive scheme of Goritz, Ober, Braun and Weil to re-establish the German repertory only a year after the cessation of hostilities in a season at the Lexington Theatre. Sembach studied singing first in Vienna and later, like Slezak, went for special coaching to Jean de Reszke in Paris. At the precocious age of nineteen he made a successful debut at the Vienna Imperial Opera, where he remained five years before accepting an engagement in 1905 as a leading tenor at the Dresden Opera. It was there, in 1909, that he created the role of Aegisthus in the world premiere of Strauss's *Elektra* with Annie Krull, Schumann-Heink and Siems. The following year he travelled to London and appeared at Covent Garden as Siegmund and Loge.

> [He] made a particularly vivid and mercurial Loge; his rapid, fluttering movements carried on the suggestion of his theme and he illustrated both by the colour of his voice and by gesture the insinuating nature of the character.[6]

He returned twice in 1914; for the season of German opera at the beginning of the year and again in the summer. He was commended for singing 'beautifully' the title-role in Méhul's *Joseph*, then came Walther, Lohengrin, Loge and Parsifal, in which he succeeded Hensel in the first performances of the work in London. The consensus of opinion was that he had worked a great improvement on his previous form and now showed a command of 'real mezza voce'.[7]

In the autumn of 1914 he arrived in New York and made a definite impression in his first appearance in the title-role of Parsifal. Thereafter he was Tamino, Loge, Siegmund, Florestan, Walther and Adolar in *Euryanthe* with Hempel, Ober and Weil under Toscanini's direction.

quality, though most agreeable, is enhanced by the perfect blending of the registers—this is a characteristic of the Robinson pupils—which shows it off to its best advantage. Some movement in the tone is only natural and it is the poise and suave line in Lohengrin's 'Farewell' (one of the Swedish titles) that really makes him sound like a knight in shining armour. His fine musicianship and graceful style are very telling in Roméo's 'Salut! tombeau' from Gounod's opera (again in Swedish); the sweet quality and portamento style are of the essence in so romantic a piece. He gives a demonstration here of how any language is musical if the singing is; thus when the words are correctly placed in a pure singing tone, they will be clear but not obtrusive. Radamès's 'Holde Aida' may come as something of a pleasant surprise to those who had supposed it was simply an apostrophe to the gallery. He treats it as a love song and is able to avoid a muscular effect in the upper range using an artful measuring of head resonance. Only the high B flat at the end somewhat

Mr Sembach made a chivalrous and knightly figure of Adolar—his singing had much beauty in many passages, both in restrained and in full voice—more beauty and more style than many German tenors have been able to offer.[8]

In the following two seasons he added the title-role in *Siegfried*, Lohengrin, Lucentio in Goetz's *Widerspenstigen Zähmung*, Pylades in *Iphigenia auf Tauris* and Chaucer in Reginald de Koven's *Canterbury Pilgrims*. In this last his English was apparently clearer than many of his English-speaking colleagues. It was to stand him in good stead when he returned in 1920, for though the Met had reinstated Wagner's operas, in order to smooth the way with a still vociferous dissident lobby, they were given in English; Sembach sang an English Tristan, Lohengrin and Parsifal. The following season he sang Lohengrin (again in English) on the second night, but after the debut of Jeritza in Korngold's *Die Tote Stadt* given in the original, the dam was broken and a German *Tristan* and German *Walküre* followed quickly. *Parsifal*, however, remained in English and in *Lohengrin* though the principals sang in German, the chorus still used English. His last appearances at the Met were in 1922, but he returned to New York nine years later to sing Loge and Siegmund once again at the Mecca temple in a season organised by Johanna Gadski; his powers were apparently still intact.

In Sembach's day for a tenor to embrace a repertory that included Wagner's Tannhäuser, Siegmund and Lohengrin as well as Mozart's Tamino was not so unusual; Slezak was a famous interpreter of all of them and Karl Jörn, many of whose roles Sembach had succeeded to at the Met, sang them too. Mozart undoubtedly gave greater fluency and accuracy to their delivery of Wagner, and Wagner in return lent a not inappropriately heroic timbre to what is often, and mistakenly, sung with a white tone and in an effete manner. The achievement, though difficult, seems so logical that it would be pleasant to hail Sembach as a master of the classical style; alas, a recording of Tamino's 'Picture' air greatly disappoints. True, the execution is clean, the natural quality of the voice pleasing, but the incessant tremolo greatly distracts and the tight emission adversely affects his intonation. There is nothing ingratiating about his 'Ach so fromm' from *Martha*, and this music relies on a little charm. Making allowances for the bleating delivery, Schumann's 'Du bist wie eine Blume', though not imaginatively sung, has the virtue of a cleanly focussed tone and neatly graced line.

The records of a singer of remarkable technical skill, HERMANN JADLOWKER (1877–1953), have always been much sought after by collectors and it is easy to hear why; he was a virtuoso able to despatch the most difficult and elaborate music with prodigious ease and accuracy. Born in Riga, as a young man he sang in the choir of the town's leading synagogue. The cantorial training he acquired there profoundly affected his vocal style and technique throughout his career. After overcoming initial parental resistance, he went to Vienna for further study with Josef Gansbacher, whose pupils also included Felice Kaschowska, Leopold Demuth and Thila Plaichinger. In 1897 he ventured a debut at Cologne as Gomez in Kreutzer's *Nachtlager von Granada*; nobody, it seems, was much impressed and he spent the best part of the next decade in provincial engagements at Königsberg, Rostock and Stettin. It was not until 1906 when he came to Karlsrühe and took the part of Georges Brown in Boieldieu's *Weisse Dame* that he had any real success. Afterwards he confirmed this as Raoul in *Hugenotten*, Faust, Don José and Ottavio; thenceforth and until the outbreak of the war his name was prominent on the Karlsrühe roster. During these years he made guest appearances at Cologne, as soloist in Beethoven's *Missa Solemnis*, and at the Opera in Budapest and Vienna.

In 1910 he was brought to the Metropolitan, where he stayed for three seasons. He was liked as Rodolfo in *Bohème*, disliked as Max in *Freischütz* and also sang: Faust, Turiddu, Canio, Pinkerton, Lohengrin, created the Prince in the world premiere of Humperdinck's *Königskinder* and took part in the first US performances of Blech's *Versiegelt* as Bertel, in Wolf-Ferrari's *Le Donne Curiose* as Florindo, and the title-role of Thuille's *Lobetanz*. As part of the Gatti-Russell agreement on the exchange of artists, in Boston he was heard as Cavaradossi, Alfredo, Faust and Pinkerton. When the Met trooped to Paris in 1910, he added Fenton in *Falstaff* under Toscanini's direction. Through all of this activity it was less a matter of what the critics said, good or bad, than what they did not say at all. In a company that, during part at least of those years, boasted the services of Smirnov, Constantino, Clément, Bonci, Slezak, McCormack and Caruso, of whom the first two were outright failures, the second two had a mixed reception and only the last three were unqualified successes, it says something for Jadlowker that he was only ignored.

At the end of three years he accepted an invitation to the Berlin Imperial Opera and returned to

Europe; once again he was the big fish. To his previous repertory he added: Tamino, Almaviva in *Barbier von Sevilla*, the Duke in *Rigoletto*, Wilhelm in *Mignon*, Nureddin in *Barbier von Bagdad*, Bacchus in *Ariadne auf Naxos*, which he created at the Stuttgart world premiere and repeated in Berlin, Don Carlos in Verdi's opera of that name, Florestan, Eleazar in *Judin*, Manrico, Radamès, Otello, Tannhäuser and Parsifal. Not surprisingly by 1914, as

184 Hermann Jadlowker as Gérald in *Lakmé*

the records show, the voice was in evident decline, and his operatic career virtually ended in 1919 when he was only forty two. He had been warned of the dangers of undertaking too dramatic parts and in particular, after a concert in Berlin, cautioned to give Wagner 'a wide berth', but he persisted and no voice could have sustained such a regime. Throughout the twenties he was still busy as a concert and recital singer, and occasionally even sang on stage in operetta in *Zigeunerbaron*, *Frasquita* and Reinhardt's production of Suppé's *Schöne Galathée*. After 1929 he returned to Riga to become Chief Chazan at the same synagogue where he had sung as a boy. Between 1936 and 1938 he taught singing at the Conservatory there, then moved to Israel where he continued to teach until his death in 1953.

Perhaps no other tenor on record displays so complete and astonishing a command of fioritura as Jadlowker, and there is no faking, it is all done in full voice—at least in the lower range. We cannot know how Raaff sang 'Fuor del mar' from Mozart's *Idomeneo* but it would hardly have been possible for him to have got his voice round the notes with greater alacrity or more accurately. The same expertise is on show in two of Belmonte's arias from *Seraglio*, Ottavio's 'Il mio tesoro' and Almaviva's 'Ecco ridente'. He had too an extraordinary facility in falsetto singing, of which there are several examples on record, but it is most appropriate in Fra Diavolo's 'Meine Freunde', where he duets with himself. He is similarly accomplished in awkwardly written, fast moving passages; in, for example, the concluding measures of Florestan's Prison aria from *Fidelio* and Tannhäuser's 'Dir töne Lob!', both of which we are accustomed to hearing sketched in the most approximate fashion. One gets quite breathless listening to him; like watching the lady on the high wire, jumping up and down, juggling with one hand and holding up a colleague with the other, it is truly astonishing. How, we want to know, is it done? The answer is simple: by practice.

Much of this was accomplished in his youth as a soloist in the synagogue choir, which is the main reason why in opera it often astounds, but does not satisfy; it derives from an alien tradition, and as a result it is not stylish and only rarely suits the music. As we can hear in recordings of liturgical music made by various cantors of the Russian school in the early years of this century, the often elaborate ornamentations are delivered with great emotional fervour, extravagance of manner and with an extraordinary doleful quality which at times the singer intensifies almost into a howl; it is very affecting and suits the music perfectly but there is no conception of beautiful tone as such, which is at the basis of bel canto. When the florid style was introduced into opera in the seventeenth century, from a parallel oriental tradition, it was tempered and disciplined, acquiring a severity and grace of utterance hitherto unknown; at once as elaborate and refined as that which we can see in baroque architecture.

Jadlowker's experience in the opera modified his early training yet it remains true that he was most at home in a bold style approaching the canto di bravura, as we can hear in 'Fuor del mar'; though his singing lacks variety of expression or brilliance, for his voice, like that of most cantors, has a guttural quality. Brilliance is impossible when the registers are not fully blended; Jadlowker was able to do spectacular things with the head and chest voices separately but never managed to integrate them. This is strikingly demonstrated in his first (and German) recording of 'Salut! demeure' from *Faust* where there is a drastic change in timbre when he moves up to a high C in the head voice; by the time he came, eight years later, to make the second the separation is virtually complete, the aria delivered in a throaty almost baritonal voice and the high C taken in pure falsetto. His dramatic ambitions in the years between had made apparent what was always incipient.

In Almaviva's 'Ecco ridente' his general manner and execution is tasteless. He despatches the music with devastating aplomb, includes the trills and several measures that are customarily omitted, but of any trace of the canto di grazia, there is none. The aria is a serenade not a firecracker; his rendering would only seduce an audience that neither knew nor cared for what the words meant or what the dramatic situation called for. Instead of gracing the line, the coloratura becomes the whole raison d'être. Much the same can be said of his Ottavio. It may be argued that McCormack's famous interpretation is a little lacking in assertiveness and more spirit would not have come amiss, but it is the only possible criticism to make of it, and in any case if it is personality the listener wants, he will go to Tauber; for here, as elsewhere, Jadlowker's singing quite lacks any. It is true that his execution is more fluent than McCormack's, but how ugly is the tone, the difficult sustained notes are tightly gripped and on the flat side, nor is there any of the fine phrasing and characterful delivery that makes Tauber's singing so richly musical and satisfying. We are aware

only of the mechanics, of the art that does not disguise the craft.

Over the years his preoccupation with Tannhäuser, Parsifal and Otello coarsened the voice. And the odd thing is that he had nothing to offer in these roles, as recordings reveal plainly; he sings Tannhäuser's 'Dir töne Lob!' quickly and accurately but there is none of the phrasing that even a routine German tenor might attempt to suggest, and his Lohengrin is an unromantic stick. The American experience, as with Frieda Hempel, removed certain provincial mannerisms and cost him his high notes, for he became infected with the ambition to sing like Caruso. This exaggerated the throaty tone and, as we can hear in an utterly charmless rendering of 'Una furtiva lagrima', it is easy to copy a great singer's mannerisms, even something of his phrasing, and yet quite fail to recapture the musical essence of the performance. Jadlowker was a remarkably accomplished technician, a competent, routine musician and uninspired artist.

185 Ottokar Marák as rodolfo in *Bohème*

51. East European Tenors

The Czech tenor OTTOKAR MARAK (1872–1939) was a student at the Prague Conservatory before making his debut in the title-role of *Faust* at Brunn in 1899. From 1900 for two years he was a principal at the German Opera, Prague, during which time he created the role of the Prince in the world premiere of Dvorak's *Roussalka*. In 1903 at the invitation of Mahler he joined the Vienna Imperial Opera. Three years later he moved to the Berlin Komische Oper and it was there in 1911 that he sang Gennaro in another world premiere, that of Wolf-Ferrari's *Gioielli della Madonna*. During these years he made various guest appearances; in Paris, Brussels, Munich and, in 1908, at Covent Garden. His debut, opposite Tetrazzini as Alfredo in *Traviata*, was not a success; in particular his vibrato was strongly disliked. He seems to have made little effect in his other roles, either as Canio, which was considered too strenuous for him, Turiddu or Don José. He reappeared in London at His Majesty's Theatre in

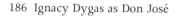

186 Ignacy Dygas as Don José

Beecham's 1913 season and sang Bacchus in the local premiere of *Ariadne auf Naxos*, but after only one performance was replaced by Robert Hutt. He sang one performance too in the 1913/14 season at Chicago as Parsifal. There at least he was successful in finding a wife; he married the American soprano Mary Cavan. In 1914, whether with or without Mary is uncertain, he returned to Prague to become the first tenor with the National Opera. He remained there more than twenty years and sang over fifteen hundred performances. Upon his retirement he came again to Chicago to teach, but the move was a failure and, penniless, he was obliged to find a livelihood selling newspapers on the street. When news of his predicament reached Prague, a subscription was raised to bring him home. He died soon after his return.

It was a voice of characteristic timbre, lyric in quality and the emission, as the London critics noted, hardly suave, but he makes an appropriately appealing effect in the First Act aria from Smetana's *Dalibor*.

The Polish tenor IGNACY DYGAS (1881–1955) was a student at the Warsaw Conservatory under Szczepkowsky and made his first stage appearance in the baritone role of Valentin, but he was not a success and went to another teacher, Alexandrowicz, who re-trained the voice in the tenor range. His tenor debut took place at the Warsaw Opera in 1905 as Jentek in Moniuszko's *Halka*. Thereafter he journeyed to Italy and made some reputation for himself as an interpreter of Wagnerian roles; as Lohengrin, Tannhäuser, Walter, Siegmund, Siegfried and Tristan. He sang in various Italian theatres: at the San Carlo, Naples, the Costanzi, Rome, at Palermo, Turin, Genoa, Padua and the Dal Verme and Lirico, Milan. While in Italy he took a further course of instruction from the younger Lamperti in Milan. In 1910 he was engaged in Madrid, and the following year returned to Warsaw where he remained until 1914, though spending some part of each season in Italy. Upon the outbreak of war he moved to Moscow and joined Zimin's Opera where he sang leading roles until 1918. In that year the independence of Poland was established and he was engaged as principal tenor at the Warsaw Opera; his career continued there until his retirement in 1937. His was a wide repertory embracing German and Italian works as well as leading Polish operas: Moniuszko's *Halka* and *Haunted Castle*, Zalewski's *Konrad Wallenrod*, Statkowski's *Maria* and Szymanowski's *Hagith*, in which he appeared in the opera's first performances in 1922.

The voice has, as many Polish tenors do, something at once Russian and German about it; the typically plaintive quality of the Slavs with a pinch of Teutonic tightness thrown in. He sings neatly and attractively, though the voice hardly seems to have the power or thrust for Wagner, save possibly in a small theatre or with the orchestration pruned. A piece from Moniuszko's *Haunted Castle* cast in a melancholy mood is interspersed with snatches of cheery dance music, recalling Newman's remark about doing everything in central European countries to characteristic rhythms: 'you shave yourself to a Krakoviak, cut a man's throat to a Mazurka and bury him to a Czardas'.[1]

Great things were expected of the Austrian born tenor JOSEPH MANN (1883–1921); negotiations were under way to bring him to the Metropolitan when he dropped dead on the stage of the Berlin State Opera during a performance of *Aida*. This was less than three weeks after the death of Caruso, a number of whose roles it was expected that Mann would take over. He was born in Lemberg in Galicia, a city with a long and noble operatic tradition and, as in so many of the eastern provinces of the Austrian Empire at that time, made up of many different nationalities. He studied there with Strozeckiej and Wysocki and made his first appearances in concert as a baritone. It was Professor Kicki, however, who realised his full potential and converted him into a tenor. He made his debut at the local opera as Jontek in Moniuszko's *Halka* in 1909 and then moved to Warsaw before accepting an invitation from the Vienna Volksoper, where he remained until the end of the war. During that time he made several guest appearances at the Imperial Opera. In 1918 he joined the Berlin State Opera. Only a short time after his arrival he created Palestrina in the local premiere of Pfitzner's opera. During the last years of his life he sang in Munich, Frankfurt and Budapest.

His is a big, rather brassy instrument, of no particular quality, the production typically German; secure but not suave and with a tendency to tighten in the upper range. Although hardly an elegant singer, he manages to get his voice round the graces and difficult intervals of Riccardo's 'Di tu se fedele' with a certain measure of accuracy, despite the German translation. Pedro's Dream from d'Albert's *Tiefland* is mostly a matter of declamation, which is not quite secure enough and he is unable to give shape to the piece, or establish the presence of any underlying music; perhaps there is none. In the 'Erzählung des Assad' from Goldmark's

187 Joseph Mann

Königin von Saba he surprises us with some soft high notes but here we need a more glamorous voice. The Love Duet from *Aida* with Mme Kemp sounds a strenuous affair; she is very forceful—too much so for the good of her voice or the music—and he has a nasty way of going at the high notes, scooping up to them rather than using portamento correctly. Though fairly observant of the composer's markings, neither singer has a smooth enough style, sufficient control or the imagination to make out of the scene anything at all memorable. Though he has not a real legato style, he is at his best and makes a moving and soulful effect in 'Recha als Gott dich einst' from Halévy's *Jüdin*. No comparisons with Caruso are called for, nor are they necessary. On this evidence it is hard to believe that New York missed much and that he would have made a greater effect than, say, Kemp, and she barely lasted out a season.

A popular 'Italian' tenor and favourite singer at Dresden, Berlin and Vienna—though there he had competition from Piccaver—TINO PATTIERA (1890–1966) was not, in fact, Italian but from Dalmatia and never sang in Italy. As a citizen of Austro-Hungary, when he decided to take up a career as a singer he was not able to turn left at the bottom of the Alps, but obliged to continue on over them to Vienna where he became a student of von Horboucki-Ranieri. As a result, on records, he sounds like a German but since his name looked Italian and his career was spent principally in the service of Italian opera—though mostly translated into German—in Germany and Austria at any rate he was thought of as an Italian singer. In 1914 he secured an engagement at the Dresden Opera but the war intervened and it was not for another two years that he made his debut as Manrico in *Troubadour* in company with Siems and Horvat. He was an immediate success with his voice 'fresh as a daisy [and] of excellent timbre'.[1] Soon afterwards he was heard in *Aida* and *Carmen* and made guest appearances in Leipzig, Magdeburg, Prague, Graz, Düsseldorf and Duisberg. Dresden was to be his operatic home throughout his career. His repertory embraced Andrea Chénier, Don Carlo, Otello, Hermann in *Pique Dame*, Bacchus in *Ariadne auf Naxos*, Erik in *Fliegende Holländer*, Tannhäuser, Alvaro, Turiddu and Canio. After 1919 he was often in Vienna, at both the Volksoper and the Staatsoper—on one occasion he managed to sing Cavaradossi at one house and Canio at the other on the same day. Between 1924 and 1929 he divided his time about equally between Dresden and Berlin, where he was particularly successful in Verdi roles.

In 1924 he was invited to Covent Garden, but in the event did not appear. He was a member of the Chicago Opera in the 1921/2 season. His roles included Cavaradossi, Radamès and Rodolfo. He was commended for his striking good looks, fine voice—especially the way he took the high notes—and his singing generally pleased, but he did not make the kind of impression on the public he had done in Germany; the competition was so very much stiffer. Though contracted to return the following season, he preferred to remain at home. He made three films: *Der Bettelstudent*, which he also sang on stage in a season at Berlin, *Eine Nacht in Venedig* and *Fra Diavolo*, this last apparently with Auber's music 'syncopated'.[2] He continued to sing into the 1930s, though less frequently, and lived in Dresden until the war. In 1950 he was appointed Professor of singing at the Academy of Music in Vienna.

Pattiera inclined increasingly as time passed towards dramatic roles; records suggest—as did the Chicago critics when he sang there—that he would have been wiser to stay with the lyric repertory. His was a voice of exceptional natural quality; the famous teacher August Iffert pronounced it a gift from God, even preferring it to Caruso's. Unfortunately the guttural German technique that he acquired did not take long to remove most of its

quality. This throatiness, especially in later recordings—the Brindisi from *Cavalleria*, for example—and the consequent forceful delivery is often distressing to listen to and gives the sensitive listener a sore throat in sympathy. This is all the more regrettable for Pattiera was a singer of genuine artistic intentions. His is not, on the evidence of 'La donna è mobile', the most refined or elegant Duke, but his manner is engaging. He knows how to make an effect in this music and though the rhythm is not elegantly pointed he moves the voice accurately and with appropriate spirit through the traditional cadenza. In Raoul's Romance from *Ugonotti* Pattiera is hardly the beau chevalier. He makes a genuine attempt to sing in a romantic style but the guttural quality of the voice and the tremulousness are not aids to pleasurable listening, and then he has the

188 Tino Pattiera as Riccardo in *Maskenball*

greatest difficulty with the climax in the cadenza. He gets full marks for the effort, even if it nearly kills him. By the later twenties the voice has become less tremulous but stiffened and an attractively phrased rendering of Tosti's lovely 'Vorrei morire' made in 1927, sung with genuine feeling and subtle range of expression, finds the tone beginning to catch in the middle range. In a live recording made the following year of Manrico's 'Mal reggendo' (in German), we can hear how the voice is drier, no longer responsive, the intervals are not clearly articulated, and the purity of the vowels always in some degree compromised.

52. Heldentenors

In the fashion of many heldentenors, RICHARD SCHUBERT (1885–1969) began his career as a baritone; at Strasbourg in 1909. After only a season, however, he returned to his teacher, Rudolf von Milde, in order to re-study the voice in the tenor range. He made his tenor debut at Nuremburg in 1911, two seasons later he moved to Wiesbaden where he was a principal Wagnerian tenor until 1917. In that year he secured an engagement at the Metropolitan in New York; the death of Rudolph Berger two seasons previously had left the company with only two principal tenors in the German repertory, Jacques Urlus and Johannes Sembach, and the latter did not sing all of the more heroic parts. However, before Schubert had time to leave Europe, the United States entered the war and his contract was automatically null and void. He went to Hamburg instead, and there began a career which was to last until 1935 and where he created the role of Paul in the world premiere of Korngold's opera *Die Tote Stadt* in 1920. In that year he made his Vienna debut and for the next nine seasons divided his time between Vienna and Hamburg. He also found time for guest appearances elsewhere, at Budapest, Barcelona, Paris, Munich and Buenos Aires, where he sang a solitary performance of Max in *Freischütz* during the 1926 season at the Colon. He eventually arrived in the United States in 1921, but with Chicago Opera and not the Met; he sang Tristan, and Tannhäuser with Raisa and Schwarz. This last part he repeated at the Manhattan with the company on its annual visit to New York. In the later years of his career Schubert was busy as a stage director at Stettin and Osnabruck; after the Second World War he taught singing in Hamburg.

189 Richard Schubert as Tannhäuser

Despite his baritone beginnings Schubert's voice has a fine tenor ring and there is nothing equivocal about it. It is a good, expressive instrument and has sufficient colour and point for the exacting demands of Siegfried and Tristan's music. As we can hear in Siegmund's 'Winterstürme' he has the skill to sing the piece by turn vigorously and tenderly and shows an incisive command of rhythm and proper breadth of expression in the long phrases. With the big but dull voiced baritone Theodor Scheidl he duets in 'Solenne in quest'ora' from *Forza del Destino* (in German); it represents the best Verdi singing in Germany at the time; assured and convincing though the legato is sometimes a bit pressured, especially in upward intervals.

Within half an hour of the curtain falling on the last performance of the Bayreuth Festival in the summer of 1914, Parsifal—WALTER KIRCHHOFF (1879–1951)—could be seen pacing the platform of the railway station waiting for the train that was to take him to rejoin his regiment; before becoming an opera singer he had been an officer in the cavalry and on the outbreak of war was appointed to the staff of the Crown Prince of Germany. It was at the instigation of the Intendant of the Berlin Imperial Opera, Baron von Hülsen, that he had left the army to take up a career on the stage. He studied in Berlin with Robert Weiss and Lilli Lehmann and then went to Milan for coaching in the Italian repertory. A debut at the Berlin Imperial Opera followed in 1906 in the title-role of *Faust*; he remained there until 1920 establishing himself as one of the company's leading Wagnerian tenors.

> Kirchhoff was following Berger as Siegfried and I must confess I did not expect much of him. In the event I was pleasantly surprised, his voice has developed greatly in brilliance. He managed the innocent as well as the heroic aspects of the character. All his interpretation needs to be numbered among the best, is a little more rhythmic vigour in the first two acts.[1]

His range also included certain Italian roles, and he was Alfredo in *Traviata* with Battistini 'but he had not the bel canto style necessary'.[2] During the immediate pre-war period he sang with various other German companies: Tannhäuser in Dresden in 1912 and Samson in a staging of Handel's oratorio at Düsseldorf the next season. His first visit to Bayreuth was in 1911 as Walther in *Meistersinger* and he repeated the part the following year. With his wife he appeared in recitals and was much praised for his interpretations of the songs of Taubert, Schumann and Hugo Wolf.

In February 1913 he went abroad for the first time to sing Walther at Covent Garden in Beecham's season.

> Mr Kirchhoff gives what one so rarely gets in a Wagnerian tenor, a combination of vocal power and manly personality, which is essential to a satisfactory representation.[3]

But it was not until after the war that his international career got under way. In 1922 Weingartner brought him to Buenos Aires for the first German *Ring* cycle at the Colon, and he was also heard as Parsifal and as a German Don José; the year after he added Tristan, Lohengrin, Aegisthus in *Elektra* and Herod in *Salome*, the last two under the composer's direction. In 1924 at Covent Garden again he was an 'outstanding'[4] Loge and 'masterly'[5] Herod. His Metropolitan debut took place in the

1926/7 season as Loge; it introduced, according to Henderson, one of the finest interpretations of the role heard in New York and, since his memory went back to the days of Heinrich Vogl, Ernst van Dyck and Carl Burrian, that was praise indeed. Kirchhoff was a prominent figure in the company's Wagnerian wing until 1931. To the principal roles in the *Ring* he added Walther, Lohengrin, Tannhäuser, Erik and Tristan—but in this, though he looked well, there was much tired and strained vocalism. He appeared in a number of novelties: as Alfonso in the seventeen-year-old Korngold's *Violanta*, one of several vehicles staged for Jeritza's benefit, Kirchhoff gave a fine performance. Later he replaced an indisposed, and apparently inadequate, Laubenthal as the cuckolded Menelaus in Strauss's *Aegyptische Helena* with Jeritza, but not even her face could launch this one and after a season it sank without trace. He was Max in *Jonny spielt auf*, in which

190 Walther Kirchhoff as Loge in *Rheingold*

Krenek attempted to cash in on the jazz vogue and managed to write a bad opera as well as bad jazz, and finally Pietro in another piece for Jeritza: von Suppé's *Boccaccio*. By the end all of his skill could not disguise a wavery voice and the fact that the time had come to say 'Good-bye'; the presence of Melchior made it easy for the Met to do so.

His singing on records confirms many of the good opinions of him held by his contemporaries, for he was an artist. In Lohengrin's 'Atmest du nicht' and 'Nun sei bedankt' he sings in affecting style, imaginatively, with a fine command of mezza voce, the enunciation beautifully clear yet without a trace of the Bayreuth bark. The voice is firmly produced, an attractive instrument, if rather persistently plaintive in quality and nasal, especially in the upper range where the tight attack accounts for certain lapses in the purity of his intonation and an infirm rhythm in vigorous passages.

When nature created LAURITZ MELCHIOR (1890–1973) she broke the mould and having done so threw it away: never before had there been such a powerful tenor voice, at the same time so dark and so brilliant, and to this day he has had no successor. If we compare his records to virtually all the other Heldentenors, genuine or so-called, what they only manage in large measure by fine skill, Melchior surmounts with casual, almost insolent ease. He had his faults but these were much exaggerated by jealous rivals—conductors as much as singers, for no orchestra could drown him out. Criticising him is like trying to knock the Great Wall of China. Just look at a photograph with his wife and Toscanini on board a trans-Atlantic liner; he called her 'Kleinchen', not inappropriately, yet next to the maestro she looks quite a big girl, both, however, are grouped about the Colossus of Rhodes. Francis Robinson has compared him to Niagara: a great natural phenomenon: Melchior inspires gigantic allusions. And the man and his voice were all of a piece. His singing technique was a perfect rationalisation of his own prodigious resources and if it lacked the character of the traditional German school, it was also without its vices. He was perhaps the first great modern singer; though born before the days of free milk, orange juice and a high protein diet, he had a physique that in his youth was considered quite extraordinary, but which over the last half century in the United States and Western Europe had become relatively commonplace. Traditionally opera singers tended to fat, but nowadays they are as notable for their stature, height and breadth and many of them, by older, more modest

standards, seem like a race of supermen and superwomen. This has not brought any refinement to their art but it has given them the stamina to stand up to the boisterous and intemperate playing of modern orchestras and at the same time permitted them to indulge the audience's taste for sheer decibels of sound.

To begin with Melchior trained as a baritone, and no teacher could be blamed for misdirecting him; even in his maturity the voice still had in the lower range much of the weight and colour of a baritone. He made his debut at the Copenhagen Opera in 1913 as Silvio in *Pagliacci*. During the next four years he sang various small roles in *Traviata*, *Carmen*, *Freischütz*, *Parsifal*, *Faust*, *Tannhäuser* and *Der Rosenkavalier*. At length in the summer of 1917 on a tour of Sweden he was promoted to di Luna in *Trovatore*. It was the Azucena of these performances, the American contralto Mme Charles-Cahier, a pupil of Jean de Reszke, who first saw Melchior's real potential; she advised him to become a tenor and offered to help him make the conversion. Although he was apprehensive and declined, he soon began to feel that she was right and decided to seek further opinions. Under the guidance of the famous Danish tenor Vilhelm Herold he commenced a period of re-study. By the autumn of 1918 he felt ready for a new start and made his first appearance as a tenor, again at the Royal Opera, Copenhagen, in the title-role of *Tannhäuser*; in the event, however, the still very dark and heavy quality of the voice and his complete inexperience told against him and for the next two seasons he moved, uncomfortably, between the two ranges. It was in 1920 that he accepted an invitation to visit London. He sang in the first radio concert with Melba but it was at a Promenade Concert that he made his first big impression on a British audience. 'His manly appearance appealed almost as much as his voice'[6] and Wood recalls the only objections were when he persisted in singing everything in Danish. The novelist Hugh Walpole heard him and determined to assist him; he raised enough money so that Melchior would be able to acquire a thorough musical and dramatic training. Thereafter he went on a tour of teachers, to Victor Beigel in London, Ernst Grenzebach in Berlin, Anna Bahr-Mildenburg at Bayreuth and Hermine Kittel at Munich. Throughout this period he continued to accept engagements and in 1924 was offered a contract at Covent Garden as Siegmund in *Walküre*.

The quality of his voice gained immediate recognition but, surrounded by such experienced artists as Leider, Lehmann, Olczewska and Schorr

191 Lauritz Melchior as Otello

his performance was pronounced 'uneven'. From London he journeyed to Bayreuth, where he sang Parsifal for the first time. He greatly pleased Siegfried and Cosima Wagner and returned often in the course of the next seven years for performances of *Walküre*, *Siegfried*, *Götterdämmerung*, *Tannhäuser* and *Tristan* and during that time completed his education with the help of Karl Muck, Erik Schmedes and Cosima herself: she acclaimed him 'The Great Dane' and 'The Greatest Parsifal'. In 1926 he was brought to the Met by Bodansky, who had

heard him at Bayreuth. He did not set the Hudson on fire; that had been tried earlier on the same day at the matinee when Marion Talley had made her debut amid a whirl of publicity that she never did live up to; the critics had had enough of sensations. The beautiful quality of his head voice was commented upon but so too was his awkward stage presence and a tendency to force; at best it did not look as though he would be more than 'a useful addition' to the company's Wagnerian wing. During the next few seasons by dint of hard work he steadily improved; Siegmund fared little better than Tannhäuser but Siegfried, which he had sung only twice before, marked a distinct upward turn and though his Parsifal was less effective in dramatic moments his singing showed great promise. It was not however until 1929, as Tristan, that he entered into his heyday and thenceforth knew no competition.

His Met career lasted with one interruption until 1950; in that theatre alone he sang 385 performances, broken down as follows: 51 Tannhäusers, 53 Lohengrins, 40 Parsifals, 95 Tristans, 62 Siegmunds, 41 Siegfrieds in *Siegfried* and 43 in *Götterdämmerung*. His energy was unflagging; when a friend once commented on it, he remarked apologetically that he had had to cancel three performances on tour recently: the first time when a bad knee made it impossible for him to stand and on the other two occasions when he had eaten too much. He returned to Covent Garden in 1926 and was praised for the great improvement since his previous appearances. He sang there every season until the outbreak of the Second World War, a record not equalled by any other tenor. In London he was also heard as Florestan in *Fidelio* and in the title-role of *Otello*. He did in fact sing one act of the latter at Gatti-Casazza's Farewell in 1935, but Gatti remarked at the time that he was too old and had his hands full with his Italian tenors as it was and did not dare ask Melchior to sing the role in the regular season. He travelled widely in the United States and on tour in South America at the Colon, Buenos Aires, and elsewhere. In Europe he appeared in Berlin, Paris, Hamburg, Brussels, Amsterdam and Barcelona, chiefly in the Wagnerian repertory but on occasion as Samson, Otello, Canio, Radamès and John of Leyden in *Prophet*.

We still see it sometimes repeated that Melchior was not really a great singer, but only shouted, and that his musicianship was slovenly and suspect; he was reproached for carelessness in the treatment of note values, for shifting accents and generally for being a law unto himself. It is hardly possible without having heard him often in the theatre to rebut these claims in full, but, as john Steane was the first to point out, recordings made in the studio, and from Met broadcasts and at Covent Garden, hardly substantiate them; rather the contrary. At a time when general standards of execution were deteriorating and there was little concern for detail or finish, compared with most other Wagnerian tenors then active, Melchior was a model, in spite of having to manoeuvre such a big

and heavy voice. In Siegfried's Forging Song we have to go back to Jean de Reszke on the Mapleson cylinders or Ivan Erschov to find marcato singing so solid, brilliant and accurate, while the declamation of Tannhäuser's Rome Narrative for nobility of tone, clarity and poise has not been equalled. In *Lohengrin* he sings with a fresh, cantabile line, the mordents and graces turned without trace of aspirates. There is the same precision of detail, which we hear so rarely, in Tannhäuser's exacting music in the Venusberg and here, as elsewhere, his intonation is pre-eminently correct, the attack clean and precise—unlike most German singers.

A clue to the origins of many of the complaints probably lies in Melchior's background. He sang a limited repertory of extremely onerous music, more often than any other important singer hitherto and with less relief. During the difficult and early years of his career he spent a great deal of time working until he had mastered the roles exactly the way he wanted them, and then like many great performing artists, from Pasta to Rachmaninov, having done so was disinclined to change anything. We may imagine that this did not endear him to certain conductors who had their own ideas. In the usual way they would have had no difficulty intimidating a singer, but Melchoir's prestige, the size of his voice, and the man, made that difficult as well as undesirable; it is not surprising that they chose to disparage him with finicky criticism. He made it easier for them by his generally indifferent stage deportment; acting did not come easily to Melchior, he preferred to do most of it with his voice. He would take the opportunity of walking off stage when he was not singing for long stretches of *Parsifal* and *Tristan*, though Wagner's stage directions required that he should remain (not that stage directors have ever taken those very literally). It was not difficult to believe that he was as casual musically. We have only to listen to two of his early song records, Wagner's 'Träume' from the Wesendonck Lieder, always a Melchior favourite, and Strauss's 'Cäcilie' to hear how consummate a singer and how sensitive a musician he really was. The Wagner is rapturously sung, the long melting line shaded down to pianissimo, full of expression and an intensity hinting at latent reserves. These he discloses with superb vigour in 'Cäcilie', the tone focussed, full of colour, and with that passionate emotional quality that communicated so surely. He never lost it and brought it to everything he did, even *Rose Marie*, but that dates from the Hollywood postscript to his career and will keep. . . .

Glossary

Terms are here defined as they are used in connection with vocal music. Bracketed numbers refer to the Bibliography.

Acciaccatura. Here refers to an ornament related to the appoggiatura (q.v.): a short, crushed note produced on the beat, immediately before an essential note of a melody.

Appoggiatura. An important ornament. The general use of the term describes a 'leaning' or supporting note, which prepares and delays the main note. In the body of this book, the term is used with a more particular meaning. A convention of musical notation from the seventeenth to the early nineteenth centuries led composers to write recitatives particularly, but also arias, in such a way that the phrases ended on two equal short notes; for example, Susanna's 'Giunse alfin il momento'. The appoggiatura here means the raising or lowering of the penultimate note by an interval that depends on the musical line of the phrase. Failure to observe this rule means the performance of arias by Handel, Mozart or Rossini with hundreds of wrong notes. In Susanna's 'Deh vieni non tardar o gioia bella', only the insertion of the appoggiaturas (heard in the records of Sembrich and Lotte Lehmann) reveals the musical line completely and authentically.

Arpeggio. Where the singer sounds the notes of a chord successively in the fashion of a harpist.

Aspirate. A common technical frailty, where a note instead of being attacked cleanly is preceded by an audible exhalation of breath. In rapid coloratura (q.v.) intrusive *hs* make it impossible for the singer to execute all the notes accurately and smoothly.

Bel Canto. Although the term can be found in one or two texts of the late eighteenth and early nineteenth century, it clearly meant only what it said—'beautiful singing'. Its use to describe a vanished school of Italian singing dates from the later part of the nineteenth century. We find it employed by German, English and, later, Italian writers to describe the art of those singers—in particular Adelina Patti—which remained unaffected by the verismo or Bayreuth styles, and still exemplified the classical virtues set out by Tosi, Mancini and the other great singing teachers of the eighteenth century. (See *The Record of Singing* Volume One, p. 8.) Nowadays, through misuse, it has come to mean pretty well anything the writer likes.

Cadenza. A brilliant, usually unaccompanied passage introduced at the fermata (q.v.) preceding the cadence proper. In the seventeenth and eighteenth centuries it was of the singer's own invention, designed to show off virtuosity and skill in composition, within the particular character and style of the music. From the middle of the nineteenth century composers have taken to writing out cadenzas in full. Those of many famous singers and singing teachers of the past survive in the common lore and are still in general use, e.g. those for the Mad Scene from *Lucia* by Fanny Persiani (the first Lucia) and Mathilde Marchesi. Certain composers wrote cadenzas for particular singers; Rossini composed a number for Patti to sing in *Barbiere* and *Semiramide*, and for operas by Bellini and Donizetti. The term is often used instead of the more correct 'embellishment' to describe any kind of addition to the composer's vocal line.

Cantilena. A smooth and flowing melody.

Cavatina. Originally an entrance aria, but the term is nowadays interchangeable with aria.

Coloratura. Literally, coloured. Not an Italian word, but apparently Italianised from the German 'Koloratur', it refers to those passages of ornamentation—divisions, cadenzas, embellishments and so on—which may be said to colour the vocal line. It is often incorrectly supposed to be a type of voice, the light, high soprano more properly termed soprano leggero.

Continuo. Refers to a practice in baroque and classical opera, where the simple chords providing the harmonic bass indicated by the composer in the score were extended by unwritten elaborations ad libitum on various instruments, chiefly the harpsichord.

Corona. See Fermata.

Division. Literally the dividing up or breaking down of long notes into figures compounded of shorter connecting notes. A particular feature in baroque music—as in the opera and oratorios of Handel—it was a harmonic as well as melodic amplification.

Embellishments. Term describing ornaments and graces used to decorate a given melody. In the seventeenth and eighteenth centuries embellishments were largely the singers' prerogative. Garcia in the second part of his *L'Art du chant* (33) gives the most reliable guide to the conventions in the late Classical and early Romantic opera.

Falsetto. The falsetto in modern terminology generally refers to the upmost notes in the man's range, the remains of the boy's unbroken voice. For a full discussion of voice registers, see *The Record of Singing* Volume One, pp. 6, 7.

Fermata or *Corona.* Literally, a pause.

Glissando. Where the voice is drawn across an interval between one note and another; similar to the portamento, but while that is accomplished smoothly, in the glissando the steps are marked in whole or half tones.

Gruppetto. See Turn.

Intonation. Refers to the singer's ability to keep to the correct pitch, i.e. sing in tune.

Legato. A smooth, flowing vocal line. This is only possible where the voice is correctly supported by the breath. See also Portamento.

Marcato and *Martellato.* Literally where the notes are marked or hammered out. Although these are non-legato markings, the breath support must remain smooth and continuous. There should not be, in Sir Henry Wood's words, 'shock of diaphragm, or aspiration'. Undoubtedly two of the most difficult effects to contrive, depending as they do on complete control of the breath supply.

Messa di voce. The art of swelling and diminishing a note.

Mezza voce. In half voice.

Morendo. A favourite vocal effect, where the singer gradually diminishes a note to a mere thread of tone.

Opera buffa. Comic opera.

Opera seria. A term in general use until the time of Rossini's *Semiramide* (1823) and Meyerbeer's *Crociato in Egitto* (1824) to describe operas treating serious subjects as distinct from opera buffa.

Parlando. Where the singing is subordinate to the patterns of speech. An effect used especially in opera buffa, see Recitative.

Portamento. This term will be found used in the text with two distinct meanings. Today it generally has a narrow instrumental sense: the linking of two or more intervals together to create a special effect of legato. It has come to be regarded as an ornament, whereas it is in fact an indispensable part of the melodic style of almost all music up to the First World War. However, such writers as Giustiniani, Mancini, Agricola, Tosi and Burney used the term portamento in its literal sense, viz. 'carrying' the voice on a complete mastery of the breath. (See *The Record of Singing* Volume One, p. 8.)

Recitative. Term used to denote the more or less extended passages of singing in baroque, classical and early romantic opera where the story is advanced between the arias and other set pieces. Garcia distinguishes the recitativo parlante, used exclusively in opera buffa, in which note values are determined by the natural rhythms of speech, from the recitativo strumentale, where the manner of delivery reflects the character of the music, as it would in an aria or set piece.

Sprechgesang. A declamatory style where the quality of speech is introduced into song at the expense of lyricism. It seems to have originated in Bayreuth in the period after Wagner's death.

Staccato. A note that is cut off quickly. Although this is a non-legato marking, the execution should be accomplished smoothly, without exaggeration and without disturbing the flow of breath. Garcia distinguishes between staccato, a sound released immediately after the attack, and picchettato, a sound not only quickly released but attacked delicately, 'pure and velvety, like the notes of the glass harmonica'. The picchettato slightly prolonged becomes the flautato.

Tessitura. The prevailing range in which a vocal part is written.

Timbre. The quality or tone of a voice.

Tremolando. A deliberate trembling of the voice, or variation of intensity in the sound, in order to contrive an emotional effect.

Tremolo. See Vibrato.

Trill or *Shake.* The rapid alternation of two notes, sometimes a semi-note apart, sometimes a whole tone; it is possible to trill even in thirds.

Triplet. A rhythmical unit divided into three equal parts.

Turn. The Italian term is gruppetto. A four-note ornament, using the note above, the note itself, the note below and then concluding on the note itself—or vice versa.

Verismo. From the Italian, meaning truth. An operatic style originating in Italy in the later part of the nineteenth century. Its preoccupation with 'ordinary' people, naturalistic style and usually contemporary settings (e.g. in *Cavalleria Rusticana*), at the time made it seem the epitome of realism; nowadays much of it seems merely sensational.

Vibrato. A deliberate or uncontrolled vibration of the voice. For a full discussion of the historical use of the terms tremolo and vibrato, see *The Record of Singing* Volume One, p. 14.

Voce bianca or *voix blanche.* When the voice is not properly supported by the breath and the throat is not fully opened, the tone develops a 'white' colour. As an expressive device, in Lieder singing for example, it has come to be considered a legitimate effect, but since it invariably affects the intonation, it should be used very sparingly.

Bibliography

The following is a (very) Select Bibliography, including only those works which I consulted most often.

1. ALBANI, Emma. *Forty Years of Song*; London, 1944
2. ALDA, Frances. *Men, Women and Tenors*; Boston, 1937
3. ALDRICH, Richard. *Concert Life in New York*; New York, 1941
4. ALVAREZ, Marguerite d'. *Forsaken Altars*; London, 1954
5. ARDITI, Luigi (ed. Baroness von Zedlitz). *My Reminiscences*; London, 1896
6. BAUER, Roberto. *New Catalogue of Historical Records 1898–1908/9*; London, 1947
7. BISPHAM, David. *A Quaker Singer's Recollections*; New York, 1921
8. BLOOMFIELD, Arthur J. *San Francisco Opera, 1923–61*; New York, 1961
9. BUKOFZER, Manfred. *Music in the Baroque Era*; London, 1948
10. BURNEY, Charles. *Musical Tours in Europe*; London, 1773
11. BURNEY, Charles. *The Present State of Music in France and Italy*; London, 1773
12. BURNEY, Charles. *The Present State of Music in Germany*; London, 1773
13. CAAMANO, Roberto. *La Historia del Teatro Colon, 1908–68* (3 vols); Buenos Aires, 1969
14. CACCINI, Giulio. *Le Nuove Musiche*; Florence, 1602
15. CAPELL, Richard. *Schubert's Songs*; London, 1928
16. CELLETTI, Rodolfo. *Le Grandi Voci*; Rome, 1964
17. CHALIAPIN, Feodor (ed. and trans. Nina Froud and James Hanley). *An Autobiography as told to Maxim Gorky*; London, 1968
18. CHALIAPIN, Feodor. *Man and Mask*; New York, 1932
19. CHORLEY, Henry F. *Modern German Music: Recollections and Criticism*; London, 1854
20. CHORLEY, Henry F. *Thirty Years' Musical Recollections*; London, 1862
21. CONE, John Frederick. *Oscar Hammerstein's Manhattan Opera Company*; Oklahoma, 1966
22. DAVIS, Ronald L. *A History of Opera in the American West*; Englewood Cliffs, N.J., 1965
23. DAVIS, Ronald. *Opera in Chicago*; New York, 1966
24. DAWSON, Peter. *Fifty Years of Song*; London, 1951
25. DONINGTON, Robert. *A Performer's Guide to Baroque Music*; London, 1973
26. DOWNES, Olin (ed. I. Downes). *Olin Downes on Music*; New York, 1957
27. DUEY, Philip A. *Bel Canto in its Golden Age*; New York, 1951
28. EATON, Quaintance. *The Boston Opera Company*; New York, 1965
29. EATON, Quaintance. *Opera Caravan*; New York, 1957
30. FARRAR, Geraldine. *Such Sweet Compulsion*; New York, 1938
31. FINCK, Henry T. *My Adventures in the Golden Age of Music*; New York, 1926
32. GAISBERG, F. W. *The Music Goes Round*; New York; 1942
33. GARCIA, Manuel. *L'Art du chant*; Paris, 1847
34. GARDEN, Mary & Louis Biancolli. *Mary Garden's Story*; New York, 1951
35. GATTI-CASAZZA, Giulio. *Memories of the Opera*; New York, 1941
36. GELATT, Roland. *The Fabulous Phonograph*; London, 1956
37. GOUNOD, Charles François. *Autobiographical Reminiscences: with Family Letters and Notes on Music*; London, 1896
38. GOUNOD, Charles François. *Mozart's Don Giovanni; a Commentary*; London, 1895.
39. GUNSBOURG, Raoul. *Cent ans de souvenirs . . . ou presque*; Monaco, 1959
40. HANSLICK, Edouard (ed. and trans. H. Pleasants). *Music Criticisms 1846–99*; London, 1951
41. HENDERSON, W. J. *Early History of Singing*; New York, 1921
42. HENDERSON, W. J. *The Art of Singing*; New York, 1938
43. HURST, P. G. *The Golden Age Recorded*; London, 1963
44. JERITZA, Maria, *Sunlight and Song: a Singer's Life*; New York, 1924
45. KEY, Pierre. *Enrico Caruso, a Biography*; Boston, 1922
46. KLEIN, Herman. *An Essay on the Bel Canto*; London, 1923
47. KLEIN, Herman. *Great Women Singers of My Time*; London, 1931
48. KLEIN, Herman. *Musicians and Mummers*; London, 1925
49. KLEIN, Herman. *The Golden Age of Opera*; London, 1933
50. KLEIN, Herman. *The Reign of Patti*; London, 1920
51. KLEIN, Herman. *Thirty Years of Music Life in London: 1870–1900*; London, 1903
52. KOLODIN, Irving. *The Story of the Metropolitan Opera*; New York, 1966
53. KUTSCH, K. J. & Leo Riemens (trans. Harry Earl Jones). *A Concise Biographical Dictionary of*

Singers; Philadelphia, 1969

54. KUTSCH, K. J. & Leo Riemens. *Unvergangliche Stimmens: Sangerlexikon*; Berne, 1975.
55. LAURI-VOLPI, Giacomo. *Voci Parallele*; Bologna, 1977
56. LANG, Paul H. *Music in Western Civilisation*; London, 1942
57. LEBLANC, Georgette (trans. J. Flanner). *Souvenirs (1895–1918): My Life with Maeterlinck*; New York, 1932
58. LEDBETTER, Gordon. *The Great Irish Tenor*; London, 1977
59. LEHMANN, Lilli. *How to Sing*; New York, 1942
60. LEHMANN, Lotte. *Wings of Song*; London, 1938
61. LEIDER, Frida (ed. and trans. C. Osborne). *Playing My Part*; London, 1966
62. LEISER, Clara. *Jean de Reszke*; London, 1933
63. LEVIEN, John Mewburn. *The Garcia Family*; London, 1931/2
64. LIFF, Vivian. *Singers at La Scala*, unpublished MS
65. MACKENZIE, Barbara and Findlay. *Singers of Australia from Melba to Sutherland*; London, 1968
66. MACKINLEY, Malcolm Sterling. *Garcia: the Centenarian and his Times*; London, 1908
67. MANCINI, Giambattista. *Pensieri, e riflessioni pratiche sopra il canto figurato*; Vienna, 1774
68. MARCHESI, Blanche. *A Singer's Pilgrimage*; Boston, 1923
69. MATZ, Mary Jane. *The Many Lives of Otto Kahn*; New York, 1963
70. MERCER, Ruby. *The Tenor of his Time: Edward Johnson of the Met.*; Toronto, 1976
71. MOORE, Edward C. *Forty Years of Opera in Chicago*; New York, 1930
72. MOORE, Gerald. *Am I Too Loud?* London, 1962
73. MOORE, Gerald. *Farewell Recital*; London, 1978
74. MOORE, Grace. *You're Only Human Once; the Autobiography of Grace Moore*; London, 1947
75. NEWTON, Ivor. *At the Piano*; London, 1966
76. O'CONNELL, Charles. *The Other Side of the Record*; New York, 1947
77. OSBORNE, Charles. *The Opera of Verdi*; London, 1969
78. PLEASANTS, Henry. *The Great Singers*; New York, 1966
79. POUND, Ezra. *Ezra Pound on Music*; London, 1978
80. PURITZ, Elizabeth. *The Teaching of Elisabeth Schumann*; London, 1956
81. READ, O. & W. L. Welch. *From Tin Foil to Stereo*; New York, 1959
82. RONALD, Landon. *Variations on a Personal Theme*; London, 1922
83. ROSENTHAL, Harold. *Two Centuries of Opera at Covent Garden*; London, 1958
84. RUSSELL, Henry. *The Passing Show*; London, 1926
85. SAINT-SAENS, Camille (trans. E. G. Rich). *Musical Memories*; 1921

86. SELTSAM, William H. *Metropolitan Opera Annals*; New York, 1947
87. SPALDING, Albert. *Rise to Follow*; London, 1946
88. STRAUSS, Franz and Alice & Willi Shuh ed. *A Working Friendship: the Correspondence between Richard Strauss and Hugo von Hofmannsthal* (trans. H. Hammelmann and E. Osers); London, 1961
89. STRONG, L. A. G. *John McCormack*; London, 1949
90. THOMPSON, Oscar. *The American Singer: a Hundred Years of Success in Opera*; New York, 1937
91. TOSI, Pier Francesco (trans. J. E. Galliard). *Observations on the Florid Song*; London 1742
92. WAGNER, Charles. *Seeing Stars*; New York, 1940
93. WALSH, T. J. *Monte Carlo Opera, 1879–1909*; Dublin, 1975
94. WALTER, Bruno. *Theme and Variations*; New York, 1946
95. WOLF, Stephane. *L'Opéra au Palais Garnier 1875–1962*; Paris, 1962
96. WOLF, Stephane. *Un demi-siècle d'Opéra-Comique*; Paris, 1953
97. WOOD, Henry J. *My Life of Music*; London, 1938

NEWSPAPERS AND PERIODICALS

98. *Boston Evening Tribune*
99. *Chicago Tribune*
100. *Le Courrier Musical*
101. *Le Guide Musical*
102. *The Illustrated London News*
103. *The Times* (London)
104. *The Sunday Times* (London)
105. *Le Maschère*
106. *Le Menéstrel*
107. *Le Monde Musical*
108. *Monthly Musical Record*
109. *Musical America*
110. *Music and Musicians* (G.B.)
111. *Music and Musicians* (U.S.A.)
112. *Musica e scena*
113. *Musical Courier* (U.S.A.)
114. *Musical Times*
115. *Die Musik*
116. *New York Daily Tribune*
117. *New York Sun*
118. *New York Telegram*
119. *New York Times*
120. *Orfeo*
121. *Philadelphia Evening Bulletin*
122. *The Record Collector*
123. *Record News*
124. *La Revue Musicale Mensuelle*
125. *Vita Teatrale*

MISCELLANEOUS

126. Author's conversations with André Turp
127. Sleeve notes to EMI record
128. Sleeve notes to IPA record
129. Sleeve notes to Rubini record

Notes

The first number throughout refers to the bibliography, which is numbered; the second to the page.

Introduction
1. 85: 222
2. Quoted 42: 104–5
3. Quoted ibid.: 103–4
4. 91: 59
5. 41: 40
6. 42: 167/171
7. 126
8. 129: 11.1912
9. 46: 17
10. ibid.
11. ibid.
12. 77: 392
13. 42: 90–1
14. 42: 90–1

PART I Revolution and Russian Singing

1. Chaliapin
1. 124: 4.1922
2. 116: 21.11.1907
3. 116: 10.12.1921
4. 73: 38–9
5. 39: 141
6. 119: 14.11.1921/4: 681
7. 127: COLH 141
8. ibid.
9. 28: 65
10. Quoted 28: 65
11. 98: 26.2.1910
12. Quoted 122: XII, 12
13. Quoted 28: 65
14. 109: 19.3.1910
15. Quoted 23: 129

2. Smirnov
1. Quoted 129: GV 74
2. Quoted 52: 226
3. 103: 27.6.1914
4. 107: 1.1923
5. 107: 12.1923
6. 107: 31.1.1931

3. Kouznetsova to Koshetz
1. 101: 26.10.1913
2. 106: 6.5.1911
3. 101: 26.10.1913
4. 102: 9.7.1910
5. Quoted 122: xii, 7
6. 107: 7.1913
7. 101: 1.3.1914
8. 103: 9.6.1914
9. Quoted 23: 111
10. 106: 14.11.1919
11. 128: IPA 116
12. ibid.
13. 3: 652/668
14. ibid: 653
15. 128: IPA 116

4. Two 'Coloraturas'
1. 101: 6/13.6.1909
2. Quoted 28: 63
3. 52: 213
4. 106: 24.12.1926
5. Quoted 28: 57

6. ibid.
7. Quoted ibid.

5. Contraltos
1. 101: 23/30.5.1909
2. ibid. 8/15.6.1913

PART II The French Tradition in Decline

6. Franz, Ansseau and Fontaine
1. 101: 7.2.1909
2. 103: 7.5.1910
3. ibid.: 17.5.1910
4. 83: 361
5. Quoted ibid.: 387
6. 114: 1.7.1914
7. ibid.: 1.7.1912
8. Quoted 83: 370
9. 124: 8.1912
10. Quoted 83: 400
11. 106: 14.10.1921
12. 101: 23/30.7.1911
13. ibid.: 1.2.1914
14. 106: 30.4.1920
15. 3.618

7. A Quintet of Lyric Tenors
1. 101: 14.2.1909
2. 21: 256
3. 114: 1.7.1910
4. 106: 2.4.1926
5. 101: 5.5.1912
6. 107: 11.1924
7. 106: 7.11.1919
8. 112: 1. 1926

8. Baritones at the Opéra
1. 103: 17.5.1911
2. 108: 8.1911
3. Quoted 83: 408
4. 103: 6.6.1924
5. 3: 383

9. Journet and the Basses
1. 101: 15.1.1911
2. 124: 1.5.1923
3. 106: 18.11.1921
4. ibid.: 6/13.6.1909
5. Quoted 52: 193
6. 3: 219
7. 21: 179
8. 116: 29.1.1909
9. 3: 618

10. Singing Actors
1. 28: 201
2. 103: 4.5.1905
3. 82: 332
4. Quoted ibid.: 331
5. 82: 352
6. 28: 126
7. 26: 40
8. 28: 184
9. 26: 41
10. 107: 3.1922
11. 100: 15.1.1911
12. 107: 7.1922
13. 3: 430
14. Quoted 23: 170
15. 124: 4.1922
16. 107: 1.1922
17. 42: 114
18. 107: 3.1922
19. 103: 23.5.1913
20. 103: 8.7.1914
21. 106: 1.4.1921

22. 101: 7/14.6.1914
23. Quoted 82: 447
24. 105: 5.3.1921
25. ibid.: 9.1.1921

11. Contraltos
1. 106: 9.4.1920

12. Five International Sopranos
1. 114: 8.1913
2. 108: 7.1909
3. ibid.
4. Quoted 82: 352
5. 28: 185
6. ibid.
7. 103: 19.6.1909
8. ibid.
9. 106: 16.4.1920
10. 107: 1.1922
11. ibid.: 6.1922
12. 55: 59
13. 124: 1.1922
14. 106: 29.10.1920
15. 55: 59
16. 100: 12.1924
17. 106: 19.11.1926
18. 52: 281
19. 3: 620
20. 23: 128
21. 124: 1.1922
22. 107: 11.1923
23. Reported 82: 447
24. Quoted 82: 447

13. Lyric Sopranos at the Opéra-Comique
1. 100: 15.5.1910
2. ibid.: 1.5.1912
3. 100: 1.12.1911
4. ibid.
5. ibid.
6. 114: 1.1912
7. 108: 1.2.1912
8. 8: 119
9. 101: 7/14.6.1914

14. A Trio of Concert Singers
1. 106: 26.3.1920
2. ibid.: 2.7.1920
3. ibid.: 26.3.1920
4. 100: 15.11.1911
5. 42: 23
6. ibid.

PART III The Heyday of Verismo

15. The 'Duse' of Song
1. Quoted 22: XVII, 199
2. 120: 25.10.1910
3. ibid.: 31.5.1911
4. ibid.: 7.4.1912
5. Quoted 122: XVII, 198
6. 35: 255
7. 103: 7.5.1914
8. Quoted 82: 387
9. 103: 22.7.1914
10. Quoted 122: XVII, 199
11. 114: 1.7.1914
12. 3: 525
13. Quoted 52: 267
14. Quoted 122: XVII, 200
15. Quoted 52: 271
16. ibid.: 272–3
17. ibid.: 273
18. Quoted ibid.: 267
19. ibid.

20. ibid.
21. ibid.
22. Quoted 122: XVII, 207

16. Raisa and some Dramatic Sopranos
1. 120: 22.9.1913
2. 23: 106
3. 103: 20.5.1914
4. 35: 315
5. Quoted 52: 275
6. 120: 8.10.1911
7. ibid.
8. 21: 177
9. 106: 23.1.1913
10. 21: 135
11. 121: 8.3.1909
12. 112: 1.1.1911
13. 120: 16.4.1911
14. 120: 19.5.1912
15. 103: 20.6.1912
16. 120: 14.1.1912

17. Verismo Sopranos
1. 35: 250
2. 55: 85
3. 103: 21.6.1920
4. 117: 7.12.1909
5. 28: 85
6. ibid.: 83
7. ibid.: 87
8. 103: 16.6.1913
9. 112: 26.3.1911
10. ibid.
11. ibid.
12. 55: 62
13. 112: 1.3.1919
14. 103: 18.5.1920

18. Galli-Curci and the 'Coloraturas'
1. 112: 26.1.1913
2. 120: 26.3.1911
3. 52: 276
4. 71: 156
5. 92: 180
6. 92: 192–3
7. 71: 156
8. Quoted 52: 275
9. ibid.
10. ibid.
11. 3: 560
12. 52: 281
13. ibid.
14. ibid.: 288
15. ibid.: 301
16. 117: 16.11.1921
17. 119: 16.11.1921
18. Quoted 52: 339
19. 112: 17.3.1912
20. 71: 156—7
21. 4: 256
22. 124: 1.6.1922
23. 114: 1.7.1914
24. 2: 74
25. 119: 1.2.1916
26. 52: 279
27. 124: 1.1.1924
28. 120: 23.4.1911
29. 112: 23.4.1911
30. 120: 24.1.1913
31. 112: 15.1.1918
32. Quoted 122: XVII, 82
33. Quoted 83: 409
34. 103: 13.5.1920
35. ibid.: 7.6.1920
36. Quoted 52: 213
37. 120: 26.11.1911

19. Bori
1. Quoted 122: XXI, 161
2. 3: 416
3. 116: 12.11.1912
4. Quoted 52: 235
5. Quoted 122: XXI, 152
6. 119: 4.1.1914
7. ibid.: 29.1.1921
8. Quoted 52: 293
9. Quoted ibid.: 329

20 Italian Contraltos
1. 120: 20.8.1911
2. 92: 11.12.1919
3. 119: 6.12.1919
4. 105: 14.3.1920
5. 112: 10.3.1916

21. Lyric Tenors
1. 70: 205
2. 112: 1.3.1919
3. Quoted 52: 288
4. 120: 26.11.1911
5. 52: 273

22. Tradition and the Italian Tenor
1. 120: 27.7.1913
2. 112: 15.11.1914
3. 119: 27.11.1920
4. Quoted 52: 326
5. 112: 1.2.1915
6. ibid.
7. 105: 20.2.1921
8. ibid.
9. 55: 131
10. 120: 29.11.1913
11. 103: 10/17.5.1914
12. Quoted 83: 385
13. 112: 25.3.1916
14. 103: 17.5.1919
15. Quoted 83: 403
16. Quoted ibid.: 437

23. Four Dramatic Tenors
1. Quoted 122: XVIII, 54
2. Quoted ibid.: XVIII, 55
3. Quoted ibid.: XVIII, 58
4. ibid.
5. ibid.
6. ibid.
7. Quoted ibid.: XVIII, 52
8. 120: 30.10.1910
9. 110: 3.1.1914
10. 35: 233
11. 112: 10.4.1916
12. 103: 23.4.1912
13. ibid.: 20.6.1912
14. 114: 1.6.1914
15. ibid.: 1.8.1914
16. 116: 21.11.1913
17. Quoted 52: 246
18. 119: 21.11.1913
19. Quoted 122: XXI, 235
20. 4: 265
21. 16: 514
22. Quoted 122: V, 175

24. Principal Baritones
1. Quoted 86: 294
2. Quoted ibid.: 351
3. Quoted ibid.: 385
4. Quoted ibid.: 408
5. Quoted ibid.: 500
6. Quoted 122: XII, 270
7. ibid.
8. 120: 12.11.1911
9. Quoted ibid.: 471
10. 103: 12.6.1928

25. Mardones
1. 116: 13.11.1925

PART IV Singers From the English-Speaking World

26. Alda and Mason
1. 116: 8.12.1908
2. Quoted 52: 208
3. Quoted ibid.: 271
4. 28: 85
5. Quoted 52: 245
6. 52: 238
7. 3: 487
8. Quoted 52: 286
9. 3: 555
10. ibid.: 519–520
11. Quoted 52: 259
12. 106: 2.1.1920
13. ibid.: 26.3.1920
14. Quoted 23: 136
15. Quoted ibid.: 185
16. Quoted ibid.: 219

27. American Concert Sopranos
1. 116: 24.12.1909
2. 3: 423
3. ibid.: 518–9
4. ibid.: 519
5. ibid.: 299
6. ibid.: 410
7. ibid.: 510–11
8. 124: 1.2.1921
9. 3: 620–1
10. 124: 1.5.1925

28. American Lyric Sopranos
1. 112: 5.4.1914
2. 125: 22.3.1914
3. 3: 499
4. Quoted 23: 93
5. ibid.: 93
6. Quoted 52: 231
7. 113: 1.4.1908
8. ibid.: 14.4.1909
9. 28: 152
10. 101: 14/21.5.1911

29. Gramophone Singers
1. 108: 7.1910
2. ibid.: 6.1910
3. ibid.: 5.1912

30. A Quartet of 'Coloraturas'
1. Reported 28: 121
2. 119: 24.11.1919
3. Quoted 52: 248
4. Quoted ibid.: 252
5. ibid.
6. Quoted ibid.: 280

7. 108: 1.7.1913
8. 83: 538

31. English Lyric Sopranos
1. 103: 3.2.1908
2. Quoted 83: 348
3. 103: 12.6.1908
4. 103: 12.6.1928

32. Miura and Bryhn Langaard
1. 97: 264
2. 3: 618
3. Quoted 13: 330
4. ibid.: 334

33. Ponselle and Easton
1. 119: 16.11.1918
2. 117: 19.1.1919
3. ibid.: 17.11.1927
4. 119: 13.11.1925
5. 90: 343
6. 117: 17.11.1927
7. 104: 15.6.1930
8. 118: 17.1.1931
9. 117: 17.1.1931
10. 90: 345–6
11. 119: 28.12.1935
    42: 474
    52: 393
12. Quoted 122: XXI, 208
13. Quoted ibid.: XXI, 199
14. 103: 22.1.1909
15. 114: 1.6.1913
16. Quoted 122: XXI, 204–5
17. Quoted 52: 272
18. Quoted 122: XXI, 206
19. 116: 18.11.1922
20. 119: 25.3.1922
21. Quoted 83: 478
22. 119: 2.3.1936
23. Quoted 122: XXI, 215

34. Contraltos
1. 114: 1.4.1910
2. ibid.: 1.3.1913
3. 79: 124
4. 103: 23.5.1919
5. 52: 295
6. 3: 490
7. Quoted 83: 307
8. ibid.: 306
9. 21: 69

35. A Quartet of American Tenors
1. Quoted 52: 191
2. 114: 1.7.1910
3. 90: 261
4. 114: 1.3.1912
5. ibid.: 1.1.1912

6. Quoted 52: 286
7. 3: 655
8. ibid.: 685
9. 112: 15.1.1918
10. 119: 6.12.1919
11. Quoted 52: 295
12. 118: 4.3.1938

36. A British-born Trio
1. 23: 124
2. Quoted 52: 288
3. 119: 17.11.1922
4. 3: 636–7
5. 103: 6.6.1924
6. ibid.: 15.5.1920

37. High Cs and Heroic Voices
1. 103: 31.5.1927
2. Quoted 122: VII, 5
3. Quoted ibid.: VII, 10
4. Quoted ibid.: VII, 10
5. ibid.
6. Quoted ibid.: VII, 11

38. The Ballad and Oratorio Tradition
1. 73: 42
2. 114: 1.12.1911
3. ibid.
4. ibid.
5. Quoted 114: 1.5.1912
6. Quoted 83: 330
7. Quoted ibid.: 332
8. Quoted ibid.: 420
9. 114: 1.1.1914

39. McCormack
1. Quoted 21: 241
2. 97: 322

40. Baritones and Basses
1. 3: 290
2. Quoted 52: 280
3. 103: 17.9.1931
4. Quoted 65: 50

PART V The German Style in Evolution

41. Lyric Sopranos
1. 103: 30.1.1913
2. ibid.: 3.2.1914
3. 83: 382
4. 108: 1.10.1913
5. 101: 5.5.1912
6. 107: 4.1924
7. 119: 23.11.1922
8. Quoted 83: 437
9. ibid.: 497
10. 117: 23.12.1937
11. 103: 6.6.1927

12. Quoted 52: 342
13. 119: 3.11.1927

42. Lyric-Dramatic Sopranos
1. 105: 25.3.1921
2. 116: 2.3.1923
3. 52: 311
4. ibid.: 315

43. Dramatic Sopranos
1. 119: 20.2.1915
2. 117: 2.2.1915
3. 116: 2.2.1915
4. 117: 5.2.1915
5. 103: 26.4.1912
6. ibid.: 30.4.1912
7. 119: 17.1.1928
8. Quoted 52: 343
9. ibid.: 382
10. 116: 5.12.1932
11. ibid.: 17.1.1933

44. Schumann
1. Quoted 122: XXI, 236
2. 119: 21.11.1914
3. 3: 453
4. 82: 427
5. 104: 88–9
6. 101: 29.1.1911
7. 114: 1.7.1914
8. 23: 150
9. 99: 26.12.23
10. 94: 209
11. Quoted 52: 307
12. 103: 5.6.1924
13. 103: 5.5.1927

45. Jeritza and Lehmann
1. 88: 441
2. 83: 436
3. Quoted 86: 384
4. Quoted 83: 427
5. Quoted ibid.: 435
6. ibid.: 455
7. Quoted ibid.: 467
8. Quoted 23: 188
9. 119: 12.1.1934
10. ibid.: 5.1.1935
11. 123: IV, 401

46. Five Contraltos
1. Quoted 52: 246
2. 3: 410
3. Quoted 52: 246
4. 3: 446
5. Quoted 83: 357
6. 114: 1.1.1911
7. 83: 498

47. Two Great Lieder Singers
1. 108: 1.7.1912

2. 3: 351
3. 72: 101
4. 3: 351–2
5. 100: 1.3.1911
6. 97: 249–250
8. 114: 1.6.1911
9. 3: 384
10. ibid.: 449–50
11. ibid.: 384

48. Baritones
1. 105: 30.1.1913
2. ibid.: 7.7.1925
3. 115: 2.1913
4. Quoted 83: 374
5. Quoted 52: 263
6. 3: 447

49. Basses
1. Quoted 52: 330
2. 116: 2.3.1923
3. 52: 326
4. Quoted ibid.: 318
5. ibid.: 330
6. 101: 7/14.6.1914
7. Quoted 83: 381
8. Quoted ibid.: 425
9. Quoted ibid.: 426
10. 103: 5.5.1927
11. Quoted 83: 427
12. Quoted ibid.: 434
13. Quoted ibid.: 435
14. Quoted ibid.: 449
15. 119: 3.11.1927
16. Quoted 52: 259
17. ibid.: 252
18. Quoted ibid.: 252
19. 119: 6.1.1940

50. Tauber and the Lyric Tenors
1. 122: XVIII, 248
2. ibid.: 253
3. ibid.:
4. ibid.: 254
5. Quoted 83: 533
6. 103: 26.4.1910
7. 83: 381
8. 3: 446–7

51. East European Tenors
1. Quoted 86: 431
2. Quoted 122: XVII, 271

52. Heldentenors
1. 115: 5.1913
2. ibid.: 3.1913
3. 103: 23.2.1913
4. Quoted 83: 425
5. Quoted ibid.: 428
6. 97: 312.

Index

Numbers in **bold** refer to extended discussion of a singer in the text.